*For Kenneth and Alberta –
With much love to
my dear friends –*

Ingrid

–>•<–

Coffee Made Her Insane

For Kenneth and Alberta –

On The occasion of

Kenneth's 80th birthday.

Best wishes.

Peg Meier

May 1988 –

—>•<—

Coffee Made Her Insane

& Other Nuggets from Old Minnesota Newspapers

Compiled by
Peg Meier of the Star Tribune

Published by Neighbors Publishing
P.O. Box 15071
Minneapolis, Minn. 55415

First printing

Copyright 1988, Neighbors Publishing

ISBN 0-933387-01-6

Neighbors Publishing
P.O. Box 15071
Minneapolis, Minn. 55415

For Wilmott Ragsdale and Lester Hawkes, my two favorite journalism professors at the University of Wisconsin in the 1960s. They showed me that newspapers and the history of journalism can be great fun.

Contents

–>•<–

Introduction

My mother was in a toss-it-all-out mood. I wasn't. It was 1974, and my parents were moving to an apartment from the house where my sister and I grew up. Among the things I rescued from the garbage was my mom's scrapbook from her high school years — the late 1920s — in Plymouth, Wis. I liked the old photos, the playbills, the valentines. I especially enjoyed the old newspaper stories, from the enthusiastic accounts of basketball victories to the sappy obituaries.

I was a newspaper reporter in Minneapolis by then, and I had written hundreds of obits. None was like the one in my mother's scrapbook about her 17-year-old classmate. The second paragraph read:

"She contracted a cold last fall which seemed to stay with her and left her in a weakened condition and this spring it was thought a blood transfusion might help and it did for a time but her condition again was such that she was removed to the hospital about 10 days ago where a second transfusion was performed but her condition grew worse until the sad news of her death was learned and came as a shock to her large circle of friends and sympathy goes out to her surviving relatives who are prostrate with grief."

Whew!

That was all *one sentence*. In tone as well as structure, the obit was completely unlike today's. We latter-day journalists are taught to write sparely and without emotion. Ours are fairer accounts, but drier; less lurid, but also less vivid.

Some months after I read the scrapbook, I helped myself to microfilm of old Minneapolis Tribunes and started reading. Immediately, I was hooked. The papers provided an easy, entertaining way to learn about Minnesota and its history. They were more interesting to me than many history and journalism books.

I was caught up in the immediacy and drama, even about events long past. Never before had I told President Lincoln out loud that he shouldn't go to that theater.

Some years after I poked around in the old Tribunes, Dave Wood and I traveled around Minnesota to gather stories for the Neighbors section of our paper. In the newspaper office of practically every town we visited, we found bound volumes of old issues, many from around the turn of the century. I would browse long enough — five or 10 minutes — to find an old item of interest to run with our stories about the town. In every newspaper my eyes fell upon, there would be *something* of interest. Usually there was something good enough that I would say to someone, anyone, "Hey, look at this!" After an hour or two, I would have to pull myself away.

I began to search for a way to spend a great deal of time reading old newspapers. If I could put together a book, I could justify taking a year away from my reporting job to sit in front of a microfilm reader and revel in old newspapers.

–>•<–

The old Minnesota newspapers ran charming stories and horrifying stories. They ran the bizarre and the poignant. They ran romance and adventure. They had stories about generosity and a slower pace of life that lend validity to the idea of the Good Old Days, and they had stories about child brutality, racial and ethnic hatreds, loneliness and terrifying crimes that made me ponder the cruelty in human hearts and the unfairness of life.

No matter what your theory of life, you can find evidence for it by reading old newspapers.

My simple view is that life is a mixed bag. Consequently, you'll see here a variety of story subjects and writing styles, a mix of advertisers and art. This is no Chamber of Commerce glorification of Minnesota. Nor does it convey the despair of "Wisconsin Death Trip," in which the author chronicled the miseries but none of the pleasures of one town, Black River Falls, in the 1880s and 1890s. Newspapers always have concentrated on the unusual, the they had happy stories about good people and ordinary life.

The choice of articles and ads in this book is purely subjective. These are pieces that *I* like, that tug at *my* heart. I like funny stories. I like colorful writing. I like stories that speak strongly of a particular place and time; the late 1800s are especially good for that. I like stories about children. I like to know how people handle adversity, and what happens when they can't. I like obituaries, not so much for the facts of deaths as for the details of lives. I like picky little minutiae about how people live and have lived.

I'm less fascinated by politics, foreign affairs and business, so they are sparse here. Also, those stories are harder to decipher for today's readers than are human interest stories.

This selection is hit and miss. One week, for example, I decided to "go" to Madison in 1910, Park Rapids in 1911, Two Harbors in 1914 and Lindstrom in 1916. I roamed about in the state's newspapers as my whims took me. If a newspaper bored me, I went on to the next. If that one struck my fancy, I read many issues.

The Minnesota Historical Society has preserved (mostly on microfilm) about 3 million issues of the state's newspapers. Although I spent a year with them, I skimmed only a tiny part. I opened only a small window on Minnesota's past. I couldn't try to treat every Minnesota city favorably, or even fairly. If I missed your town or your people or your memories, I'm sorry. I can only suggest that you scrounge around in old newspapers and find your stories.

There's so much wonderful material in the old papers. You could set out on the same old-newspaper project and come up with a totally different tone and assortment of items than I did. My hope is that you'll like some of what I like.

–>-<–

Newspapers, of course, don't tell the whole story of a place or a time. Historians use them as only a part of their research. Newspapers have errors (it's appalling how often we journalists get even the name of the subject wrong) and major omissions (Twin Cities newspapers didn't do much about bootleggers and crime figures living here in the 1930s). Newspaper people get so caught up in the here-and-now that often we miss the chance to put things into context. Our predecessors did worse.

Back a few generations, readers knew the politics of the editor and how he (or, more rarely, she) viewed life. Stories were biased, but the readers knew it. They expected it. Editorials and opinion pages are fairly recent inventions; then newspapers' positions were apparent in the news columns. By our standards, some of those positions were less than responsible. Nonetheless, the reports were spellbinding — flashy, ruthless, exciting, bawdy. Rarely did newspaper editors of yore call for "more study."

but they definitely have personalities. The older newspapers had stronger personalities than today's. No way would a reporter now write of an accused murderer that he "is not spoken well of by people who used to know him," and no copy editor would write a headline that says, "Froze to Death; Another Drunkard Gone."

No editor today would run a gory, graphic story about the skinning alive of a criminal in China. I'm sorry I read it. I'm sorrier I can't get it out of my head. Lucky for you, I'm not reprinting it here. Nor the 1891 story from the Fertile, Minn., Journal about a man who cut out his tongue with a razor. That newspaper, by the way, had a regular column called "Ways of the Wicked" about criminals around the world.

With our "enlightened" perspective, we read some of the old stories differently than did our ancestors. We're amused that in 1901 an Aitkin writer thought many of the world's problems were licked. We're outraged that fire codes didn't exist to prohibit the use of candles in fresh evergreens in 1906, when children were horribly burned in a Christmas program at church near Montgomery. We giggle when we see the 1895 St. Paul article headlined "Coffee Made Her Insane." At first, this strikes us modern coffee-chuggers as amusing. But then we realize it's the tragic story of a mentally unbalanced woman. Perhaps just as our grandparents did, we end up shaking our heads in sympathy.

While the old papers are fun to read today, I wouldn't want to depend on their kind of journalism to tell me what's going on in the world now. In many ways, today's newspapers are far superior to yesterday's. Ours have more depth, greater subtlety, less sentimentality. They try to avoid the gruesome and the sensational. They report more of "ordinary" life; there's more to newspapers than the old formula of "blood, money and broads." Newspapers today are more straightforward and informative. Sometimes reporters are given time to investigate and to write well; their works do qualify as "literature under pressure" or "literature in a hurry."

Hurry. Today readers are in so much of a hurry. Newspapers as well as radio and television have to give information in little pieces, easy for the mind to digest. A news story must be written with the main elements in the first few paragraphs. No longer will readers wade through a chronologically told tale, in which the number of dead or the fate of the hero isn't revealed for many, many inches of type.

Check out the article in this book on the 1876 Northfield bank robbery; it's a well-told story, but would you sit still to read it in your morning paper?

–>-<–

A few words about how I gathered the items in this book:

The best times I had were putting a new reel of microfilm on the machine and randomly "exploring" another town; it's easy to figure out who the big-shots were and if the mayor had lots of power and if the editor had a sense of humor.

Sometimes, though, I wanted specific information. For example, in one newspaper I spotted a brief reference to a Rochester-area family that had lost six children to diphtheria in one month of 1878, and I had to learn more. I searched the Rochester Post until I found it.

For the big stories such as the Hinckley forest fire and the murder of Kitty Ging, I read several newspapers and chose for you the one I think is best.

Newspaper indexes helped. I was able to track down stories on early automobiles through an index of old Minneapolis Journals, kept at the Minneapolis Public Library. The Works Progress Administration's newspaper index of selected early Minnesota newspapers was useful; that index is at the Minnesota Historical Society. The WPA, fortunately, translated portions of the state's foreign-language papers. Your local newspaper may have an index; many weeklies and small dailies in Minnesota do.

–>-<–

As I worked my way through the decades of old newspapers, I sometimes got stuck in the past. I remember an acquaintance casually asking about my life with the words, "What are you up to, Peg?" To which I responded, quite seriously, "1911."

I hope you, too, will be caught up in the work of Minnesota's long-gone newspaper reporters and editors. Here's to them all.

Peg Meier
Minneapolis, Minn.
January 1988

–>•<–

Note to Readers

Dear Reader (a nice little phrase from the past):

Some of the words and punctuation in this book are likely to strike you as odd. That's because the stories are printed here much as they originally ran in old newspapers.

You'll find such spellings as "cranberrie" and "aeroplane" and "every body." Some place names were capitalized and spelled differently, as in "lake Harriet," "Wenona" and "Minnesotaens."

Headlines on articles in this book are as they appeared when they were first printed. Today we regard some as strange, some racist and some humorous.

Unless the original article had an obvious error or was terribly confusing, I have reprinted it as it was. Sometimes I added a bit of punctuation. In places where I helped you with definitions or explanations, I marked them with brackets [like this]. Parentheses (these things) were in the original stories.

I have resisted the temptation to rewrite, clean up, move the good stuff to the top of the story. What you see here is what earlier generations of Minnesotans saw.

— **Peg Meier**

1840s

Minnesota Pioneer, St. Paul, April 28, 1849

Congress created the Minnesota Territory in March 1849. A month later, the first newspaper, the Minnesota Pioneer, was printed in Minnesota. Frontier editors were much like today's Chamber of Commerce heads, praising their towns and encouraging settlement. Promises of good land and good health enticed people here. In 1849 there were fewer than 5,000 whites and 25,000 Indians in the Minnesota Territory, an area twice the size of the present state.

1840s
-›•‹-

Immigration to the Minnesota Territory

James M. Goodhue of the Minnesota Pioneer was the first newspaper editor on the Minnesota frontier, and he saw his role as attacting settlers. Editors then were more interested in promoting their towns than they were in reporting the news, keeping watch on government or advertising goods and services.

Letters of Inquiry Respecting Minnesota.

BELOW WILL BE seen specimens of letters of inquiry about our Territory, of which we receive more or less every mail. We have answered some of them by private correspondence, but they flock in so fast that we now adopt the expedient of caging what we have on hand together, and sending the answers back in one covey.

Our readers would be astonished at the multitude and constantly increasing evidences which come to our hand, of the wide-spread interest manifested in our young Territory. Every week several papers not on our list appear with a request for the Pioneer in exchange. [That is, other newspapers ask for a free copy of the Pioneer in exchange for one of theirs.] Of course we do not mention this fact with any motive of vanity — we ascribe it to the pervading curiosity of a multitude of people of other meridians who are thinking to emigrate. Unquestionably, if they can satisfy themselves of the productiveness of our soil, they will, under the additional and all important consideration of health, prefer this direction to any other. We here insert a part of a letter addressed to us in behalf of himself and others by one in Crawford Co., Pa.:

"I have been requested by several persons who think of emigrating to your Territory, to address you and obtain the aforesaid information. At the same time, by forwarding one or two numbers of your paper as specimens, you will confer a kind favor, &c [etc.].

"N.B. [nota bene, note well] — Please state whether the Odd Fellows have any lodges in the Territory."

Here is another, from a gentleman in behalf of himself and others in Calhoun Co., Michigan:

"ED. PIONEER — Dear Sir: Being solicited by many citizens of this place, and having a great desire myself to learn something of the prospects and present condition of your country and village, I have taken the liberty to address you with inquiries respecting your Territory. Will you, Mr. Editor, furnish me with a short description of your country and village? Is your land susceptible of growing wheat generally? Can fruit be raised, such as apples, peaches, &c? Are your winters long and severe? Are there many settlements in the country round about St. Paul? Are building materials, such as lime, lumber, stone and brick, to be got near? Are the people of St. Paul mostly Eastern? Have you a full supply of mechanics and tradesmen? How many stores, hotels, tin shops [to make cups, buckets, water dippers, etc.], groceries, &c? Is there a regular line of steamboats up the Mississippi to your place daily? Lastly, I would inquire whether a stock of ready made clothing, in your opinion, could be sold this fall? If not, what commodity would be the best to bring to dispose of readily? If you see fit, Mr. Editor, you may answer this in your paper and set me down as a subscriber for one year, and on the receipt of it, I will remit you the money, or be in St. Paul soon, and see you in person. I think your paper would be taken by a number, if once introduced, for a large portion of our population have suddenly been seized with the Minnesota fever, and the Pioneer no doubt, would be an excellent thing for that disorder.

"P.S. — I would ask if provisions are plenty, the price of board per week, and whether, in your opinion, that climate would be congenial to bilious [gassy] and rather delicate constitutions."

A gentleman in Kentucky makes the following inquiries:

"Minnesota is large enough for every body."

Minnesota Pioneer, April 28, 1849

"ED. PIONEER — Dear Sir: I wish to purchase a lot of ground within the suburbs of your town, St. Paul, containing several acres, and as I have a knowledge of the character and prospects [of] this place, derived principally from extracts from your paper, I have taken the liberty of writing this letter to you, with a view of gaining some additional information from you in a more direct and private way in reference to the growth, population, and situation of St. Paul, and also to ask you to do me the favor to refer me to some resident citizen of the place, through whom I can negotiate the contemplated purchase above mentioned. I shall before a great while, I hope, be in your Territory, but I cannot say when I can make suitable preparations for going. Please inform me what is the present population of your town? What is the character of its location, and what is the nature of the country around? Is the land which lies around it rich and productive? I should like very much to know what a large sized lot of ground, containing say about ten acres, within the suburbs of St. Paul, would cost me at present in cash, and whether there are any such for sale?"

We will proceed to answer these several interrogatories, by way of a general statement respecting Minnesota and her prospects, without going far into detail.

First, Minnesota is large enough for every body. All her lands east of the Mississippi, except the comparatively small number of sections already entered, are in market. Probably, in the course of a year or two our enviable domain will include the lands now occupied by the Sioux Indians. When the Indian title is extinguished, all that tract of country included within the northern line of the State of Iowa, and the Mississippi and Missouri rivers, extending as far west as Nebraska, will be open to settlers, like other parts of Minnesota.

There are excellent localities for farmers unoccupied, upon the eastern — i.e. our — side of the river; and considering the relations of these sections to our river trade and our present towns, they probably present equal advantages with the Sioux lands, which at present we are not allowed to "take up." These Sioux lands are the admiration of every body, and the mouth of many a stranger and citizen waters while he looks beyond the Mississippi's flood upon this fair Canaan beyond. . . .

St. Paul, which is the principal commercial town on the Mississippi, is situated upon a bluff some seventy-five or a hundred feet above the river on its outward sweep, commanding a view of the stream for a distance of some two miles. The face of the country in the rear, that is, north of the town, is quite uneven; and is made up of oak-openings, mir-

"Our country is proverbially healthy."

---

rored by numerous little ponds.

St. Paul has about eight hundred inhabitants, most of whom have sprouted up within the last few months. We have already most of the material comforts of life; we are usually visited by four steamboats a week, and Galena, Dubuque and St. Louis, though the latter town is some eight hundred miles south of us, seem like neighbors. Their citizens frequently "drop up" to make us a call. The mechanic arts in St. Paul are in many of the departments abundantly represented. We have no immediate want of ordinary carpenters nor blacksmiths, though their journey work obtains from $1.50 to $2 per day and found [food and lodging].

We need no more merchants. There is already too great a supply of all sorts of merchandise adapted to this market. If any merchant is so set upon trying this market as not to take our word for it, let him come and see.

We want farmers. We are almost ready to offer a bounty on farmers. And we recommend them to come — come as soon as they can. Corn and oats have retailed here during most of the present season at 50 and 75 cents. Potatoes at 75 [cents] and $1. A ready market will be found for agricultural produce during the whole time the Territory is being settled, and probably long afterwards, for the supply of the lumber trade. Three nations of Indians, too, are supplied with provisions yearly, by the U.S. Government, which now brings their supplies from below.

The Territory is settling very fast with immigrants from the eastern and middle States. We should probably have had a fuller flood of immigration had it not been for the cholera in the towns

Minnesota Pioneer, Aug. 2, 1849, and Sept. 2, 1849

along the way. Young men can do well to work for wages almost anywhere in the Territory, and in the pine region they can get from $15 to $26 per month.

Whether winter wheat is a sure crop, we can find but one citizen who has resided here long enough to inform us. He has a small extent of ground sowed with winter wheat which bids as fair as can be desired. Apples can be raised here unquestionably in great perfection. We doubt whether peaches would survive the winters. The winters are long and cold, but the temperature is so equable, that they are said to be agreeable. Lumber is abundant at St. Anthony's Falls, seven miles above St. Paul, and at St. Croix, some forty miles N.E. We have a brick yard and good quarrying stone near at hand. As to commodities for trade, probably Indian corn would pay the best profit. It has sold heretofore, in the winter at one dollar per bushel. The climate is almost precisely like that of New England. Bilious diseases are rare, and agues [fevers] have no home here. Our country is proverbially healthy.

Town and suburb lots are for sales by Mr. H.M. Rice, & Co., Gen. S. Leech, Mr. J. Irvine, Mr. Randall, Smith & Whitney, Rev. Mr. Hoyt, and various others whose names do not now occur. Lands in the suburbs of St. Paul are worth from ten to one hundred dollars per acre.

As to the order of the Odd Fellows, we have not heard of any, but there are a great many smart bachelors, who will have to continue odd if their other halves do not come along with you immigrants.

We have hotels enough and a good tin shop. Board at the hotels is about one dollar a day, and from two and a half to five dollars per week. Wash-

"Would any one believe that in the nineteenth century, our Government would limit Minnesota, situated here in the very heart of the Republic, to one mail a week?"

---

ing is from seventy-five cents to one dollar and a half per dozen. We have some eighteen stores and twenty-five groceries of the first water; we have sev- eral excellent ministers and one good school.
Minnesota Pioneer, St. Paul, Aug. 16, 1849

→>•<←

We say to the INVALIDS of the great western valley, who have been devoured by fevers and debilitated by malarias ... seek the vicinity of the Falls of St. Anthony and St. Croix, as a residence ... its acres recently brought into market — the population as yet sparse, so as to afford room for the enterprize of the earlier comers; a soil as capable of staple grains as Michigan or New York — forests of pine reaching Northward beyond the prairie region — the streams affording the best sites for mills, and above all, a bracing climate. ...The Maine emigrants have here renewed the lumber trade...But the charm of Minnesota life is HEALTH — HEALTH! The winters are not more severe than many parts of New York and New England, while the diseases of southern latitudes are avoided.
Minnesota Register, St. Paul, April 27, 1849

→>•<←

Never enter a sick room in a state of perspiration, as the moment you become cool your pores absorb. Do not approach contagious diseases with an empty stomach nor sit between the sick and the fire, because the heat attracts the vapor.
Minnesota Pioneer, St. Paul, April 28, 1849

→>•<←

Newspapers. — Every subscriber thinks the paper is printed for his special benefit, and if there is nothing in it that suits him, it must be stopped — it is good for nothing. Some people look over the deaths and marriages, and actually complain of the editor if but few people in his vicinity have been so fortunate as to get married the previous week, or so unfortunate as to die. An editor should have such things in his paper whether they occur or not. Just as many subscribers as an editor may have, just as many different tastes has he to consult. One wants stories and poetry, another abhors all this. The politician wants nothing but politics. One must have something smart, another something sound. One likes anecdotes, fun and frolic, and the next door neighbor wonders that a man of sense will put such stuff in a paper. We only wish that every man, woman and child who reads a paper, were compelled but one single month to edit one. They would find that it is not so easy a matter as they first supposed it to be.
Minnesota Chronicle, St. Paul, May 31, 1849, reprinted from the Liverpool Mercury

→>•<←

Land For Sale. [Advertisement] For sale by the subscriber, land in the immediate vicinity of St. Paul, by the acre, in lots to suit purchasers. Price, from ten to twenty-five dollars per acre. Terms, one fourth in hand, the remainder on time with six per cent per annum. Said land is suitable for cultivation, mowing and pasture.
B.F. Hoyt
Minnesota Chronicle, St. Paul, June 21, 1849

→>•<←

Good Limbs. — Dr. Dotwood, in his "Hints to Young Mothers," recommends patience and care in teaching *boy* babies to feel their "footies." He says that for the sake of seeing them tottle, they are put upon the floor too soon, which has a tendency to furnish them with an everlasting pair of parenthetical shanks. "It is not of so much consequence about the *girls!*"
Minnesota Pioneer, St. Paul, June 28, 1849

→>•<←

The military band of Fort Snelling, who delighted us so much at the dinner and ball on the 4th, the first celebration of Independence Day in Minnesota, really deserve a puff for the quality of their music, and their efforts to promote harmony and good feeling on the occasion.
Minnesota Chronicle, St. Paul, July 6, 1849

→>•<←

The Mails. Would any one believe that in the nineteenth century, our Government would limit Minnesota, situated here in the very heart of the Republic, to one mail a week? We ought to have mails at least tri-weekly during the summer by steamboat, between Galena and Fort Snelling. In the winter, mails ought also to be tri-weekly and ought to be conveyed between Galena and St. Paul, in two days each trip. Are we to be blocked in here half the year, and is the rest of the world to be cut off from that communication with Minnesota which is now so essential to their welfare, for a whole week together, for the sake of saving a few hundred dollars of expense for mail service? The other Territories and the thirty States in the Union have abundant reason to complain of being thus exiled from Minnesota; and we hope their presses will speak out boldly for the reform we ask for. Nor is it alone of the want of more mail service up and down the riv-

"The best distinction between the sexes is the beard."

er, that we have reason to complain; we want internal mails also. — We want a mail from St. Paul to Stillwater and back, at least twice a week. . . .

Does Congress expect us to assume the functions of Government, to legislate, to hold elections, to promulgate laws, to print newspapers, to make speeches, to do all that an organized Territory of freemen may of right do, without furnishing us with mail facilities? Must we make brick without straw? Give us mails — sustain them now and soon they will sustain themselves and afford revenue.

Minnesota Pioneer, St. Paul, Aug. 2, 1849

→·←

Dr. Johnson, speaking of a lady who was celebrated for dressing well, remarked: "The best evidence that I can give you of her perfection in this respect is, *that one can never remember what she had on.*" — Delicacy of feeling in a lady will prevent her putting on any thing calculated to attract notice; and yet a female of good taste will dress so as to have every part of her dress correspond. Thus, while she avoids what is showy and attractive, everything will be so adjusted as to exhibit symmetry and taste.

Minnesota Pioneer, St. Paul, Aug. 23, 1849

→·←

The *best* distinction between the sexes is the beard. Why do not all men wear their beard, or some part of it? A smoothly shaved, or beardless, man meets our ideas of manhood about as well as a square-shouldered, shingle-shaped woman meets our notions of womanhood. There is very little difference between the mental formation of man and woman, still there is a difference; but the physical structure is another matter. Nature has made the lines of difference very marked and strong, and the more perfect the development of either, the greater the dissimilarity. A Venus with the muscles of a Hercules would be a fright. Art should not interfere with Nature's arrangements. Let men keep their distinct apparel, their strength, and their ugliness.

Minnesota Pioneer, St. Paul, Dec. 12, 1849

→·←

Minnesota Register and Chronicle, St. Paul, Sept. 15, 1849

1840s
-›•‹-

The Beauty of the Falls

St. Anthony Falls is on the Mississippi River in what is now Minneapolis.
The area near the falls was called St. Anthony and was incorporated
as a city in 1855. In 1872 it consolidated with Minneapolis.

Saint Anthony.

The importance of the subject, and our want of full and definite information about it, is the only reason we have not yet attempted to describe the Falls and to set forth the unrivalled advantages of that locality for business. Here it is, that after a progress of four hundred miles from above, through a channel in which no obstructions occur to steamboat navigation worth mentioning, that the whole volume of the Mississippi pours down in a precipitous sheet from a bench of limestone rock, to the depth of eighteen or twenty feet. . . . The cataract of St. Anthony is but little less wonderful than that of Niagara. The roar of this immense volume of falling water is often distinctly audible at St. Paul, a distance of eight miles, and probably at a much greater distance. Some one said that men could make towns, but it took God to make the Falls. At any rate it is an admirable piece of workmanship. The shores along the Falls present the same beautiful appearance of benches, table lands, and swelling hills, interspersed with groves that characterize the features of the land along the river for some distance above and below the Falls.

THE WATER POWER.

At a distance of more than half a mile above the Falls, the stream becomes very rapid, and is divided by an island [now known as Nicollet Island] planted upon a base of rock and crowned with trees. This island runs parallel to the east shore at a distance from that shore of about fifteen rods, and extends below the Falls. It is by extending a strong dam, fastened into the ledge at the bottom with immense iron bolts, from the foot of this island to the east shore, that the hydraulic power of the river is controlled — a power which has no limit that an engi-

neer would ever have occasion to compute. . . . A very large saw mill is erected, capable of making two millions of lumber per annum; and another mill of the most substantial and thorough description, is in the process of erection. It is the plan . . . to erect mills enough to employ eighteen or twenty saws, besides using all the water that may be wanted for other machinery. Lumber, for the present, will be the leading interest. The saws went into operation last autumn, and have had no rest since, night or day, except Sundays, and the demand for lumber at the Falls and at St. Paul, has not nearly been supplied. . . .

THE PINERY.

. . . Between the Falls of St. Anthony and the Pokagomon Falls — another St. Anthony, 400 miles north — is a vast body of pine timber, perhaps the most extensive in the world, into which the axe has yet made no inroads. This region of pines is watered by the Crow Wing river, The Rabbit, The Pine, Leech Lake, and many other streams, and embosoms in its sombre shades of evergreen trees, Winnipic Lake, Cass Lake, Leech Lake, Pokagomon Lake, and many other fine sheets of water; and is interspersed with many tracts of fine rich lands which are destined to be cultivated and inhabited by our countrymen. . . .

SCENERY, &C.

The beauty of scenery at St. Anthony cannot be exaggerated. We are particularly delighted with that bench of table land back of Water street, some 30 feet high, parallel to the river, which overlooks the island and the Falls. Along the bench, a row of houses has sprung into existence since our last visit. A healthier spot than St. Anthony cannot be found this side of the White hills [of New England].

*"There is not a grog shop in town.
They go in for water, and they won't have anything else."*

Most of its inhabitants are from the lumber regions of Maine — people of industry, energy and enterprize. Those who are loafers and tipplers by trade, will find no encouragement at St. Anthony.— Every person there works for a living. — There is not a grog [liquor] shop in town. They go in for water, and they won't have anything else.

PROPRIETORSHIP OF THE FALLS.

This water power was first claimed by Mr. Franklin Steele, 12 years ago. Mr. Steele is the Sutler [storekeeper for the military] at Ft. Snelling, a most worthy officer, and a man who has done not a little for Minnesota. He built the first house ever built in Minnesota. [Not true, but Steele did set up claims, build a dam in 1847 and a sawmill in 1848.] He built the first mills on the St. Croix river. He is emphatically a pioneer. Laboring under disadvantages which no man can imagine, in obtaining labor and tools and materials for the work, he succeeded in time in building the dam and getting things in motion. He has expended at the Falls over fifty thousand dollars. . . . A finer agricultural region than that which surrounds St. Anthony cannot be found. . . . All crops do well. Corn is a sure and an abundant crop. If we were to specify the crop that is most excellent and abundant, however, it would be the potato crop. . . .

CONNECTION WITH THE ATLANTIC.

When we consider how soon the upper Mississippi will be placed in direct communication with the Atlantic by railroad extending east from Galena and by steamboat through the Wisconsin and Fox rivers and the Lakes — a work already well in progress — is it too much to predict for this young Territory and for the manufacturing interest of St. Anthony, a rapidity of growth unparalleled even in the annals of Western progress?

Minnesota Pioneer, St. Paul, Aug. 16, 1849

→•←

"This cave is so large, you can walk erect in it for thirty or forty yards, when suddenly you find yourself in a room more beautiful than could be made with all the wealth of Astor."

Steamer Dr. Franklin, Oct. 4, 1849

Messrs. Editors — I have just come aboard this boat which is lying at the Lower Landing at St. Paul, and will start for Stillwater soon. While they are rolling on these barrels of cranberrys, I will tell you something about the cranberrie trade here. There have already been *three thousand* barrels shipped from St. Paul and Mendota this season, and probably more than half as many from Stillwater. They are gathered by the Indians who exchange them for goods. They are nearly twice as large and much more delicious than any cranberries I ever ate East. Those shipped from St. Paul are gathered from cranberry marshes, twelve and sixteen miles North and North-West from here. They are here worth $4 per barrel.

Now we are off — but instead of going down the river, we are going up. The Captain says we are going to "Carver's Cave," which is two miles above, to take on some cranberries — .... While they are rolling on those barrels I will tell you about the cave. The boat has stopped at the mouth of a fairy little dell where a beautiful little crystal stream runs into the Mississippi. You follow this stream a few rods, stopping every step to admire the grassy, rocky sides of the ravine — when you come to a white sandstone rock at its head. This rock is about 30 feet high — forming three-fourths of a circle, and it is crowded with grass and trees. In this rock is a cave, with a semi-circular mouth, about 30 feet wide and 20 feet high; and from its beautiful white sand floor flows a most beautiful crystal stream. This cave is so large, you can walk erect in it for thirty or forty yards, when suddenly you find yourself in a room more beautiful than could be made with all the wealth of Astor. It is

Minnesota Pioneer, May 5, 1849

circular, about 15 feet in diameter, and high enough for the greatest beauty. Its floor, and walls, and siding, are all formed of this almost snow-white rock. In its centre is a large vase, smooth and white, and polished as marble, three or four feet in diameter, and about a foot in depth, into which the water falls about two feet, filling the room ceaselessly, with its delicious music. After you leave this room by creeping some distance, you

"Our cold weather is dry, bracing, exhilarating — gives us an appetite and makes us fat."

find yourself in another room; and then for the rest of the way is only large enough for you to crawl on your hands and knees. It gives rise to strange feelings to be in that narrow, winding passage, three hundred yards under ground, without room to turn around. Most of the way, the stream has worn a channel about a foot wide. If your light should happen to go out you have only to crawl down the stream, and you will certainly find your way out. I know the depth of water in this channel, for I measured it in several places, by slipping into it up to my knees. It was supposed that is was the Cave in which [explorer Jonathan] Carver encamped some days during his travels in this region [in 1766], and from this it derives its name. But this Cave does not at all answer to the description of the Cave in which Carver encamped. That is two miles below St. Paul, and the mouth of it is nearly obstructed. On [explorer Joseph] Nicollet's map, the Cave which I have been describing is called "New Cave." It should be called Fountain Cave. [Later, parts of Carver's Cave were cut away for the railroad. In what is now the Dayton's Bluff area of St. Paul, the remaining portion is closed to the public in order to protect both cave and people.]

While I am writing, the boat is on its way, and we have reached Red Rock, five miles below St. Paul. . . . A few miles [beyond], on the West side of the St. Croix, is Cottage Grove, a little village, surrounded by a beautiful and fertile country. There is no finer land for farming than a greater part of this point between these rivers. Corn grows as well as in Southern Ohio. Oats will average fifty bushels to the acre. Cabbages grow four feet six inches in circumference. Onions from the seed this year measure one foot in cirumference. And the turnips

are as large as I ever saw any where. . . . Every foot of a medium quality of this land in four years will be worth six dollars per acre. . . .

You will see I am dull, from the manner I write. I have not time to transcribe, and therefore send you my notes, without alteration or correction, hoping that you will be able to read them. I will write you as soon as I can, and tell you something of Stillwater.

Yours truly,
HESPERIDES

Minnesota Pioneer, St. Paul, Dec. 12, 1849, reprinted from the Cleveland, Ohio, Democrat

→·←

Vindicated at Last. The character of Minnesota for cold, stands redeemed at last. On Monday morning, Fahrenheit's thermometer indicated 20 degrees below zero, in Saint Paul. The air was still as death. In fact, we have no wind; so that we actually suffer less in the coldest weather, than they do in the cutting winds of Illinois, at a much milder temperature, as indicated by the thermometer. Where there is no wind, the body soon generates and carries along with it, a warm atmosphere. Our cold weather is dry, bracing, exhilarating — gives us an appetite and makes us fat.

Minnesota Pioneer, St. Paul, Dec. 19, 1849

→·←

[For more on Minnesota's first newspapers, see George S. Hage's "Newspapers on the Minnesota Frontier, 1849-1860," published in 1967 by the Minnesota Historical Society Press.]

LIST OF LETTERS.
LIST OF LETTERS remaining at the Post Office, Ft. Snelling, Sept 30, 1849.

Alexander Mrs M A	Lowery Mrs E M
Briggs A J	Lewis Dr Wm 2
Breurtein Julius	Lumley John
Bureand Mons Jean	Lynch Thos H
Braily Chas	McMullon Hugh
Bruce Col Amos J	Mansuer Chas
Blake Edward Esq	Mason John McK
Bootes Lt. L C,U S A	Neilly Lt. U S A
Clainnn Jacob	Nobles Rev Lemuel
Camron Hugh	Otto G.
Cainron Peter	Perry Thomas
Convers Wm 2	Parle Thomas
Chapman D P Esq	Roorback Uriah
Doe Hilton	Reese Bennet
Edwards David F	Radford Lt R C W
Foyles James	Scott Gilbert
Fisher Jos S	Sullivan Mortimer
Frish Elijah N	Spencer Mrs C S
Grant Geo M	Strohl Levi
Gordon Wm B	Schriner Jacob
Hall Mrs Cyrus	Sparks Mrs Theresa
Howard O C	Shumard Dr B F
Hall Lt C, U.S.A. 3	Turner Dr U S A
Hatch Lt.J.P, USA	Turner Chas
Heath Lt. H'y U SA	Turner Robt
Jones Greenbury	Taper Chauncey
La Point Charles	Wells Geo W 2

F. STEELE, P. M.
Ft. Snelling, Sept 30, 25 3t.

Minnesota Pioneer, Nov. 22, 1849

1850s

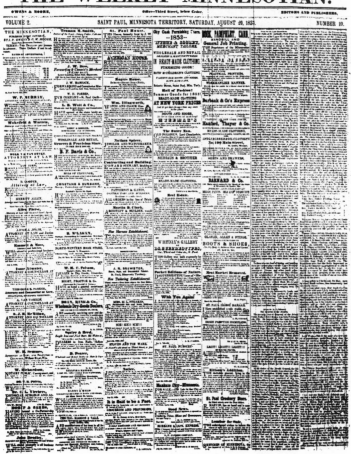

Commercial steamboating was inaugurated on the Minnesota River. The Dakota and Ojibway signed away most of their lands to the whites. The capital was located at St. Paul, the university in St. Anthony (later part of Minneapolis) and the penitentiary in Stillwater. Large-scale immigration began in the mid 1850s, and a real estate boom resulted. A nationwide financial panic in 1857 brought the boom to an end. Minnesota became a state in 1858, during hard times. Logging and milling were important, but the state's main business was farming. Immigrants were mostly from New England and New York.

Weekly Minnesotian, Aug. 20, 1853

1850s

—>•<—

Steamboating on the Upper Mississippi

A traveler wrote this glowing report of Minnesota for the St. Louis Republican and for St. Paul's Weekly Minnesotian.

AN EXCURSION on the Upper Mississippi during midsummer, is an agreeable escape from the heat and dust of a crowded city. The scenery along the river above Keokuk [Iowa] to St. Paul, is beautiful. The country along is thickly settling with energetic and industrious people. Most of the towns are improving rapidly. We noticed in Galena [Illinois], a large number of stores and dwelling houses, which, from their appearance, had evidently been built this year or last, and many fine edifices in the course of construction. . . . Between Galena and St. Paul are a number of flourishing towns.

St. Paul presents the most astonishing growth for a four-year-old town that can well be imagined. We were informed by Mr. Owens, editor of the Minnesotian at St. Paul, that when he settled there in May, 1849, there were but six or seven houses in the place. Now, to make a guess, there are some six or seven hundred — the most of them large and elegant. The town is laid out upon a liberal scale, and presents a handsome appearance. The population is estimated at between three and four thousand. The place has been rather deficient in hotel accommodations, which is being remedied by the construction of two large houses. One is nearly completed, and the other will be ready by next spring. These hotels are owned by wealthy citizens of the place, and they design to have them furnished and kept in such a style as to give satisfaction to those who may sojourn in St. Paul. — The country around St. Paul is beautiful, and although settled but recently will compare favorably with many older settlements in the number and beauty of its farm houses and the improvements around them. St. Paul is undoubtedly destined to become a place of great importance, being at the head of regular river navigation on the Mississippi, and the seat of government of Minnesota Territory. The U.S. Government has erected, adjoining the town, a large and handsome building for the accommodation of the Territorial Legislature and the Government officers.

There are many picturesque sights in the neighborhood of St. Paul. A few hours ride over a handsome country, will bring you to the Falls of St. Anthony, several beautiful lakes, lake Calhoun, the newly discovered lake Minnetonka, lake Harriet, "Little Falls" [Minnehaha], Fort Snelling, and the Mammoth Cavern, which will amply repay the traveler for the few hours spent in visiting them. On the road, about midway between Fort Snelling and the Little Falls, is the "St. Louis Hotel" kept by Mr. J.W. Downer. This house has been recently enlarged, improved and elegantly fitted up by the owner of the house and grounds, our townsman, Mr. Kenneth Mackenzie. The house is well arranged and properly kept by an accommodating host, and will, no doubt, be found a pleasant resort.

About six miles below St. Paul, on the Mississippi river, at the "Little Crow Village," is still to be found about three hundred Sioux Indians, living in their rude bark huts. Although Government has purchased their lands, and by the treaty they should have removed some time since, they still linger near their old hunting grounds and the graves of their fathers. An annuity is to be paid to them by the Government, at Traverse des Sioux, on the 15th of August, and an effort will be made to induce them to remove before that time; so that it will be but a short time before their rude huts will be taken possession of by the grasping hand of the white man. On the hills adjoining the village can be distinctly seen six or seven long square boxes, perched upon poles, about three feet above the ground, containing the bodies of Indians who had recently died. One box was shrouded with crimson cloth, and upon a pole near it was hung the feather head dress and the war implements of the de-

"The infant child of the Rev. Mr. Hoyt, of St. Paul, fell backwards into a pan of coals and ashes, on Wednesday morning last, and died next evening."

---

ceased. Upon the brow of the hill were seated two Indians with their heads covered with their blankets apparently mourning for some friend or relation.

To those who are fond of fishing and hunting, there are various places on the Upper Mississippi which will furnish them ample field for amusement. Grouse and other small game, and fish, are abundant. There are many streams in the neighborhood of Point Prescott, at the foot of lake St. Croix, and about Stillwater that abound with fine speckled brook trout. A party of seven of us visited Rush River, and bagged, in part of an afternoon and morning's fishing, nearly four hundred, ranging from six to sixteen inches in length.

Regular packets [boats] ply between St. Louis and Galena, connecting with packets of the first class to St. Paul, leaving Galena on Tuesday, Thursday and Saturday. The Nominee leaves Galena on Thursday, and travelers will find her a fast boat, with an accommodating Captain and Clerk, and excellent fare.

St. Paul Minnesotian, Aug. 20, 1853

—→•←—

Married. On the 13th inst. [of this month], by Rev. E.D. Neill, Mr. ISAAC BURRILL to Miss MARY J. NOTWELL, all of Saint Paul.

> She was lovely, she was fair —
> As mild as summer even;
> An angel from a spirit bright,
> A star that dropped from Heaven.

(Well she was!)

Minnesota Pioneer, St. Paul, Feb. 20, 1850

—→•←—

Casualties. The infant child of the Rev. Mr. Hoyt, of St. Paul, fell backwards into a pan of coals and ashes, on Wednesday morning last, and died next evening.

Mr. Whitmore, one of the mail carriers between Red Wing and Prairie la Crosse (on the river) was on the last trip severely injured by the running away of his horse. He was in a cutter which upset, causing the horse to run off, when he became entangled in the reins, and was dragged a considerable distance on the ice. He will probably recover.

Minnesota Democrat, St. Paul, Dec. 24, 1850

—→•←—

[Here a writer poked fun at legislators:]

We would respectfully suggest to the members of the lowest of the two lower houses [of the Minnesota Territory's Legislature], to allow their Sergeant-at-Arms mileage for his daily travels about St. Paul in search of "absent members." — He should also receive some extra pay for the arduous labor performed by him in pulling the Representatives out of bed every morning.

Watab Reveille, St. Paul, Jan. 29, 1851

—→•←—

Regents' Meeting. The Regents of the University of Minnesota hold their first meeting today at the St. Charles Hotel in this village. It is greatly to be desired that there should be a full attendance, as it is absolutely essential to the success of the University that prompt measures should be taken for the selection of a site, and the establishment of a preparatory department. If a suitable building can be erected, able and experienced teachers stand ready to open an Academy which shall

---

North-Western Democrat, St. Anthony, July 5, 1856

"What do you expect will come of that son of yours, who is loafing about town?"

do honor to the Territory, without asking any pecuniary aid from our citizens. Now is the time to begin. We should start with the determination, that not a single youth of either sex shall be permitted to leave this Territory to acquire an education, for want of an institution at home fully endowed to meet the wants of this class. Nature has here furnished one of the most beautiful sites in the Union for the establishment of a University.

St. Anthony Express, St. Anthony Falls, May 31, 1851

→›•‹←

Train up your Children to Work. There is a subject, which is not exactly political, nor religious, but which is not foreign, either to politics or religion upon which we have often reflected and will now express our opinions; deeming the subject one of vital interest to the welfare of all parents and children, who read our journal.

Neighbor A., what do you expect will come of that son of yours, who is loafing about town? Do you intend that he shall enter upon the great profession of loafing? (the largest, by far, in the United States.) If so, you are taking the right way to learn him that business thoroughly. Do you think it sufficient that he has learned to read and write, acquired a smattering of geography and grammar and arithmetic, or learned a little latin, perchance? Do you call *that* education? You cannot commit a more fatal error; your son, or your daughter, has to learn something infinitely more important than any and all of these things — and that is, patient industry, steady application, and business habits. Your child — every child, has a living to make. Remember that. No matter what honest pursuit your child may be taught, or may follow through life — that is of very lit-

Daily Minnesotian, St. Paul, June 17, 1857

tle consequence, since industry will afford a competence in any business he may follow — the main thing is, to put him *in harness* and learn him to *work*. Failing to teach him industry, you make him a drone and an inveterate loafer through life. There are scores of active, smart boys and girls, in Saint Paul, who are growing up in idleness and in ignorance of any way under heaven to make a living, because their parents are too proud to put them to trades, or because they think they are too young and tender to be put to work. There is not a more miserable, worthless

dog in the world, than a young man raised in affluence, without industry, without self-reliance, no matter what his knowledge of *books* may be, who is turned out into the world to struggle for a subsistence. It would be just as sensible to tie a boy in a chair and feed him there, from his infancy, to prepare him to run foot races at the age of 21 years, as to raise him in idleness, from infancy, to prepare him to wrestle with poverty and the hardships of life, when he is of age. A child that is old enough to *learn* is old enough to learn something useful. — It is only for want of being

"They caught 300 lbs. of black bass, and killed 63 prairie chickens."

taught some *useful* employment, that a boy ever learns to play cards or billiards. Teach your children, (for they can understand you) the value of time and industry. Make them understand *how* and *why*, industry and frugality are indispensable to their respectable subsistence. Make your boy earn a hat or a pair of boots, by his own industry; and it will be the best lesson you can teach him.

Minnesota Pioneer, St. Paul, June 26, 1851

→>·<‑

Little Falls — On the road from here to Ft. Snelling are what is called the Little Falls. A clear, bold stream a few yards wide, and about two feet deep, falls perpendicularly more than 60 feet over a semi-circular overhanging rock. It is a perfect miniature of Niagara on the Canada side. You can go behind the sheet just as at Niagara. The Indians call it "Minne-ha-ha," or the laughing water. "Minne" is the Dahcota [Dakota Indian] word for water, and certainly "ha-ha" is laughing.

St. Anthony Falls Express, June 28, 1851

→>·<‑

Great Hunting and Fishing. — Four gentlemen of St. Paul enjoyed a day sport at hunting and fishing last week, on Rice creek and Rice lake. They caught 300 lbs. of black bass, and killed 63 prairie chickens.

Minnesota Democrat, St. Paul, Aug. 26, 1851

→>·<‑

Consistency is a Jewel. — How much more forcible other people's sins strike us than our own. "Look at those boys," said our friend Jones, on Sunday last; "not a week passes over their heads without their violating the Sabbath, with their d‑‑‑‑d ball

Stillwater Messenger, Oct. 12, 1858

playing, and yet the police take no more notice of the desecration, by thunder, than if they were so many d‑‑‑‑d heathens." Jones looks upon himself as quite a moral man, and yet he

"Should a fire occur let every citizen repair to the scene of conflagration with a bucket of water and much property may be saved thereby."

committed more sin in speaking of the boys, than the boys were committing with the ball playing. Jones' remarks on the Sabbath reminds us of the Yankee captain, who told his cabin boy to wait until he got done praying and he "would knock his d————d head off." Queer world this.

St. Anthony Express, St. Anthony Falls, Oct. 25, 1851

—›•‹—

Fire! St. Paul is entirely destitute of means for extinguishing fire, and should any of our buildings in the more densely populated portions of town take fire, a large number might be destroyed before the conflagration could be arrested. Measures should be taken to form a hook and ladder company — immediately.

Should a fire occur let every citizen repair to the scene of conflagration with a bucket of water and much property may be saved thereby.

Minnesota Democrat, St. Paul, Nov. 18, 1851

—›•‹—

THE ITASCA HOUSE, ITASCA, BENTON COUNTY, MINNESOTA

It gives me pleasure to inform the traveling public that I have taken and refitted in excellent style, the above old and well known stand; and am determined to make it the best public house above St. Anthony. My table will be kept supplied with venison and other game in season, and the bar with the choicest liquors. The best accommodations — couches fit for a tired prince — will be found by all who may have occasion to visit this region, or the upper country during the fine sleighing of the present winter. Being situated midway between St. Paul, St. Anthony and Sauk Rapids, and but a moderate drive from each, I invite a call from one and all, whether business men or pleasure seekers. I will treat you well and charge you moderately.

(Signed) William B. Vincent

Minnesota Democrat, St. Paul, Dec. 10, 1851

—›•‹—

Caught — Messrs. Castner, French and Bryant, our efficient town police, have caught one of the rascals engaged for some time past in robbing the outhouses, clothes lines, kitchens and store houses of our citizens. The fellow's name is Thomas, a villainous looking rascal, who, with his two sons, lads apparently 12 and 14 years of age, have been carrying on quite large business in nocturnal stealing for the last three months. The police made a search of Thomas's house, on Monday evening, and found a wagon load of stolen goods; embracing clothes of all kinds, blankets, quilts, table covers, crockery ware, whiskey, axes, saws, carpenter tools, &c., and the butter lately stolen from Revd. E.D. Neill.

The stolen property was deposited in French's auction store, where a large crowd assembled yesterday, and many of them recognized and claimed articles that have been stolen from them.

There are one or two others in town, suspected of being engaged in the same business as

MINNESOTA RIVER PACKET.

THE new and splendid Steamer MINNESOTA BELLE, HUMBERSTONE, Master, will run as a regular packet between St. Paul, and the ports of the Minnesota river, during the present season of navigation. The Minnesota Belle is an entirely new boat, just completed at Pittsburgh, having been built expressly for this trade and will be found equal in every respect to any steamer on the western waters.

April 15, 1854.

1—tf

Minnesota Pioneer, June 15, 1854

*"Minnesotans, believing that there is a time to dance,
are resolved to make the winter pass merrily."*

Thomas. The police, aided by our citizens, are wide awake, and after the rascals. They cannot escape. — With these exceptions theft has been almost unknown in this community.

Minnesota Democrat, St. Paul, Dec. 10, 1851

⇥·⇤

Balls. — The first of a series of balls to be given every other week, during the winter, will take place at Lott Moffets' Hall this evening. Minnesotans, believing that there is a time to dance, are resolved to make the winter pass merrily.

Minnesota Democrat, St. Paul, Dec. 10, 1851

⇥·⇤

Soon as there is sufficient snow to admit of running sleighs, Burbank & Co. will make two trips per week between this place and Galena. Their days of departure will be Monday and Thursday. They have good sleighs and horses; and there are comfortable accommodations along the road. — Mr. B. says they will make their trip to Galena in six days. Price of passage $16 to Galena [Ill.]; $13 to Prairie du Chien [Wis.]. Freight from Galena $5 per 100 lbs.

Minnesota Democrat, St. Paul, Dec. 17, 1851

⇥·⇤

Statisticians inform us that a woman's chance of getting married is at its maximum between the ages of twenty and twenty-five. After thirty, her chances, as might have been supposed, dwindles away to zero: hence the great length of time that most ladies take in arriving at that age.

St. Anthony Express, St. Anthony Falls, Dec. 27, 1851

⇥·⇤

Died. On the 19th inst. [of this month], BIRDIE, infant daughter

TWENTY-FIVE FARMS FOR SALE.
TO PRACTICAL FARMERS.

THIS notice is to *real* Faamers, not to speculators who pretend to be farmers.

To practical Farmers, I wish to say that I have on hand now twenty five farms for sale, (and always have from ten to twenty-five) which range from two to ten miles from St Paul.

From a long residence in this Territory, and from personal inspection of all the lands near this City, I am enabled to make the best selections.

I therefore invite all persons wishing to cultivate the soil, to give me a call.

My Farms have various degrees of improvement, and flatter myself that I can please all.

Terms made to suit purchasers.

HENRY M'KENTY,
Dealer in Real Estate.

Office—Old Post Office Building, 3d street.
May 5, 1854.

Minnesota Pioneer, Sept. 26, 1854

of William F. and Harriet B. Corbett.

At St. Paul, on Wednesday, Feb. 18th, HARRIET LOUISE, daughter of Nelson and Abigail Gibbs, aged 5 years the 25th day of last January.

At St. Paul, M.T. [Minnesota Territory], on Saturday morning Feb. 14th, LUCY ANN, daughter of Edwin and Catharine Perkins, aged 10 years and one week.

Beautiful indeed has been the tender flower to look upon, and truly short has been the race of our departed friend. The withered rose and the drooping lily, when reflected upon, may cast the lengthened shadow of gloom o'er the gayest heart, but oh, how truly sad to behold the tender flower, which brightly has bloomed amid the wreath entwined around the hearts of parent and child, sister and brother, withered by death's chilling touch and consigned to the cheerless grave. Mild and affectionate in her manners, she won the esteem of all who associated

with her, and will long be remembered by them all. No more, bereaved parents, will the smiles of your child brighten home's fireside; she is gone to a land of spirits, from whence no man returneth, and where sickness and sorrow are unknown; all your earthly ties are ended, you may be once more united; but in a world beyond the skies.

C.E.S.

Harrisburg papers please copy.

Minnesota Pioneer, St. Paul, Feb. 26, 1852

⇥·⇤

Side Walks. — A good plank side walk and railing, will be built this week, along the bluff, from Wabashaw to Hill street. The expense of constructing it, is made up by voluntary subscriptions of our truly public spirited townsmen.

Minnesota Pioneer, St. Paul, March 18, 1852

⇥·⇤

*"It appears according to her simple story,
that she was in search of a truant husband . . . "*

The Weather. Such glorious weather as that with which we have been favored this month, we venture to say has not been enjoyed in any part of the country. O ye mud-engulphed Suckers! ye sposh-affected Hoosiers! — Ye fog enveloped, mist drenched Buckeyes! Ye snow-buried, rain sleet-and-hail assailed Yankees and Knickerbockers! Come to Minnesota, if ye would enjoy the perfection of a winter clime. For the last six days we have enjoyed an uninterrupted succession of warm, unclouded days — thermometer ranging about 30 degrees during the day, atmosphere pure and exhilarating, just about as stimulating as the nectar of Olympus, and heavens of such a deep, lustrous blue, at evening flooded with such a mellow, golden sunset light as no Italian skies can surpass. Strangers passing their first winter in the territory, entertaining the false and absurd notions that prevail at the east respecting our winter climate, express their unmeasured disappointment and delight between the representation and reality of a Minnesota winter. The inch of snow with which December opened, has disappeared under the influence of an April sun — no mud takes its place — the wheeling is superb. ... Summer, Autumn and Winter are each so delightful in this climate, that you are puzzled to decide which you prefer. The latter, however seems to have a majority in its favor.
St. Anthony Express, St. Anthony Falls, Dec. 10, 1853

⟶•⟵

An Incident. A few days ago, a matronly looking woman entered our office, daguerreotype [a photograph made by an early process on a light-sensitive, silver-coated metallic plate] in hand, and respectfully submitting it for our inspection, modestly asked if we

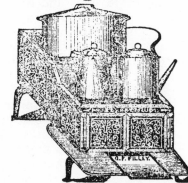
had seen a man answering to the description which the shadow portrayed. It appears according to her simple story, that she was in search of a truant husband, who had disposed of his farm near Adrian, Mich., and started for Minnesota to better his fortunes, promising that he would return and accompany her to their new home within a certain specified time. As the set period for his return had long transpired, and hearing that she had been supplanted in his affections by another, with feelings breathing love or vengeance, she had left home armed, not with a pistol or dagger, but a more formidable weapon, consisting of simply a daguerreotype, which when once seen would ever be remembered, to see if she could not find the guilty couple, and either win him back to his former allegiance or hand them over to the tender mercies of the law.

When we took the proffered picture to examine it, our mind was full of poetic fancies, and forms of angelic beauty flitted across our imagination, and we mentally thanked our visitor for her kindness in entertaining us with some rare specimen of revealed loveliness, but we confess that we were most egregiously disappointed when, instead of a likeness embodying all the charms of the graces, our eyes fell on a grim Cyclops, whose physical and moral deformity could be read at a glance. Why a woman would take the trouble to seek after such a mean apology for a man, and leave home, friends and acquaintances for one who had forfeited all claims to her respect, is an anomaly not to be explained, except in the constant unchanging love of woman. We for our part conceive her extremely fortunate in getting rid of so miserable a specimen of humanity, and think that the greatest misfortune that could befall her would be to restore the heartless renegade to her former confidence or esteem.
St. Anthony Express, St. Anthony Falls, July 15, 1854

⟶•⟵

Our Observations in Minnesota. The renowned grandeur and beauty of the scenery of the Hudson, the St. Lawrence, and of Italy, has been extolled time and again by the press and the tourest, while but few have as yet satiated their love for the beautiful in natural scenery by a trip on the upper Mississippi. Our own imagination had scarcely reached the starting point of what the re-

"The habitual use of tobacco was never calculated for health or substantial comfort, or to prolong life."

ality opened to it the 17th of May last, the day after we had taken passage, on board the Nominee, for Wenona, a new but lovely little town, about 250 miles above Galena, and which was to have been our abiding place in this land of promise. A continual variation of scene now opened to the view, marred only by an occasional ungraceful slew or marsh which placed the opposite high lands at a more remote distance from the steamer as she gracefully moved up the winding channel. We have not time nor space to notice the numerous worthy places between Galena and Wenona, none of which, however, left so great an impression on our mind as the latter. As we neared it the evening of the third day after our embarkation, the beautiful prairie on which the town had been located, put on the most lovely appearance, the buildings which dotted its surface filling their appropriate places in the scene, as if to enliven which, numerous tenements were in progress of erection, the workmen pausing now and then to watch the progress of the boat as she neared the landing. Here was life and activity, politeness and civility, where the rude state of border life had been expected. . . .

Minneapolis, which is just opposite St. Anthony, stretched forth her arms to receive us. The rich soil of Hennepin county, of which she is the county town, promised great things. Her inhabitants are full of enterprize and intelligence — just such as would successfully invite us to her embrace. Here we pause for language to convey the thoughts that crowd forward for expression. We have adopted Minneapolis as our home — as the place where we would live and die; in the bosom of whose citizens we would rest our future prosperity. Home. It is here thou art found. Old and tried friends do not greet us as we walk abroad; that warm grasp of the hands of those who are near and dear is missed, still the sacredness of home is here enjoyed. The christian, the generous friend, and all those who are necessary to comprise the home neighborhood in completeness are here. The enlightened and industrious mechanic and farmer, the professions and tradesmen are well represented, and the sciences and fine arts are soon to take their appropriate places among us. To doubt this would be to disbelieve what our eyes have actually seen: viz, fifty substantial buildings which have gone up within a year past, all but four being dwellings and business houses, and there are between fifteen and twenty more now in progress of erection, two of them substantial bricks. A new church edifice overlooks all from an elevated position.

North-Western Democrat, St. Anthony, Aug. 19, 1854

→-←

A late writer, in speaking of sour krout, says, "it is the connecting link between damaged cabbage and pickled manure."
St. Paul Minnesotian, Sept. 13, 1854

→-←

Tobacco. — The habitual use of tobacco was never calculated for health or substantial comfort, or to prolong life. It destroys all these. Notwithstanding the slow and insidious manner in which it poisons the vitals and undermines the constitution, it is yet seen that it occasions everywhere a frightful loss of life. In the United States, intelligent physicians have estimated that 20,000 die every year from the use of tobacco; and in Germany, where the streets as well as the houses are literally befogged with tobacco smoke, the physicians have calculated that of all the deaths which occur between the ages of 18 and 35, one half originate in the waste of the constitution by smoking! Such opinions as these from men who ought to know, should startle all the world, and bring chewers and smokers to their senses, in regard to the

Minnnesota Pioneer, Sept. 26, 1854

"Our streets are daily full of German Emigrants on their way into the interior of the Territory."

powers of this Indian weed, and the effects of habits which too many have been inclined hitherto, to call harmless.
St. Paul Minnesotian, Oct. 11, 1854

→⟩•⟨←

German Emigrants. Our streets are daily full of German Emigrants on their way into the interior of the Territory. — A great number of this class have come among us this season, and a great majority of them intend to cultivate the soil. They inform us that many more are on the route. Several of them in advance of the wagons, filled with women and children, were sauntering along the street, with their matchlocks [guns] on their shoulders, and singing the popular German song of Arudt. ... Their spirit-stirring tunes went ringing on the clear air, while their little ones and wives listened with melancholy pleasure, for the scenes doubtless brought back many fond reminiscences of the past. Only those who have left the scenes of their childhood for some foreign shore, and heard in that distant land, the familiar songs of their youth, can appreciate the feelings of emigrants as they wander amid strangers in a strange land.
St. Paul Times, Nov. 7, 1854

→⟩•⟨←

In Minnesota, the four seasons of the year are distinctly marked and well divided, tho' summer and winter are somewhat longer than spring and autumn. The almanac maker has one calendar; Nature has another.
Minnesota Republican, St. Anthony Falls, March 1, 1855

→⟩•⟨←

Bury Your Dead! — We are informed that a number of dead animals are lieing above ground, in various parts of the city, viz:

Three or four dead horses on Boom Island, a hog, near the Catholic church, several hogs near the shop of Mr. Leaming, and some putrid fish on the bank of the river above the planing mill. The man who will thus leave the body of an animal to lie and putrify within city limits, deserves the reprobation of all honest men. Burial is the only proper disposition that can be made of such things. Do not throw them into the river, but bury them.
St. Anthony Express, St. Anthony Falls, May 12, 1855

→⟩•⟨←

"At 4 o'clock, P.M. we consigned the body of our loved child to the grave."

Extracts from a Journal kept by a Citizen of Stillwater.

Wednesday, Aug. 27, 185-. After a week of severe suffering with dysentery, accompanied with hydrocephalus [fluid on the brain], our dear L---- J---- left us this evening. Poor Dear Babe! I felt I scarcely could give her up, but her suffering was so great that it was a relief to see the breath leave her little body. I know not why it is that I am the fourth time left childless. I am a great lover of children, but have tried not to make an idol of them: I, by faith, *know it is best,* but the struggle to be *resigned* is a hard one. But I can, *I do say, "Thy will be done."*

Our kind friends have aided and sympathized with us. This we needed, strangers as we were, in a strange land. Long will we remember Mrs. B----, F----, B----, C----, and F----. May God always raise up *friends* for them when they are needed!

Thursday, Aug. 28. At 4 o'clock, P.M. we consigned the body of our loved child to the grave. I felt my heart struggling to show its rebellion against the grave as it fell upon the coffin, and hid it from sight. O, how the ties that bind us to our children instinctively refuse to be sundered! But they *must sever.* Farewell, dear Babe!

Thursday, Sept. 4. I would abhor myself for indulging a murmuring spirit for one moment, but I almost fear I do so in reference to my dear L----'s death. Whenever the thought of her enters my mind, my *heart* refuses to consent that she is dead, though my *judgment* is convinced she has been buried now a full week. I have buried three lovely babes, before, and could, from the hour of burying them, look back on their little graves with pleasure, as their resting place; but this time my foolish heart envies the grave its treasure. I feel always at

Minnesota Pioneer, July 12, 1855

"Hog's lard, rubbed freely on bedsteads. . . is the best preventative we know against bed-bugs. . ."

first though *I must have her back.* I never would have re-called one of the others if I could, but this time I feel it a hardship that I cannot. The oth-ers I scarcely expected to keep — this one I did — she lived longer and was healthier than the others, and was called for my only sister. But, alas! in a strange land, in so short a time [the writer had emigrated to the Territory only two weeks before], she was taken. I know it is all right, but it seems that *I cannot do without her.* My heart bleeds, my cheer-fulness in a great degree is gone. There seems little for me to live for. My dear companion feels her loss as keenly as I do. The Lord forgive us, graciously, any thing that may be wrong in these feel-ings — remember that we are but flesh and blood!

Sunday, Sept. 7. My dear little child, I think, is now *fully* given up. I can, with pleasure now think of her as being "absent from the body — present with the Lord," and her two little brothers and sister. No more pain will ever affect her body, or damp the joys of her mind. O that we may so live as to see them there!

Tuesday, Dec. 2. There is nothing, however, in my feelings like despondency. On the con-trary, I feel quite cheerful the greater part of my time; but since the grave closed over all that was tangible of my Dear L———— J————, I feel little comfort in human society. I enjoy myself much bet-ter with a book than with a friend. Perhaps one of the great-est reasons for this is that, that grave, though more than a mile distant, is always in sight. I can scarcely lift up my eyes but that the white palings of the bluff at-tract them. Then I think of her smart face and form — of her pain and patience — her last groan, and of that awful silence, when with intense interest I looked for another gasp, which

came not; and then of the still more painful conviction that she would breathe no more with mortal lungs. And so one thought follows the preceding till I fancy her among miriads like her — in-fant Angels — around the bril-liant throne of Jesus, offering him the praise of human lips nev-er contaminated with sin. Then I think of the happy hour when my four Angel Babes may be permit-ted to welcome their unworthy Father to those realms of glad-ness. [Yes, the writer is a man.] Can I be gloomy? No. Thanks to God for the hopes of the Chris-tian that when a few years more of toil and disappointment are past, he may enter into rest, not alone, but with the loved ones of Earth.

Saint Croix Union, Stillwater, June 2, 1855

→ • ←

Farming. — If a young man wants to engage in business that will insure him in middle age the greatest amount of leisure time, there is nothing more sure than farming. If he has an indepen-dent turn of mind, let him be a farmer; or, if he wants to engage in a healthy occupation let him become a farmer. In short; if he would be really independent, let him get a spot of earth here in Minnesota, keep within his means to shun the constable; be temperate, to avoid the doctor; be honest that he may have a clear conscience; improve the soil, so as to leave the world bet-ter than he found it; and also to leave an unimpoverished legacy to his children.

St. Peter's Courier, June 7, 1855

→ • ←

Fleas, Bed-Bugs, &C. — A writer in the Gardener's Chroni-cle recommends the use of oil of wormwood to keep off the in-sects above named. Put a few drops on a handkerchief or a

piece of folded muslin, and put in the bed haunted by the ene-my. Neither of these tribes can bear wormwood, and the hint is especially commended to travel-lers who are liable to fall among the topers [drinkers] of blood.

Hog's lard, rubbed freely on bedsteads, says another writer, is the best preventative we know against bed-bugs; for as long as it remains, they do not come near. Before applying it, bedsteads should be well washed with a cloth and cold water. — Scalding with hot water, and spoiling them, is needless.

St. Peter's Courier, Aug. 30, 1855

→ • ←

Come to Minnesota.

A lady writes to Col. Fuller, the editor of the N.Y. "Mirror," propounding a query as to where she shall settle in the West. She says:

"I am one of those unfortu-nate individuals whose whole life, or rather the best part of it, has been made indescribably wretched by marriage. I have an interesting family, who cling to me, and I have sufficient means (I think) to obtain an indepen-dence, if well appropriated. You will, I hope, excuse me for ad-dressing you; and I feel assured you will not be displeased at my boldness, in asking you for ad-vice in relation to purchase of land. I fear *imposition* and wish to know how to avoid it. I have a son, or rather three sons, who all say they will be farmers, and knowing you to be a gentleman in the true sense, and that you have opportunities of obtaining reliable information I hope you will do me and my family the fa-vor or a reply."

The Colonel in reply, states:

"So far as our personal obser-vation may be worth anything to the lady, we will say that during the trip she alludes to, we saw nothing so charming or so invit-

"The principles of some [legislators] may have undergone a change."

---

ing as the region of the Upper Mississippi. The soil, the climate, the scenery, in the vicinity of St. Paul is all that an agriculturalist or artist could desire; and the young man who finds himself the owner of a hundred acres in that neighborhood to-day, can hardly help being a rich man ten or fifteen years hence. Had we to 'begin life anew,' a Minnesota farm should be the paradise we should pray for. What a luxury to live up there in the pure atmosphere of its grain-clad hills, among its simple hearted people, its beautiful horses, fat sheep, and honest looking cows and oxen."

To which the "St. Paul Pioneer and Democrat" pertinently adds:

The Colonel is correct. To a person desiring to begin life, by pursuing agricultural pursuits, Minnesota offers rare inducements. The "three sons who say they will be farmers," are just the class of people we want here. There are in the Territory, millions of acres of land to be had at government price, which, for fertility, is unsurpassed. A good market for all that the "three sons" can produce, is to be found at home. Our climate is healthy, invigorating — everybody likes it. Our people are intelligent and enterprising — they have made Minnesota what it is. But the class of population which we particularly require, at present, to insure our future prosperity are agriculturists. As evidence of the high repute for fertility, which Minnesota soil has, we may state that at the recent land sales, wild land brought a high premium over the government minimum. The sales attracted to the land offices, the enterprising men of the East, who could not help observing that the admirable geographical situation of Minnesota, the character of its soil, and the intelligence of its people, will make

MINNEAPOLIS FERRY,
Six Tickets for a Dollar.

Z. M. BROWN, - - PROPRIETOR.

THE above ferry has been improved, and is well conducted. A good and faithful ferryman is always in attendance, who will use all diligence in preventing delays or accidents in crossing. The hills on either side are being improved so as to render it easy for teams to get off and on the boat.

Inducements for Crossing at this Ferry.

Persons visiting Minneapolis for pleasure or business, from St. Paul, save near two miles of travel, and if they desire to go back through St. Anthony, have an opportunity of seeing the whole of the picturesquely beautiful Minneapolis without driving back and forth, the bridge from Minneapolis to Nicollet Island being at the extreme upper end of town. Teams going to St. Paul or goods or otherwise, unless they have business in St. Anthony, will find it a great saving in distance and time to cross at this ferry.
Minneapolis, July 7, 1855. 51tf

North-Western Democrat, Sept. 8, 1855

the future State the great producing region of the north west. We may add, that no fears need be entertained that the actual settler will not be able to secure his land at government price. There is not a foot of land in the Territory, belonging to government, surveyed or unsurveyed, which is not subject to preemption, and the provisions of the law granting that privilege, amply guards the right of the settler to the land which his labor may make valuable.

Southern Minnesota Herald, Brownsville, Nov. 15, 1855

-›-‹-

The great and General Assembly had adjourned *sine die* [for the session], and the members of that long-to-be-remembered body of Law makers had returned to their respective abodes under various circumstances. Their habits, morally and physically, may have been the same as when they were sent to the capitol by their constituents; but the principles of some may have undergone a change.

Sauk Rapids Frontierman, April 17, 1856

-›-‹-

Important if True. — We have heard it stated that the practice of wearing hoops will become very general as soon as the fall fashions arrive. Should this be true, and our ladies determine on

"Everything was in that wagon, sure enough, an infant city in embryo! — chairs, tables, wife, children, stock, houses and all!"

bringing them into universal use, we trust our city fathers will be duly advised of the fact, in order that pavements hereafter constructed may be built of greater width, in order to accommodate the fair pedestrians. As it is now, they are entirely too narrow.

The question of hoops or anti-hoops is fast becoming one of the leading questions of the day, and it will soon become necessary for candidates for political preferment to clearly define their positions on this.

St. Paul Pioneer and Democrat, Sept. 3, 1856

→•←

We saw a funny incident, yesterday. A long, four-wheeled barge sailed by our office in the mud, and for its cargo was a lot of motley merchandize. May we often look upon its like! — Guiding the oxen was a stalwart yeoman and by his side chatted a plain, sensible-looking woman, with hope in her eye and a bouncing baby in her arms, while under and around the seat cuddled a lot of other children, "the very picture of their father." A pile of furniture and domestic goods came next, including tubs, tables, chairs, carpets, brooms, bedsteads, stoves, axes, rifles, pails, porridge pots and pudding sticks — everything necessary for primitive house-wifery. In the body of the wagon was lumber — boards and posts — with which to complete a house for the winter, while in the hind end a two year old yearling stood demurely chewing his cud, evidently very much surprised at the growth of our city. Everything was in that wagon, sure enough, an infant city in embryo! — chairs, tables, wife, children, stock, houses and all!

Minnesota Times, St. Paul, Oct. 22, 1856

→•←

A Pill for Old Fogies! The lot opposite the Winslow House, corner of St. Anthony and Fort streets, was sold yesterday by Mr. Nathan Myrick, of this city, to B.H. Campbell, Esq., of Galena for $19,000! — five years ago the lot cost Mr. Myrick just $200! Mr. Campbell's business relations have brought him to this city frequently during the last six years, and had he taken advantage of the opportunity, he might have

INVENTIONS

Potato Digger. — We have been shown an ingenious machine, by this name, invented by F. Jones, Esq., of Otter Lake [Ramsey County]. It is very simple in its construction, and so far as we are able to judge, cannot fail to answer the purpose admirably. It is estimated by farmers and others versed in such matters, that one man and two horses, with this machine, can dig from three to five acres of potatoes per day, or from six to eight hundred bushels.

Minnesota Pioneer, St. Paul, Feb. 7, 1855

→•←

Gas in St. Paul. — The Minnesotian of yesterday morning, states that Messrs. Greenleaf & Chappell, Jewellers, on St. Anthony street, have introduced gas into their store. It is manufactured upon the premises, and when lighted, emits from the burners a jet of pure flame equalled only by that made at the expensive works of large cities. It is said to be cheaper than oil or fluid.

St. Paul Pioneer and Democrat, Nov. 15, 1855

→•←

Important if True. — We understand that Mr. Peter J. Clark, a well known citizen of this place, has lately invented a flying machine, and also, that he intends soon to take passage up Crow River in a canoe, in search of some retired place, where he can more quietly perfect his invention. We learn that compressed air is to be the principal motive power, although the machine will be so constructed that a certain quantity of steam can also be used, if necessary. In order that the inhabitants of Minnesota may be convinced that his invention is no humbug, Mr. Clark will first fly from the top of Cheever's Tower to St. Paul, after which he contemplates passing over the Rocky Mountains, to San Francisco in California. He estimates the speed of the machine at thirty miles per hour, but thinks it may be safely increased to forty. We understand that his arrangements will probably be completed about the first of September. From the well known energy and inventive talent of Mr. Clark, we presume there can be no doubt but the experiment will prove successful. [Guess again. If Clark had made it, we would have learned his name instead of the Wright Brothers'. They flew in 1903.]

St. Anthony Express, July 12, 1856

"The washerwoman is a power in society."

purchased, within that time, the whole ground upon which St. Paul now stands, for the money he yesterday paid for a single building lot, almost on the outskirts of the city! Yet, even now the lot is obtained at a bargain, and in a few years, will sell readily at five times that amount. Men are coming to our city every day who "came very near starting some years ago," and are discovering that though our land sells at a higher price than it did a month ago, it does not *yet* cost *half* as much as a lack of confidence! Experience will teach the lesson.

Minnesota Times, St. Paul, Oct. 24, 1856

→›‹←

The Washerwoman. The washerwoman is a power in society. Princes are amenable to her. Your Beau Brummels [Brummel, an Englishman, set the style for men's clothes and manners in the early 1800s] and D'Orsays [D'Orsay was a French society figure and patron of the arts] are her handicraft. She is old and ugly, perhaps, as such a potent witch should be, but from the ingredients of her "charmed pot" she conjures a spell more powerful than Hecate and all her hags. From the steaming tub and seething boiler, in the dingy caboose without a window or a name — where with

"double toil and trouble Fires burn and cauldrons bubble,"

from chaotic heaps of dirty linen and the spurned cast-offs of a week's grime and sweat, the washerwoman distils the essential respectability of society, and reinstates it in the pride of wristbands and the dignity of shirt collars. She hears the burden of our sins. In penitential suds and saponaceous contrition she shrives us weekly of our follies, vices,

Minnesota Pioneer, June 14, 1855

"Princely fare and first class accommodations [will] be provided for any who wish to spend a few days in that beautiful place."

and world stains. She is the appointed guardian of our fame. She retrieves the tarnished character with a little lye, and gives us back a spotless bosom for eight cents. She turns blackguards into gentlemen. She creates the whole difference between men. Through the medium of pearl buttons and by the combined influence of starch and soap and soda, she exercises a control almost supreme over our social relations. She breaks at will our most important engagements; gives or denies us the *entree* into fashionable circles. Are we invited to dine with the President of the Mankato Bank? We take our washerwoman into our confidence. Are we appointed to make an extempore speech at an oyster supper? It is our washerwoman who lends to our peroration the splendor of her best wristbands, and invests our periods with the magnificence of a white Marseilles. Our cravat is a speech in itself — her speech. Our cambric handkerchief is a broad parenthetical sweep of rhetoric — her interpolation. Generally speaking, we are a compilation from her clothes-horse, and should be put in quotation marks. She is our best friend or our worst enemy. Our fate is in her hands. As long as a man's reputation is in his shirt, and dress is the measure of social distinction, the washerwomen will rule the destinies of mankind.

St. Paul Financial, Real Estate and Railroad Advertiser, June 14, 1856

⇥•⇤

Grading Streets. — In St. Paul, this term means the digging out and carting of earth from a particular locality, by order of the City Surveyor, one day and hauling it back the next. All very interesting to tax-payers!

St. Paul Minnesotian, Aug. 29, 1856

"GARDING SASS."

HOE! all who intend planting gardens—who are disposed to "mind your PEAS and q's"—who have faith in cabbage—tailors not excepted,) who "know beans when the bag is opened"—who "acknowledge the corn" in the roasting ear—who believe in the good time coming—when new potato-ses and ripe tomato-ses —fence rail cucumbers, and inclined-plane squashes, will please the eye and administer to the appetites of the "toiling millions."

This special proclamation, greeting: If you wish fresh Garden Seeds, come and get them of
BOND & KELLOGG,
At the Old Brown Drug Store.

North-Western Democrat, Oct. 28, 1854

Never Repress Your Tears. — A lengthy dissertation has recently been published by a physician of France, on the beneficial influence of groaning and crying on the nervous system. He contends that groaning and crying are the two grand operations by which nature allays anguish — that he has uniformly observed those patients who give way to their natural feelings, more speedily recover from accidents and operations, than those who suppose it is unworthy a man to betray such symptoms of cowardness as either to groan or cry. He is always pleased by the crying and violent roaring of a patient during the time he is undergoing a violent surgical operation, because he is satisfied that he will thereby soothe his nervous system so as to prevent fever, and insure a favorable termination. He relates the case of a man who, by crying and bawling, reduced his pulse from one hundred and twenty-six to sixty, in the course of two hours. That some patients often have great satisfaction in groaning, and that the hysterical patients experience great relief from crying, are facts that no person will deny. As to restless and hypochondriachal subjects, or those who are never happy but when under some medical or dietetic treatment, the French surgeon assures them that they cannot do better than groan all day and night.

Valley Herald, Shakopee, May 20, 1857

⇥•⇤

White Bear Lake. — This retreat, always famous for its beautiful scenery and romantic seclusion, and always a favorite with sportsmen, tourists, and invalids, has been lately rendered doubly attractive from the fact that John Lamb, Esq., has opened a first rate hotel there. Not only will princely fare and first class accommodations be provided for any who wish to spend a few days in that beautiful place, but the proprietor has a choice supply of boats, fishing tackle, guns, nets &c at all times for his guests. Strangers anxious to see the country, and have a glorious time generally, had better call on

*"There is something cordial about a fat man.
Everybody likes him, and he likes everybody."*

John. They will find him a clever landlord.

St. Paul Minnesotian, May 27, 1857

—>·<—

Fat Men. There is something cordial about a fat man. Everybody likes him, and he likes everybody. . . . Fat does a man good: it clings to him; it fructifies on him; he swells nobly out; and fills a generous space in life. He is a living, walking minister of gratitude to the earth, and the fullness thereof; an incarnate testimony against the vanity of care; a radiant manifestation of the wisdom of good humor. A fat man, therefore, almost in virtue of being a fat man, is, *per se,* a popular man; and commonly he deserves his popularity. In a crowded vehicle, the fattest man will ever be the most ready to make room. Indeed, he seems to be half sorry for his size, lest it be in the way of others; but others would not have him less than is; for his humanity is usually commensurate with his bulk. A fat man has abundance of rich juices. The hinges of his system are well oiled; the springs of his being are noiseless; and so he goes on his way rejoicing, in full contentment and placidity. A fat man feels his position solid in the world; he knows that his being is cognizable; he knows that he has a marked place in the universe, and that he need take no extra pain to advertise to mankind that he is among them; he knows that he is in no danger of being overlooked. It does really take a deal of wrong to make one really hate a fat man; and if we are not always as cordial to a thin man as we should be, Christian charity should take into account the force of prejudice which we have to overcome against his thinness. A fat man is nearest to that most perfect of figures, a mathematical sphere; a thin man to that most limited of conceiv-

Minnesota Pioneer, June 14, 1855

able dimensions, a simple line. A fat man is a being of harmonious volume, and holds relations to the material universe in every direction; a thin man has nothing but length; a thin man, in fact, is but a continuation of a point.

Emigrant Aid Journal, Nininger, June 20, 1857

[The town of Nininger was built by Minnesota politician Ignatius Donnelly, who wanted it to be a culturally enlightened city, the "New York of the West." The townsite near Hastings was divided into 3,800 lots. Extensive advertising promised a hotel, ferryboat and library. Land prices went up and about 500 people moved in. But the Panic of 1857 hit, and Nininger was severely crippled. It went under in the next decade.]

—>·<—

Look Out for the Circus. Notice in another column, the advertisement of Major Brown's Colosseum, and great American Circus, which will exhibit at this place on the fourth of August next. — The canvas will be erected on the block, which is in front of our office.

We would recommend a full attendance. Ladies must not wear hoops, as the tent will be crowded. Children must stick close to their parents. Castello it is said, is the greatest clown in the world.

We have seen Oliver Bell in St. Louis. — He can throw himself higher, turn over oftener, and come down lighter, than any other man in the known world. Madam Mathias, the accomplished equestrienne, will appear in her favorite characters.

Valley Herald, Shakopee, July 22, 1857

—>·<—

Mammoth Salad. — We were presented by Mr. Higgins up Straight river with a fresh, tender head of lettuce, four feet and three inches in circumference.

"I shall substitute another man in his position."

Our sense of taste has also been gratified with the good things grown on the farm of S. Henderson, Esq., of Circle Lake.

Don't a generous soil tend to make liberal hearts?

Faribault Herald, July 23, 1857

->-<-

The town never witnessed a more healthy state of improvement. The erection of substantial buildings has become so extensive that we cannot report them. Those interested must come and see.

Faribault Herald, July 23, 1857

->-<-

Notice. Whereas my husband, John Brown, has left my bed and board without just cause or provocation for the term of three years, therefore I, Sophia Brown am determined and do hereby declare in the event of his non-appearance or continued silence, that I shall substitute another man in his position.

SOPHIA JONES

Red Wing Republican, Sept. 11, 1857

->-<-

Emigration of Women to the West. — An association has been formed at Philadelphia for the purpose of sending to the West the surplus female population of that city. It is to be managed exclusively by the ladies, prominent among whom is Mrs. Sarah J. Hale, editress of the Lady's Book [the first women's magazine in the United States, begun in 1830 by Louis Godey]. The idea of the founders is to open one or more offices, at which ladies will attend to register the names of the applicants, make inquiries with regard to character, so that none but respectable and proper women shall be taken, and then open a correspondence with the editors of newspapers at the West, to learn the points where females are most needed. Agents

Wholesale & Retail Straw Goods.
E. HATCH & CO.

St. Anthony Street near the Presbyterian Church, St. Paul.

LADIES BONNETS.—Neapolitan, Soft Straw, Leghorn, Florence, Braid, Chip, Swiss, Straw, &c., &c., at all prices.

LADIES SILK BONNETS.—Satin, Poult de Loi mode.

CHILDRENS' BONNETS.—Leghorn, Neapolitan, Swiss, Chip, Pedal, Soft Straw, and Leghorn Flats.

LACES, &c., &c.—Ladies Lawn Bonnets, various colors, styles and prices.

CHILDRENS' HATS.—Cassimere, with plumes, plain do.; also trimmed with colors, Leghorn, Pedal, Shell Straw, &c., &c. French Flowers, Wreaths, Linings, &c., wholesale and retail, cheap for cash.

Gentlemens' Hats.

White Drab, Beaver and Black, do.; Black Moleskin, Le Bon Ton, do.; Le Midaille Cassimere Hats, Nankeen Marios de, White Dernier mode do, Panama Hidalgo do, Nankeen Planters do, L Expositor dernier '55 do; Brush and Felt Hats all qualities, also Caracoa Maracaibo, Panama, Leghorn, Pedal, Sennet Nankin and Straw of all kinds and all prices. Caps, Cloth, Silk, Leather, Morocco, Glaized, Wool, &c, &c.

Umbrellas all qualities; also parasols.

Retailers would do well to call and examine our stock, before ordering from the east, as we can sell cheaper than the goods can be bought at the present rates of freight.

We propose to wholesale within ten per cent. of Eastern prices.

North-Western Democrat, June 7, 1856

"Do not sit down to spend the evening with the accumulated perspired matter producing a stench that is exceedingly disagreeable to your family, and ought to be to you."

---

will be employed to forward the emigrants, see to their wants, provide places, defray expenses, etc.

Southern Minnesota Herald, Brownsville, Nov. 21, 1857

→•←

The person who left a plug of villainous tobacco on our table, will please call, claim the same and remove it.

Daily Minnesotian, St. Paul, Jan. 1, 1858

→•←

The Legislature. We give no detailed report of this body this week. We cannot afford to wade thro' the mass of motions, resolutions, amendments, &c., for the sake of presenting to our readers the *very little* that is weekly accomplished.

Faribault Herald, Feb. 3, 1858

→•←

Those of our readers who may have a curiosity to hear about Indian eloquence, will read the speeches made by the Chippewa Chief, Flat Mouth, and Mahjegahbo. Flat Mouth is one of the best Indian orators now living, and has many a time astonished his white brethren with his eloquence.

Sauk Rapids Frontierman, March 4, 1858

→•←

Water and Comfort. — Be careful how you use it as a drink. Be careful and use it on your body. Few farmers — we speak from observation — seem to know how much it may add to both comfort and health. Do not sleep in the garment you have worn through the day, but wash yourself all over and put on a clean one. Do not sit down to spend the evening with the accumulated perspired matter producing a stench that is exceedingly disagreeable to your family,

"Dr. A. is enlarging his conservatory, and improving his grounds, already the finest private garden in the North-west."

---

and ought to be to you. Do not say it is too much trouble. The added comfort, to say nothing of your own feeling of respectability, will soon cause you to anticipate the clean shirt and quiet happy evening hour.

Southern Minnesota Herald, Brownsville, July 24, 1858

→·←

Fine Flowers. — The lovers of flowers (and who are not?) will be interested to learn that Dr. Alfred E. Ames, of Minneapolis, has just received direct from the gardens of James Booth & Sons, Hamburg, Germany, a choice lot of European flower seeds and plants, embracing some seventy varieties of the best roses, such as Bengal Bourbon, Noisetts, Thea, etc., and several very fine Fuchsia; also over two hundred varieties of flower seeds and bulbs. Dr. A. is enlarging his conservatory, and improving his grounds, already the finest private garden in the North-west.

St. Paul Pioneer and Democrat, April 13, 1859

→·←

Immigration to Minnesota not only continues brisk, but is large-ly on the increase. On last Thursday evening sixty-five persons landed at the [port in Winona], all designing to locate either [in Winona] or the interior. And it is so with almost every packet [boat] from below. They all bear hither considerable numbers of immigrants from the East; not speculators or mere lookers-on, but mostly tillers of the soil and skillful mechanics — just the kind of population we most stand in need of, and the class which will enrich itself here more rapidly than any other. With these valuable accessions to our population, and the renewed and persistent energies of those already here for a few months longer, we shall soon witness the gradual but sure disappearance of the intense financial gloom which has hovered over our State ever since the crash of 1857. Faint hearts may droop under the ordeal to which we are temporarily subjected; but notwithstanding this, we feel daily more assured that there is a career of prosperity in store for this . . . State.

Rochester Free Press, May 5, 1859, reprinted from the Winona Republican

→·←

Hog Shooting. — A widow lady residing in this town, being exceedingly "pestered" by the hogs making depredations in her garden and becoming disgusted by the non-action of the city officials, with regard to enforcing the "Hog Ordinance," concluded to take the law into her own hands, and on Wednesday she, herself, "individually and collectively," without trepidation or remorse, shot, killed and destroyed a porker belonging to one of the many hog owners about town, while the animal was actively en-

"This great day — celebrated by rich and poor, poet and peasant, in all civilized portions of the globe — passed off very quietly indeed, at the City of Rochester."

gaged in the destruction of various and sundry tender vegetables with which her garden abounds. Owners of live pork in this town, will please take notice of this fact and govern themselves accordingly.

Rochester Free Press, May 21, 1859

→-←

Fourth of July. — This great day — celebrated by rich and poor, poet and peasant, in all civilized portions of the globe — passed off very quietly indeed, at the City of Rochester. The spirit of '76, usually displayed on this ever-memorable day, was somewhat *dampened* by a disagreeable and chilly rain. The shooting of fire crackers ... and the smell of gun-powder resulting therefrom, was all that could be seen or heard that would indicate in the least that there was such a day as the Fourth of July.

There was a celebration at Pleasant Grove, in this county, and one at Mantorville, Dodge Co. No report from either, but are inclined to the opinion that they must have enjoyed themselves hugely. ...

The picnic at Joscelyn's Grove, was postponed, on account of the bad state of the weather, until a more auspicious time. On the morning of the 5th, the sun shone out in all its splendor, the air was balmy, pure and bracing — just such a day as we are wont to have on an old fashioned Fourth. Therefore a goodly number of citizens from town and country assembled at the grove beneath the shade of beautiful forest trees — "God's first temples" — to enjoy the songs, speeches, toasts and dinner. Hon. C. H. Lindsley, delivered the oration, which was said to be, by those who heard it, a masterly

North-Western Democrat, Aug. 18, 1855

effort. The dinner was spoken of highly, and it is generally understood that there was a "grand old time."

Rochester Free Press, July 16, 1859

→-←

Fortunate. — There is not a negro living in Mankato, nor do we believe in the whole of Blue Earth county. ... It is often remarked by visitors that we are peculiarly blessed in this respect.

Mankato Weekly Record, Nov. 15, 1859

→-←

v on Wednesday evening , by which a number of jured. The accident was ; so that the whistle of it train would not work. til two o'clock Friday

—Friday morning about train from Chicago on oing towards Joliet, Mr. was instantly killed.— a bridge between Ma- eased for some cause was or had his head suffi- ars that the bridge came ctly behind the right ear

—The Chicago *Democrat* n that left that city for lnesday night, the 10th alf past twelve, at the ur; and by the displace- ross the turn table, the e transverse, and buried brick wall of BRADY ie concussion opened all made a general distri- nace, and Mr. GOBLE, from a terrible death g itself over his head, l supply of water. Mr. ster, had a very narrow ters of the freight and etty well demolished.— not yet located.

ublisher of the Cincin- last week, a fine silver party of " Know Noth- merican principles.

f Brooklyn voted upon

Steamers.

Through Line—St. Louis and St. Paul.
Regular Packet!

THE NEW AND ELEGANT LIGHT Draught Steamer ADMIRAL, JOHN BROOKS, Master, will run as a regular Passenger Packet between St. Paul and St. Louis, during the searson, making regular trips.

The ADMIRAL is a new and staunch built craft, of superior freight and passenger accommodation, and is the fastest as well as the safest boat on the Upper Mississippi; having been built under the requirements of the late Steamboat law, and being provided with Life Boats, Life Preservers, Steam Guages, &c.

The Admiral touches at Galena, Dubuque, and all other intermediate ports.

For Freight or Passage, apply on board, or to
J. C. BURBANK & CO.,
JOHN M. LAMB, St. Paul.
WALL & WIDEN, or.
OTIS WEST, St. Louis.
my1d&w6m   T. D. CONNER, Galena.

Galena and Minnesota Packet Co.

ARRANGEMENT FOR
1854.

THE GALENA AND MINNESOTA PACKET COMPANY will run a daily line of Boats during the ensuing season, between Galena, Stillwater and St. Paul, stopping at all intermediate landings, leaving Galena at 12 M., daily, xcept Sundays.

The line will consist of the

NOMINEE,	CAPTAIN R. BLAKELY.
WAR EAGLE,	" D. S. HARRIS.
GALENA,	" D. B. MOREHOUSE,
ROYAL ARCH,	" E. H. GLEIM.

All first class boats, and commanded by experienced and accommodating officers.

These boats will connect, at Galena, with the Saint Louis and Galena daily line of steamers, which line connects at Rock Island with the Chicago and Rock Island Railroad.

This Company's boats being United States Mail Steamers their punctuality can be confidently relied upon.

Freight shipped at St. Louis, or between St. Louis and Galena, on the St. Louis and Galena line of Boats to points above Galena, will be re-shipped at Galena free of charge for drayage or forwarding without delay.

The Railroad between Galena and Chicago, connecting with the various Eastern Roads, is now completed within a few miles of Galena, and the unfinished portion of the Road stocked with comfortable Stage Coaches.

manufactory, where Grave Stones, Monum lar St. Louis prices.

May 12tf.

POCKET KNIVES. Pocket Cutlery. an manufactory. So

POCKET BOOKS.

SCHOOL BOOKS of tory, at

PICTURES. A fe frames. Sold at

STATIONERY of ev

FISHING TACKLE— at

NEW MUSIC. A l music, just rece

MON
TEN thousand doll on 3, 6, 9 and 1 Call at the office of may 25 tf

FASHION. MRS. MARVIN Paul, that she large, varied, and spl latest Summer Style amination, it will be of Millinery, Flowe brought into the Ter Dress Silks, &c., &c. PRICES than the sam this market,

SAINT PAUL I Third Street SERVANTS of every for city or count Merchants, Hotel kee clerks or laboring me calling or sending th will be sent to any wanting them will s money to pay girls fa &c., &c.
Females in want of of charge.
Young men with o ness, can be accomm office.
All letters must be Box 412, St. Paul Po:
WARREN BRTOL.

BRISTO

1860s

Minnesota had been a state just three years when the Civil War began with the attack on Fort Sumter in April 1861. A year later, Minnesotans faced war on the homefront — an uprising by the Dakota Indians. The state also struggled with a financial depression. Foreign-born people made up about 30 percent of the state's population in 1860. The federal census that year numbered 172,023 Minnesotans. 1867 opened a new period of prosperity, bringing railroad building, real estate inflation and heavy immigration, especially from Germany and Ireland.

1860s

–>•<–

Civil War

*Few Minnesotans were active in the fight to abolish slavery in the
United States. Even those opposed to the spread of slavery did not
want to interfere with it in the southern states. In Minnesota, the
most outspoken crusader against slavery was Jane Grey Swisshelm,
editor of a St. Cloud newspaper. She had been a well-known
journalist in Pittsburgh before she came to Minnesota in 1857.*

*H*ER STRONG *feminist and abolitionist
stands so antagonized some of St. Cloud's
leading citizens that a vigilante committee
threw her printing press into the river and made
her promise to stop publishing her paper, the St.
Cloud Visiter. What she did was change the name
to the St. Cloud Democrat; it appeared on schedule
the next week.*

*This is her newspaper's account of a Mississippi
slave who was brought to Minnesota by her vaca-
tioning master. Many Southerners, eager to escape
the heat, spent summers here. The signature "S" at
the end of the account probably means the writer
was Swisshelm herself. The writer makes no attempt
to conceal her opinion of the event.*

Correspondence of the St. Cloud Democrat
From Minneapolis.

Minneapolis, Aug. 22d, 1860

Yesterday was a lively day in this place. Preparations had been made the night previous for freeing
a colored woman held as a slave by a Col. Christmas, of Mississippi, who was stopping at a private
boarding house near Lake Harriet, four or five miles
back of town. The slave woman while stopping
with her master at the Winslow house, had informed some persons in St. Anthony of her desire
to be free, and measures had been taken for giving
her assistance, when the unexpected removal to
Lake Harriet disconcerted the plans of the slave.
Finding it impossible to communicate with her
while she was at the Lake, and learning that her
master proposed to return South, a warrant was obtained from Judge Vanderburg for taking her out of
the hands of her master. As large numbers of Southerners are at present stopping at the hotels here
and at St. Anthony, and also at the different private
boarding houses around the lakes, from whom op-
position might be expected, and to prevent the
slave being slipped off into the woods or conveyed
out of our reach, a posse of twenty-five men accompanied the Sheriff. Some good Democrats in the
place, learning that something was in the wind,
sent off parties to warn the slave-owners to be on
their guard. But their information was uncertain,
and fortunately their suspicions were directed
more particularly to another point. Still, as we have
since learned from the slave, about ten o'clock in
the forenoon, two men from this place came to the
house and warned them to be on the look out; and
at various times during the day when persons were
seen approaching the house, the girl was sent into
the woods back of the house. After the party started
and their direction was fully ascertained, two persons left with a fast horse taking a different route
from the Sheriff's party, to notify the people at the
house. In order to intercept them, three or four of
our company left the wagons and taking a short cut
across the fields, came out just in front of their car-
riage, when the worthy gentlemen not caring to become too conspicuous in their dirty business,
turned off by a side path and returned to town.
When the Sheriff and posse approached the house
— which they did from different directions — the
girl was hurried off into the woods; but their coming was too sudden to allow the concealment effectual; besides, the slave girl, while not daring to dis-
obey, yet only went a few rods, hoping thus to favor
the finding of her. The party in the house were very

49

"When the girl was found in the woods, she said in a low and earnest voice, 'I want to be free, but don't tell master I said so.'"

willing to have the house searched, and while the Sheriff performed this operation, others of the party searched the woods.

The girl was soon found, and the party returned to town, where the case was tried before Judge Vanderburg. A large crowd was present. The news had gone all over Minneapolis and St. Anthony, and large crowds of Southerners and their lick-spittle toadies were present to aid and comfort Col. Christmas. It was expected that when the slave girl would be discharged an attempt would be made to carry her off, and care was taken that no favorable opportunity for such an attempt should be offered.

When the Judge declared her free to go where she pleased, Col. Christmas went to her and said, "Come, Eliza; your mistress is at the Winslow House and wants to see you." But Eliza said "no;" and after vainly *entreating* — a style of speech which among other benefits a Minnesota air has given him — his former property for about ten minutes, he was obliged to communicate the unfortunate state of affairs to the disconsolate "missus" at the Winslow House. The slave was then taken to Mr. W.D. Babbitt's, accompanied by twenty-five or thirty persons as protectors of her new found freedom. At night she was placed where she will be safe. — During the night an attack was made on the house of Mr. Babbitt. Windows were broken; and a person who left the house for aid, was fired at two or three times. Measures will be taken to discover, if possible, the perpetrators of this outrage.

In connection with the slave, I should say that her freedom was promised her years ago, but the promise was broken. A new promise was made that if she would be faithful, she should have her freedom when the [master's] child, whose care was her especial business, was seven years old. This child was seven years old a few weeks since, but Col. Christmas had refused to keep his word a second time. When the girl was found in the woods, she said in a low and earnest voice, "I want to be free,

St. Paul Pioneer, Dec. 8, 1864

but don't tell master I said so." So difficult is it for them to divest themselves of the habitual spirit of submission and obedience, and so little confidence have they in the ability of any persons to protect them from their masters, that many slaves who have implored aid in escaping from slavery, would quail before the eye and the word of their masters, and even deny that they wish to be free. This was not the case in the present instance. She is happy in her freedom, and those who helped her congratulate themselves on this open and manly vindication of our laws and of the rights of humanity. Certain classes of our community are doleful enough — particularly those who are afraid that the "Southerners won't come here because they can't bring their slaves;" and so the poor, miserable, mercenary souls will lose that filthy gain for which they are anxious to barter what little manhood they have.

S.

St. Cloud Democrat, Aug. 23, 1860

[Eliza retained her freedom. The Underground Railroad helped her to get to Canada.]

→•←

[When Confederate forces shelled Fort Sumter on April 12, 1861, and the Civil War began, Minnesota Gov. Alexander Ramsey happened to be in Washington. He offered President Lincoln 1,000 men, giving Minnesota the distinction of being the first state to offer troops to the Union cause. Soon, volunteer companies formed in all parts of the state. Nearly every able-bodied man joined the fight. Minnesota provided 24,000 men, and this from a state whose population was only 172,000.]

"It seemed to me as if Dame Nature was weeping over the impending fate of those poor infatuated rebels who by their madness have brought disgrace on themselves and the country."

To Farmers. — Now is the time for the farmers to make money. The country is at war. A half million of men instead of being producers will become consumers. Flour, beef, pork, beans — the substantials — will be wanted in large quantity. Europe is convulsed, and the indications are that there will be a general outbreak across the water; if so, America must supply the armies of France, Italy and England with food. Let the farmers prepare for a great demand; let every cultivator put in an extra acre of corn or wheat, and carry his tilth [tilling] to the best possible perfection; let every calf be saved from the butcher's hands, for there will be a great demand for beef. Farmers, every where, now is your time!
St. Paul Pioneer and Democrat, May 15, 1861

-> - <-

[Early in the war, the mood was upbeat. An example was this letter to a Faribault newspaper from a soldier whose regiment was treated to a picnic by the ladies of Minneapolis.]
Head Quarters First Reg. M.V. [Minnesota Volunteers]
Fort Snelling, May 23, 1861
DEAR [Faribault Central] REPUBLICAN: — Since my last [letter] the weather has been wretched — rain, rain, rain, for three or four days. It seemed to me as if Dame Nature was weeping over the impending fate of those poor infatuated rebels who by their madness have brought disgrace on themselves and the country to which the ingrates belong; but now the clouds have cleared away and the heavens seem to predict a glorious future for us of the North and West — the land of the bold and free.

The feature of the week has been the regimental excursion to Minneapolis and St. Anthony. Eight companies were ordered to "march" — the "Faribault

N.B.
Prof. Leonnard's
CELEBRATED
NECTAR
BITTERS

A CERTAIN PREVENTATIVE OF

FEVER AND AGUE,

AND A SURE CURE FOR

DYSPEPSIA, CONSTIPATION,

COLIC, CHOLERA MORBUS,

Cramps, Nervous Headache, Debility, Depression of Spirits, Loss of Appetite and Liver Complaint.

FOR SALE BY

J. C. Raguet & Co.,

P. F. McQuillan,

J. I. Beaumont.

CASSILLY & CO.,

St. Paul Pioneer, Sept. 3, 1864

Guards" being one of the number, and in good spirits we all started "oph" [off] — flags flying, "drums a beating" — for the scene of the day's festivity, which we reached about 11 o'clock.

Minneapolis might very appropriately be termed the city of magnificent expectations (if not distances). There are some very fine buildings, but they are "few and scattering," while the rest are inferior to the majority in our own little town. The suspension bridge is a magnificent structure — well worthy of attention — spanning the "Father of Waters." Above the falls of St. Anthony the visitor has a fine view of the River, and, if inclined to calculation might form some idea of the vast amount of power that is running to waste.

We had dinner in the grove on Nicollet Island, a beautiful place for such purposes. The ladies and gents who had the affair in charge deserve great praise for the manner in which they discharged their duties. — The tables were supplied with plenty to have fed two regiments, and the materials were all of the choicest kind: sandwiches, bread — as white as the fair hands that made it — and butter as delicious as the lips of the ladies who passed it around; but why particularize when everything was excellent — sweet milk and beer as drinkables. So much beer was furnished that after we had drank all we wished there were sixty kegs untapped.

Before partaking of the dinner our Colonel gave the command to "uncover" [remove their caps], and a benediction was invoked by a venerable clergyman of Minneapolis. Owing to the distance between us I did not hear a word he said. After dinner Col. Gorman, in behalf of the Regiment, returned thanks to the citizens and committee in his usual happy style. It was responded to by Col. Aldrich of Minneapolis. After complimenting the officers and men, he said, "success would surely attend our arms. — We were engaged in a glorious and holy cause — the cause of freedom and humanity."

Three hearty cheers were given by our soldier boys for the ladies of St. Anthony and Minneapolis, which was sent back with a will by the citizens, including

*"The day was fine; the ladies beautiful;
the soldiers performed their evolutions gracefully."*

the ladies, the waving of whose scented pocket handkerchiefs seemed to load the air with perfume.

I think it was the happiest thing in the shape of a picnic that I ever attended. The day was fine; the ladies beautiful; the soldiers performed their evolutions gracefully, and everything passed off to the satisfaction of all concerned.

The march home was not quite so pleasant, but it was accomplished, and tired and weary we waited for "tattoo" [lights out], which was hardly over ere we turned in to sleep.

Tomorrow we go to St. Paul to receive our regimental flag. I will try to give you an account of our reception there in my next.

Faribault Central Republican, June 5, 1861

-→•←-

[The following is part of a letter from a Minnesota private, who didn't sign his name, at Camp Stone in Maryland.]

Yesterday I made an experiment. I had heard a good deal about taking French leave [going AWOL], and I determined to try it myself. As the call was given to fall in and go to hear Rev. E.D. Neill's sermon, I left camp (without leave, of course), and proceeded to one of the neighbor's, who preserves a prudent silence on all secesh [Secessionists, that is, rebel or Southern] movements — and here in company with two boys of company B, we had a magnificent dinner at the rate of twenty five cents per capita. We returned safely to camp in time for dress parade. Hence I have made the important discovery that military regulations, like all other arbitrary regulations, can be violated with perfect impunity, provided, however — and it is quite an important proviso, too

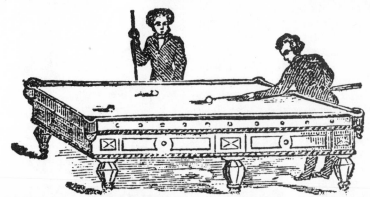

Tontine Billiard Room,

RAMSEY STREET, NEAR LEVEE,

Hastings, Min.

Everything is in complete order connected with the Room to make it a comfortable place for Billiard Players.

LAWRENCE NESSEL, Proprietor.

Hastings, Feb. 13, 1867.

Dakota County Union, Hastings, Dec. 11, 1867

— that you can do so without detection.

St. Paul Pioneer and Democrat, Nov. 15, 1861

-→•←-

[Excitement waned as announcements such as this were published.]

Death of Samuel M. Parker.

We briefly noticed last week the death of this young soldier, at the battle of Mill Springs.

Samuel M. Parker was born in Bradley, Penobscot county, Maine, Jan. 1, 1843; killed at the battle of Mill Springs, January 19, 1862; aged 19 years and 19 days. He enlisted in Co. I, 2d Regiment Min. Volunteers, Sept. 13, 1861.

The following is a copy of the letter from his brother, conveying the sad news to his parents in this city:

Camp Logan [Kentucky]
January 20th, 1862
Dear Parents:

I am weary and lonesome and hardly know what to write to you. We have had a great battle with Zollicoffer's forces, one mile and a half from this camp, but I am safe and well. Ten of our poor boys are killed, and some fifteen or twenty wounded. Dear father and mother! how can I tell you — (but you will hear it before this gets to you) — Samuel has gone to his God. He now sleeps the sleep that knows no waking on

"I cannot write you the particulars of the battle, for I am so lonesome and sad, that I have no mind to do anything."

this earth, beneath the cold soil of Kentucky. He died charging bravely on the enemy, from a bayonet wound in the left groin, which passed through the kidneys. He died in about fifteen minutes after receiving the thrust. He died calmly and easily, without much pain. — One of the drummer boys offered to call the doctor, but he said, "If you call him he will leave some poor fellow that will die, and it may as well be me, as any one."

When he was laid in his grave, he looked as natural as if asleep.

I cannot write you the particulars of the battle, for I am so lonesome and sad, that I have no mind to do anything. I have a board at the head of his grave, with his name, regiment and company cut on it.

Oh! dear father and mother, may God help us to bear up under this our affliction. Good bye, my dear parents.

From your sorrowing son,
ALBERT.

Minnesota News, St. Anthony, Feb. 1, 1862

-> - <-

INVENTIONS

-> - <-

To those who have become disgusted with star and tallow candles, (and who has not?), and are no longer willing to risk the lives of their children by using burning fluid, we would say that Mr. Richard Marvin has a large supply of the best article for illuminating that has ever been brought to the city. It is Kerosene — refined to such an extent that it is as colorless as alcohol, and without smell. It is the cheapest article that can be used, and the light is better than gas. He has also a large assortment of lamps that are offered very low.

St. Paul Pioneer and Democrat, Nov. 2, 1860

-> - <-

Stereopticons [an early type of slide projector] are all the rage in Eastern cities.... There has been a perfect rush for weeks together to see them. At last we are to have one in Saint Paul. One of our own citizens has purchased one at a cost of several hundred dollars, and proposes to exhibit it in Saint Paul and through the State this winter. It will be on exhibition some time next week.

St. Paul Press, Dec. 25, 1863

-> - <-

Among the latest novelties is an ironing glove, to protect the hand from heat when ironing. The under part is composed of several thicknesses of flannel.

Minneapolis Tribune, Nov. 12, 1868

-> - <-

Bicycles were known in America in the 1860s and became immensely popular in the 1870s and 1880s, when manufacturers greatly improved them. By the late 1880s bicycles were everywhere and were used for business, sport and excursions. Cylists were among the first people to clamor for good roads.

Velocipedes. — Minneapolis has at last a velocipede — a genuine bicycle or two wheeled machine, just such an one as has been creating such a sensation throughout the eastern cities. It is no joke, but a fact. We saw it yesterday and tried it, and must say the velocipede is a fine institution. This is almost a fac similie of the celebrated Hanlon Improved Velocipede, and was made by Mr. E.N. Hamilton and L.L. Leathers, two enterprising young men of this city. The iron work was made at the blacksmith shop of Mr. Geo. F. Libby on First street, where the machine was on exhibition yesterday and tested. During the afternoon a large number of visitors thronged the shop to inspect it. A considerable of skill is necessary to ride, but we presume a few days' practice will encourage some amateur so that he will venture upon the streets. It will be a strange sight to see these two wheeled machines kiting around our city. We learn these gentlemen design getting up a three wheeled velocipede for ladies.

Minneapolis Tribune, Feb. 12, 1869

-> - <-

Hair curler. — Mr. Geo. W. Dudley, of this city, has invented a hair curler, which is rather a novelty in its way. It consists of a hollow tin tube, attached to a reservoir at one end, which is filled with hot water. The hair to be curled is then wrapped around the tube, in the same manner as a common curling tong. The advantage claimed for it is, that while it curls the hair, it does not burn or injure it. A patent has been applied for, and at an early day they will be manufactured in this city.

Minneapolis Tribune, Feb. 21, 1869

". . . the bristly-backed, vermin-skinned, rotten-hearted, loathsome, dirty, filthy, cowardly sneak . . ."

We wish the bristly-backed, vermin-skinned, rotten-hearted, loathsome, dirty, filthy, cowardly sneak, who borrowed a barrel of choice family flour from our back kitchen a few nights since, much joy, and will guarantee to him and his another barrel just as good, if he will favor us with another visit, "free gratis for nothing." We respect a thief, but not of that class who would purloin the cents from a dead man's eyes, the linen from a sacrament table, that would exhume a corpse for the ring it wore, or enter the habitations of helpless women and children whose husbands and fathers are absent battling for their country and pilfer their only frock and last palatable morsel. This is the class of brutes in human shape that have been infesting this community more or less for the past two years, and are likely to in future for all the present authorities will do to the contrary. We do not wish to speak in favor of aught save civil law, but we do say that as the law and its officers have thus far totally failed to get *even a clue* to the dastardly band of house robbers, we will be *one* that will pull on the hemp that will stop effectually their cowardly raids.

Shakopee Argus, Feb. 18, 1865

→❯-❮←

[The war ended. The heartache didn't.]

The Great Sorrow of the Hour.
Human life is full of contrasts. — Light and darkness, joy and sorrow, life and death continually alternate. — From the summit of prosperity, we are often hurled in a moment down to the deepest pit of adversity. Our hearts swell with joy to-day; they throb with unutterable anguish to-morrow. As with individuals, so is it with nations. So is it with our country to-day. Yesterday the tide of victory and joy lifted the nation to the skies; to-day it sinks in the

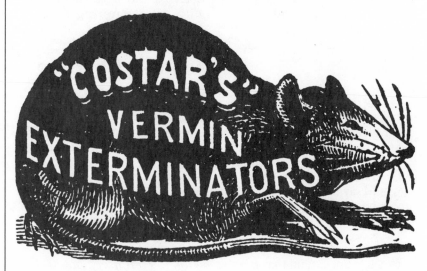

To Destroy——Rats, Roaches, &c.
To Destroy——Mice. Moles and Ants.
To Destroy——Bed-Bugs.
To Destroy——Moths in furs, Clothes, &c.
To Destroy——Mosquitoes and Fleas.
To Destroy——Insects on Plants and Fowlers.
To Destroy——Insects on Animals, &c.
To Destroy——Every form and species of Vermin.

THE
"ONLY INFALLIBLE REMEDIES KNOWN."
Destroys Instantly
EVERY FORM AND SPECIES OF
VERMIN.

Minnesota State News, Minneapolis and St. Anthony, July 12, 1862

lowest abyss of sorrow.

The strong hand that through four years of storm and tempest, has with gentle yet firm and steady grasp held the helm of the nation, has relaxed its hold forever. The pilot is stricken down in sight of the harbor, and the ship of state is left upon a troubled sea to be guided by an untried hand.

Abraham Lincoln is dead. Dead when his country seemed to need his life the most; dead ere the great work to which he was specially called — and

"Abraham Lincoln is dead."

---

which he of all men seemed most fitted to finish — is fully completed; in the vigor of his manhood and the maturity of his wisdom, dead by the hand of an assassin.

Had he fallen — as multitudes of others in the same cause have — on some bloody battle field, though the loss would not have been less, the horror with which it has thrilled the nation would not have been so great.

But to fall thus in the hour of victory and rejoicing; when events were just beginning fully to vindicate the wisdom and justice of the policy he had pursued; when his and his country's enemys baffled, beaten and crushed were at his feet; when he had almost reached the goal towards which, through four years of toil, suffering and blood, he had been struggling to conduct the nation — thus to perish by the hand of a traitor and an assassin seems a grief almost too great for utterance.

But though he did not fall upon the battle field, Mr. Lincoln is none the less a martyr to the great cause of American nationality and constitutional liberty. Indeed of all the noble lives that have been sacrificed in the great contest for Union and Liberty against Treason and Slavery, his has been the most precious, and in the truest and noblest sense his death is a martyrdom. Not so much on account of any superior intrinsic worth in him, but because he, more than any other man, has been the most conspicuous representative of those great principles of Truth and Justice. . . .

Abraham Lincoln is dead; but the great principles which he represented, thank God, cannot die. They are as vital and imperishable as Truth, Justice and humanity. The just of every past age have transmuted them as a perpetual legacy to their posterity;

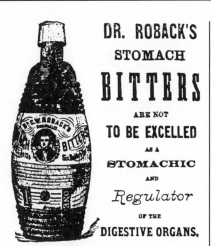

DR. ROBACK'S
STOMACH
BITTERS
ARE NOT
TO BE EXCELLED
AS A
STOMACHIC
AND
Regulator
OF THE
DIGESTIVE ORGANS.

These Bitters are not offered to the public as a medicine which will cure all the "ills which flesh is heir to," but as a remedial agent — a great Regulator of the system.

In the Bilious districts of the West and South there has, for a long time, been much needed an article of Stomach Bitters, which, if taken in proper quantities, and at the proper time, are a sure preventive of

Bilious Fever,
Fever and Ague,
Liver Complaint,
Dyspepsia,
Indigestion,
Jaundice,
Kidney Complaints,

and all diseases of a similar nature.

These Bitters are composed of rare and powerful roots and herbs, which make them

Highly Tonic.

Minnesota Courier, Austin, April 29, 1863

and to maintain and diffuse them will be the duty and pleasure of good men in all time to come.
Taylors Falls Reporter, April 22, 1865

→•←

[After the war, some Minnesota newspapers called for humane treatment of blacks.]

Cicero Africanus. — Those of our citizens who were present were favored on last Tuesday evening with a description of the slave life of one, H. H. Thomas, who for twenty-five years was a chattel and suffered the abuse of twelve masters. He depicted in a clear and forcible manner his sufferings while under the effects of the "institution," his attempts to escape and his final success. He is an "Oberlin" graduate, and a very fair lecturer. During his travels he has been almost constantly subject to all kinds of coarse and insulting remarks and not particularly flattering allusions to his complexion, mostly from individuals who were really not his equal, and as is almost invariably the case, those who raise the greatest hue and cry about negro equality, are those who actually fear that should the negro have his rights he would soon excell them.
Taylors Falls Reporter, Sept. 16, 1865

→•←

Riot. — On Thursday night a party of young fellows, whose names are as yet unknown, attacked the building on Wabashaw street known as the "Negro Rookery" and behaved in an outrageous manner, maltreating the inmates, breaking furniture, &c. The only crime of these poor people is that they are poor and live in a very humble manner, but have always been orderly and industrious. The attack on them was merely the result of a low prejudice.
St. Paul Pioneer, June 9, 1866

→•←

Inhumanity. — Several days since the small pox broke out in a family of negroes living on 7th street, back of the City Hall, and

"Here the poor sick people, unable to move or help themselves, remained four days, almost without attention, and almost without shelter."

six of them were taken sick with that loathsome disease at one time. The neighbors of course, could not permit them to remain in that crowded locality, and as the health officers made no effort to help remove the unfortunate family, they took them outside the city, and left them in a swamp near the Lake Como Road in a rude and hastily constructed hut — a mere tent of boards — scarcely that, in fact. Here the poor sick people, unable to move or help themselves, remained four days, almost without attention, and almost without shelter. Fortunately the weather was very warm and mild, or they would have suffered much more than they did.

Why the health officers did not take measures to care for the unfortunate parties, or procure a proper place to put them in, is beyond conception. The board of health officers are clothed with almost despotic powers (vide [see] their action in the Cholera epidemic). Certainly a hovel somewhere could have been rented, confiscated, or built, that would have answered for a pest house.

The above mentioned cases of small pox are all that have occurred here this season. Fortunately the disease did not spread. But a pest house must be secured without farther delay. Humanity must never be shamed again by carting sick people out of town and leaving them to die by the road side, for the honor and good name of our Christian city.

St. Paul Pioneer, Oct. 7, 1866

→•←

[Kenneth Carley's "Minnesota in the Civil War," published by Ross and Haines in 1961, is the best book on the war.]

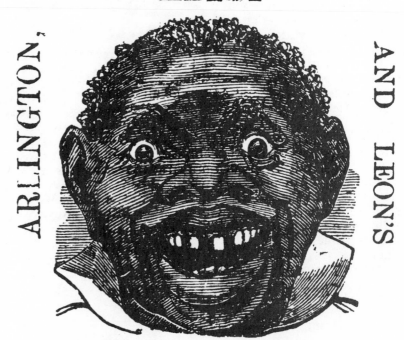

COURT HOUSE !
One Night Only !
Monday Eve., August 28.
KELLY

ARLINGTON,

AND LEON'S

MINSTRELS !
From the Academy of Music, Chicago.

Everywhere acknowledged by the press and public the Sovereigns of the Profession.

ADMISSION, - - . 50 cts

Doors open at half past seven ; Concert to commence at a quarter past eight.

Winona Democrat, Aug. 26, 1865

56

1860s
—>•<—

Dakota War

One of the United States' worst Indian/white conflicts occurred in Minnesota in 1862, during the Civil War. In six weeks of brutality, more than 450 white people died. More than 100 white women and children were taken captive, and some 15,000 white settlers were forced to flee their homes. Nobody knows how many Dakota Indians were killed, but probably even more than the whites.

In retrospect, historians can see why the Dakota people rebelled. Most immediately, they were hungry. The food, supplies and money that the government had promised them didn't arrive. And in a larger sense, the Dakota were fighting for their homeland and way of life.

While whites reaped the riches of lands that had been the Indians' only shortly before, the Dakota had been confined to a small reservation, pressured to abandon their culture and religion, cheated by traders and treaty-makers time and again, faced with food shortages and humiliated almost daily. Newspaper editors considered Indians subhuman and routinely called them "savage foes" and "infidels."

About one hundred and twenty-five Sioux Indians are encamped some three miles above the city. . . . Many of our young people are availing themselves of the good sleighing on the river, to visit the teepees. The Indians are at present resting from their labors till they can dispose of their game, and sell the moccasins which are now being made by the squaws. They are perfectly harmless and strictly honest — never taking anything which is out of their reach.

Red Wing Sentinel, Jan. 21, 1860

—>•<—

[War broke out between the Dakota and the whites on Aug. 17, 1862. The Dakota drove out many settlers and attacked the town of New Ulm. After the massacres of whites began, editors called for revenge. Here's what the Faribault Central Republican had to say:]

The Indian Outrages
Horrible Massacres

At no period in the annals of our State has there been a week of more intense excitement and alarm, than during the one just passed. Little did we dream that almost in our very midst was a slumbering volcano, ready at any moment to burst forth. Yet such it seems is too true, and now while assailed on the one side by a ruthless, desperate foe [Southern forces], struggling for the overthrow of our Government and its glorious free institutions, we turn to find ourselves plunged into the horrors of a savage struggle with the inhuman barbarians that have wrongfully been permitted to occupy a large portion of the most beautiful sections of our State. Men, women and children, peaceably pursuing their daily avocations, have been cruelly and inhumanly mangled and murdered by these fiends in human shape. There seems to have been a general and preconcerted uprising of all the tribes of the Sioux in our State, and it is feared that the Chippeways and other powerful tribes are also united with them in their bloody work of carnage and death. . . .

Of the total number that have been murdered by these savages, we have no definite knowledge. Some [soldiers fighting the Dakota], in their letters from the scene of conflict, place the number at over a thousand persons, but this must be exaggerated, at least we hope so. Gov. Ramsey, upon the first alarm, immediately dispatched Col. Sibley with four companies of infantry to the frontier. — Other forces are now hurrying to the rescue. A proclamation by the Governor calling upon the militia of the Minnesota Valley and the border counties, to take horses and

"A poor frightened woman . . . thought she saw savages skulking in the bushes near her house, and uttered these now fearful words, 'The Indians are coming!'"

arms and join the expedition under Col. Sibley, has been issued, also one calling upon the militia of the Valley of the Upper Mississippi to rendezvous at St. Cloud and there organize for the protection of the frontier in that vicinity.—

We trust and pray that this may be a war of extermination. We ask that every warrior may be speedily despatched; let us wipe out the treacherous, accursed vipers or drive them far beyond our borders, that peace and security may once more reign.

Faribault Central Republican, Aug. 27, 1862

→‣‹—

[White settlers were seized with panic, much of it justifiable, some of it exaggerated. Here a newspaper writer describes the reactions of the whites of Monticello with not a Dakota in sight.]

Monticello, August 23, 1862.

Editors of the Press:

I write amid the lowing of cattle, the barking of dogs and the crackling of firearms. Monticello is all excitement — general confusion is the order; the streets are full of men, women and children. The whole country between Silver Creek and Crow river, as far back as Forest City, an area forty by twenty miles, has been on the move since 6 o'clock yesterday evening. The people have arrived, and are quartered with the families and in the empty houses; about three hundred have taken up quarters in the Academy building.

The cause of this seems to have originated in the excited imagination of a poor frightened woman, who thought she saw savages skulking in the bushes near her house, and uttered these now fearful words, "The Indians are coming!" The public mind had been prepared by recent outrages, and the excitement was most intense. It reached Monticello about 10 o'clock Friday night — loaded wagons arrived and sounded the alarm. The families were all aroused, and the women and children taken to the hotel; men ran in every direction for guns, pitch-

PIONEER

LIVERY STABLE,

GEO. WARREN, Proprietor,

Corner 3rd and Washington Streets, above the Huff House,

WINONA, MINNESOTA.

My horses, carriages, buggies, cutters, sleighs, etc. are superior to any in Southern Minnesota. Good horses, and careful and sober drivers furnished for pleasure parties on short notice, day or night. 39

Winona Democrat, July 15, 1865

forks, &c.; wagons kept coming, but nobody could be found who had seen an Indian. Morning came — the excitement increased; it was said the houses in the Big Woods were on fire. . . .

At our approach, some of the women took us for Indians, and fled for the thick woods. One woman endeavored to reach the lake that she might drown herself and child in order to escape the scalping knife; children hid themselves in the thick brush; one woman and two children have not been found up to this time. We do not know of a family left between this place and Forest City, and teams are coming in from the prairie beyond.

St. Paul Press, Aug. 30, 1862

→‣‹—

[Unlike most newspapers, the St. Paul Press raised questions about whether the Dakota had been maltreated and pushed to violence. A portion follows of the front-page article called "Who is to Blame?"]

The hoarded vengeance of an injured, oppressed and defrauded people has at length burst upon our defenseless settlements; and the terrible retribution for a thousand outrages is meted out with indiscriminate hate alike upon the guilty and innocent. . . . Are there any [whites] upon whose heads descend the blood guiltiness of these appalling crimes? Are there any to whom the welfare of the red man was intrusted, — and how have they discharged their trust? Has there [been] any one whose duty it was to have foreseen the danger and provided against it? These to many persons in high official station are startling questions. . . .

Our blood curdles in our veins as we read of hearthstones made desolate, infants torn from their mother's breasts, women outraged and violated, millions of property destroyed, unoffending settlers driven from their happy homes, or led to a hopeless captivity. But have we never heard of the long series of outrages which prompted these avenging blows?

"A Sioux scalp . . . was on exhibition at the Furniture Store of John Stees."

Do the annals of Indian Agencies show no records of fraud, pillage and rapine [plundering]? Have no wigwams been desolated? Have no women been ravished? Have not the moneys and property of the red men poured in an incessant stream into the coffers of unscrupulous traders and mercenary agents? . . . Has not their intercourse with the whites taught them the vices of the latter, and destroyed the savage virtues of their own race? . . .

Let those whose crimes have incited these terrible deeds, and who now stand trembling at the fury their misdeeds have invoked, cease the futile attempt to screen themselves at the expense of another, and unite with him and every loyal citizen in defending our beautiful State, now menaced with disaster and ruin.

St. Paul Press, Sept. 11, 1862

→›‹←

First Arrival. A Sioux scalp captured by Lieut. Chas. Stees of the Sixth Regiment, at the battle of Wood Lake, was on exhibition at the Furniture Store of John Stees, on Third street. Another lot is expected in a few days.

St. Paul Pioneer, Sept. 27, 1862

→›‹←

[Just two days after the Dakota surrendered on Sept. 26, 1862, a military court began holding trials. More than 300 Dakota were sentenced to die. But President Lincoln himself reviewed the records and concluded that proof did not exist to condemn most of them. He changed most of the sentences to prison terms. The day after Christmas, 38 Dakota were hanged at Mankato, in what is believed to be the largest mass execution in the history of the United States.

[A correspondent for the St. Paul Press reported on Dec. 27, 1862, that Mankato was jammed with eager observers the day before the executions. Hotels and private houses were overflowing. The city was placed under martial law. Saloons were closed. The scaffold was ready: "It is so constructed as to drop at the severing of the rope, launching the whole thirty-nine (there was one last-minute reprieve) into eternity at once. The arrangements are thought to be all perfected, so that the programme may be promptly carried out at ten in the morning."]

The Sioux War.

Further Particulars of the Execution.

Want of space in our last issue, prevented us from giving as full an account of the execution last Friday as we first contemplated. . . .

On Friday morning, we accompanied the Rev. Father Ravoux to the prison of the condemned. The whole number were sitting and lying about, in

pairs, and disposed as comfortably as their chained condition would permit. There was very little conversation kept up among them, though occasionally one would mutter a few words to another in an unintelligible jargon. As a crowd they sat and lay there, smoking their pipes as unconcernedly as if they were engaged in council over some unimportant matter of tribal concern. Absolutely impassive, smoking and rarely muttering as if their lease on life was eternal, and not bounded by three or four short hours.

The Reverend Father spoke to them of their condition and fate, and in such terms as the devoted priest only can speak. He tried to infuse them with courage — bade them to hold out and be

"They had evidently taken great pains to make themselves presentable for their last appearance on the stage of life."

strong, and to show no sign of fear. — While Father Ravoux was speaking to them old Tazoo broke out in a death-wail, in which one after another joined, until the prison room was filled with a wild unearthly plaint, which was neither of despair or grief, but rather a paroxysm [sudden outburst] of savage passion, most impressive to witness and startling to hear, even by those who understood the language of the music only. During the lulls of their death-song, they would resume their pipes, and with the exception of an occasional mutter, or the rattling of their chains, they sat motionless and impassive; until one among the elder would break out in the wild wail, when all would join again in the solemn preparation for death.

Following this, Rev. Dr. Williamson addressed them in their native tongue; after which they broke out again in their song of death. This last was thrilling beyond expression. The trembling voices, the forms shaking with passionate emotion, the half uttered words through set teeth, all made up a scene which no one who saw can ever forget.

The influence of the wild music of their death-song upon them was almost magical. Their whole manner changed after they had closed their singing, and an air of cheerful innocence marked all of them. It seemed as if during their passionate wailing, they had passed in spirit through the valley of the shadow of death, and already had their eyes fixed on their pleasant hunting grounds beyond.

As their friends came about them, they bade them cheerful farewells, and in some cases there would be peals of laughter, as they were wished pleasant journeys to the spirit-land. They bestowed their pipes upon their favorites, and so far as they had, gave keepsake trinkets to all. Major Brown said there was as much of laughter and fun as if they were going to a feast.

While we were there, the chains were cut from them and their hands bound behind them. White-Dog begged to be left free, without tying, and it seemed a mortification to all when they were bound. One, right in front of us, with a smiling face which nothing seemed to change, trembled all over even while he smiled, as the irons were struck from him, and his arms were pinioned. The half-breeds were most visibly affected while these preparations for the gallows were in progress.

They had evidently taken great pains to make themselves presentable for their last appearance on the stage of life. — Most of them had little pocket mirrors, and before they were bound, employed themselves in putting on the finishing touches of paint, and arranging their hair according to the Indian mode. All had religious emblems, mostly crosses, of fine gilt or steel, and these were dis-

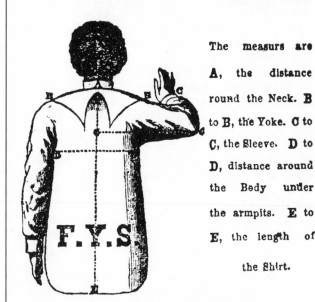

Minnesota Courier, Aug. 12, 1863

played with all the prominence of an exquisite or a *religieuse*. Many were painted in war style, with bands, and feathers, and were all decked as gaily as for a festival.

None were admitted within the prison besides the priests, the reporters, and the officers and men of the provost guard. They expressed a desire to shake hands with the reporters who were to write about how they looked and acted, and with the art-

"Then ensued a scene that can hardly be described and which can never be forgotten."

ist who was to picture their appearance. So we had to go through the ordeal of shaking hands with the thirty-nine. The hands of most were of the natural warmth, while those of others were cold as ice. Nearly all, on shaking hands would point their fingers to the sky and say as plainly as they could, "Me going up!" White Dog told us it was Little Crow who got them into the scrape, and now, they had to die for it. [Little Crow was the Dakota leader.] One said to us there was a Great Spirit above who would take him home, and that he should die happy. Thus the time passed away during the tying of hands, and striking off the manacles.

At a little after nine o'clock, the Reverend Father Ravoux entered the prison again, to perform the closing religious exercises. The guard fell back as he came in, the Indians ranging themselves around the room. The Father addressed the condemned at some length, and appeared much affected. He kneeled on the floor in their midst, and prayed with them, all following and uniting with him in an audible voice. They appeared like a different race of beings while going through these religious exercises. Their voices were low and humble, and every exhibition of Indian bravado was banished.

THE HOUR CALLED.

While Father Ravoux was yet speaking to the Indians, and repeating for the hundreth time, his urgent request that they must think to the last of the Great Spirit before whom they were about to appear, Provost Marshal Redfield entered and whispered a word in the ear of the good priest, who immediately said a word in French to Henry Milord, a half breed, who repeated it in Dacotah to the Indians, who were all lying down around the prison. In a moment every Indian stood erect, and as the Provost Marshal opened the door, they fell in behind him with the greatest alacrity. Indeed, a notice of release, pardon, or reprieve could not have induced them to leave the cell with more apparent willingness than this call to death. We followed on behind them, and as those at the head of the procession came out of the basement, at the opposite

B LACKSMITHING.

Lafayette street

Near Postoffice

T. CHAPPELL is prepaaed to do all kinds of Blacksmithing on the shortest notice and reasorable terms. This is the place for farmers to get their work done- **Satisfaction Warranted.**

Winona, Oct. 1, 1864.   3tf

Winona Democrat, Jan. 7, 1865

side of the gallows, and directly in front, we heard a sort of a death-wail sounded, which was immediately caught up by all the condemned and was chanted in unison until the scaffold was reached. At the foot of the steps there was no delay. Capt. Redfield mounted the drop, at the head, and the Indians crowded after him, as if it were a race to see which would get up first. They actually crowded on each other's heels, and as they got to the top each took his position, without any assistance from those who were detailed for that purpose. They still kept up a mournful wail, and occasionally there would be a piercing scream. The ropes were soon arranged around their necks, not the least resistance being offered. — One or two, feeling the noose uncomfortably tight, attempted to loosen it, and though their hands were tied, they partially succeeded. The movement, however, was noticed by the assistants, and the cords rearranged. The white caps, which had been placed on the top of their heads, were now drawn over their faces, shutting out forever the light of day from their eyes. Then ensued a scene that can hardly be described and which can never be forgotten. All joined in shouting and singing, as it appeared to those who were ignorant of the language. The tones seemed somewhat discordant, and yet there was harmony in it. Save the moment of cutting the rope it was the most thrilling moment of the awful scene. And it was not their voices alone. Their bodies swayed to and fro, and their every limb seemed to be keeping time. The drop trembled and shook as if they were all dancing.

The most touching scene on the drop was their attempts to grasp each other's hands, fettered as they were. They were very close to each other, and many succeeded. Three or four in a row were hand in hand, and all hands swaying up and down with the rise and fall of their voices. One old man reached out each side but could not grasp a hand. His struggles were piteous, and affected many beholders. We were informed by those who understand the language, that their singing and shouting was only to sustain each other — that there was nothing defiant in their last moments, and that no "death song," strictly speaking was chanted on the

"It is unnecessary to speak of the awful sight of thirty-eight human beings suspended, in the air."

gallows. Each one shouted his own name, and called on the name of a friend, saying in substance, "I am here! I am here!"

THE EXECUTION.

Captain Burt hastily scanned all the arrangements for the execution, and motioned to Major Brown, the signal officer, that all was ready. There was one tap of the drum, almost drowned by the voices of the Indians — another and the stays of the drop were knocked away, the rope cut, and, with a crash, down came the drop. One rope broke, but not until the neck of the victim was dislocated, whose body came down with a heavy *thud,* and a crash of the boards. There was no struggling by any of the Indians for the space of half a minute — the only movements were the natural vibrations occasioned by the fall.

In the meantime, a new rope was placed around the neck of the one who fell, and it, having been thrown over the beam, he was soon hanging with the others. After the lapse of a minute, several drew up their legs once or twice, and there was some movement of the arms. One Indian, at the expiration of ten minutes, breathed, but the rope was better adjusted, and life was soon extinct. It is unnecessary to speak of the awful sight of thirty-eight human beings suspended, in the air. Imagination will supply what we refrain from describing.

REMOVING THE BODIES.

After the bodies had hung for about half an hour, the physicians of several regiments present examined the bodies and reported that life was extinct. Soon after several United States mule teams appeared, when the bodies were taken down and dumped into the wagons without much ceremony, and were carried down to the sand bar in front of the city, and were all buried in the same hole. The half-breeds were buried in one corner of the hole, so they can be disinterred by their friends.

MILITARY.

. . . The whole military part of the program was carried out in the best style. There was no confusion, and every detachment knew its appointed place, and stuck to it. We have never before seen a finer military display in the State. Many detachments came from a long distance, and had a hard tramp of it, and also were not very comfortably quartered in Mankato. Much credit is due to Col. Miller, as well as to all other field officers, for the excellence of their arrangements for the execution, and the good order which everywhere prevailed.

Everything was conducted in the most orderly and quiet manner. As the drop fell the citizens

STILLWATER MESSENGER.

A. J. VAN VORHES, EDITOR.

STILLWATER:

Tuesday, - - - - - May 22, 1860

FOR PRESIDENT,
ABRAHAM LINCOLN,
OF ILLINOIS.

VICE PRESIDENT,
HANNIBAL HAMLIN,
OF MAINE.

EDITORIAL CORRESPONDENCE.

STEAMER ITASCA, }
May 15th 1860. }

Stillwater Messenger, May 22, 1860

could not repress a shout of exultation, and the soldiers joined. A boy soldier, who stood beside me, had his mother, and brothers and sisters, killed; his face was pale and quivering, but he gave a shout of righteous exultation when the drop fell.

The people, who had gathered in great crowds, and who had maintained a degree of order which had not been anticipated, quietly dispersed as the wagons bore the bodies of the murderers off to burial. Few, we take it, who witnessed the awful scene, will voluntarily look upon its like again.

FURTHER PARTICULARS.

The bodies of the thirty-eight Indians hanged on Friday of last week, were buried among the willows on the flat in front of the town, bordering on the Minnesota river. They were all placed in one grave, about thirty feet long, twelve wide and four or five deep. They were laid in two rows, their feet together and their heads to the sides of the grave. Their blankets were then placed over the bodies and dirt thrown over them.

So great was the desire of soldiers and visitors to obtain some relic of the occasion, that in some cases the crucifixes, wampum and other ornaments

"A number of orders for bodies have been received here."

were taken from their bodies before they were interred. Some visitors carried off a few beads, others a lock of hair, and we have heard of several instances where pieces of clothing were taken for preservation.

"THE RESURRECTION."

On the day of the execution, a number of physicians from different parts of the State were here to procure bodies for scientific purposes. Before midnight on Friday, at least eight or ten bodies were taken up and carried off. Others were taken on Saturday, Sunday and Monday nights, for the same purpose; and very few, if any, remain in the grave at the present time.

An eminent physician from an adjoining town obtained the bodies of old Cut-Nose and the large Indian that had broken his rope; and he has had them scrubbed, their hair cut, and transformed generally so that were they to return to life again they would not know themselves. [The legend is that the physician was Dr. W.W. Mayo of Rochester.]

A number of orders for bodies have been received here — one from Chicago by a physician for several bodies, for which he proposed to pay the *extravagant* sum of $10 each, delivered in that city.

Mankato Weekly Record, Jan. 3, 1863

—>•<—

[Race relations remained dreadful. The Shakopee Argus proclaimed on May 6, 1865, "As a rule Indians are entitled to no more clemency than should be given to wolves or any other wild beasts of the forest."]

Lo! The Dead Indian. — Pat. Leonard informs us that while coming to this city a few days since ... they discovered a frozen Indian lying near the roadside. We sympathize with Pat. in profound regret that the entire Chippewa tribe were not found in the same condition.

Stillwater Messenger, Feb. 13, 1866

—>•<—

The Indians are having a grand old time again. We mean the Sioux and the Chippewas. They are killing each other at every opportunity. May that opportunity be every minute of the day.

Minneapolis Tribune, June 19, 1869

[Many hundreds of Indians were exiled from Minnesota. The Dakota who eventually returned found themselves treated as outsiders in their former homeland and suffered decades of discrimination and neglect.

[For more on the Dakota War, see "The Sioux Uprising of 1862" by Kenneth Carley, published in 1976 by the Minnesota Historical Society Press. "Little Crow: Spokesman for the Sioux" by Gary Clayton Anderson, published in 1986 by the Minnesota Historical Society Press, tells the story of the Dakota leader and his people.]

—>•<—

[Of course, much was happening in the 1860s that was unrelated to the Civil War or the Dakota War. Let's look at the more ordinary life during the decade.]

Minnesota Hunter. Our friend N. Haughton, of Winnebago Agency, started northward, on a hunting expedition last Friday. He is recognized as one of the best shots and most successful hunters in Minnesota, and withal a noble, generous hearted gentleman. So far, Mr. H. has killed about two thousand deer, besides countless amounts of other game. His father, living in Sherburne county, has killed over four thousand deer; and his brother, captain of the steamer Antelope, counts his deer scalps by hundreds.

Mankato Weekly Record, Feb. 14, 1860

—>•<—

Two Minute Sermon to the

HOUSEHOLD HINTS

Half a cranberry bound on a corn [on the foot] will soon kill it.

Stillwater Messenger, Feb. 14, 1865

—>•<—

To Clean Papered Walls. — The very best method is to rub them with stale bread. Cut the crust off very thick, and wipe straight down from the top; then go to the top again, and so on; the staler the bread the better.

Goodhue County Republican, Red Wing, July 17, 1868

"Take early morning exercise, let loose your corset string, and run up the hills on a wager, and down again for fun."

Girls. Ladies — caged birds of beautiful plumage, but sickly looks — pale pets of the parlor, who vegetate in an unhealthy atmosphere like the potato germinating in a dark cellar, why do you not go out in the open air and warm sunshine, and add lustre to your eyes, bloom to your cheeks, and elasticity to your steps, and vigor to your frames? Take early morning exercise, let loose your corset string, and run up the hills on a wager, and down again for fun; roam the fields, wade the brooks, climb the fences, leap the ditches, and after a day of exhilarating exercise and unrestrained liberty, go home with an appetite acquired by healthy enjoyment. The blooming and beautiful young lady — rose-cheeked and bright-eyed — who can darn a stocking, mend her own frocks, command a regiment of pots and kettles, feed the pigs, milk the cows, and be a lady when required, is the girl that young men are in quest of for a wife. But you pining, screwed-up, wasp-waisted, doll-dressed, consumption-mortgaged, music-murdering, and novel-devouring daughters of fashion and idleness — you are no more fit for matrimony than a pullet is to look after a brood of fourteen chickens. The truth is, my dear girls, you want less fashionable restraint and more liberty of action, more kitchen and less parlor; more leg exercise and less sofa; more pudding and less piano; more frankness and less mock modesty. Loosen your waist strings and breathe in the pure atmosphere, and become something as good and beautiful as nature designed.

St. Peter Tribune, Feb. 22, 1860

–>•<–

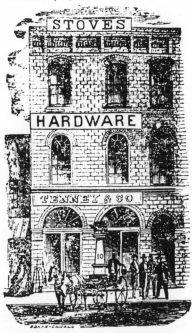

Winona Democrat, Aug. 19, 1865

I Wish I Was an Editor.

I wish I was an editor —
I really do indeed;
It seems to me that editors
Get everything they need.
They get the biggest and the
best
Of everything that grows,
And get in free to circuses
And other kinds of shows;
And when a mammoth cheese
is cut,
They always get a slice,
For saying Mrs. Smith knows
how
To make it very nice.

The largest pumpkin, longest
beet,
And other garden stuff,
Is blown into the sanctum by
An editorial puff.
The biggest bug will speak to
them,
No matter how they dress—
A shabby coat is nothing — if
You own a printing press.

At Ladies' Fairs they're almost
hugged
By pretty girls, you know,
That he may crack up every-
thing
The ladies have to show.
And thus they get a blow-out
free
At every party feed —
The reason is — because they
write,
And other people read.

St. Cloud Democrat, Aug. 30, 1860

–>•<–

Contemptible Means. — We understand that the telegraph operator at St. Paul shut up the telegraph office at 9 o'clock on election night, and refused to transmit any election news whatever to the daily papers of that city, unless they would raise him a bonus of $50. This the several publishers very properly refused to do, and therefore no news of

*"If you wish to improve the moral characters of your neighbors,
give them a good dinner on Thanksgiving day."*

election, except a few lines to private individuals, was received in St. Paul until brought by the mails. —

Thus we have been kept back from the news one week. When it is considered that each of the St. Paul dailies pay $10 per week for the daily news over the line it will be seen what an unwise move it was in the operator, to attempt extortion, as the three offices now declare they will not receive another item by telegraph until THAT operator slides. He had better agitate his pedal extremities and get scarce as soon as possible.

Wright County Republican, Monticello, Nov. 17, 1860

→•←

Thanksgiving — Remember the Poor. — It has been recommended that collections be taken up in the churches on Thanksgiving day, for the benefit of their pastors, and also for the benefit of the people of Kansas [where civil strife was taking place], and while we would not discourage contributions to either of those objects, we earnestly hope that no one, be he a church-going man or otherwise, will forget the poor, whom we have amongst us always. Let them have a share of your abundance, wherewith to make contentment in their households, for one day at least, and involuntary thanksgiving will be the result. It requires more philosophy and more christianity than the majority of people have to render thanks for blessings which they are not conscious of possessing. If you wish to improve the moral characters of your neighbors, give them a good dinner on Thanksgiving day — and above all "Let not your right hand know what your left hand doeth" — in other words, don't let anybody know of your good deeds.

St. Paul Pioneer and Democrat, Nov. 28, 1860

→•←

German Celebration. — One of the most pleasant of all our Christmas festivals was that of the German Methodist Church in this city. The Germans have transplanted the beautiful Christmas tree of the fatherland. — All its emblems are as significant here as across the waters. The tree . . . was beautifully ornamented. The songs, speeches and dialogues were well performed. Love of liberty and of religion ran through all. . . . The music was led by Prof. Seebich. An abundance of sweetmeats were provided for the little ones, and apples and candies were handed to all in the house. We are right glad to see our German friends so happy among us.

Goodhue County Republican, Red Wing, Dec. 28, 1860

→•←

The Fur Trade. — The value of the Fur Trade of St. Paul cannot be over estimated. Sleigh loads come in daily from trading points one and two hundred miles distant, some of which are worth a thousand dollars. This money is mostly spent again for goods, groceries and merchandize, helping to keep trade brisk and circulate money. Then our dealers have a fair profit, which leaves a balance of exchange in our favor. Many persons in the interior settlements of the State, who cannot work at their trade in the winter season, become trappers, and make considerable money.

St. Paul Pioneer and Democrat, Jan. 22, 1861

→•←

A Suggestion. — We notice that our Horticultural Society has taken the initiatory steps to procure shade trees for our principal streets. They have advised that said trees should be planted

twelve feet from the line of the houses. Our eighty foot streets are to have twelve foot pavements, and our avenues sixteen feet. The trees ought to be placed at least one foot inside of the outer edge of the pavement. This would secure them from being injured by passing vehicles. It is to be hoped that no one will be so reckless as to fasten their horses to these trees. It is no use to plant trees if they are to be destroyed in this way.

St. Paul Pioneer and Democrat, April 19, 1861

→•←

Marriage at Minnehaha. — On Friday morning, a gentleman and lady, who had been stopping for several days at one of our hotels, took a trip to Minnehaha and while there, were united in marriage under the rock from which the laughing water falls. The scene is said to have been quite interesting, but the romance of it will be better appreciated a thousand miles distant, than in St. Paul.

St. Paul Pioneer and Democrat, Aug. 27, 1861

→•←

Easy Tooth Pulling Illustrated. — Before the day of chloroform there was a quack who advertised tooth drawing without pain. The patient was placed in a chair, and the instrument applied to his tooth with a wrench, followed by a roar from the unpleasantly surprised sufferer. "Stop," cried the dentist, "compose yourself. I have told you I would give you no pain, but only just gave you that twinge as a specimen to show you Catwright's method of operation." — Again the instrument was applied, another tug, another roar. "Now don't be impatient; that's Dumerge's way; be seated and calm; you will now be sensible of my superiority over those I have named." Another

"How boldly we struck out upon the smooth ice."

tug, another roar. "Now pray be quiet; that is Parkinson's method; you don't like it, and no wonder." By this time the tooth hung by a thread, and whipping it out, the operator exultingly exclaimed, "That is my mode of tooth drawing without pain, and you are now enabled to compare it with the operations of Catwright, Dumerge and Parkinson."
St. Peter Tribune, May 28, 1862

⤚➤•⤙

One of the most delicious warm weather beverages is the lemon and sarsaparilla pop manufactured in this city by Mr. J. Lines. It is cool, refreshing, and withal cheap, and we most heartily commend it to the attention of those looking for an article which exhilarates, but not intoxicates.
St. Paul Press, June 3, 1862

⤚➤•⤙

Police Court. — Two more boys were brought up for swimming in the day time — fined one dollar each and costs. Served you right, boys. Keep your clothes on and stay out of the water next time.
St. Paul Press, Aug. 1, 1862

⤚➤•⤙

Pay of School Teachers. — At the meeting of the Board of Education the other evening, a resolution was adopted establishing the pay of School Teachers from the commencement of the present term as follows: Teacher the Boy's Secondary Department, $60 per month; Girls Secondary, $35; Upper Primary, $30; Lower Primary, $30. This we believe is an increase of $5 per month for the female teachers, and $10 per month for the teachers of the Boy's Secondary, presided over by male teachers.
St. Paul Press, Jan. 16, 1863

⤚➤•⤙

Chewing. — The habit of tobacco chewing is a loathsome, filthy, injurious, expensive, and wholly uncalled for habit; and we are sorry that it is our misfortune to be given a leetle to the weed ourself. But you may take all the evils and disadvantages of tobacco chewing, as above mentioned, and multiply them by ten and you have the exact product of the evils of GUM CHEWING; a habit that is now so fashionable, especially with the female portion of humanity, that it is fast becoming hereditary to such an extent that the first word a child utters nowa-days is "come, old dad, where's the gum?"
Shakopee Argus, Nov. 26, 1864

⤚➤•⤙

Skating. — Hurrah boys, now's the time for your iron shoes, before too much snow falls to prevent the enjoyment of this grandest of all grand sports — so considered by many at least, but for us, we can't see it. Never shall we forget the first and only time we were persuaded to imagine the sport of skating No. 1 of all other sports, and how boldly we struck out upon the smooth ice, and how we were congratulating ourself that we had been so kindly and correctly informed as to its merits, when all of a sudden — oh, horror of horrors — we saw with our starspangled vision a new and strange firmament, lit up with all the hues of the rainbow, the view alternating between beauty indescribable, and all the hob-gobblin hideousness that imagination

"While engaged in adjusting a belt on one of the wheels, [he] was caught and dragged into the machinery and instantly crushed to pieces."

could conjur; but soon our dream was brought to an end, by a tingling sensation in sensitive portions of our person, and we made the remarkable discovery that we had got a fall; and was sitting our whole weight upon a terrible sore spot in the ice; after sitting a moment, heaping epithets upon the head of the *friend* who had thus seduced us, and wishing ourself of sufficient calibre to whip the man who made the skates, we betook our remains to our home, fully convinced that stocks in ice and skates were considerably below par, so far as *this* American was concerned.

Shakopee Argus, Nov. 26, 1864

–✈·✠–

Fatal Accident. — On last Monday a most shocking accident occurred at Spring Lake, in this county. The victim was a Mr. Ringrose, who was employed in the sawmill at that place, while engaged in adjusting a belt on one of the wheels, was caught and dragged into the machinery and instantly crushed to pieces. — There was no one near at the time, and he was found a few minutes afterwards by another of the employees of the mill, a frightfully mangled corpse. He was a returned soldier, and had been at home but a few days when he was thus torn from family and friends, just as his security from death seemed to have become the most perfect. He leaves a wife and several children to mourn his untimely fate.

Since the above was in type we have learned some of the particulars of the sad affair. — It appears that the belt wheel had no flange and the belt frequently ran off the wheel as it did in this instance, and had to be put on again while in motion; the deceased upon seeing the belt come off, went to put it on, and did so, but just as it snapped on to the wheel it caught his left

Minnesota State News, May 3, 1862

"Froze to Death. Another Drunkard Gone."

CHATFIELD PAPER

[A particularly well-written and spicy newspaper full of local news and views was published in Chatfield, Minn., in the late 1860s. Its language was colorful; for example, it told of a man "as fond of handsome ladies as a pig is of a warm jam." Articles in those days rarely carried the name of the writer, but one may assume that many in the Chatfield paper were written by J.S. McKenny, the editor until his death in July 1868. Here's a sampling:]

A Naughty Man — A gay and festive little rooster, who formerly edited one of the Rochester papers, has been disobeying one of the commandments lately. The rantankerous little cuss is married, has a charming wife and lives in a beautiful cottage, where there also did dwell a handsome, buxum "hired gal." The ex-editor acted queer. Wife smelt one or two large sized mice, but laid low. One Sabbath started for Church, ex-editor was sick, couldn't go. Wife smelt a wharf rat — returned for a handkerchief — walked slowly to kitchen window, peeped carefully in — saw husband and the girl standing in the corner. A row ensued, of course, right and proper it should, which the ex-editor attempted to quiet by assuring his wife and her friends that "he and the girl were just measuring to see which was the tallest." — Wife couldn't see it, and the ex took the first train for the East.
Chatfield Democrat, Jan. 17, 1867

→•←

Froze to Death. Another Drunkard Gone. — Mr. Thomas Warner, a man of superior intelligence and information and once a minister of the gospel, froze to death, while in a helpless state of intoxication, near Elysian, Le Sueur county, on the night of the 16th of January. The day previous to his death and most of the night he had spent in a saloon in the village and left for his home, near morning, in a state of intoxication. When within one hundred rods of home, he commenced falling down every few rods until at last he was obliged to crawl on his hands and feet, which he did until he got within ten or twelve rods of his own door, but could get no farther, then falling forward from his crawling position died. He leaves a very interesting family.

Thus another victim to intemperance has gone — perished in a snow bank, almost at his own door, and the tears of the widow and orphan are falling and aching hearts are almost bursting in breasts that know no comfort.

We have been fearful for the past winter or two that we should have a similar case to the above to report, as having occurred in this village, but so far, thank God, all have escaped, but no one knows for how long.
Chatfield Democrat, Feb. 2, 1867

→•←

Men Wanted. The great want of this age is men. Men who are not for sale. Men who are honest, sound from circle to circumference, true, to the heart core. Men who will condemn wrong in friend or foe. Men whose consciences are steady as the needle to the pole. — Men who will stand to the right if the heavens totter and the earth reels. Men who can tell the truth. Men who neither brag nor run. Men who can have courage without whistling for it. Men careless of man's applause. . . . Men who do not strive nor cry, nor cause their voices to be heard in the streets, and who will not fail nor be discouraged. Men who know their message and tell it. Men who know their duty and do it. Men who know their place and fill it.
Chatfield Democrat, June 15, 1867

→•←

Apology. — We dislike to make apologies to our readers, but fear that some might notice that we fail this week on our usual amount of interest, especially in the local department, we would remind them that this has been 4th of July and circus week, and it has been more than we could do to keep the boys at work, or to do much ourselves. Besides this we have been otherwise embarrassed in mind and body, and hope all may overlook our short comings this week, at least.
Chatfield Democrat, July 6, 1867

→•←

Happy Homes. — Do not be afraid of a little fun at home. Do not shut up your houses lest the sun should fade the carpet; and your hearts, lest a hearty laugh should shake down some of the musty cobwebs there! If you want to ruin your sons, let them think that all mirth and social enjoyment must be left on the threshold when they come home at night. Young people must have fun and re-

"The wife rose, intending to reveal the infidelity of her spouse."

CHATFIELD PAPER

laxation somewhere. If they do not have it at their own hearth stones, it will be sought in other and less profitable places. Therefore let the fire burn brightly at night, and make the home ever delightful, with all those little arts that parents' sons perfectly understand. Do not repress the buoyant spirits of children; half an hour of merriment round the lamp and fire light of home blots out the remembrance of many a care and annoyances during the day, and the best safe-guard they can take with them into the world is the unseen influence of a bright little domestic sanctum.

Chatfield Democrat, May 9, 1868

–>•<–

The funniest story of the age is told by a Detroit paper. A lady suspected her husband of improper intimacy with the hired girl. — Without informing her husband of her intentions, she sent the girl off, and that night went to sleep in the girl's bed. She hadn't been there long when somebody came and took the other half of the bed. About two hours after, the wife rose, intending to reveal the infidelity of her spouse, struck a light, when lo! it was the hired man.

Chatfield Democrat, Dec. 12, 1868

–>•<–

Assault with Attempt to Kiss. — The case of the State of Minnesota vs. Charles N. Paine, for an assault with attempt to kiss the wife of G.W. Bolster, mentioned in our last issue, was tried before a jury in this place on Saturday last, and resulted in the conviction of the Defendant, who was fined $25 and costs. Take it altogether this is rather an expensive luxury when indulged in without leave or license, and should serve as a warning to all who are in the habit of "sticking in their bills" where they are not wanting. Not any for us if you please, at such prices.

Chatfield Democrat, Dec. 12, 1868

–>•<–

Phunny. An old Bachelor named Buckinghan, aged 58, and a young lady by the name of Baker, aged 18, both of Jordon Township, this county, were married a few days ago, and when last heard from were "doing as well as could be expected," under the circumstances.

Chatfield Democrat, Aug. 21, 1869

–>•<–

[The writing in the Chatfield Democrat was lively, but some of it was extremely racist. This, believe it or not, is not the most virulent example.]

Rape. — The St. Paul papers give the particulars of a rape case that took place in the suburbs of that city a few days ago. The victim was a Sweed woman who had but recently arrived in St. Paul, and the fiend a nigger by the name of Combs, about 20 years of age. The nigger was arrested and is now in jail awaiting his trial. If the laws of Missouri were in force in this State a material change in the physical proportions of this Mr. Nig would be the result of his conviction. We hope the Sweeds of this State who are sweet upon the nigger, will please make a note of this transaction. This is the second outrage of the kind that has been committed upon Sweed women by *niggers* during the past year in Minnesota.

Chatfield Democrat, June 19, 1869

---

arm, when he was instantly rolled in between the belt and the wheel, which was going at the rate of sixty revolutions per minute. The owner of the mill, Mr. Turner, was upstairs at the time, and noticed a curious action in the machinery and heard an occasional thud, but attributed it to some trifling cause; in about fifteen minutes after he had first noticed it he determined to go below and see the occasion of the noise, when he found the body in the position described. — He immediately stopped the mill and, with assistance, extricated the body of the unfortunate man. His arms and legs were broken into twenty or thirty pieces, and the flesh literally stripped therefrom, pieces of which were found in every direction; his body was ground to a pumice and blood was thrown thirty feet. One of his feet was found the next day, and pieces of flesh were picked up for several days after in and about the mill.

Shakopee Argus, July 22, 1865

–>•<–

Sale of Farms. — Mr. Jared Lewis, living about five miles north of Mankato, sold his farm of 300 acres, and improvements, to Mr. Bradley, of Illinois, for $5,000. This farm is in a good state of cultivation, and contains

"The Minneapolis Base Ball Club have received their full dress suits which they ordered from the East some time since."

a comfortable dwelling and all the necessary out-houses.

St. Paul Press, Aug. 23, 1865

→·←

A Quaker Woman's Sermon. — "My dear friends, there are three things I very much wonder at. The first is, that children should be so foolish as to throw up stones, clubs and brick bats into fruit trees, to knock down fruit; if they would let it alone it would fall itself. The second is, that men should be so foolish, and even so wicked, as to go to war, and kill each other; if let alone, they would die themselves. And the third and last thing I wonder at is, that young men would be so unwise as to go after the young women; if they would stay at home the young women would come after them."

Brownsville Free Press, Feb. 2, 1866

→·←

The Influx of Strangers. — We have not seen the city so full of strangers for several years as it is now. The hotels are jammed to overflowing — every boarding house is a regular bee hive, and still the throng presses on. ... The want of accommodations here ... is causing them to pass on. Most of them would stop here a few days if they could get lodgings, and many would settle here permanently. Thus we are losing population by the thousand for want of accommodations for them.

Nearly all of those who come, come with plenty of money, and with the design of staying here. Most of them are seeking homesteads, and our real estate dealers are fast clearing off their old lists. We hear of sales every day at figures actually startling. So it is all over the State, and by fall we will doubtless have a population of 300,000.

St. Paul Pioneer, April 24, 1866

THE LATEST
BY TELEGRAPH.

GLORIOUS NEWS FROM GEN. SHERMAN'S ARMY.

CAPTURE OF ATLANTA

A Battle Fought by Gen. Sherman with General Hood.

REBEL ARMY CUT IN TWO WITH A VERY HEAVY LOSS TO THE ENEMY.

The 500,000 Call Reduced to 300,000.

Grant Wants 100,000 Men to Take Richmond.

He Thinks the Present Call will Finish the Rebellion.

St. Paul Pioneer, Sept. 4, 1864

→·←

The City Council held a meeting last Monday evening, at which they passed an ordinance in reference to the streets, making it unlawful for persons to blockade the streets or walks with boxes, barrels, wood or anything else. Also one prohibiting the running at large of "hogs and other animals." Cows are, however, exempt, and have the liberty of the city. Also an ordinance taxing dogs, and obliging the owners to keep them muzzled, and it is perfectly lawful for anybody catching any dog running at large without a substantial muzzle to forthwith dispatch said dog.

Minneapolis Chronicle, April 3, 1867

→·←

Concerning Cribs, &C. — About three months ago one of our enterprising furniture dealers caused ten dozen cribs to be manufactured in their factory at St. Anthony, supposing that number would be sufficient to supply the demand for this peculiar article for six months at least. They informed the reporter yesterday that the call for cribs had been enormous, and that thirty days ago they had parted with the last one of the hundred and twenty. On top of this startling information comes the intelligence that one of the great drug firms of this city has sold upwards of 50 dozen of bell-shaped bottles during the past four months. In view of this unprecedented occurrence, it may well be asked whether the climate of this State is in any way connected with, or accessory to the demand for cribs or bell-shaped bottles.

Minneapolis Chronicle, May 16, 1867

→·←

Base Ball Suits. — The Minneapolis Base Ball Club have received their full dress suits which they ordered from the East some time since. Their caps are red, something after the jockey style, and the shirts blue and trimmed with red, the pants blue and the shoes white. Their belts are blue with the name of the club in raised letters on the back side and the initials of the wearer in front. It is a beautiful suit and the boys will be apt to make fair hearts flutter while on their trips to Red Wing and Hastings.

Minneapolis Tribune, July 13, 1867

→·←

Huge Bear. — Henry Lamb, who keeps the St. Paul meat mar-

"Children are like toothpicks."

ket, on Jackson street, bought a dressed bear yesterday, that weighed 305 pounds. This huge animal was killed a few days ago by a boy on Kettle river, and was brought to this city by Mr. S.A. Martin, from whom Mr. Lamb purchased him. To-day he will be dished up to customers who desire a rarity for Christmas dinner.
St. Paul Press, Dec. 24, 1867

→·←

Bakeries. We know of but three bakeries in the city . . . and with one exception, [they] do a small business. . . . This is a flour city. Three hundred and thirty-seven thousand dollars are invested in its manufacture, and what is more to the point, nearly every family manufactures its own bread.
Minneapolis Tribune, Feb. 21, 1868

→·←

A lady was urged by her friends to marry a widower and as an argument they spoke of his two beautiful children. "Children," replied the lady, "are like toothpicks. A person wants her own."
Minneapolis Tribune, May 5, 1868

→·←

The Language of the Handkerchief. — An exchange [newspaper] says that fans and flowers have each their language, and why not handkerchiefs? No reason having been discovered, it has transpired that handkerchief flirtations are rapidly coming in fashion. As yet the "code of signals" is confined to a select few, but we do not intend that they shall enjoy the monopoly any longer, and accordingly publish the key. Our informant says that it may be used at the opera, theatre, balls, and such places, but never in church; and we hope that this restriction will be observed, and are quite sure that it *won't.*

Drawing across the lips — Desirous of an acquaintance.

Drawing across the eyes — I am sorry.

Taking it by the center — You are too willing.

Dropping — We will be friends.

Twirling in both hands — Indifference.

Drawing across the cheek — I love you.

Drawing through the hands — I hate you.

Letting it rest on the right cheek — Yes!

Letting it rest on the left cheek — No!

Twirling it in the left hand — I wish to be rid of you.

Twirling it in the right hand — I love another.

Folding it — I wish to speak with you.

Over the shoulder — Follow me.

Opposite corners in both hands — Wait for me.

Drawing across the forehead — We are watched.

Placing on right ear — You have changed.

Placing on left ear — I have a message for you.

"In our day, books are so cheap that a man may every year add a hundred volumes to his library for the price of what his tobacco and his beer would cost him."

Letting it remain on the eyes — You are cruel.

Winding around forefinger — I am engaged.

Winding around third finger — I am married.

Putting it in the pocket — No more at present.

Minneapolis Tribune, Oct. 10, 1868

→•←

Death from Rattlesnake Bite. — On Wednesday night last Mr. Abel Folsom, of Zumbrota township, came home at a late hour and his wife got up from bed in the second story to admit him. She came down to the first floor in the kitchen, and immediately screamed for help, saying that a snake was fastened to her foot and she could not shake it off. Another woman, sleeping in the house, struck a light and admitted Mr. Folsom. By this time Mrs. Folsom had shaken off the snake which stuck to her by its fangs so that it was only by violent effort she threw it off. The snake was found making its way towards the second story, half way up stairs, and killed. It was a rattlesnake of the prairies, such as is sometimes called a massasaugar. Such help was given Mrs. Folsom as could be had in the way of stimulants, and a physician obtained as soon as possible, but she died, after great suffering, on Saturday evening.

Red Wing Argus, June 25, 1868

→•←

Bookless Houses.

We form judgments of men from little things about their houses, of which the owners perhaps never think. Flowers about a rich man's house may signify only that he has a good gardener, or that he has refined neighbors, and does what he sees them do. But men are not accustomed to buy books unless they want them. If, on visiting the dwelling of a man of slender means, we

St. Paul Pioneer, Sept. 4, 1864

find that he contents himself with cheap carpets and very plain furniture, in order that he may purchase books, he rises at once in our esteem. Books are not made for furniture, but there is nothing else that so beautifully furnishes a house. The plainest row of books is more significant of refinement than the most elaborately carved sideboard.

Give us a house furnished with books rather than furniture. Both, if you can; but books at any rate. To spend several days in a friend's house, and hunger for something to read, while you are treading on costly carpets, and sitting upon luxurious chairs,

and sleeping upon down, is as if one were bribing your body for the sake of cheating your mind.

Books are the windows through which the soul looks out. A house without them is like a room without windows. No man has a right to bring up his children without surrounding them with books, if he has the means to buy them. It is a wrong to his family. Children learn to read by being in the presence of books. The love of knowledge comes with reading, and grows upon it. And the love of knowledge in a young mind is almost a warrant against the inferior excitement of passions and vice.

Let us pity those poor rich men who live barrenly in great bookless houses. Let us congratulate the poor that, in our day, books are so cheap that a man may every year add a hundred volumes to his library for the price of what his tobacco and his beer would cost him. Among the earliest ambitions to be excited in clerks, workmen, journeymen — and, indeed, among all that are struggling in the race of life — is that of owning, and constantly adding to, a library of good books. A little library, growing larger every year, is an honorable part of a young man's history.

It is a man's duty to have books. A library is not a luxury, but one of the necessaries of life.

Hastings Gazette, Jan. 9, 1869, reprinted from the "Episcopalian"

→•←

Wanted, a Mother! — We are informed that in September last, a well dressed and respectable appearing woman, giving her name as Mary Lassoe, called at the residence of a Mrs. Myers, in St. Anthony, and desired to leave with her an infant about four months old (which she carried in her arms), and did finally do so, agreeing to pay Mrs. Myers $3 per

"Two bruisers with their friends went out on the Como road yesterday, and punched each other's heads for amusement."

week while the child remained with her. The woman's story seems to have been rather indefinite — her home was "on Rum river," and she was a widow, her husband having died one month before her babe was born. Whether her statements were true or false, she never paid a second visit to Mrs. Myers, nor did she pay the stipulated $3 per week. Up to the present time, the County Commissioners have allowed Mrs. Myers $12 per month, but unless the child's mother calls for it ere long, they propose transferring it to the county house, where it can be cared for at less expense.

Minneapolis Tribune, Feb. 6, 1869

→•←

Prize Fight. — Two bruisers with their friends went out on the Como road yesterday, and punched each other's heads for amusement. The parties were Mike King and a man by the name of McDonald. They fought seven rounds in twenty minutes, and owing to a foul blow by McDonald, the fight was decided in favor of King. Both, according to accounts given by spectators, were pretty thoroughly punished. The fight was witnessed by about twenty-five bruisers, who went out quietly from town escaping the attention of the police.

St. Paul Press, March 2, 1869

→•←

Minnesota State News, May 3, 1862

1870s

The population reached 439,706 by 1870. Duluth and St. Paul were connected by railroad. By the end of the decade, railroads reached the northwest part of the state, carrying settlers to the Red River Valley. The national Panic of 1873 slowed booming expansion. A devastating grasshopper invasion lasted five years. The legendary Northfield Bank Robbery got lots of press in 1876. Minneapolis emerged as the world's flour-milling center; in 1878 three flour mills exploded and 18 men died. Streetcars and telephones came onto the scene. Rivalry between Minneapolis and St. Paul was flagrant. Diphtheria reached epidemic proportions by the late 1870s.

Minneapolis Tribune, Sept. 8, 1876

1870s

–>•<–

Northfield Bank Robbery

Northfield, Minn., became known across the nation when townspeople foiled the plans of a gang of bank robbers. Two outlaws were left dead on the street, and the bank's bookkeeper was killed for refusing to open the vault. The robbery was Sept. 7, 1876. This is the story the Minneapolis Tribune ran the next morning.

THE NORTHFIELD BANK robbery has continued, to-day, to be the one all absorbing topic of conversation, and every particle of news, every rumor afloat on the street was caught at with eager interest, every one is astounded at the boldness of the attack and the prompt and effective effort of the attacking Northfield men. Nothing has excited such widespread and universal interest in Minnesota since the Indian outbreak, and there is no abatement to the feeling. . . . The Tribune emissary returned from Northfield this morning at 11 o'clock, and is therefore prepared to present the fullest, most graphic and accurate account of the affray yet published.

The Scene of the Robbery.

Northfield is, be it stated for the information of those not acquainted with the fact, a quiet little city of about two thousand inhabitants, situated in Rice county and on the line of the Iowa and Minnesota division of the Milwaukee & St. Paul railroad, about 40 miles from this city.

The inhabitants are peacefully disposed, and the morals of the city are notably of the undemonstrative character; its people prosperous and happy. Naturally, then, the bold attack, the fatal result to one of the bravest and best men in the city, and the shooting of two of the highwaymen, has created the

WILDEST EXCITEMENT.

It is impossible to portray the excitement and interest that prevails. All yesterday afternoon and this morning groups of men were gathered at every street corner, in every store door, about the bank, about the room where the bodies of the two dead robbers lay [actually, the bodies were outside], examining eagerly the marks of bullets that are everywhere to be seen, where the

BRIEF AND BLOODY

skirmish occurred. Farmers, this morning, learning for the first time of the affair, were swarming into town; every man encountered had his story to tell, and the reporter had but to make known his mission and forthwith were opened upon him the flood gates of information.

The scene of the short and decisive affray is the very centre of the business portion of the city. The village proper, or rather the main portion of it, lies east of the Cannon river. The main business street runs parallel with that stream. Intersecting the main street, is another, to which access is gained by crossing a small bridge. The intersecting street is rather an open square two or three hundred feet wide each way. About this square are grouped the leading business houses, and on the northwest corner is a stone block occupied by Lee & Hitchcock, and in the immediate rear is

THE FIRST NATIONAL BANK

fronting on the main street. It is a small, neatly furnished room, not different from other banking rooms, and in its arrangement much resembles the Hennepin county savings bank. The vault occupies a position to the centre and right of the room. Around it is an ordinary counter, with high glass protection, an opening at the corner, and another at the end next to the wall, where is the desk of the cashier and where was seated the murdered man when the robbers entered. The other two occupants of the bank, the wounded man Bunker and

"The shots were fired in every direction, as the marks upon the buildings indicate."

NORTHFIELD'S SENSATION.

Full and Graphic Account of the Bank Robbery.

With a Sketch of the Scene and Particulars.

The Excitement in Northfield, This City and Elsewhere.

The Wonderful Execution of the Brave Men of Northfield.

Hoy and His Party in Hot Pursuit and Close After Them.

The Attack, the Flight, the Pursuit and Its Incidents.

Something of the Dead Bank Official— A Former Minneapolis Man.

Another Victim of the Tragedy—The Wounded Swede.

Rumors that Hoy Met the Robbers at Three O'Clock This Morning.

And Made Them Come Down Repulsed and Probably Cornered.

Minneapolis Tribune, Sept. 8, 1876

Mr. Wilcox, occupied positions at the other part of the desk and directly in the line of the door. This description is necessary that the manner of the attack be better understood further along.

Appearance of the Robbers.

As early as ten days ago one of the men shot and a man who appeared to be one of the leaders of the gang of desperadoes, arrived in Northfield and made inquiries concerning the price of land, and appeared to be desirous of purchasing. He rode a fine animal, which was quartered at the livery stable, and remained a day or two. Other members of the party were seen in the vicinity at different times.

On Wednesday three of them rode in from Millersburg and met a fourth member of the gang. All tied their horses near the depot, where they were observed by fanciers of fine stock as remarkably fine animals, but the belief was then entertained that they were

CATTLE DEALERS

from the cities, and their appearance would have led to that supposition very naturally. But there was nothing in their appearance that would open them to suspicion that they were the daring desperadoes their conduct has since proved them to be. Yesterday morning three of the party rode into town. They took dinner at a restaurant on the west side of the Cannon River, which flows through the town, took everything in a leisurely manner, ate heartily, discussed politics among themselves, paid their bill, and one of the number, to all appearances the leader of the gang, offered to bet the restaurant proprietor one hundred dollars that this state would go Democratic. The bet was not accepted, and the three men mounted their horses and drove

ACROSS THE BRIDGE.

They tied their horses near Lee & Hitchcock's corner, very nearly in front of the bank. For a few moments they stood leisurely talking among themselves at the corner, afterwards moving towards the bank, which they entered. At the very same time there rode across the bridge into the large open square, three men

MOUNTED AND ARMED

to the teeth, and heading their horses into a gallop commenced yelling and firing their revolvers, ordering every one inside. The shots were fired in every direction, as the marks upon the buildings indicate. The square was at once cleared, store doors closed, and surprise that produced only compliance with the sudden and desperate command

76

"Damn you! open that door, or we'll cut your throat from ear to ear."

prevailed. Simultaneously there rode down from the west into the main street, two or three other men, who observed the same kind of tactics as the three that had crossed the bridge. At this part of the narrative there is some disagreement. Some state the number who rode down into the main street was three, others but two, but as near as can be ascertained there were

ONLY EIGHT

men engaged in the affray. Of this number three entered the bank, and the other five continued to shoot and shout to every one on the street to get out of the way, and not to endeavor to interfere, using the most profane and threatening language. It was all done in a less space of time than it takes to tell it, and occurred about two o'clock on yesterday afternoon. Meantime the three that entered the bank had been

DOING RAPID WORK.

Without a word of warning all three jumped over the counter at the opening at the corner. The rest of the story of their attack is better told by Mr. Wilcox, the clerk in the bank, who was the only eye witness to Mr. Haywood's murder accessible to the reporter's inquisitiveness. Mr. Bunker [is] still suffering from the wound he received, and the excitement of the affair.

MR. WILCOX'S STORY

is as follows: "Mr. Haywood occupied the cashier's seat at the desk which you see at the end of the counter. Mr. Bunker and myself occupied seats at the desk, Mr. Bunker being nearest the opening at the corner. The first thing we knew the three men were upon or over the counter with revolvers presented at our heads. They ordered Mr. Bunker and myself to

HOLD UP OUR HANDS,

and we could not do otherwise than comply. The robbers stated briefly that they intended to rob the bank. I believe this was stated by the small man of light complexion, who seemed to be in command, and who was first in getting behind the desk. The second man was a large, heavy built fellow with black heavy moustache cut rather stubby short. The other one I did not particularly observe, but believe he was also a large man and wore no beard. The man in command approached Haywood and inquired if he was the cashier, and he replied that he was not. He demanded of him that he

OPEN THE SAFE.

He replied that he could not. The demand was

also made of Mr. Bunker and myself in succession. We were asked if we knew the combination. We replied that we did not. The outer vault door stood open. An attempt had been made to drag Mr. Haywood to it, and meantime the leader of the gang had entered the outer vault. Mr. Haywood jumped forward and endeavored to shut the door and shut the desperado in. One of the ruffians interfered, however, and prevented it.

During this time one of the party continued to cover Bunker and myself with his revolvers. Bunker thought that he had an opportunity, and cut and

RAN FOR THE BACK DOOR.

The robber whom I mentioned as the third man followed, firing one shot which made the hole shown you in the blind door, one half of which was closed. That shot did not take effect. He followed Bunker to the door, and as he stood in the door fired again at Bunker, who was making down between the two buildings in the rear, the ball

TAKING EFFECT IN THE SHOULDER,

I am told, and inflicting nothing more serious than a flesh wound; I saw him this morning, and he is doing nicely. The other two continued their demand of Haywood to open the safe, but he persisted in refusing. They seemed to think he was the man, and paid but little attention to me. One of the number drew a knife, and presenting it at his throat, exclaimed, "Damn you! open that door, or we'll cut

YOUR THROAT FROM EAR TO EAR,"

at the same time inflicting a slight scratch upon the neck. But Haywood refused to comply. Meantime, the firing had continued to increase outside, and one of the number who were upon the outside shouted to those in the room to come out. It was evidently getting

TOO HOT FOR THEM.

Almost immediately they took the alarm and somehow jumped over the counter, making their exit. The small man was last to go. He mounted a desk at the front, and as he turned to go fired a shot at Haywood, which I do not think is the one that took effect. Haywood dodged behind his desk, or sank into his chair (Haywood's desk stands at right angles to the bank desk, and he sat sideways to the opening at the front, with his back next to the wall) and as the robber made over the desk railing he turned, and placing his revolver to Haywood's head, fired,

SHOOTING HIM DEAD.

He staggered forward and fell behind the

"While all this had been going on inside the bank, an exciting interchange of leaden courtesies had been going on outside."

counter. The robbers made out of the door. I do not remember much more that followed."

IN THE BANK.

A huge spot of deep-red clotted blood and blood stain upon the matting behind the counter told where the murdered bank official had fallen. Upon his desk there lay a blotter besmeared with blood and small particles of brains. His desk was also similarly smeared with the brave man's brains. The wound was a fearful one and must have produced instant death. The muzzle of the heavy navy revolver used, shooting a 44-ball, was placed within six or eight inches of his left temple and fired, literally

BLOWING HIS BRAINS OUT.

The ball was lodged in the head. When the robbers had taken their departure and the firing ceased, there was a rush of citizens for the bank, and the ghastly spectacle of the murdered man lying prone upon his face, with his brain and blood oozing slowly from a hole in his right temple, but fired the excitement. It was scarcely possible to appreciate the terrible tragedy that had been enacted.

The Fight in the Streets.

While all this had been going on inside the bank, an exciting interchange of leaden courtesies had been going on outside. With a promptness that speaks volumes for the bravery of several of the citizens of Northfield, and an intuition of what the intent of the desperadoes was, that is simply remarkable, they armed themselves and did effective service. Dr. Henry Wheeler, a young physician, suddenly recollecting that there was an old breech loading carbine in the Damphier House, fronting on the open square, where the robbers were dashing about and firing shots in every direction, issued from a drug store, and braving a

FUSILLADE OF BULLETS

from the robbers, ran for his life down half a block, secured the rusty old weapon, loaded it, and from a position in one of the hotel windows commenced to fire on the intrepid horsemen. Meantime Mr. A.R. Manning, who keeps a store four doors from the corner, had also secured a rifle, and Joe Hyde brought up the rear with a shot gun. Geo. D. Bates took a position in the door of Hanam's clothing store, directly opposite the corner, and under the window occupied by Wheeler, and with an empty revolver sought to intimidate the robbers. The firing commenced in sharp earnest.

THE ROBBERS

had in the interim congregated in front of or about the bank, and had vacated the square. Mr. Manning took a position at Lee & Hitchcock's corner, and slipping out at intervals discharged his rifle. When he first put his head out he discovered several [robbers] crouching behind a horse presenting a broadside to Mr. Manning. He let fly and

KILLED THE HORSE,

thus summarily disposing of that fortification. One more shot he got in and which he believes brought down a horseman who had adopted the Indian tactics of hiding behind his horse's neck and firing running fire. Boyd had meantime succeeded in discharging his shot-gun. Wheeler held the window, and is believed to have

KILLED ONE OF THE MEN,

who up to that time had occupied a place in front of the bank, and gave the alarm to the robbers inside. He fell directly in front of the bank, and a spot of blood still marks the spot. The other man fell from his horse about one hundred feet distant and on the other side of the street. By this time all were mounted. As the horseman fell he threw up his arms, another of the robbers dashed up to him, said something, and seized from his belt one of his navy revolvers and

DASHED UP THE STREET.

While this was going on Manning was placed under the surveillance of two of the robbers, who watched his movements so closely and covered him so with their revolvers that he dare not attempt to fire again from around the corner. A flight of stairs in a measure protected him. It is riddled with bullets, and tells of the hot fire the robbers sent at the intrepid and self-possessed Manning.

He adopted other tactics and made through Lee & Hitchcock's store and renewed the fire from the back door. Meantime Wheeler continued to do good service from his position in the hotel windows, and as the robbers dashed down the street, coming from the scene of the bloody affray,

HE WOUNDED ANOTHER MAN.

He checked his horse, called to his companions "For God's sake don't leave me," and well nigh fell from his saddle. The other robbers pulled up slightly, spoke to him, and then all dashed on down the main street, the wounded man

WITH DIFFICULTY

retaining his seat in the saddle.

"Allen got out of the way in remarkably good time."

OTHER INCIDENTS.

Immediately after the first attack in the street, but one man other than the robbers was to be seen. A man named Shepley stood, paralyzed with fear, holding his horses in front of Lockwood's store, about a block distant from the bank. He was uninjured. A Swede, who evidently understood but little English, was passing down the street. He was ordered to stop, but paid no attention, and one of the horsemen fired a shot

Sketch courtesy of the Minnesota Historical Society

which inflicted a wound upon his head, which was not believed to be serious. The Swede beat a hasty retreat. Later advices state that his injuries promise to prove fatal.

Mr. J.S. Allen, at about the time the fray commenced, started to the bank. He was met at the door by one of the men killed, who presented a revolver at his head and said,

"DAMN YOU, TURN BACK,

I'll blow your head off if you squeal." Allen got out of the way in remarkably good time.

The Flight.

The desperadoes started their horses into a dead gallop, but checked them about a mile and a half out of town, and dressed the wounds of their companion. At Dundas, three miles distant, another halt was made and the wounds washed. When the highwaymen were observed on this occasion two were riding upon one horse, and leading the riderless horse of the injured man. On beyond Dundas another halt was made and the wounds again washed and dressed. Just beyond Dundas the highwaymen met a man in the employ of Mr. Emphry, who was drawing in a load of hoop poles. Revolvers were presented at his head, one of the desperadoes knocked him

INTO THE DITCH,

cut the harness from the best of the two horses and appropriated the animal. The wounded man was seated and they rode on, the frightened Scandinavian continuing his way into town with one horse and his load.

About three miles on beyond Dundas, the rob-

bers met a farmer named McMurtee, and two men in his employ. One of the number, a man named Sargent, stated to The Tribune reporter that they were stopped, their horses examined, but the highwaymen evidently believing their own horses as good as either of the two driven by McMurtee, went on and let the farmers proceed. At that time the party consisted of six persons. One of the number had his leg bandaged, also his arm, and sat in the saddle holding in his right hand the ends of the fingers of the left; blood was trickling from the finger tips. His horse was being led by another of the party.

The Pursuit.

A number of the citizens of Northfield, lead by Dr. Wheeler, who did such good service, started shortly after, in pursuit. They were well armed and equipped. Wheeler did not even stop to put on his boots. It was reported this morning that his horse had given out and he would be obliged to return. Capt. Hoy and party went on to Faribault, and at 9:10 last evening information was received that shortly after six o'clock the highwaymen were

SEEN AT MORRISTOWN,

ten miles distant. They started in pursuit at once, with good and fresh horses.

The posse of police from St. Paul, headed by John Brisette, stopped off at Northfield, and left soon after the arrival of the train for Morristown. Scott, son of the circus man, who resides at that village, brought in the report.

The three men met on the road beyond Dundas report that the pursuing party from Northfield was

ONLY TWENTY MINUTES BEHIND

the robbers yesterday afternoon between three and four o'clock.

RUMORED ENGAGEMENT.

A rumor was received this morning about eight o'clock that the bank robbers were encountered by Hoy and party near Morristown about three o'clock this morning and one robber wounded and one

"A wife and one child mourn his loss."

Sketch courtesy of the Minnesota Historical Society

horse shot. The robbers, it was said, had been driven toward Northfield.

THE DIRECTION OF THE FLIGHT.

It is evident that the robbers took a southwesterly course, following the belt of timber that extends down through the state, without interruption towards Winnebago City into Iowa. Capt. Cole, representative of John Oswald's house, is with Hoy, and is familiar with every foot of the ground.

The Minneapolis police are armed with Henry rifles. The St. Paul posse are not so equipped. Hoy most certainly is near on to the highwaymen, and his well known grit is surety that he will miss no opportunities.

The Murdered Bank Official.

Mr. J.L. Haywood, the murdered bank official, was a man about 34 years of age, and married. A wife and one child mourn his loss. He was acting cashier in the absence of Mr. Phillips, now in the east. It was his intent upon the return of Mr. Phillips to leave with his wife for the Centennial. He formerly resided in this city, and was in the employ of Capt. John Martin. At the opening of the Northfield Bank four years ago, he accepted a position there, and has since been made city treasurer of Northfield, and also treasurer of Carleton College. He was a man of

INDOMITABLE PLUCK,

and though given up as long as ten years ago as a hopeless consumptive, he has simply persisted in living up to the time of his tragic death. Mr. L.S. Haywood of this city, and Mrs. John Brooks, are his brother and sister. Mr. and Mrs. Brooks, and Mr. and Mrs. Haywood arrived in Northfield this morning by the early train. They are deeply stricken with grief at the horrible fate of their brother. The remains will probably be interred to-morrow.

The Robbers.

No better description of the robbers that escaped and the ones that lie dead than is embraced in the telegram reprinted from the morning paper can be given. The two deceased desperadoes resemble each other greatly. They are about the same size, and both have short curly auburn hair, high cheek bones, and small, soft, white hands. They appear to be no novices in their

BLOODY PROFESSION.

On the person of the best dressed of the two, the one attired in a new suit of clothes, was found a map of the western states, a pocket compass, a box of salve, $4.50 in money, a watch, and gold sleeve buttons and studs. There was nothing that would indicate his name or from whence he came. He is the one that fell a victim of Wheeler's fire in front

"The man had previously been connected with the notorious James boys."

of the bank. On the person of the other was found simply a scrap of paper bearing the advertisement of Hall's safe, in which a burglar is pictured as giving it up on discovering the make of the safe. There was also found the business card of a St. Peter livery stable, with a table of distances on the back. He is Manning's victim.

Other Facts and Rumors.

ARE THEY JAMES BOYS?

Officer Patrick Kenny, of the police force of this city, stated to a gentleman of this city two months ago, that he had seen in this city one of a gang which he had encountered and aided in the arrest of in Iowa several years ago. The man recognized Kenny and spoke to him. He stated that he had been released from custody and was doing better now; that he intended to go to the Black Hills. The man had previously been connected with the notorious James boys. It is almost certain that the eight raiders came from the south, and are probably the same as have been operating in Missouri and Iowa.

A telegram from St. Paul states that it is positively known that two of the gang

PURCHASED THEIR EQUIPMENT

in that city. Their purchases included two horses, saddles and bridles. Members of the party have also, beyond doubt, been in this city during the past weeks. All kinds of

WILD RUMORS

are afloat, but it is safe to say that none are true. There is certainly no truth in the report that Officer Hoy or any of his force have been wounded, or The Tribune would be informed of the fact by its correspondents.

Minneapolis Tribune, Sept. 8, 1876

[The eight bank robbers were indeed Missouri's infamous James-Younger gang — Jesse and Frank James; three brothers named Younger: Cole, Jim and Bob; William Stiles; Clel Miller, and Charles Pitts. Already well-known for a decade of robbery and murder, they didn't expect the resistance they met from the citizens of Northfield.

[In front of the bank lay the dead horse and the body of Clel Miller; half a block away was Stiles' body. Of the three deaths, only that of the horse was said to make spectators sad.

[Within 24 hours of the raid, newspapers across the country carried accounts of the shoot-out in Northfield. Some 500 men were on the robbers' trail within two days. That number doubled. The

Bank robbers and victim, living and dead
Photo courtesy of the Minnesota Historical Society

pursuit lasted two weeks and resulted in the capture of the Younger brothers and the killing of Pitts. The Youngers were sentenced to life in prison. Bob Younger died in Stillwater Prison in 1889. His brothers were pardoned after 25 years, and Jim Younger, unable to adapt to independence, committed suicide the next year, 1902. Cole teamed up with Frank James in a wild west show. And Jesse James? Six years after the Northfield raid, he was shot from behind while dusting a picture in his Missouri house. His killer was a fellow gang member, motivated by promise of a reward.

[The murdered Joseph Lee Heywood, the bank's acting cashier whose name was misspelled in newspaper accounts for the first few days, immediately became a hero. To this day, his name is recognized by many Minnesotans.

[Strictly speaking, Heywood was correct in telling the robbers that he couldn't unlock the safe. It was unlocked all the time.]

⇥•⇤

[For more on the Northfield bank raid, see "Robber and Hero" by George Huntington, published in 1986 by the Minnesota Historical Society Press.]

"Hardly anyone here talks about anything but the hard times."

Mr. Editor:

Hardly anyone here [Norseland, in Nicollet County] talks about anything but the hard times, and this is only natural as the price of wheat, the farmers' most important product, remains at 45-50 cents per bushel, while he is forced to pay the same high prices for clothes and groceries as well as in hiring farm hands. . . .

It appears as if the businessmen are doing their utmost and are prepared to use extreme measures to collect outstanding debts, even to the extent of sending the sheriff to confiscate all of their personal property. In this instance, however, the law of the State of Minnesota restrains them. . . .

A short time ago, a storekeeper in St. Peter sent the sheriff to a German farmer to seize 800 bushels of wheat to satisfy a debt of $300, and did not allow the farmer to haul the wheat to the market, but paid high prices to others to have it done. Shortly after this incident the businessmen of St. Peter had a meeting and decided that all outstanding debts must be paid before Dec. 20, and that against those who failed to do so they would "apply the word of the law to its fullest extent." It was further agreed that all credit should be limited to 30 days, and, if further extension was granted, to charge interest from the debt-or. These measures have angered the farmers who feel that these hard times are not the proper times to take such steps.

During the so-called good times such things were unheard of. On the contrary, the farmers were encouraged to buy under any circumstances and credit was cheerfully given for almost any length of time. It is not the intention of the farmers to avoid paying their debts, at least not the farmers of this region, who are all making the greatest efforts to pay them, but it seems that a little more consideration ought to be due them in view of the hard times at hand. We hope that these debts will soon be paid up but to prevent anything like this from happening again the farmers at Lake Prairie and New Sweden have held a meeting, where, after some discussion 50 of the participants formed an association, which will attempt to sell their grain to eastern markets, and to order their necessities from that part, or try to establish a Farmers Union Store. A committee of five men was selected, which will acquaint itself with the previously formed farm associations in Vasa, Goodhue county and Lansing, Iowa. Something ought to be done in this direction, and something can be done if we only unite and see our energy in the best way. I should like to see the farmers of Lake Prairie, New Sweden, Bernadotte and Granby unite and make a real effort at this and if this came to pass, 200 - 300 members could be expected to take part in the movement. If these then could raise a fund of $50 - 100 it would be possible to run a store in a manner that would be profitable both to the members as well as the settlement as a whole. As things now stand, we are entirely dependent on the businessmen, and their meetings and conferences have indicated that they are bound to take as much advantage of the farmers as possible. . . .

S. Svenson

Nordisk Folkeblad, a Danish-Norwegian newspaper, Minneapolis, Jan. 12, 1870, translated by the Works Progress Administration

→•←

In Wright county there lives a young mother, who at the age of eleven years and eight months gave birth to a fine, healthy child, and at last accounts both were doing well. The husband of this smart young mother is only nineteen years of age. She is undoubtedly the youngest mother in the State of Minnesota.

St. Anthony Falls Democrat, Jan. 14, 1870

→•←

Lettuce. — Think of lettuce in

"Dave's fiddle soon struck up a cotillion."

Minnesota in April, with snow still lingering in the ground. And yet it is true. Mr. Buckendorf of Dr. Ames' garden, has been supplying his customers for several days with this popular relish, right from his hot beds. This is not such a cold country after all.

Minneapolis Tribune, April 3, 1870

—✦—

At the meeting of the Hennepin County Eclectic Medical Society yesterday afternoon, at Dr. Stanton's office, Dr. Elliott exhibited a tape worm taken from one of his patients at Long Lake, which measured twenty-five feet in length.

Minneapolis Tribune, April 7, 1870

—✦—

That Party —

At Henry Hipple's, on Friday evening last, was a splendid affair, if that expresses a real good, jovial, social and nice time. That party came into existence about 5 times quicker than any other party we ever knew. It was 1st thought of about 30 minutes before it came off, and Snell went 'round and told the folks it was thought of.

When we arrove there was Fred and his girl, Patten and his 2 girls, Snell's girl and her beau, McClure and somebody's girl, Megquier's baby and its pa and ma, Miss Orvord and her fellow, Mrs. Hall and no fellow, the blacksmith, Weed with his slippers, Dave's fiddle with him, the editor's wife with her baby and him along, Floris Legg, and several other odd couples. Dave's fiddle soon struck up a cotillion, but nobody terpsichored for everybody was waiting for somebody to call off. Some said Snell, and some said Patten, and some said Fred, and some said Weed, and all said they couldn't, but finally Snell did, and away we all went into a cotillion, like a parcel of boys in swimming. And it

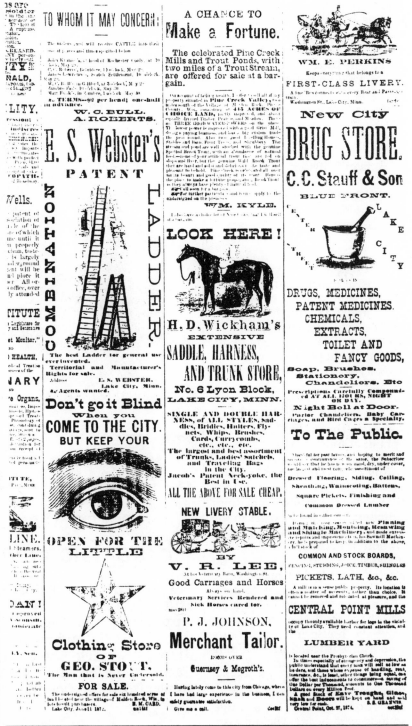

Lake City Leader, May 20, 1876

was Cotillions, and Waltzes, and Polkas, and French 4s, and Schottisches, etc., till the midnight clock chimed 12, when the party expired, and the girls all took their beaux home, except the blacksmith.

When we want another right

"There was a great commotion among the pots and kettles, which caused the inmates to leave the house in a great hurry with each particular hair standing erect."

good time we would as soon have it at Hipple's as anywhere, for he enjoys a party about as well as anybody we know of, and when he builds another new house we'll go in for another party at Hipple's.

Beaver Falls Gazette, Renville County, July 15, 1870

→×·×←

A family living at Prairie Island, Goodhue county, includes 19 children, all under 21 years of age. The name is Souter.

Minneapolis Tribune, Jan. 22, 1871

→×·×←

The Mankato Review learns that Mr. David Buckmaster, who lives in the vicinity of Madison Lake, in that county, has recently lost five children by typhoid fever, and another is lying quite ill, with slight hopes of recovery.

St. Paul Pioneer, March 1, 1871

→×·×←

Ghost. — One night last week, at the house of Charles Sprain, at Meyer's Grove 7 miles from this place, the inmates consisting of the family and two visitors, shortly after retiring for the night, were startled from their slumbers by strange noises in the kitchen, but not being able to ascertain the cause, they settled down again, and all was quiet till just as the clock struck twelve when there was a great commotion among the pots and kettles, which caused the inmates to leave the house in a great hurry with each particular hair standing erect. The whole party numbering six, after holding a consultation outside, concluded to enter the room where the strange sounds were heard. The old man, armed with an ax, advanced, followed by his better half, who was provided with a club. In the kitchen there was an old fashioned fire-place, and they had just entered the door when some-

thing descended the chimney with a great racket, and again the party beat a hasty retreat, trembling in every limb. After again consulting for a few moments, a bright idea struck the old man, and he told the old woman to take the ax and go ahead, that it must surely be a mean ghost, entirely devoid of gallantry, that

"As handsome a drive as can be found in the State of Minnesota is to be found on Park Avenue."

would harm a woman. The old lady accordingly advanced, followed by the whole posse, and this time the mystery was solved. They had been making sausages the day before, and had hung them in the chimney to smoke. The strings had given away and let the sausages drop into the kettles which had been left setting in the fire-place below. The party breathed a sigh of relief and, after fastening up the ghostly sausages, retired, and were no more disturbed by the spirits.
Sauk Centre Herald, March 4, 1871

→·‹·←

The Lake City Sentinel says a sort of a sea monster was seen in Lake Pepin near that place on Monday: "It was between the size of an elephant and rhinoceros, and moved through the water with great rapidity. The same thing, whatever it may be, has been seen on one or two other occasions." Perhaps it was a cow?
St. Paul Pioneer, April 28, 1871

→·‹·←

On the 4th inst., [of this month] as the Brainerd stage was ferried over the Nokopissi, the horses became frightened and jumped off the boat, taking the coach with them. There were seven passengers in the stage, who escaped with a "ducking" merely.
Minneapolis Tribune, June 13, 1871

→·‹·←

Found. — On Saturday evening, June 17th, on Seventh street, between Jackson and College, a small piece of a gentleman's whiskers, tied with a scrap of red ribbon. The owner can hear of the whereabouts of his property by calling at this office.
St. Paul Pioneer, June 20, 1871

→·‹·←

A correspondent says Mankato now boasts of two cornet bands,

one composed of Germans and the other of Americans.
St. Paul Pioneer, June 24, 1871

→·‹·←

Park Avenue. — One of the most pleasant drives in the suburbs of Minneapolis, and we may say, as handsome a drive as can be found in the State of Minnesota, is to be found on Park avenue, which lies between Chicago and Portland avenues, west of the city limits. It is one hundred feet in width, and one mile in length, turnpiked, and made as level as a race course, for the entire distance. Property holders upon either side have lined the street with shade trees, which, if properly protected, will in a few years add greatly to the beauty of the avenue. We regret to see that cattle allowed to run at large in that vicinity are destroying these trees, and suggest that it would be a good idea to restrain the cattle, or otherwise protect the trees, if possible.
St. Paul Pioneer, July 19, 1871

→·‹·←

A Nuisance. — We labor under the impression that we have on some previous occasion alluded to the unpleasant necessity of tying horses in the gutters along Main street. During a rainy spell, when flies are legion, horses will stamp vehemently, and as a consequence, muddy water is splashed on the clothing of passers-by.
Stillwater Gazette, Aug. 22, 1871

→·‹·←

From Red River. — Major A.B. Brackett returned from an absence of twenty days to the Northern Pacific and Red river country yesterday morning. His main business has been to look after timber thieves on railroad and government lands. . . . He reports Morehead [Moorhead] as a bustling, driving, thriving village

of some hundreds of inhabitants already. From twenty-five to thirty buildings are in process of erection, several are completed, and others contemplated. The Major has no doubt but Morehead will eventually be the largest town in Northern Minnesota. All of the gamblers, pimps, bullies and harlots that have been following up the N.P. road have been driven out of Morehead, and are now located at Fargo, the new town on the Dakota side of Red river, opposite Morehead.
Minneapolis Tribune, Oct. 12, 1871

→·‹·←

St. Paul and Pacific Main Line. — The opening of the main line of this great railroad from this city to Breckinridge [Minn.], 206 miles, almost to the extreme limit of civilization, is an important event, and was celebrated yesterday by many old settlers in this city and Minneapolis, who returned home to-day with enlarged ideas of the rapid progress of the internal development of Minnesota and of its growing population.
St. Anthony Falls Democrat, Oct. 26, 1871

→·‹·←

Earth Closets.
Colonel Geo. E. Waring, Jr., in his work on earth closets [indoor toilets which used dirt to cover wastes] and sewage, makes the following drive at what he calls those "graves of decency which disfigure almost every country house in America, and rise their suggestive heads above the garden walls of elegant town houses.

"What is not generally understood is their pernicious effect upon health. The influence of subterranean stores of fecal matter in the propagation of disease has already been referred to; but that which produces in the aggregate far worse results — the ag-

"It is universally admitted that nothing is more injurious to health than irregularity."

gravation of the difficulties of delicate females — has attracted less attention than its importance deserves. It is universally admitted that nothing is more injurious to health than irregularity, and the undue retension of the rejectamenta of the intestines. Admitting the justice of this view, let us see what chance a woman has to escape the direst evil that delicate health has in store for its victims. The privy stands perhaps at the bottom of the garden, fifty yards from the house, approached by a walk bordered by grass, which is always wet except during the sunny part of the day, overhung by shrubbery and vines, which are often dripping with wet, and exposed frequently to the public gaze. In winter snow-drifts block the way, and during rain there is no shelter from any side. The [out]house itself is fearfully cold, if not drifted half full of snow, or flooded with rain. A woman who is comfort-

ably housed during stormy weather, will, if it is possible, postpone for days together the painful necessity for exposure that such circumstances require. If the walk is exposed to a neighboring workmanship window, the visit will probably be put off until dusk. In either case no amount of reasoning will convince a woman that it is her duty, for the sake of preventing trouble, of which she is yet ignorant, to expose herself to the danger, the discomfort, and the annoyance that regularity under such circumstances implies. I pass over now the barbarous foulness and stifling odor of the privy vault. It is only as an unavoidable evil that these have been tolerated; but I cannot too strongly urge attention to the point taken above and insist on the fact that every consideration of humanity, and of the welfare, not only of our own families, but of the whole community, demands a

speedy reform of this abuse."

At G. Webster Peck's House-Keepers' Emporium, 232 Third Street, St. Paul, earth closets may be purchased, ranging in price from $10 to $20. There should be at least one in every house. Mr. Peck supplies prepared earth closets to purchasers at actual cost. Referring to this well known house, we have at this time but one word to say to our readers, and that is, if any of them intend visiting St. Paul to purchase holiday goods, we can assure them it will be to their interest to call in at 232 Third street, before buying elsewhere, and that no one can make a more suitable present to his family this Christmas than by presenting them with one of the earth closets, of which Mr. P. is agent.
St. Cloud Journal, Dec. 7, 1871

[Yes, that was an ad, disguised as a news story.]

–>–<–

ENERGY

"**Light, More Light.**" We don't mean sunlight, nor moonlight, nor starlight — but, beyond the shadow of a doubt, the time has come in Minneapolis when there is great need of more *gaslight*. So much as we already have will possibly bear a little improvement in *quality,* but it is the *quantity* which we are after now. We are not blaming the Gas Company for this lack; indeed we are not blaming anybody. The fact is simply this: *Our streets are not well lighted.* It partakes of the farcical to say that they are lighted at all. There are in all about two or three dozen lamp posts scattered at remote corners in the business portion of the city. The rays from these lonely lan-

terns penetrate the gloom as far as the laws of optics will permit, but it is hardly sensible to expect them to illuminate the streets for more than one or two blocks distant.
Minneapolis Tribune, June 11, 1872

–>–<–

Burning Coal. It seems almost incredible that in this "wooden country" coal is so fast becoming the principal article of fuel, but such is the fact. During the past two or three winters our citizens have been experimenting with coal stoves, and it has been fully demonstrated that with the "base burning" coal stoves, coal at $13 or $14 per ton is cheaper than wood. And then

there is this great advantage in favor of coal — that with an "Oriental" coal stove an even temperature is easily maintained, which is very desirable in this country; also that the stove has to be loaded with coal but twice in twenty-four hours.
Minneapolis Tribune, Oct. 19, 1872

–>–<–

Fuel is so scarce in St. Paul that on Saturday night a gentleman actually could not buy any and chopped up a chair to boil the tea kettle with.
Minneapolis Tribune, Nov. 19, 1872

–>–<–

*"A woman in New Ulm was arrested last week and locked up
in jail for beating her husband."*

The Blue Earth City Post speaks of a woman residing in Minnesota Lake Township who is the mother of twenty-seven children and still it is with difficulty that she can find a comfortable place to spend the few remaining years of her life. Certainly "she hath done what she could" and is deserving of better treatment than this.

Mower County Transcript, Austin, Jan. 25, 1872

-›-‹-

The Shakopee Mirror reports the death of a child three years old, caused by the bursting of a mince pie, which his mother was conveying from the oven. The pie being surcharged with steam — having no vent in the crust — exploded, throwing a considerable quantity of the scalding contents about the little unfortunate's face and neck, burning it so badly as to throw it into convulsions resulting in death.

Mower County Transcript, Austin, Feb. 15, 1872

-›-‹-

Well Done. — The higher department of the Sauk Centre school was spelled down last week by Miss Tilly Ward, a colored girl 14 years old.

Sauk Centre Herald, March 30, 1872

-›-‹-

[Dolly Varden performed on the flying trapeze and was considered the queen of the American circus. Everything from chocolates to shoes to trout was named for her, and the Sauk Centre newspaper editor was sick of the fad.]

Dolly Varden. If this Dolly Varden mania is not put a stop to, the peace of families will be imperilled and the lunatic asylum enlarged. Everything is Dolly Varden, and Dolly Varden is everything. There are Dolly Varden hats, Dolly Varden coats, Dolly

This standard article is compounded with the greatest care.

Its effects are as wonderful and as satisfactory as ever.

It restores gray or faded hair to its youthful color.

It removes all eruptions, itching and dandruff. It gives the head a cooling, soothing sensation of great comfort, and the scalp by its use becomes white and clean.

By its tonic properties it restores the capillary glands to their normal vigor, preventing baldness, and making the hair grow thick and strong.

As a dressing, nothing has been found so effectual or desirable.

A. A. Hayes, M.D., State Assayer of Massachusetts, says, "The constituents are pure, and carefully selected for excellent quality; and I consider it the BEST PREPARATION for its intended purposes."

Price, One Dollar.

Lake City Leader, June 23, 1877

Varden trousers, Dolly Varden drawers, Dolly Varden shoes, Dolly Varden shirts, Dolly Varden back hair [long hair at the back of the neck], Dolly Varden front hair, Dolly Varden night gowns, Dolly Varden bustles, Dolly Varden panniers [skirts], Dolly Varden garters, Dolly Varden hugs, Dolly Varden kisses, Dolly Varden babies, Dolly Varden cocktails, Dolly Varden mothers-in-law, Dolly Varden walks, Dolly Varden dips in the "valse deuxtemps." Turn where you will, these two maddening words, "Dolly Varden," meet the eye in business, dry goods, crockery, clothes, society, "the world, the flesh and" — Dolly Varden!

Already Dolly Varden has brought one man to a silent tomb in Kentucky; so no more of Dolly Varden.

Sauk Centre Herald, May 25, 1872

-›-‹-

A woman in New Ulm was arrested last week and locked up in jail for beating her husband. After 24 hours imprisonment, she was tried and discharged with an admonition to leave the poor fellow alone in the future.

Sauk Centre Herald, June 15, 1872

-›-‹-

Horrible Suicide! Jacob Dietz Dies by his Own Hand. Our readers will recollect the attempted suicide of Mr. Jacob Dietz of Watertown, which took place on the 9th of May last. After recovering from the injuries sustained on that occasion, Mr. Dietz seemed to have recovered his usual health of body and mind, and his friends had mainly dismissed their fears of a repetition of the attempt.

Within the past month, however, his unfortunate appetite for intoxicating liquors again overcame him and he had been drinking heavily, although for a few days next preceding his tragic death, he had been induced to abstain. He seemed to be haunted by fears that a conspiracy to murder him had been formed, and in various ways manifested the unsound condition of his mind. He was closely watched by his wife to whose control he seemed to yield readily; but the fatal germ was growing, and on Wednesday morning he was seen to start from his house to the barn with a large knife which he had taken from the kitchen. His wife, fearing the worst, ran after him, at the same time calling to a hired man who was near at hand. She caught her husband by the arm, within a few feet of the door, whereupon he drew the

"There is nothing so important in one's life as to live under one's own roof."

knife across his throat, inflicting a fearful wound. He fell to the ground and expired in a very few moments. Mr. Dietz was widely known, and the business of his brewery was in a prosperous condition. His terrible death must be carried to the fearful balance that stands against the Rum Demon.
Big Woods Citizen, Delano, July 26, 1872

→‣•‣←

A little boy named George Killian, aged six years, lost his life on Thursday last under most painful circumstances. In company with a younger brother he was playing upon a plank across the flume of Engle & Co's. mill, from which it is supposed he fell into the water. The smaller boy missed him, and supposing he had stolen away, ran off in search of him. His inquiries excited alarm and Mr. Engle caused the gate to be closed, when it was found to be obstructed. The mill was stopped by choking the stones, and upon search, the body — except one leg, which had been severed and floated away — was found lying upon the top of the wheel, which is of the Turbine pattern, and has a lateral motion. It is supposed that the leg was forced into one of the buckets — they being too small to receive the whole body — and by contact with the case, in which the wheel revolved was crushed off. It was not found until after the body was interred. Coroner Barnes held an inquest which resulted in a verdict of "accidental death by drowning."
Mower County Transcript, Austin, Aug. 1, 1872

→‣•‣←

A House of Our Own. Next to being married to the right person, there is nothing so important in one's life as to live under one's own roof. There is something more than a poetical charm

in the expression of the wife:

"We have our cozy house; it is thrice dear to us because it is our own. We have bought it with the saving of our earnings. Many were the soda fountains, the confectionery saloons, and the necessities of the market we had to pass; many a time my noble husband denied himself of comforts, wore his old clothes, and even patched up boots; and I, O me! made my old bonnet do, wore the plainest clothes, did the plainest cooking; saving was the order of the hour, and to have a 'home of our own' was our united aim. Now we have it; there is no landlord troubling with raising the rent, and exacting this and that. There is no fear harbored in our bosom that in sickness or old age we will be thrown out of house and home."

What a lesson do the above words teach, and how well it would be if hundreds of families would heed them, and instead of living in rented houses, which take a large share of their capital to furnish, and a quarter of their

earnings to pay the rent, and the rest to dress and eat accordingly, would bravely curtail expenses, and concentrating their efforts on having "a home of their own." *Better a cottage* of your own than a rented palace.
Sauk Centre Herald, Sept. 28, 1872

→‣•‣←

Duluth Overrun by Rats. — That Duluth is becoming civilized is evident from the fact that those pestiferous accompaniments of civilization — rats — are now, and for some two or three months have been, holding high carnival in this city. Indeed, we have rarely seen these insufferable nuisances in more plenty in any place than they are here now.
Duluth Tribune, Oct. 24, 1872

→‣•‣←

No person has ever yet died in the prosperous town of Windom, and yet the newspapers and people of that community hanker after a graveyard. Even the railroad company seems to be anxious to

"Marshall is a musical little burg."

---

have a good place in which to deposit any chance corpses which may be found along its line, and generously offers to donate the town of Windom sufficient land for a cemetery, though the people are apparently not over anxious in accepting the grave responsibility.

St. Paul Press, Jan. 15, 1873

⇥•⇤

The organ grinders — with their delightful notes, which prompt the occupants of rooms in the fourth story of buildings to heave a brick therefrom upon the heads of the artists — are again waking up the suspended agonies of the soul.

St. Paul Press, May 7, 1873

⇥•⇤

Marshall is a musical little burg. The violin, organ, flute, and other musical instruments, swept by master hands, are frequently heard by the passer-by upon our streets. The fact that there has never been a quarrel in town is doubtless owing to the prevalence of good music. Certain domestic animals seem to have caught the inspiration, and frequently vie with each other in their efforts to produce pleasing harmony. But we fear their efforts are very poorly appreciated. There is probably nothing so damaging to a man's nerves as a feline midnight serenade on the woodshed and no boot-jack handy.

Prairie Schooner, Marshall, Aug. 30, 1873

⇥•⇤

Somebody's child living out here on somebody's farm had a finger cut off the other day, but we are unable to learn names and other particulars. Hope it is done aching by this time. If anybody else will cut off a finger we will lend them a good sharp knife, will pay for having it (the finger) sewed on, and will give a good square notice of the affair in the Schooner. Locals [local news items] are scarce and getting scarcer.

Prairie Schooner, Marshall, Sept. 13, 1873

⇥•⇤

Mr. S.E. Ives, of the City Music Store, has received a large invoice of new music, among which is "The Farmer's Song," a Solo by Julia Leverett; a new and popular song by J.H. McNaughton entitled " 'Twas a Story;" a song by George W. Morgan, called "Youthful Lays," and a piece for a soprano voice, entitled "My Guiding Star," by Mrs. Slade.

Minneapolis Tribune, Oct. 28, 1873

⇥•⇤

Female Physicians. At the Annual Meeting of the State Medical Association which met at St. Paul on the 3rd and 4th insts. [of this month], the application of Miss Preston for membership, which had been laid upon the table at a previous meeting, was taken up for consideration. Dr. A.B. Stuart presented her case in a strong argument, showing that she was a graduate of a college in Pennsylvania of high standing, and cited numerous cases where women were admitted into medical societies, and that their practice has brought no discredit to the profession. He also stated that under a resolution adopted by the Society last year, which declared that applicants are to be admitted irrespective of color, race or sex, that they were bound to admit her to membership.

By a vote of 13 to 27 the application was refused. . . .

Minnesota cannot afford to permit [its reputation] for a supe-

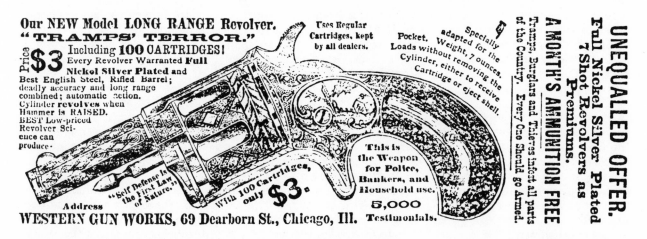

"They were penniless and entirely unable to speak the English language."

rior plane of education, and liberal opportunities for mental culture, to wane in an era when other States declare that the field is open for competition to all. . . .

Nature has made woman a nurse by instinct. What should prevent her from acquiring the art of healing which is but secondary to the primary trait of soothing attention? History has demonstrated that women, as a class, have more nerve in delicate cases, at the bed-side, than her more muscular adversary; and, too, as keen a perception of the intricacies of anatomical research and pharmacology, as the most practical of the profession. . . .
Duluth Minnesotian, Feb. 14, 1874

->-<-

The other day a little girl of Marshall, in tearing to pieces her father's old vest with which to make a doll, discovered a twenty-dollar greenback snugly tucked away in one of the pockets. It had lain there nearly a year during which time the owner had his "suspicions" that it went into another fellow's vest pocket. It is needless to say that since that little piece of good luck every old vest in town has been turned wrong side out more than twenty times. Can't say how it is with the rest, but our old vest pockets don't pan out worth a cent, disclosing nothing but rents.
Prairie Schooner, Marshall, March 5, 1874

->-<-

A neat little stand is being built next to the sidewalk adjoining Cochrane & Walsh's office on Wabashaw street, wherein is to be deposited a barrel, said barrel to be kept constantly supplied with pure ice-water for who so thirsteth.
St. Paul Dispatch, May 27, 1874

->-<-

Rev. J. Juszkenitz, a Polish preacher of Winona, has sued 32 of his church members for pew rent. They refuse to pay because he called them empty heads in the pulpit. This is a light excuse for not settling pew rent.
St. Paul Dispatch, May 28, 1874

->-<-

Just What He Deserved. A low fellow named McNeil was treated to a good thrashing on Thursday which he well deserved. He has been a nuisance in the vicinity of Fifth Avenue South and Fifth street by making indecent exhibitions of himself for about two years past, and though he has been watched for, he was never caught by any of the male population until Thursday, when Mr. Chas. Hoyt chased him into a barn and after pounding him with his fists, hit him on the head with a piece of iron as a parting reminder. McNeil owned up and promised to leave town.
Minneapolis Tribune, July 11, 1874

->-<-

A man named Hell keeps a saloon in Owatonna. Some of the young men of the city are said to go to Hell pretty often.
St. Paul Pioneer, Sept. 8, 1874

->-<-

Nearly a Homicide. On Sunday last Julius Lang aged 16 years and several other boys were playing ball at Green's farm, when several Swede boys came along, and one of them said to the players: "You fellows don't know how to play ball." This with other remarks so exasperated the temper of Lang that he turned to one of the boys who was playing ball and asked him for his pistol, saying he would shoot some of the Swedes. The boy refused to let Lang have it, but he being much the stoutest, took the weapon by force, and then turning on the Swede boys shot Edward Hogan,

lodging about a dozen small bird shot in his breast and stomach, one shot entering just above the abdomen was at first supposed to be dangerous, but nothing serious will occur from the wounds.

Lang was brought before Justice Fleischman on Tuesday, and after a hearing, was committed to the County jail in default of $300 bail to appear at the next term of the District Court.
Duluth Minnesotian, Sept. 12, 1874

->-<-

Is there no way by which the entrance to the Opera House can be kept clear of the crowd of loafers who invariably line the steps and walls of the hall each night there is a performance there? They are a great nuisance and their impudent staring is a great annoyance to ladies who have to run the gauntlet of their ill bred manners, both going in and coming out. The nuisance should be abated.
St. Paul Pioneer, Oct. 10, 1874

->-<-

The school board of Dundas have resigned because parents objected to their hiring a teacher who would thrash the boys.
St. Paul Dispatch, Nov. 6, 1874

->-<-

It is never too late to marry or to mend.
Blue Earth City Post, Nov. 7, 1874

->-<-

A Frenchman, his wife and six children, ranging from two to eight years old, arrived at the St. Paul & Pacific depot night before last. They were penniless and entirely unable to speak the English language. The children, all of which looked as near alike as two peas, slept on a piece of carpeting in the ladies waiting room during the entire night.
Minneapolis Tribune, March 21, 1875

1870s
-›•‹-

Explosion of the Flour Mills

Growing and milling wheat were among the chief occupations in Minnesota by the 1870s. Twenty mills were clustered about the waterfalls of Minneapolis when a huge explosion occurred the evening of May 2, 1878. In a headline the next day, the Minneapolis Tribune called the tragedy "The Most Direful Calamity Which Has Ever Befallen the City of Minneapolis."

The city was startled at twenty minutes past seven last evening by a concussion which shook every building for miles from the scene of the terrible disaster, the smoke of which has not yet cleared away, and the terrible realization of which has but begun to dawn on the community. The shock was distinctly felt in the very suburbs of the city. In the business part of the city solid business blocks were shaken, and the massive plate glass windows in many of them utterly destroyed. No adequate idea can be given of the terrible force of the shock which startled the community into the belief that a

TERRIBLE EARTHQUAKE

had occurred, marking its work of destruction. The shock had hardly subsided before the whole population were in the street. Men, women and children flocked to doors and windows with terrified faces and consternation in every movement. An ominous flame from the centre of the milling district told the first story of a disaster the like of which Minnesota has not before known, and the full extent of which it is not possible to estimate. The fact that an explosion had occurred dawned on the community after the first

CONFUSION OF SURPRISE

had passed away. But not until the excited crowd had surged down to the scene of the disaster was the full extent of the work of devastation in any measure realized. It was found that the explosion had occurred in the big Washburn mill, that it had been followed by the demolition of the Humboldt and Diamond mills situated in the rear thereof; that

one wall and the roof of the Washburn B mill had been carried away, the solid stone wall carried from the side of the Galaxy mill, the Milwaukee & St. Paul round house more or less damaged and the stone planing mill of Smith & Parker destroyed. The explosion was followed in less time than it takes to tell it by flames which enveloped the ruins of all the buildings, communicating to the mill of Pettit, Robinson & Co., the Zenith and Galaxy mills opposite, and threatened the entire milling district and the extensive lumber yards situated further down the river.

THE ORIGIN.

Every imaginable theory was advanced as to the cause of the explosion. The first report noised about was to the effect that the big mill used gas manufactured within its walls. It was found that this was false, the city gas being used in the mill exclusively. Then it was charged upon the boiler, but the engine room is situated outside of the mill, and there was but about twenty pounds of steam on at the time. The excited crowd meantime clamored for an explanation, and every theory that was in any measure tenable was advanced. . . . The latest and probably the most current theory is that the explosion was the result of natural causes, not unknown to the milling business, which may be stated as

SPONTANEOUS COMBUSTION.

It is the theory of Mr. J.A. Christian, the head of the firm operating the big mill, that the fire originated in the [grinding] stones from flour dust; that a gas was created that filled the elevators and every

"Burned and blackened was he, bleeding, too."

LIKE A BESOM.

The Terrible Explosion Last Evening Which Carried With it Death and Destruction.

The Most Direful Calamity Which Has Ever Befallen the City of Minneapolis.

Five Flouring Mills and Other Valuable Buildings Scattered in Countless Fragments.

Relentless Flames Finish the Work of Devastation With Horrible Completeness.

Sixteen Persons Known to be Killed —The Bodies of the Poor Victims Consumed.

Terrible Force of the Explosion– The Intense Excitement Throughout the City

The Spectacle Last Night During the Progress of the Conflagration - Painful Scenes.

Wild Despair of the Wives, Parents, and Children of the Poor Victims.

The Fuller Realization of the Extent of the Calamity This Morning.

Evidences of the Tremendous Force of the Explosion Found in All Parts of the City.

Minneapolis Tribune, May 3, 1878

part of the mill, and the explosion followed. . . .

[The deaths of the workers trapped inside the mills had not yet been mentioned. After much more type, the story gets to the victims. The number of dead varies in the article.]

THE NIGHT FORCE

here usually consists of fifteen men. By fortuitous circumstances two of this number were absent at the time of the disaster and thirteen men suffered death. It is reported that one of the thirteen managed to escape, but the story seems improbable, and the more so since he has not been discovered up to the hour that this is penned. . . . In the Zenith mill there were two men, one of whom escaped badly burned and the other went to a horrible death, while the watchman, who was the only occupant of the Galaxy mill, miraculously escaped by jumping from the third story window into the canal below, borne down by the additional weight of a Babcock fire extinguisher which he bore upon his back.

THE SCENES

about the fire beggar description. One poor fellow, believed to be John Boyer, employed in the Diamond mill, was seen to struggle with all the desperation of love of life out from the ruins of the Diamond mill, through flame and smoke, to the very edge of the pile of rubbish and almost out from the hungry flames. Burned and blackened was he, bleeding, too, from wounds upon his body and head, but he struggled on with all the delirious desperation of a battle for life. Human endurance was not sufficient, and when almost released from the seething cauldron he fell dead. A rope had been thrown to him by the excited crowd, but it came too late and he could not reach it. An attempt was made to reach his mangled remains, but the flames for three hours

RELENTLESSLY HELD BACK THE CROWD,

during which the dead, mangled and charred remains lay within sight of the crowd. It was taken out of the ruins last night, and was the only body so rescued. In the crowd were the distracted wives and mothers of some of the missing men, whose shrieks mingled with the cries of firemen, noise of the crowd and the crackling of flames. One distracted woman would have thrown herself into the flames but for the restraining power of the arms of two strong men. The majority of the employes in the mills were married men, who had an hour before gone forth from happy homes, leaving loving wives who had no thought of the horrible disaster that was to usher their loved ones into eternity

"The whole affair is so horrible, so sickening of contemplation that it makes the heart sick."

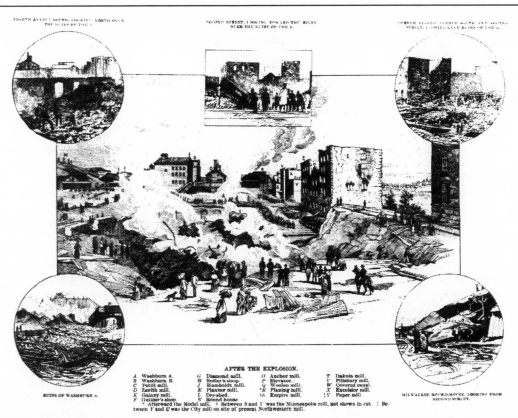

Sketch courtesy of the Minnesota Historical Society

Proposals.

NOTICE TO CONTRACTORS.

I invite proposals for rebuilding of the walls of

"MILL A."

The material and style of walls will be similar to those of the mill destroyed.

The size of the mill on the ground will be 100 feet by 250.

The sides fronting the Canal, Second street and Seventh Avenue South, will be of blue limestone range work. The other side a rubble wall.

C. C. WASHBURN.

July 16, 1878.

Minneapolis Tribune, Aug. 9, 1878

without a moment's warning. The realization of the destruction of life, comparatively small though it be to what might have been the case had the explosion occurred during the day, has fallen like a pall upon the entire community.

ALL NIGHT LONG

did the firemen battle with the flames, the crowd watching the lapping work of destruction and the grief stricken friends of the dead men haunt the scene of the disaster and conflagration. The whole affair is so horrible, so sickening of contemplation that it makes the heart sick. Those who went to their homes last night went there with the realization that sixteen mortals had met a sudden and terrible death, and that more than one-third of the milling capacity of Minneapolis had been swept out of existence almost before it was possible to realize it, and that a loss had been entailed thereby which will not aggregate far from a million and a half of money.

Minneapolis Tribune, May 3, 1878

[Historians say that the correct number of dead was 18 and that nearly half the city's milling capacity was destroyed.]

"The most marvelous invention of the day — the phonograph."

INVENTIONS

Arnold's Automatic Clothes Washer. — We have given this simple and unpretending, but really useful, invention, a fair trial in our family, and find that it fulfils all that it promises, if carefully used according to instructions. It diminishes the labor of washing to a considerable extent, but its strongest point is in saving the wear of the clothes, which, in many cases, suffer much more from the hard rubbing they get on the wash-board than they do on the backs of their owners. This is particularly true of fine cottons and linens, and of many articles of wearing apparel. This washer may be obtained at the cost of five dollars, of Messrs. Austin & Fairfield, in this city.
Minneapolis Tribune, April 6, 1870

—>•<—

Something New. — Moore & Kinsella, in Lake House Block, have just received a stock of "Cold Water Soap," which is warranted to wash clothes as clean in cold water without boiling. It takes no more soap than the old method. Besides there is no roasting or boiling over a hot stove, which is such a dread to the ladies this warm weather.
Stillwater Gazette, June 27, 1871

—>•<—

The Electric Clock. One of the greatest novelties ever on exhibition in this city [St. Paul] are the electric clocks, invented and manufactured by Mr. Sebastian Geist, of Wurzburg, Germany, which may be seen at the store of his son, Emil Geist, No. 57 East Third street. These timepieces are wonders of simplicity and ingenuity, and are absolutely accurate. They consist of but very few parts, all of which are visible, and will run with unerring accuracy as long as the batteries maintain their power. The clocks are of beautiful design, and should be inspected by all who delight in curious and elegant things. Mr. Geist will be happy to explain them to any who may favor him with a call.
St. Paul Pioneer Press, Jan. 30, 1876

—>•<—

A new hitching post was exhibited in front of the city hall to-day. It is a safe one. If run against it yields and falls over, saving the wagon from smashing itself to pieces. When passed over it straightens up. It is strong and also yields when pulled on by a horse. Mr. John West is the owner of the invention, and it appears to be an ingenious one that ought to grow into universal use.
Minneapolis Tribune, July 14, 1877

—>•<—

Mr. Wm. Cheney has taken the agency for the type writer, and has one of them on exhibition at his office in Academy of Music block, to which he invites attention. The value of the instrument to lawyers or others having much writing to do he can demonstrate fully, and prove its capability of writing faster, more legible, and in less space than can be done in the old-fashioned way. It is a novel instrument and valuable invention.
Minneapolis Tribune, Sept. 22, 1877

—>•<—

A rare treat is offered the people of St. Paul for Tuesday evening at the House of Hope church. Professor L.W. Peck, of the State University, will lecture on the telephone, when he will give auricular [hearing] demonstrations of this wonderful invention, by entertaining his audience with music performed at Minneapolis. The only mistake in the whole matter is charging a mere quarter instead of a dollar for the opportunity of witnessing this singular invention in actual operation, and having it thoroughly explained.
St. Paul Globe, March 4, 1878

—>•<—

The most marvelous invention of the day — the phonograph, is on exhibition at No. 23 East Third street, where ladies and children, as well as gentlemen, can witness its startling performances, and have its principles explained to them.
St. Paul Globe, July 3, 1878

—>•<—

Somebody is said to have invented a process of making lumber out of straw, which can be sawed into any dimensions, which takes a polish like hardwood lumber, and which, by a chemical preparation, is rendered less combustible than wood. Such an invention is not impracticable and if brought into general use would nearly double the value of Minnesota's great staple crop.
Minneapolis Tribune, July 3, 1879

—>•<—

"Hastings has a female barber."

A match game of billiards, on which there was staked $25, took place between two experts in Pence Opera House saloon yesterday afternoon. Nearly 150 people watched the game.
Minneapolis Tribune, April 9, 1875

→•←

If the spelling mania isn't cured soon, our whole social fabric will tumble. "He's a nice sort of a boy," said a young lady yesterday, as she rolled his photograph and engagement ring for returning them, "but no well brought up girl can be expected to cling to a man who spells confectionery with an a."
Stillwater Gazette, May 19, 1875

→•←

A few weeks since Charlotte Elizabeth Dyring, about to become a mother, was taken to the Cottage Hospital, where, at the earnest solicitation of one or two citizens, she was finally permitted to remain. Sunday last, Ole Olstrom returned from the pineries, at once visited the hospital, where to his surprise he found that he was the father of a bright baby, eight days old, which on that afternoon was to be baptized by Dr. Knickerbacker. After a little persuasion he concluded to marry the unfortunate girl whom he had so wronged, and the marriage ceremony was performed by Dr. Knickerbacker just previous to the baptism.
Minneapolis Tribune, June 8, 1875

→•←

There was not a copy of the Declaration of Independence to be had in Isanti county on the occasion of the celebration of the Fourth. Hence the reading of that instrument was dispensed with.
St. Paul Dispatch, July 26, 1875

→•←

The P.-P. [St. Paul Pioneer Press] is responsible for the state-

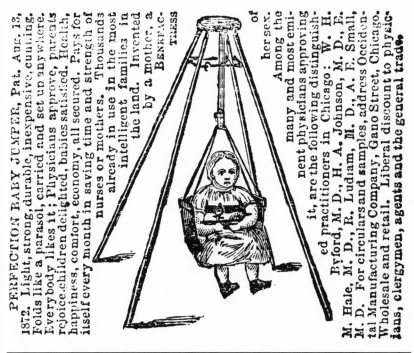

Anoka County Union, Oct. 7, 1873

ment that six murders have been committed on the road between Minneapolis and St. Paul during the past ten years, and not one of the murderers has been captured. Just reflect upon this when you have to pass over the road after nightfall, and don't forget the frequent highway robberies on the same road.
Minneapolis Tribune, Oct. 16, 1875

→•←

Hastings has a female barber. The other shops are nearly deserted.
Minneapolis Tribune, Nov. 20, 1875

→•←

Some one has been dabbling in hunting statistics, and has ascertained that, throughout the northwest there have been shot three deer, four bears, six foxes, nine wolves, one panther, two women, thirteen men and twenty-three boys. All this accomplished within ninety days.
Stillwater Gazette, Dec. 15, 1875

→•←

Here is a warning that is pertinent in St. Paul at this time: a young lady in Boston fell down upon a slippery sidewalk, and broke her leg. She instituted a suit against the man who occupied the building fronting the sidewalk, for damages to the amount of $10,000, but as her leg was only broken near the ankle, the jury reduced the amount and gave her $5,000. Let some of the ladies who want to raise a little money skip along the icy pavements of Third street, so that one or two of them may be able to prove to a demonstration that it is cheaper for people to sprinkle a few ashes on their slippery sidewalks than to pay $5,000 a piece for broken legs.
St. Paul Pioneer Press, Dec. 18, 1875

→•←

"The ebony-hued citizen who boasts a white wife, was sailing down Hennepin avenue. . ."

SPORTING EVENTS

Pigeon Matches. — The Sportsman's Club have secured one thousand live pigeons, and will have a series of shooting matches at the Driving Park. They commence this afternoon at two o'clock. It will continue every evening this week.
St. Paul Press, May 9, 1871

—>-<—

A General Invitation. — We are informed by John X. Davidson Esq. that the east half of Lake Como is frozen over. The ice is strong enough to bear a horse, and is as clear as glass. Mr. Davidson extends an invitation "to the people of the world" to visit Lake Como and enjoy the exhilarating sport of skating to their hearts content without money and without price. It is the finest skating rink in the universe.
St. Paul Pioneer, Nov. 22, 1871

—>-<—

One of the most remarkable feats of female pedestrianism that was ever brought to our notice was accomplished yesterday by two young ladies of this city. . . . The ladies, Miss Francisca Schafer and her cousin Miss Stevens, nothing daunted at the non-appearance of the gentlemen [who were to have accompanied them] determined to perform their part of the contract, and accordingly at 9:30 A.M. they started from the Park Avenue Church corner, crossed the lower bridge, and selected the University avenue route. Steadily and unfalteringly they pursued their course, disdaining to accept numerous invitations to ride tendered by persons who overtook them on the way — anybody could ride to St. Paul — and at twelve o'clock they reached their destination, accomplishing the distance, fully eleven miles, in the remarkable time of two hours and thirty minutes. They returned to the city last evening by rail, apparently as fresh and unwearied as when they started.
Minneapolis Tribune, Sept. 23, 1875

—>-<—

Last Sunday, the weather being delightful and the sleighing excellent, many people took their chances on being excluded from the kingdom of grace and glory, and disported with sleighs and jumpers and such up and down the streets. Main street and vicinity presented a lively appearance.
Stillwater Gazette, March 22, 1876

—>-<—

Owners of fast horses have succeeded in scraping a fine track on the Lake Calhoun ice, and every afternoon, especially Saturday afternoon, the flyers are out in full force, and the scene is a gay one.
Minneapolis Tribune, Jan. 27, 1879

In Plain English. English Armstrong, the ebony-hued citizen [of Minneapolis] who boasts a white wife, was sailing down Hennepin avenue, near Fifth street, accompanied by his white wife and his white wife's sister yesterday afternoon, when a bystander remarked upon what he regarded as the impropriety of such goings on. Mrs. English, for whose ears the remark was evidently intended, overheard it, and inquired if it was any of his particular-business, anyhow? And the other fellow said he thought it was, adding a further word which wasn't complimentary. Mrs. English wouldn't stand it — she hauled off and slapped his face.

The bystander didn't exactly like that, and squared up in an antagonistic way. For a moment it looked squally for the woman, but English rolled his ebony eye around, took in the situation, and in less time than it takes to tell it, dealt the fellow a left-handed blow on the sconce which sent him into the gutter with a nose bleed and enlarged ideas of the rights and privileges of American citizens of African descent. Then the fallen representative of white trash arose, shook the mud from his garments, wiped his nasal organ and meandered toward the brickyard. He had lost all interest in the war of the races, and was satisfied to allow English and his wife to walk in black and white if they wanted to.
St. Paul Pioneer Press, April 15, 1876

—>-<—

A company of German emigrants camped at Maple Plain on Wednesday night, and during the night a little child attached to the colony sickened and died. Yesterday morning the remains of the little one were deposited in the burial ground at Maple Plain, and the train moved onward to its destination.
Minneapolis Tribune, April 28, 1876

—>-<—

There are three sisters living in the town of Plymouth, the aggregate of whose children number forty-one. And yet Plymouth is not thickly settled.
Minneapolis Tribune, June 6, 1876

"The only way to distinguish a mushroom from a toadstool is by eating a specimen."

Barbara Betz, of St. Paul, who is charged with the most horrible treatment of a little girl 8 years old, had an examination on Monday. The bruised and deformed victim was placed upon the witness stand, and her testimony — given in German — was direct and positive. The testimony of the doctors was also taken, fully corroborating the girl's statement. A number of German ladies were present, who were horrified at the revelations of this woman's blood-thirsty and devilish cruelty.

Stillwater Gazette, June 21, 1876

—>-<—

Talk about hard times in St. Paul! Never within the memory of the oldest inhabitant did the people of this prosperous city enjoy themselves with so much genuine zest as they do in this centennial summer. Excursion parties of hundreds of men, women and children, are flocking to the dalles, Minnetonka, White Bear and every where else, not forgetting the Red Rock camp meeting, while amusements at home are all the rage. St. Paul is happy — hence, if you want to see hard times, go west!

St. Paul Pioneer Press, June 24, 1876

—>-<—

A large number of sidewalks about the city should be repaired at once. There are many holes in some of the walks that threaten the city with suits for damages. Some pedestrian will tumble into one of the man-traps, and then call on the city for several thousand dollars.

Minneapolis Tribune, Oct. 2, 1876

—>-<—

Two enterprising young boys this morning placed a heating apparatus on the corner of First

street and Bridge Square, opposite the city market, and commenced peddling hot chestnuts.

Minneapolis Tribune, Dec. 7, 1876

—>-<—

The Dramatic Club did so well on the former occasion, and at the request of our citizens there will be a repetition of "Ten Nights in a Bar Room," under the auspices of the Good Templars,

at School House Hall on Tuesday evening next. We can assure those who were not present on the previous rendition of this popular play that it will repay them to attend, and as the proceeds are to be donated to the Cemetery Association it is hoped the house may be filled. In addition to "Ten Nights" the Club will also perform the laughable farce of "Cool as a Cucumber," which, together with music, will make a rare evening's entertainment. Admission 15 cents; reserved seats 25 cents.

Jackson Republic, Jan. 6, 1877

—>-<—

The only way to distinguish a mushroom from a toadstool is by eating a specimen. If you live, it is a mushroom; if you die, it is a toadstool.

Hastings Gazette, Jan. 6, 1877

—>-<—

Poisoned. Last Monday evening Eddie Gutherless, a bright boy, six years old, found in the grove and ate some wild parsnip root, causing, in a short time, an alarming sickness. During the night he had twenty-five fits and three doctors, and still lives. Parents should impress it on the minds of their children that they *must not eat* roots, flowers, &c., that they know nothing about.

Dodge Center Press, May 17, 1877

—>-<—

Lunch for a Picnic. Tourist and sportsman,

There is a vast difference of opinion among different people as to what constitutes a suitable lunch for a picnic. A party who went to Lake Minnetonka the other day laid in a stock of two kegs of beer and two crackers, and when the picnic was over there was a cracker and a half, but no beer left. If any one doubts this story, just ask some one of the party who sailed to Ex-

"Place them in a room where flies are troublesome."

celsior in the Black Crook on the first day of the week.
St. Paul Pioneer Press, June 7, 1877

-→•←-

The "Fats" and the "Leans." — The game of base ball last Saturday between the adipose and the bony nines created sport enough, as was expected it would, save that the game was so well played by both nines that many were disappointed. As is usual, the "Fats" came out ahead, the score standing 13 on their side to 8 for the "Leans," a decidedly close and well played game it will be seen. Franklin's pitching, Tiffany's catching, and Knox's first base, together with strong batting, are what did the business. Even Ira Walden made two runs with his 230 pounds avoirdupois, and he caught a fly that brought the cheers from the crowd. But it was fun to see Ira make the bases. The crowd would sway back and give terra firma a fair chance and he and that "game leg," how they scooted! Jim Palmer was a good baseman — that is, the home base, which he held each time, clutch

ing the bat with a death grip, until Charley Sandon, the catcher for the "Leans," caught him out. Fields, Wood, and others of the "Leans" played well and skinned around the bases occasionally, but were not robust enough to clean out the "Fats." Tiffany made four runs during the game, which was the most made by any player, and Fields came next by making three. But there was a heap of fun and we would enjoy to see the game repeated. There is timber in those two nines for crack players.
Jackson Republic, July 14, 1877

-→•←-

Attempted Kidnapping. — Mr. and Mrs. J.N. Searles were at a party on Tuesday evening, taking their youngest child with them. During the course of the evening a strange woman made her appearance at their residence on Eighth Street and informed the servant that Mrs. Searles had sent her over for the oldest child, and that she must be dressed warm, etc. The domestic demurred and an altercation ensued, ending in the door being slammed to and

---

HOUSEHOLD HINTS

-→•←-

Death to House Flies. — Half a spoonful of black pepper in powder, one teaspoonful of sugar; mix them well together, and place them in a room where flies are troublesome, they will soon disappear.
St. Anthony Falls Democrat, Aug. 4, 1870

-→•←-

A daily moderate use of celery as a salad at meal times is said to be an effectual remedy for nervousness.
Minneapolis Tribune, Nov. 18, 1870

-→•←-

As the buckwheat season is upon us, we give the following recipe for "greasing the griddle:"
Take a turnip and cut it in halves, and rub the griddle with the inner side, and you will find the cakes come off nice and will be rid of the disagreeable odor of burning fat.
Minneapolis Tribune, Dec. 3, 1872

-→•←-

[Recipes in newspapers before the turn of the 20th century were less than complete by

our standards:]
Custard Cake. — Three eggs, one cup of sugar, one cup of flour. Bake in jelly-cake tins, two layers. Custard for the above; half a pint of milk, two tablespoons of sugar, two tablespoons of flour, one egg. Boil the custard and flavor with vanilla.
Cure for Earache. — Put a little black pepper in some cotton, dip in sweet oil and insert in the ear. This is one of the quickest remedies known.
Sauk Centre Herald, April 12, 1873

"The terrible ravages of diphtheria in the family of Mr. Wm. Holden..."

fastened. Search was made the next morning for the would-be kidnapper, but without success. The attempt was a bold one, and it is very fortunate that it did not result in an irreparable loss.
Hastings Gazette, July 21, 1877

—›•‹—

Now they have got canned Boston baked beans for sale at the groceries. If they keep on canning new things for the table, pretty soon a man will not need to get married at all. He can rent a room, buy a can opener, and live on the fat of the land, with a dog to lick off the plates.
Stillwater Gazette, Aug. 8, 1877

—›•‹—

We have had all kinds of weather the past week. Monday afternoon when it came up foggy and misty we thought we were sure to have a blizzard, and we got in lots of hay for our stock and wood into the house, but it all blowed over and Tuesday was rainy and the frost seemed to be all coming out of the ground. Wednesday we plowed all day in our shirt sleeves. Friday we were at it again, as was also our neighbor S.E. Jacobs, and we could sing that December was as pleasant as May. Simeon McCall also plowed 6 acres on Monday.
Jackson Republic, Dec. 29, 1877

—›•‹—

Susan B. Anthony. The audience that listened to Miss Anthony's lecture on Thursday evening of last week [at Thuet Hall in Dodge Center] was not a very heavy one in numbers, considering the character and notoriety of the speaker. The roads were well nigh impassable, and the few who came from the country, did so under the most adverse circumstances, but were well satisfied with the lecture. There was none of the vituperation that we had been led to expect, but the

two hours were occupied with solid argument, and sound logic. It was the old story that Susan has told for years, but which is now beginning to attract the attention of thinking men, although it is still a subject for the coarse jokes of would-be wits. Her appearance on the stage is that of a thoroughly self-possessed and earnest woman, "who knows whereof she speaks, and knowing dare affirm." ... Susan B. Anthony spoke for two hours [on an earlier day] at Rochester, and the Post says, "though approaching sixty years of age, she has all the vigor and vivacity of forty."
Dodge Center Press, Jan. 4, 1878

—›•‹—

Fasting Extraordinary. Joel L. Scott, of Salem, Olmsted county, commenced threshing his grain

Lanesboro Clarion, March 5, 1872

November 1st, piling the straw upon the remains of an old stack in his yard. Several days after he missed a large hog weighing about three hundred pounds, but all search proved unavailing, and he made up his mind that his swineship had gone where the woodbine twineth. Unexpectedly, on Dec. 21st, the missing hog made its appearance from a hole which the cattle had made in the stack. The animal had apparently lost about two hundred pounds of flesh, but was still able to navigate after its confinement without food or drink for fifty-one days.
Wabasha County Sentinel, Lake City, Jan. 16, 1878

—›•‹—

A Desolate Household. We have before spoken several times of the terrible ravages of diphtheria in the family of Mr. Wm. Holden, in the town of Haverhill [in Olmsted County]. Below we give the melancholy death list, embracing names, ages and dates of death:

Clara A., died January 3d, aged 18 years; Emily, died January 8th, aged 10 years; Eveline May, died January 9th, aged 7 years; Lonnie Mabel, died January 10th, aged 4 years; Scynthia, died January 18th, aged 8 years; Henry, died January 31st, aged 13 years.

There are four children left out of a circle of ten, all of whom, we are glad to learn, and the more especially for the sake of the stricken parents, are well and bid fair to be spared to them in their declining years.

The following lines, feelingly appropriate to the sad experience of Mr. and Mrs. Holden, are published by request:

"Six times since the New Year's dawning,
Six times o'er one saddened home
Has the dark winged angel brooded
Six times has its summons come.

"Go where you will, gloom pervades many an otherwise happy household."

GRASSHOPPERS

[Swarms of grasshoppers infested large areas of Minnesota and other Midwestern states in 1873. Farmers shuddered to see grasshoppers by the millions headed toward their fields, destroying vegetation wherever they landed. Millions of dollars of wheat and other crops were ruined. Farmers were wiped out and appealed for help. But in the 1880s, state or federal governments rarely provided aid. After five continuous years of grasshopper plagues, the government reluctantly dispensed some seed and food.]

The grasshoppers, which have been doing so much damage to crops in the upper Minnesota country, last week turned eastward, and by Friday they had reached Worthington, the county seat of Nobles, and headquarters of the national colony. They moved rapidly, reaching Worthington about one and a half hours after they did Hersey, a station eight or ten miles west. They were observed at Worthington about noon on Friday, filling the air, seeming like a dark cloud, and almost obscuring the sun. Up to Monday, the gardens in and around Worthington were pretty thoroughly destroyed, and the wheat damaged. It is hoped, however, that the latter may recover somewhat. A northerly wind setting in on Monday, the grasshoppers commenced leaving in a southerly direction, and it is hoped that Minnesota may be spared further injuries from this scourge.
Minneapolis Tribune, June 19, 1873

-> - <-

Many fields of growing wheat, corn, oats and potatoes have fallen a prey to [grasshoppers'] voracious appetites. Garden stuff they relish with a gusto.

The crops in Nobles, Rock and other surrounding counties have suffered severely. ... Considering the sparse settlement of the [counties] coupled with the short crops of the last two years, serves to discourage many in their attempts at farming. Generally poor, their crop is necessary to their winter comfort, if not safety. Hard experiences are realized along the frontier — but none more so than the loss of crops. Go where you will, gloom pervades many an otherwise happy household. Should a new invasion take place — much privation and suffering will in all likelihood have to be encountered.
St. Paul Pioneer, July 2, 1873

-> - <-

There are reported to be sixty-one families in the town of Brookville, Redwood county, wholly dependent on charity for support, and this is the work of the festive grasshoppers.
St. Paul Pioneer, Feb. 16, 1875

-> - <-

There will be a solemn service of prayer and supplication at Gethsemane Church at eleven o'clock to-day, for the purpose of imploring Almighty God to avert from our State and land the dangers threatened from the renewed invasion of grasshoppers; and also to beseech His blessing upon the labors of the husbandmen and the sowing of the seed. A general invitation is given to all who wish to participate in this service.
Minneapolis Tribune, May 5, 1875

-> - <-

Mr. Hulbert, of Dayton, returned yesterday from a trip through Blue Earth County. He reports that the grasshoppers are hatching out by millions in that section, and that there is little prospect for the farmers getting any crops. He brought along a handful of earth, and in a few hours it was alive with young grasshoppers. These destructive pests will undoubtedly sweep the ground clean of vegetation.
Minneapolis Tribune, May 20, 1875

-> - <-

Dr. Pratt has a Minnesota grasshopper that is not quite as large as an ox, but a great deal larger than a fly. He has it on exhibition.
Stillwater Gazette, Aug. 4, 1875

-> - <-

[The grasshoppers finally flew off in 1877 and did not return. For more about the horrors of the grasshopper plagues, see "Harvest of Grief" by Annette Atkins, published in 1984 by the Minnesota Historical Society Press.]

"Mothers-in-law can have sweet revenge."

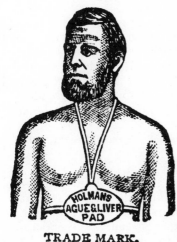
Minneapolis Tribune, Sept. 30, 1878

Yes, six times in quick succession
Have the shadows dark been cast,
Six times has the slow procession
From one darkened dwelling
passed.

Desolate is now the dwelling,
Oh, how changed since New Year's
day!
Who can speak these parents'
anguish,
O, what words their grief portray!

Sorrowing ones, in this dark hour
Of your deep, unuttered grief,
Gladly would I proffer solace,
Gladly bring your hearts relief.

But the hand that has afflicted
Can alone assuage your woe,
He hath torn and He can heal you;
Yes, in love He dealt the blow.

'Tis but little time at longest,
That death's waters can divide:
Soon a glad reunion waits you
With your loved ones o'er the tide."
Rochester Post, Feb. 8, 1878

–>-<–

Mothers-in-law can have sweet revenge on sons-in-law by sending them comic valentines to-day. The Minneapolis stock of comic valentines, with horrible odes to mothers-in-law, was exhausted several days since.
St. Paul Globe, Feb. 14, 1878

–>-<–

Industries of the Deaf, Dumb, and Blind Institute. The manufacturing business at the State Institution for the Deaf and Dumb, located in [Faribault] is getting to be quite an item. Within the last three weeks, the assistant steward of the institute, Geo. W. Lewis, has sold from the tailor shop $750 worth of goods; and the shoe shop $850 worth. Besides this, the cooper shop is turning out about 6,000 barrels a year, which find ready sale at the mills of this city, and the printing office is in nice shape and besides getting out a neat paper is doing nearly all the printing

"May they live long and prosper."

required by the institution. This work is the result of deaf and dumb pupils learning trades, at which they work from three to four hours each day, and without interfering with their studies. The profit of all goods sold belongs to the State and is used in meeting the expenses of the institution.

Sibley County Independent, Henderson, Feb. 23, 1878

—⟶•⟵—

Arrest of an Abortionist. Dr. C. Delaine, of Red Wing, was arrested last week on a charge of committing an abortion upon Christine Anderson, a young unmarried woman residing at that place. The woman Anderson fled from Red Wing and took refuge in this city, where she was found subsequent to the arrest of the doctor and escorted back to our sister city, and is now de-

---

WEDDINGS

Star-Godley. The wedding of Mr. Fred Star and Miss Mima Godley was celebrated last evening at Westminster Church in the presence of the immediate friends of the young couple whose destinies were indissolubly united by the beautiful marriage ceremony of the Episcopal church, performed by Dr. R.F. Sample. The pulpit of the church was beautifully decorated with ferns and flowers and at the appointed hour, half-past five o'clock, the wedding party entered the main door of the church, and was met at the pulpit stairs by the officiating clergyman. The groom accompanied the mother of the bride down the aisle, and the bride followed under the escort of her uncle, Mr. Phillip Godley. The ceremony was performed by Dr. Sample, amid a hushed stillness which could be felt, so intently interested in the simple service were the spectators. The wedding was unostentatious, but beautifully impressive, and the details were in such perfect taste and an air of quiet dignity pervaded the affair that will be long and pleasantly remembered by all who were present.

The congratulations of hosts of friends and the best wishes of a large circle of acquaint-ances accompany the young and happy couple in the new relations in life which they have assumed. May they live long and prosper.

Minneapolis Tribune, May 14, 1878

—⟶•⟵—

At St. Cloud the matrimonial market is so lively as to remind one of the former state of affairs in Oregon, when it used to be said that the hardy pioneers of that region, on the arrival of emigrant trains, ranged themselves in line, each one ready to take a lady new-comer "right off the wagon." Judge Evans, of St. Cloud, lately married a couple who had never seen each other until an hour before the ceremony was performed, the bridegroom meeting his bride at the [railroad] cars, and going thence straight to the judge's office. In this instance, it is proper to say, the couple had corresponded and also exchanged photographs.

St. Anthony Falls Democrat, Jan. 14, 1870

—⟶•⟵—

Less than the usual per centage of marriages are performed in church. The more common way, even for fashionable people, is to give a select party, and be married in a quiet way.

St. Anthony Falls Democrat, Feb. 18, 1870

—⟶•⟵—

Brides in good society now-a-days avoid most strictly the traditional grey and brown traveling suits formerly in vogue, and dress as unconspicuously as possible so that "all creation needn't know we've just been married."

Minneapolis Tribune, Dec. 11, 1872

—⟶•⟵—

An affair in "high life" — the marriage of Miss Lena Thompson to Mr. Frank B. Clark, at St. Paul — gives occasion for a vulgar display in newspapers, as well as on the bride's show table, of hundreds of presents, commencing with a set of "120 pieces of silverware, and closing with a $600 gold watch." And if the happy couple had been poor, and needed stoneware, or a two-dollar time-piece, they would not have been thought of in any such connection. And so goes the world, and so it will go, until the masses get their own eyes open.

The Free Flag, a Minneapolis labor newspaper, June 28, 1877

—⟶•⟵—

"The attack was a piece of pure wantoness."

CRIME

This town is infested by a considerable number of little boys who appear to have nothing else to do except to waylay in pairs any decently dressed, well-behaved boy. The better dressed the boy the more sure he is of being beaten and bruised by these good for nothing little ruffians. Yesterday afternoon a little boy was going up Wabasha street in a quiet manner, and was suddenly, and unexpectedly assaulted by three rough boys. He received two or three blows in the face, and considerable blood flowed from his nose in consequence thereof. As soon as the boys struck their victim all fled as fast as their legs could carry them around the corner into Third street. The attack was a piece of pure wantonness. It is a great pity that some of these little bruisers cannot be arrested and punished.

St. Paul Pioneer, Jan. 11, 1874

–>•<–

Young rascals in St. Peter catch five year old boys and shave their heads.

St. Paul Dispatch, March 15, 1876

–>•<–

A rather peculiar case was developed at the Chicago, Milwaukee & St. Paul depot this morning. It seems that Kate Campbell, who keeps a disreputable house in this city, brought from Chicago two girls to become inmates of her house, advancing their fares. The girls were dissatisfied, and state that Kate's place is altogether too tough a hole for them, and accordingly prepared to leave for Chicago. The girls were penniless, and Mistress Kate claimed they were under obligations to her for fare and board, and retained a portion of their clothes to secure herself against loss, but was not satisfied. She claimed further service to her in their wretched vocation. Some friend in Chicago had deposited with the Chicago, Milwaukee & St. Paul road, in Chicago, the amount of the fares of the girls, which fact came to the knowledge of Kate. Just before the morning train was to start, the woman clapped a garnishee on the Milwaukee & St. Paul company for the amount of the fare and threw the officials in so much of a doubt as to the result — the proceedings were so unprecedented — as to compel the poor girls to remain in the city. The wicked Kate went off exulting over her success, in the hope of being able to retain the girls in her hellish service, but the probabilities are they will be able to get off for Chicago this evening.

Minneapolis Tribune, June 14, 1879

tained as a witness against the abortionist.

Wabasha County Sentinel, Lake City, March 20, 1878

–>•<–

Burned to Death. — On Friday of last week Mr. Daniel Dunn, an old man about 75 years old, living with Garret Joyce of Washington Lake, went into the field to burn some brush and while so doing his clothes caught fire, and although assisted by the daughter of Mr. Joyce, before the fire could be extinguished he was so badly burned that he died in a few minutes after being helped to the house. On arriving at the house he asked for bread and coffee, but before he had tasted them death intervened.

Shot. — At Washington Lake on Sunday the 31st of March, while the family of Early, except old Mrs. Early, his mother and a little boy about 7 years of age, were at the funeral of Daniel Dunn who had been burned to death, the little boy took a loaded gun standing in the corner and in trying to carry it out doors dropped it causing it to be discharged, the contents of the gun entering the head of the old lady, killing her instantly.

Sibley County Independent, Henderson, April 6, 1878

–>•<–

A young man named Frank Bean was recently arrested in Minneapolis for committing an outrage upon a little girl, only ten years of age, whom he had decoyed into his room for that purpose. Hanging is too good for such villains.

Hastings Gazette, April 6, 1878

–>•<–

It is now quite certain that St. Paul is caught with her stock of dwelling houses sadly short of the demand. Real estate men say that we will need at least two hundred more dwellings this year than we have, to accommodate the rapidly increasing population. They say that houses neatly constructed and sensibly painted, that can be afforded at a

"Ladies' elegant silk dresses had been irreparably damaged from the untimely droppings of these soiling doves."

---

rent of from fifteen to thirty dollars per month, are in most demand, while there are occasional applicants for much more expensive houses.
St. Paul Globe, April 24, 1878

—>-<—

There are no tramps at Long Prairie, Todd county. If there is a demand for them they can be supplied from almost any other town in the State.
Minneapolis Tribune, April 29, 1878

—>-<—

Singular Case. A very singular case of poisoning occurred at Watson's Creek, Fillmore county, Friday. It seems some tramps had visited the school house at that place, on Thursday night, and stole several articles. When the teacher entered the school-room, Friday morning, she smelled a strange odor and proceeded to investigate, when she found some light powdered substance in her desk. She smelled of it; this caused her to feel faint, as well as several of the pupils who were near by. She dismissed the school and tried to get home, but fell and had to be carried to her residence.

Medical aid was at once summoned, and it was pronounced a bad case of poisoning by inhalation. Three men have been arrested, who are supposed to have left the poison there, as some of the articles taken from the school house were found in their possession. They are now in jail awaiting an examination, and the poisoned teacher is lying at the point of death.
Wabasha County Sentinel, Lake City, July 3, 1878

—>-<—

Col. Allen is disgusted with the unclean habits of the numerous pidgeons infesting the cornices of the Merchants Hotel. He related in the council yesterday

---

DAN CASTELLO'S
GREAT
CIRCUS!
AND
EGYPTIAN CARAVAN.

Great Combination Will Exhibit
AT HASTINGS,
ON WEDNESDAY OCT. 12, 1870.

POSITIVELY, THE LARGEST

Equestrian Company
EVER ORGANIZED IN AMERICA!

Among the most salient points of feature original to this establishment, is the introduction of a herd of

MONSTER CAMELS !

Driven to the largest and most

Gorgeous Chariot

Ever rolled through the Streets of America.

The following are some of the names that may be mentioned as the

LEADING ARTIST IN THE PROFESSION

MR. PALO. NATHANS.
The young and dashing Artiste, whose ambition, as well as rare merits, have gained for him the high but deserved reputation of the best living Equestrian.
MR. JOHN SAUNDERS.
The Daring and Graceful Bareback Rider.
Mrs. DAN. CASTELLO.
The Beautiful Equestrienne.
Miss ESTELLE NATHANS.
Beautiful, Graceful and Daring.
Mrs. FRANCIS DONALDSON.
Cord Volante.
Mlle. VIRGINIE.
The Graceful Equestrienne.

Dakota County Union, Oct. 5, 1870

---

how ladies' elegant silk dresses had been irreparably damaged from the untimely droppings of these soiling doves; and at his insistence permission was given by the city fathers for anyone to engage in trapping them to any extent desired. Enterprising boys will now have rare sport. Squabs make a nice dish, and the old ones will be in demand by the sportsmen at the State fair.
St. Paul Pioneer Press, July 17, 1878

—>-<—

Tenting on the beach is a delightful way to put in the time this warm weather, and nearly every day parties leave the city, for a day or week's ramble in some shady grove bordering on the lake. This week, County Attorney Hahn, Will J. Richardson and H.D. Brown, with their families, making a party of eighteen, will be found comfortably quartered on Central Point, which location commands a grand view of Lake Pepin and its surroundings, and where "roughing it" can be enjoyed to the fullest extent. The fine tents and all the necessary accoutrements for living, make a very attractive lodge and the short vacation taken by this party, will no doubt be spent in a gay and happy way, if the weather is pleasant.
Wabasha County Sentinel, Lake City, Aug. 21, 1878

—>-<—

Only one drunk in the city lock-up for the past two days, and the judge didn't have the heart to fine or imprison him, in his loneliness, so he administered the usual dose of temperance lecture, and let him go.
Minneapolis Tribune, Aug. 12, 1878

—>-<—

Wanted [by the editor]. Right away, pretty soon, something exciting, an elopement, dog fight, sewing society, fire, burglary,

"The most desirable and beneficial article ever invented for the relief of women..."

The women of New York — judging by the stir they make in the newspapers — are just now more exercised over the question of long or short dresses than they are over those more trenchant questions of Woman's Rights and Woman Suffrage.... We ... hope that the present struggle amongst the votaries of fashion will result in favor of the short dress advocates; since, however, it may be in the great cities, Minnesota is too essentially rural — there is too much call for outdoor enjoyment to hamper our fair friends with habiliments [clothing] they cannot move about readily in.
Minneapolis Tribune, May 6, 1870

—→·←—

Our attention has been called to a new article for the use of ladies, the invention of which has conferred an everlasting blessing upon every lady. We refer to the Queen City Skirt Suspenders, for supporting ladies' skirts, the most desirable and beneficial article ever invented for the relief of women, many of whom have suffered years of miserable health caused solely by carrying the weight of a number of heavy skirts, completely dragging them down. Something to support ladies' clothing is absolutely necessary. These suspenders are recommended by our leading physicians to all ladies and young girls. Every lady should have them. Thousands will testify to their excellence and the advantages to be derived from wearing them. They are sold only through lady agents. Many ladies in other localities are making from a hun-

FASHION

A. C. FRAUMAN,
MERCHANT TAILOR,
and Dealer in
CLOTHING,
HATS,
CAPS,
TRUNKS,
Valises,
GENT'S
Furnishing
GOODS,
&c.

This suit came from A. C. FRAUMAN'S.

This did not!

No. 4 Main St., Anoka.

Anoka County Union, June 18, 1872

dred to two hundred dollars per month selling these and other new articles made by the same Company, and it can be done here. We have been asked by the manufacturer for the name of a reliable lady to act as their agent in this county. We advise such to write at once to the Queen City Suspender Company, Elm and Longworth Streets, Cincinnati, Ohio.
Stillwater Gazette, April 16, 1879

"If it was difficult to get to the fair, it was more so getting away."

Lake City Leader, June 23, 1877

anything in which to find an item. It is getting terribly monotonous.
Dodge Center Press, Aug. 9, 1878

-›-‹-

The State Fair. We arrived in St. Paul on Wednesday evening, and in company with Cal. Prince, spent several weary hours trying to obtain a place to lay our weary heads. We found it at last in the Dancing Academy of Prof. Seibert, where we reposed two in a bed on the floor. In the morning we paid $1 each for the bed, voted the whole thing a contemptible extortion, and wondered if our treatment was a fair sample of St. Paul hospitality. At an early hour thousands were moving in the direction of the depot to greet the President [Rutherford B. Hayes] and his party, and as he rode up Third St. there was an occasional cheer and a great deal of stare. Mrs. Hayes was very much admired, and was called out quite as often as her husband. We did not hear the speeches at the

fair ground as we arrived just as the party were partaking of a collation [light meal], and thousands were watching the feeding. The next "show" was the shooting by Dr. Carver and Capt. Bogardus, either of whom can beat us, and that's all we can say of them. The dog show we failed to visit. There was a good exhibit of pictures, many of them choice paintings loaned by wealthy St. Paulists. The Sugar making machine, wherein was made every day, sugar from Minnesota cane, came in for its share of attention. The show of stock was not as good as at Minneapolis. That of Machinery was fully as good, and both were very fair. If it was difficult to get to the fair, it was more so getting away, the conveniences of travel not being at all adequate to the crowd. We took the Minneapolis train resolving to secure a respectable night's rest. We think that when St. Paul has her next big fair she will make provision for the accommodation of visitors, and also for a supply of wa-

ter on the fair grounds. There was a woful deficiency of drinking water, forcing the thirsty thousands to substitute beer, or the sloppy lemonade sold at the booths. The fair was a big thing, and no doubt the managers did the best they could, but it was a bigger thing than they were capable of running.
Dodge Center Press, Sept. 13, 1878

-›-‹-

A bright little fellow of four, the son of a former pastor of a flourishing church, who attends the infant class in Sunday-school, received last Sunday morning a card on which were the words, "Pray without ceasing." After his mother had explained the text, he said, "I guess I won't show this to the minister; he prays long enough now."
Hastings Gazette, April 19, 1879

-›-‹-

A Double Funeral. Friday last was the occasion of rather an unusual proceeding at Zumbrota,

"Seventeen unmarried females . . . are trying to give away their babies."

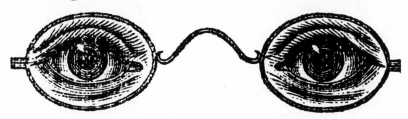
that of the second funeral service and second burial services of one of their townsmen. The circumstances as we understand them were about like the following: The deceased was Mr. Evan Houw, who, after a short illness, died about the 25th ult. [last month], and, in consequence of his recently becoming a member of the Masonic fraternity at Zumbrota, he was considered by the Lutheran society (of which he had been a life-long member) as unworthy of their continued Christian love and esteem. Therefore the good pastor of that church at Zumbrota would not admit of a regular service at the church, nor allow his remains to be interred in the place usually allotted to members of that society in their church cemetery, but merely read a prayer at the house, and only permitted them to be buried in a secluded place by the side of a suicide's grave in one corner of the cemetery grounds. This was a hard punishment and the widow, feeling grieved thereby, finally appealed to Hermon Lodge for a more suitable burial of the deceased husband. The lodge promptly responded to her request, and yesterday caused the body to be raised and buried in the village cemetery with due honors of the fraternity.

Hastings Gazette, April 19, 1879

—>•<—

Northfield, Rice county, is reported to have seventeen unmarried females who are trying to give away their babies.

Goodhue County Republican, Red Wing, April 24, 1879

—>•<—

1880s

Minnesota enjoyed boom years. The first iron ore was shipped from the Vermilion range, and iron was discovered on the Mesabi Range. Immigration was heavy, with Scandinavians, Poles, Czechs and Slovaks predominating. The 1 million population mark was passed in 1885. St. Paul people braved frigid temperatures to see the city's first ice palace and winter carnival. The state's climate was promoted as a cure for tuberculosis. The deadliest tornado in Minnesota history hit St. Cloud and Sauk Rapids in 1886. St. Marys Hospital opened in Rochester in 1889, with Dr. William Mayo and his two sons on the staff.

1880s

-›•‹-

Sauk Rapids Tornado

The tornado that struck Sauk Rapids and St. Cloud on April 14,
1886, still is ranked as the deadliest ever in Minnesota. At least 74
people were killed, some of them at a wedding reception.

Tornado Stricken
Sauk Rapids nearly annihilated by a cyclone.
Thirty-six persons numbered with the dead.
A large number wounded.
The amount of property destroyed estimated at
$289,000.
One hundred and nine buildings destroyed.
The court house, school house, mills, bridge
and depot building among the wreck.

SAUK RAPIDS is in ruins, a number of its people have met a violent and sudden death, and a still larger number are now sufferers from wounds and bruises.

It may, perhaps, be easy to tell how this melancholy and appalling condition was brought about, but no pen, however graphic, can do justice in describing the fury of the elements, and the devastation and distress which followed in its wake.

Last Wednesday, April 14th, the day dawned on a happy and prosperous community. The people of Sauk Rapids went about in pursuit of their usual avocations, and no premonitory symptoms of the dire calamity impending was apparent. Shortly after noon there was shower of short duration, accompanied with hail, and the atmosphere was close and what is generally described as muggy. The clouds were broken and did not appear threatening. Shortly after 4 p.m. the writer of this was standing in the back door way of the Sentinel office when his attention was called to a phenomenal appearance in the direction of St. Cloud. At first it appeared like a black puff of smoke, balloon-shaped, such as is emitted from a locomotive, with this difference: that it would ascend and descend; in the course of a few seconds it had assumed the form of a column, which increased in volume, and a roaring sound which increased until it became deafening. This terrible messenger approached with great rapidity, and it was apparent that our beautiful village would

before many seconds be at the mercy of a cyclone. The writer of this escaped by running in an easterly direction across the track of the storm, and after it had passed saw it depart in a northerly direction, destroying everything in its course. The scene presented can never be forgotten, neither can it be fully described.

The track of the storm was through the heart of the village, and every building within its breadth, which was from sixty to eighty rods, was leveled with the ground, the material torn to pieces, and desolation and chaos reigned supreme.

Men, women and children, wounded and bleeding, were to be seen in every direction, and it was only too painfully apparent that many had lost their lives. Those who had been fortunate enough to escape harm, were soon at work to rescue and care for the wounded, and to find the dead.

Before many hours a corps of physicians from St. Paul, Minneapolis, Anoka and Brainerd, came by special train, to render assistance, and these were accompanied by philanthropic and generous people who did all in their power to alleviate the suffering and supply the immediate wants of our stricken people.

It is impossible at this time to give an accurate and minute account of the various items and points of interest in connection with this dreadful catastrophe. We can, however, state that the aid and sympathy extended from numerous cities, towns, villages and private individuals, is such in its scope and nature that our people can only feebly express their gratitude in words. Provisions, clothing, lumber and other building material have been sent, tents erected, skilled nurses from Minneapolis, St. Paul and St. Cloud have ministered to the sick, and a hospital under direction of Drs. Kilvington and Dunn, of Minneapolis, aided by other physicians,

"Everything that skill and attention can do is being done."

has been established, and everything that skill and attention can do is being done.

The following is the list at Sauk Rapids of

THE DEAD.

EDGAR HULL, of St. Cloud, 39 years.
MRS. MATTIE FINK, 32 years.
CARL F. FINK, 10 years.
JOHN H. FINK, 8 years.
AUGUST L. FINK, 6 years.
OTELLA FINK, 3 years.
A.H. LAKE, 51 years.
A.E. SCHULER (missing).
JOHN RENARD, County Auditor.
GREG LINDLEY, Register of Deeds.
ABNER ST. CYR, 42 years.
MAURICE ST. CYR, 10 years.
OLLIE CARPENTER, 5 years.
HENRY BEHRENS, 35 years.
SAM SORENSON, 32 years.
MRS. W.E. DAVEE.
ERNEST O. ALBRECHT, 27 years.
LOUIS LANDRE, boy.
MRS. PAPPENFUS, her mother and 3 children.
MRS. SAMUEL FLETCHER.
CLARA BERG, 7 years.
ELLA BERG, 14 years.
H. CHELGREN'S DAUGHTER, 9 years.
AMELIA WOELIN, a little girl.
ANTONIA, a little girl.
WILLIE BARLNYK, 13 years.
FRED BALYNSKY, 12 years.
LULU CARPENTER, 11 years.
ANDREW WALSTED, 60 years.
EVA TEMPLIN, 18 years.
CHILD OF C. KALINOWSKI.
[The total is 35, not 36 as stated in the headline.]

LIST OF THE WOUNDED.

Dr. J.H. Dunn, the physician in charge, Friday evening issued the following report concerning the wounded. A house visitation has been made, eighteen houses being visited and thirty-six wounded found, as follows:

At A. Walstrom's house — Gracie Chelgren, aged six years, bruised about the face and flesh wounds; Leonard Chelgren, four years, slight bruises about face and scalp; Oscar Chelgren, three years, slight scalp wound.

At A.B. Anderson's house — Mrs. Henry Chelgren, thirty-four years, severely bruised about face, scalp and back; nothing needed.

At Thomas Van Etten's house — Mrs. H. Berg, thirty-six years, scalp wounds, back bruised, right arm, not dangerous.

At Jacob Ganskop's house — Mrs. Ganskop, forty-four years, bruised on left shoulder, shoulder bones broken, severe injury to lungs, critical; taken to the hospital.

At Mrs. Gaumnitz's house — Fred Bartnik, fifty-five, scalp wound, not serious; nothing needed; Mrs. Hartz needs clothes for six children; Fred Gaumnitz, twelve years, left leg broken, scalp wound, nothing needed.

At Mrs. Russell's house — Mrs. C.A. Heaton, forty years, bruised shoulder and hip, sprained ankle; not dangerous; Edith Heaton, eleven years, contusion of right eye, scalp wound; Charles Heaton, seven years, right hand slightly injured; clothes, shoes and stockings needed.

At Mr. Hamilton's house — Mrs. Florence Cormier, thirty-four years, contusion of eye and back, not serious; Fannie Cormier, thirteen years, slight bruise; Elizabeth Cormier, twelve years, scalp wound; Anna Cormier, eleven years, puncture wound of the foot; Dennis Cormier, eight years, lacerated wound of the cheek; Ella Cormier, three years, laceration of scalp; totally destitute. . . .

"They had just kneeled to engage in prayer when overwhelmed by the storm."

[There continued a house-by-house account of injuries and items wanted.]

Charles Gilman, 83 years old, who was buried in the ruins of his house, as was his daughter Lucy, and was supposed to be dangerously injured, is recovering. He didn't forget to send in a hundred dollars to the other boys whose injuries were worse than his own.

The following is the list of estimated losses at Sauk Rapids:

Stanton's mill, $62,000

Demeules's store building. 5,250

Schiele's blacksmith shop and dwelling. 1,800

North'n Pacific depot and a number of cars. 5,000

Sentinel office and W.L. Nieman's dwelling. 5,500

E. Cross' meat market. 2,200

Berg & Bros. hardware store and stock. 7,300

Bank building (injured). 400

Schouber's drug store. 2,500

A. St. Cyr's saloon. 1,000

Mrs. Jenckus's millinery store. 300

Geo. Sweet's store building. 1,900

Kern's boot and shoe store. 1,500

Skates's feed store. 200

C.G. Wood's store (damaged). 300

Goedker's saloon and dwelling. 1,200

R.J. Bell, law office. 300

Moody's drug store. 800

Beaupre Bros., groceries. 3,000

Wetzel's grocery store. 3,100

Post office building and Free Press office. 2,200

Dennis Millane, saloon and hotel. 2,000

Bell's feed store. 900

Van Etten's new store building. 400

J.W. Raeder, barber shop and cigars. 200

Fred Hart's saloon. 3,300

Brown & Sons, general merchandise. 4,000

Dr. Mayo, drug store and residence. 2,400 [Not one of the famous Drs. Mayo of Rochester]

Davis's saloon and dwelling. 2,500

Hoffman house and barn. 800

Central House. 5,700

G.S. Reeder, building. 300

G.W. Benedict, building. 700

P.N. Fink's dwelling. 2,000

Court house and jail. 10,000.

Mississippi Bridge. 10,000

Episcopal Church. 1,200.

Masonic Hall. 500.

[The list went on to three times this length.]

RICES.

Terrible Fate of a Wedding Party.

After leaving Sauk Rapids, the next heard of the cyclone is from near Rices, a station on the Northern Pacific road, about fourteen miles from the former village. Some four miles southeast of the station, at the house of a farmer named Schultz, a happy wedding party was gathered, a daughter of the farmer having been married to Henry Friday, Chairman of the Board of Supervisors of Langola. Almost before they realized it, the terrible power of the storm encircled them, and in the twinkling of an eye nine of the goodly company were mangled corpses, among the number being the groom, while the bride was dangerously if not fatally injured. The victims also include the Rev. G.J. Schmidt, pastor of the German Evangelical church of this city, a most estimable citizen and a devoted Christian, and his wife. The Rev. Mr. Seeder, pastor of the Two Rivers district, was found out on the prairie with both legs broken. Several of the wounded have since died. Twelve bodies now lie in the town house at Rices. We have been unable to learn the names of all the killed. . . .

Later information says that there were thirty-five persons at the wedding and that they had just kneeled to engage in prayer when overwhelmed by the storm.

Sauk Rapids Sentinel, April 20, 1886

→›-‹—

"Staid bank presidents are found sitting in their offices in full toboggan uniform."

132 FEET HIGH; COVERS ONE ACRE OF GROUND.

ST. PAUL ICE PALACE. 1888.

WINTER CARNIVAL OPENS JANUARY 25TH, AND CLOSES FEBRUARY 4TH, 1888.

Photo courtesy of the Minnesota Historical Society

Our Winter Festival.

The Winter Carnival in St. Paul is probably the most complete season of festival, taking all things into consideration, which is celebrated in any city in the United States to-day. For two weeks His Most Riotous Majesty Borealis I holds the undisputed allegiance of the whole city. Business gives way to him. Work stands waiting in pigeon holes till the term of his reign shall be over. Pleasure itself forgets its ordinary forms and tricks itself out in cap and bells to conform to the usages of his court. In the presence of his throne even the laws of fashion are in abeyance, as those of a tributary prince before his suzerain [feudal lord]. Even stern-faced etiquette stands uncovered and bends the knee before him. . . .

Staid bank presidents are found sitting in their offices in full toboggan uniform. High officials of railroads carry their dignity round with them swathed in blankets. Millionaires risk their valuable limbs in the perils of the slide; and solemn business men leave the counting room to take their places on the floats of the Nashkas or the Owls. King Borealis is the monarch of the most utter democracy; the jolly autocrat of a government by the mob; the despotic ruler over a land of universal liberty.

The Ice Palace is his lordly pleasure house. He has no permanent throne but in the hearts of his people.

"Massive it stands, but as light as a castle of the clouds."

The Palace itself is too lovely for even him to live in. There is a popular fallacy to the effect that the Ice Palace is built; built by mere men who saw out the blocks of ice with saws, heave them with ice-tongs and derricks into place and lay them as the commonplace bricklayer lays bricks. But this is all nonsense. Little children know better; and the fairies know better.

Look at it! Look at the light vaulting arches and stately turrets. Massive it stands, but as light as a castle of the clouds. Mysteriously beautiful and dim in its semi-translucency, and glittering from a thousand diamond facets where the winter sun strikes its angles. All the gods of Asgard [the abode of the Nordic gods] never built anything more lovely. Alph, the sacred river, flowed by no structure more majestically fairy-like.

That thing built by men? Nonsense! It rose as the walls of Athens rose, to the sound of the music of gods. . . . There was no sound heard of the hammer or the saw. But one morning the people of St. Paul awoke and found it there.

The talk about its being built with derrick and tongs, I say again, is absurd. Why should men build it? They do not live in it. They do not even put anything in it. It is only a glorified sign post which says: "This is where the fun takes place."

Northwest Illustrated Magazine, St. Paul and Minneapolis, February 1888

->-<-

The Lake City Sentinel says: "Mrs. John Judge, of Highland, has given birth to sixteen children within the past eighteen years. Since January 24, 1877, six boys have been born to her, four of whom were twins."

Minneapolis Tribune, Feb. 2, 1880

->-<-

These Rattan Rockers
Strong and Comfortable only
$2.16 EACH

Rochester Record and Union, Sept. 21, 1888

Nursing the Sick.

Some sensible person, who has evidently had experience in attending to invalids, thus speaks of the importance of decision and quietness in the sick-room:

"Consult your patient's wants, but consult him as little as possible. Your decision need not be very obvious and positive; you will be most decisive if no one suspects that you are so at all. It is the triumph of supremacy to become unconsciously supreme. No where is this decision more blessed than in a sick-room. Where it exists in its genuineness the sufferer is never contradicted, never coerced; all little victories are assumed. The decisive nurse is never peremptory, never loud. She is distinct, it is true — there is nothing more aggravating to a sick person than a whisper — but she is not loud. Though quiet, however, she never walks tip-toe; she never makes gestures; all is open and above board. She knows no diplomacy or finesse, and, of course, her shoes never creak. Her touch is steady and encouraging. She does not potter. She never looks at you sideways. You never catch her watching. She never slams the door, but she never shuts it slowly, as if she were cracking a nut in the hinge. She never talks behind it. She never peeps. She pokes the fire skillfully, with firm, judicious penetration. She caresses one kind of patient with genuine sympathy, she talks to another as if he were well. She is never in a hurry. She is worth her weight in gold, and has a healthy prejudice against physic [medical treatment], which, however, she knows at the right time how to conceal."

St. Charles Times, March 5, 1880

->-<-

Minnetonka Lake.

A general breaking up of the lake commenced last Tuesday, which is a sure indication that our long, cold winter is "busted up" at last. Fish are running at a "good hickory" and 'tis very fortunate for some of the natives. We will have a square meal if the law don't interfere. Natives can't spear a fish — 'tis against the law. Tourists can catch them by the boat load, and cast them out on the banks to spoil, but no spearing is allowed in the winter. This is called justice. Selah. [Forever.]

Rumor has it that Mr. Faller, of Minneapolis, intends putting a two-masted schooner on the lake this summer. Good for him.

G.F. Shaw, formerly of Wisconsin, is about to open a first

"Our Minnesota molasses begins to look up in the market and surely will take its place as a standard article; thereby another great industry is added to our State."

class boot and shoe shop at Long Lake. Time we had a reliable place to get our shoeing done.

N.J. Stubbs has commenced work on his house and Ed. Young is getting the lumber on his place, preparatory to building.

E. Barnes sowed wheat on the 31st. Barnes is always up to and a little ahead of the times, and says he is going to plant 50 acres of amber cane this season. Our Minnesota molasses begins to look up in the market and surely will take its place as a standard article; thereby another great industry is added to our State.

Quite a painful accident happened to Mr. Lockwood, of Medina, while chopping cord wood. His axe slipped and nearly severed his foot. Being a little anxious to get about, he has taken a bad cold which settled in his leg, and he is now in a very critical condition.

S. Dyer, of Rockford, has arrived with his fleet of new boats. He intends to have 12 boats on the lake this season. Parties that intend purchasing boats for this season would do well to call and see his.

The good people of Excelsior are band-crazy. The projected railroad is to blame for it. But crazy or not Latham is still manufacturing the best rustic chairs one can find anywhere.

Cord wood business is about played for this season. Good authority says there was not more than one half as much wood manufactured this season as last.

Farmers are about sick of doing all the hard work. For the last four years they have scarcely realized enough, many times not enough to pay their bills, and after all their hard work, can hardly afford to buy a common pair of overalls and jacket.

Hennepin County Mirror, Minneapolis, April 8, 1880

→›•‹←

"A woman cannot become a successful lawyer."

An aged squaw, whose gray hairs, sunken eyes, cadaverous expression, and dilapidated clothing bespoke her destitute condition, was passing around a paper in Winona the other day, asking alms, which read as follows:

"Look at this specimen of humanity, and think of the Pilgrims of Wm. Penn or any other person. Go to church next Sunday but don't put any money on the plate when it is passed, but keep it and give it for charity sake to this poor creature, one of the natives and former owners of this vast territory where the United States are now situated.

"This squaw's husband has gone to the happy hunting grounds of his fathers. He crossed the stream of time on a slippery log and is now in father Abraham's bosom. He was a good hunter, good husband and was humane. She is a forlorn widow, dependent on the cold world for a living.

"(Signed) J. KNIFE"

St. Charles Times, June 18, 1880

—>-<—

One is peculiarly struck with the number of cheap houses being built in this city [Stillwater] at the present time. The poorer class of our citizens have been driven from lack of tenements to put up houses, and with their limited means are doing the best they can. Some twenty-five houses, costing from $200 to $500, are being erected.

Minneapolis Tribune, July 2, 1880

—>-<—

A woman cannot become a successful lawyer. She is too fond of giving her opinion without pay.

Hennepin County Mirror, Minneapolis, Oct. 9, 1880

—>-<—

Osee Clothier [of Denmark,

Washington County] had a manure bee last Wednesday, a dozen teams were gathered together, and a little less than one hundred loads of manure were hauled out. In the evening Mr. Clothier gave the people who attended the bee in the day time a free dance; about a dozen couples were present, and enjoyed themselves well till near morning.

Stillwater Gazette, Oct. 20, 1880

—>-<—

Personal — Tom Doyle, call or send that ten dollars you borrowed last week, to Red, P.O. box "G" St. Paul, and save further advertising.

St. Paul Globe, Oct. 28, 1880

—>-<—

Gentlemen who are going to take a drive should not forget that an eight-page newspaper spread over the chest is the best chest protector that can be worn in cold weather. Put it between the under and overcoat.

St. Charles Times, Jan. 28, 1881

—>-<—

There are on an average twenty applicants for every house that is offered for rent in St. Paul.

Stillwater Gazette, April 13, 1881

—>-<—

Comfortable dwelling-houses, which can be rented for $15, $20 or $25 a month, according to size, are scarce [in St. Paul]. Two or three hundred could be rented this month.

Minneapolis Tribune, April 16, 1881

—>-<—

A new paper at Montevideo is called The Valley Blossom. Minnesota now has a "Sneezer" [Detroit Daily Sneezer], a "Blizzard" [The Bird Island Blizzard] and a "Blossom." The "Snorter" is yet to be started.

Minneapolis Tribune, July 13, 1881

—>-<—

Yesterday and last evening the first snow of the season fell in this city. It buried out of sight for

A Marvelous Display of Holiday Goods
AT THE GREAT CHICAGO BARGAIN HOUSE:

We have the Largest Stock, Best Assortment, and Lowest Prices in the County; and guarantee to save you Fifty Cents on each Dollar's worth you buy of us, and you will be better suited----We have good reasons for saying so. ☞ Call and Examine the magnificent Display. No trouble to show goods. Examine the goods and be convinced. Below

WE SHOW A FEW SAMPLES OF OUR ENORMOUS STOCK.

"Middle-aged and old people now living have witnessed wonderful revolutions in their lives."

---

the time being the filth and corruption with which the streets are covered, and in that much was a most happy relief.
Minneapolis Tribune, Nov. 5, 1881

→›•‹←

Jake Winnick, of Atwater, recently became his former wife's step-father, by getting divorced from her and marrying her mother, Mrs. Ferguson. He must like the breed.
Minneapolis Tribune, Dec. 10, 1881

→›•‹←

Another new swindle, says the Winona Tribune, is being practiced on the guileless granger. Two rogues watch the papers for estray [wandering domestic animals] notices. When one is published one of them goes and looks at the animal. Of course, on application, the unsuspecting farmer shows the beast, and the fellow decides it is not his, and then he returns to his partner and describes the animal minutely to him. No. 2 goes to the farmer, and after proving by the thorough description that he is owner of the animal, says he cannot take it away, and offers to sell it at a bargain. The farmer buys, and in a few days the rightful owner comes along and claims the animal, and, of course, the farmer is out just so much.
Mower County Transcript, Austin, June 7, 1882

→›•‹←

Saturday night a German woman, about thirty years of age, stopped at the residence of M. Teeter, about a mile and a half north of town, wishing to stay all night. She said she came from Germany with her husband about two years ago. Her husband left her last February, going west for a homestead, and where he is she does not know. He left her in Mitchell county, Iowa, working for her board. Money was given

EN ROUTE TO CALIFORNIA!!!

Lew Johnson's Black Baby Boy
Colored Minstrels
THE COMPANY THAT HAS MADE ALL AMERICA LAUGH
Will positively appear, ONE NIGHT ONLY in each of the Twin Cities.
MINNEAPOLIS, MONDAY Evening December 5th., at Freya Hall No. 5604 Washington Avenue S.
ST. PAUL, WEDNESDAY Evening December 7th., at Turner Hall. Corner Sixth and Exchange Sts.
THE GRANDEST AFFAIR OF THE SEASON

LEW JOHNSON'S MINSTRELS—8:30 to 10:30.
GRAND PROMENADE CONCERT for the audience with select music by B. B. B. Brass Band 10:30 to 11:30.
GRAND SOCIAL HOP, extra fine full minstrel Orchestra commencing at 11:40.

Western Appeal, Dec. 3, 1887

her to go to St. Paul where she was told she would receive free of charge the care she would so soon need. St. Paul parties gave her money to bring her back as far as Blooming Prairie. From there she came to Lansing, and from Lansing to Mr. Teeter's. She was tidy and of good appearance and told her story in a truthful manner. Sunday morning a baby was born and the homeless German woman is its mother. We know she will receive good care for the present from the family of our worthy friend, Mike Teeter, but, we say, God pity her. Poor woman, without husband or friends, without a dollar to provide food or clothing for herself or helpless babe. Homeless and destitute, a stranger in a strange land, in this her hour of weakness and dire necessity. Yes, God, pity her, we say, and raise her up friends, who, though they can be to her neither husband, father, mother, brother or sister, yet they can give her sympathy and supply her physical needs.
Mower County Transcript, Austin, June 21, 1882

→›•‹←

How We Progress.
It is really very remarkable, when we come to think of it. Middle-aged and old people now living have witnessed wonderful revolutions in their lives — a transition in every phase of life, almost too wonderful to believe. In the matter of artificial light, for instance. They commenced life with a pitch-pine knot, or a rag soaked in tallow, lard, or whale-oil, and believed it to be about as brilliant as need be; then, they indulged in the luxury of a tallow candle; then the improved star-candle; then the coal-oil lamp and gas, and *now* the electric light — a veritable sun, at nighttime. How odd it would seem now to hear the preacher announce that "Divine services will be held at this place this evening, at early candle light, no preventing providence — the brethren will please not forget to bring the candles." In those days matches were unknown, and if the steel got mislaid, or the spunk-wood got wet, and the fire went out, one of the family was sent a mile away to borrow a shovel full of fire from a neighbor; now, however, all you have to do is to "strike a match," and if they run out, just touch your kindling to the nose of the third man you meet. Then, the sickle and flail of the ancients; now the reapers and steam-threshers. Then, only the old primitive fire-

"The new material for dining room upholstery is elephant skin."

place and chimney-corner prevailed; now, the cooking-stove, the nickel-plated heaters, furnaces, and oil-stoves are in vogue. Then, the canal, the post-boy and lumbering stage coach; now, the flying railroad trains, the telegraph and telephone. These, and a thousand other changes in public and domestic economy, but little less wonderful, and all within the lives of thousands of people who are even yet in the hey-day of life.... At this rate of progression, in half a century more people will be flying through the air on wings and in air-ships; a man will put on his wings this morning and arrive in China yesterday — allowing difference in time; commerce will be shot through pneumatic tubes a thousand miles in a minute; and the dear [Lord] only knows *what* will come to pass in the next century. Humanity *may* become so very precocious and smart, that some morning they will wake up and find they don't know anything — their Babel will topple over and their plans become frustrated all of a sudden.

Lake City Graphic, Sept. 12, 1882

–⟩–⟨–

Litchfield Saturday Review, Dec. 21, 1889

The Faribault Democrat gives a detailed and amusing account of an amateur attempt to make a plaster-of-paris bust from a living subject. A young man condescended to be busted. A fair young creature who had graduated at an eastern conservatory, applied the plaster, surrounded by several young lady assistants. She forgot to grease the subject's face. The result was the plaster hardened and stuck — the goose quills through the nostrils for air, slipped and the subject came near being smothered. It, however, was prevented, and the cast broken off, piece-meal, bringing with it eyebrows, whiskers, mustache, ear-tips, a part of the nose, etc. After eight hours of mould agony, the young man was relieved, really busted, and put in the hands of surgeons for repair.

St. Paul Globe, Oct. 3, 1882

–⟩–⟨–

Etiquette and Decoration.
Notes on Good Manners and Beautifying the Home.
Light woods for furniture are rapidly coming into favor again.

If wax tapers are used at a dinner party, there should be as many lights as guests.

Pedestals entirely covered with plush have received the sanction of fashion.

New tables for the drawing room are square or octagonal in shape, and have light legs.

From 3 to 6 o'clock are proper hours for making calls, and a visit may be from five minutes to half an hour.

The new material for dining room upholstery is elephant skin embossed with mediaeval designs of griffins and arabesques.

A guest chamber should always be furnished with a hand glass, button hooks, pins, hair pins, brush and comb, clothes brush, and also needles, thread and scissors.

Minneapolis Tribune, Oct. 21, 1882

–⟩–⟨–

1880s
–>•<–

New York Mills Quadruplets

The Babies Named.

Mrs. Herman Blumberg, residing two miles northeast of New York Mills, on Monday of last week at 9 o'clock a.m., gave birth to a little girl and on Tuesday morning three more of the feminine sex arrived, making quadruplets weighing about three pounds apiece, and prospects of all surviving. The mother was at first reported to be doing well, but on Tuesday evening she died for want of care and proper attention. ... The father, although in needy circumstances, refuses to part with any of them. Ribbons were tied around the little ones in the order of their birth, No. 1 having one black one, No. 2 two red, No. 3 three pink, and No. 4 two black and two red ribbons; they were then wrapped up in bandages, according to the Finnish style, laid on a pillow and numbered 1, 2, 3 and 4. Their names are: No. 1, Matilda; No. 2, Helmi; No. 3, Catherine; No. 4, Ida Sophia. The mother came to America from Finland last October. She was 31 years of age and had been married ten years. The case is a very rare one and is attracting considerable attention from physicians and medical men, and although triplets are of frequent occurrence, quadruplets are very rare. It is certainly to be hoped that the little ones may continue healthy and when the proper time comes given a good education and liberal chances in life.

Perham Bulletin, Aug. 11, 1887

–>•<–

NEW YORK MILLS QUADRUPLETS

Something About the Blombergs, who Had Four Daughters Born at One Birth.

Yesterday County Commissioner Jung and Dr. Berthold, of Perham, visited New York Mills in or-der to look after the four little waifs who came into the world last Tuesday. Mr. A.S. Blowers hitched up his team and accompanied them to the residence of Mr. Blomberg [the family name was spelled several ways in the newspapers]. They found the babies all neatly dressed, lying side by side as cozy as little kittens. The doctor examined them and says they are all well developed infants and healthy and he sees no reason why they should not live if they have proper care. They are not as large as at first report-ed; they weigh from 3 1/2 to 4 1/2 lbs each. A sis-ter-in-law of the father of the children has taken the four little ones to her home and is trying to take care of them, but taking the four little ones and five more brothers and sisters all under 5 years of age with four of her own all under 6 years, in a little log house with but one room, it makes a very large fam-ily [that's 13 children under the age of 6]; yet they found everything about the place as neat as wax. These people are Finlanders, cannot speak English and are very poor, their only possession being one cow. There is one pair of twins 3 years of age, brothers to the four little girls. On the father's side there were fourteen in the family and all the moth-er's eleven brothers and sisters, all living but Mrs. Blomberg. The county commissioner made ar-rangements to have a nurse employed to take care of the four little ones, and the ladies of this village will assist in making clothing. Any little gifts will be thankfully received by these poor people. Any-one wishing to give them anything can send it to Mr. A.S. Blowers, who will see that it goes to them.

Fergus Falls Journal, Aug. 11, 1887

–>•<–

One of the quadruplets, No. 3, recently born near New York Mills, died at its home last week. The balance of the children are enjoying good health.

Perham Bulletin, Aug. 18, 1887

–>•<–

"Kissing her mother [she] said, 'meet me in Heaven.'"

Last week we announced the death of one of the quadruplets, and a few days later the other three died. The kind-hearted people at the Mills and throughout the county, have seen that the family have had proper care and a large amount of clothing has also been sent them.

Perham Bulletin, Aug. 25, 1887

→>•<—

Matrimonial.

Dr. J.W. Scott, of this city, formerly of Bladensburg, Ohio, and Miss Bessie E. Wells, Mt. Vernon, Ohio, were married on Thursday, November 9th, 1882, at Mantorville, Minn., at the residence of the bride's sister, Mrs. H. Willard; Rev. Henry Willard officiating, using the Episcopal marriage service. The following is a list of some of the presents received:

Comforts [comforter] and dried fruit, from Mrs. A.C. and Miss Violet Scott, Bladensburg, Ohio.

Damask towels and fringed table cloth, from Mrs. A.C. Scott.

Medical Works, Marseilles spread, from Dr. A.C. Scott, Bladensburg, Ohio. Pillow cases and Majolica [a type of pottery that is glazed, richly colored and ornamented] bread plate, from Miss Violet Scott.

Silver mounted fruit dish, from Mrs. Lizzie Ramsey, Bladensburg, Ohio.

Majolica sugar bowl and creamer, and $20 cash, from Mrs. R.B. Wells, Mantorville, Minn.

Decorated china tea-set, from Rev. and Mrs. Henry Willard, Mantorville, Minn.

One dozen china breakfast

OBITS

Fallen Asleep — Fannie E., aged thirteen, only daughter of Mr. and Mrs. Allan Mollison of this city, died of Spinal Meningitis, Monday morning, after an illness of three weeks. She was a great sufferer, but was patient and resigned from the beginning. The funeral was at the house at 3 P.M. yesterday, Rev. Lathrop conducting the service. Teachers, schoolmates and family friends all united their tears and sympathy with the sorrowing and deeply afflicted family. Fannie was a child of rare promise, lovely in disposition, tenderly affectionate, the idol of her parents, and beloved by all who knew her. When the end drew near she realized that death was approaching, bade father, mother and brothers "farewell" and while kissing her mother said, "meet me in Heaven." Precious child, farewell.

Mower County Transcript, Austin, May 31, 1882

→>•<—

Mrs. Ed. H. Wright. Finished her earthly life in this city on Sabbath, April 29th, Lottie, wife of Mr. E.H. Wright. She was born at Greenbush, Wis., Dec. 5th, 1863, and was married to Mr. Wright, Jan. 22d, 1884. About a year ago her health began to fail, and soon it was discovered that she was in the relentless grasp of consumption. But life was sweet to her. In the midst of her relatives; highly respected by all who knew her for her personal worth; popular with her associates, and most tenderly cared for by her husband, it was no easy thing for her to yield, nor did she, until it was clearly seen that the end was only a few hours ahead. Bravely struggling for life, she was taken to California, but not gaining by that, she was brought back to Colorado; here her strong faith in her recovery sustained her for a little time. She would live; she would send for her children; she would have a happy home there. But it was not for her to realize her hope. After a few weeks her husband saw there was but little time left for her, and leaving Colorado on Thursday last, they arrived at home on Saturday, her wonderful courage sustaining her through the journey. Sabbath it was deemed best to tell her that she had but few hours left of life. Quietly and calmly she prepared for the great change, realizing that it was her Saviour who was coming to take her to be with Him forever. We can believe that she was ready to enter into the marriage feast; so that, while the earthly home is broken up, a husband is bereaved and two little ones are motherless, with her all is well.

The funeral took place from the house yesterday afternoon, with appropriate services by the Rev. J.W. Briggs, pastor of the Methodist church. There were many beautiful flowers. The pall bearers were Messrs. J.D. Boyd, C.D. Burgan, C.F. Lamb, C.F. Hoyt, W. Edelbrock, W. Elliot.

St. Cloud Journal-Press, May 3, 1888

"40 of the poorest people in Minneapolis . . . will be invited to the lady's residence Christmas day and feasted to their heart's content."

plates, a pair of silver salt spoons and silver soup ladle, from Misses Emma and Laura Willard, Mantorville, Minn.

One dozen cans fruit and jellies, from Miss Rose Willard, Mantorville, Minn.

Silver pie knife, from Master Edward Willard, Mantorville, Minn.

Set engraved glass tumblers, from Miss Kate Winne, Mt. Vernon, Ohio.

Toilet set [vessels used with a washstand] of darned net over pale blue, from Miss Kittie Benedict, Mt. Vernon, Ohio.

Celery glass, from Mrs. H. Benedict, Mt. Vernon, Ohio.

Linen tidy, embroidered in Kate Greenaway figures, and white satin fan sachet with painted spray and motto, from Miss Mary DeVoe, Mt. Vernon, Ohio.

Silver butter knife and sugar spoon, from Mr. and Mrs. Wm. G. Linsted, Mt. Vernon, Ohio.

Comfort, and pair silver gold-lined goblets, from Mr. and Mrs. T.W. Linsted, Mt. Vernon, Ohio.

Silver sugar spoon, from Mr. and Mrs. C.W. Jelliffe, Mt. Vernon, Ohio.

Damask towels and set of Majolica butter dishes, from Mrs. S.A. Warner, Carthage, Missouri.

Perfume case with cut glass bottles, from Mr. and Mrs. A.L. Davison, Madison, Wis.

Black wrap trimmed with plush, from Mr. J.B. Wells, Utica, N.Y.

Solid silver napkin rings, from Mr. and Mrs. Philo Chamberlin, Chicago, Ill.

Silver mounted Japanese pepper and salt, from Mrs. Laura B. Ellsworth, Wentworth, N.H.

Books, from Mr. N.P. Willard, Benzonia, Mich.

Lace, from Mrs. M.M. Watson, Bradford, Mass.

Two silver gold-lined ice cream spoons, in satin-lined case, from Mrs. Judge Willard, Troy, N.Y.

Two pair silk stockings, from Miss Lizzie Davis, Mt. Vernon, Ohio.

The Times extends its congratulations.

St. Charles Times, Nov. 17, 1882

—>-<—

A gentleman last night complained to Mr. John T. Lee, agent of the Humane society, that he had seen a street car horse inhumanely treated upon the suspension bridge during the snow storm by being forced to haul a car that was too heavily laden for a single horse. Mr. Lee thereupon made a personal inspection of the manner in which the cars on several lines were being run, and upon the strength of what he saw notified the secretary of the car companies . . . that they must remedy the defects and suggested that two horses be hitched to every car or that an extra horse be stationed to help up the grades. It was promised that the defect would be remedied on the return

of the president or superintendent.

Minneapolis Tribune, Dec. 17, 1882

—>-<—

A lady of this city who wishes her name to remain unpublished, has instructed Mr. Williams, superintendent of the poor, to select 40 of the poorest people in Minneapolis who will be invited to the lady's residence Christmas day and feasted to their heart's content. Tickets have already been furnished to the superintendent, and the work of distributing them commences today.

Minneapolis Tribune, Dec. 19, 1882

—>-<—

The body of a man who died of smallpox in Nininger, Dakota county, several days ago, has not yet been buried. The officers have offered $10 for a team to take the body to the grave.

Minneapolis Tribune, Feb. 9, 1883

—>-<—

"People then thought if they had a white house with green blinds they were just about right."

The Dreaded Smallpox.

Mr. John Casey, of this city [St. Paul] arrived yesterday from one of the smallpox infected lumber camps in the northern section of the state. . . . He stated that he left Duluth on the 6th of December with a force of 80 men employed by J.H. Caldwell of that city. They located 100 miles from Grand Rapids, and 15 from Big Fork river. Shortly after their arrival John Carney was attacked with smallpox at a place called Trout Lake ranch, and died. Mr. Murdy next took the disease, and others rapidly followed, until nearly half the number in the camp were down with it. Eleven Indians, including squaws and papooses, died, and within 14 days after Carney was attacked . . . [more] . . . white men demised.

Mr. Van Cleve of Duluth arrived at the death-stricken camp and did what he could with a limited supply of medicine to aid the helpless sick and prevent the spread of the disease, but he was soon forced to abandon the camp and went to Aitkin, where a quarantine was established. Mr. Casey says Mr. Caldwell acted inhumanely toward the men, who were compelled to leave the camp along with himself (Casey), in not paying them for labor they had performed.

Minneapolis Tribune, Feb. 21, 1883

⇥·⇤

The styles of Easter cards were never so numerous as this spring, and never of such beautiful, delicate and exquisite workmanship. They vary in price, all the way from twenty-five cents up to $5 and $10.

St. Paul Globe, March 13, 1883

⇥·⇤

House Painting. "What are the popular colors now?" was asked of an intelligent house painter. "It would be very hard to say,"

Leland, 10—, 3 years old.

BROOKVILLE FARM.
Percheron Horses, Shorthorn Cattle, and Berkshire Hogs.

GOLD MEDAL STUD OF CENTRAL MINNESOTA.

Awarded One Gold Medal, Eight First Premiums, and Two Second Premiums. Have now on hand ten imported and native Pure bred Stallions—six of serviceable age. Among them are two direct sons, two grandsons, and one great grandson, of M. W. Dunham's noted "Brilliant," which is considered the king of Draft Horses—both in this country and in Europe. Our heavyweight Stallon, Sansonnet, 6991 | 8811 | took the sweepstakes, gold medal, for five best colts, over every competing stallion in the county. One of his colts, foaled last April, today (Dec. 18) tips the beam at 1015 pounds. We also have a herd of about forty pure bred and grade mares, besides a number of young colts. Those intending to purchase or breed will find it to their advantage to inspect our stock before investing elsewhere. We started with the best stock that money could buy, bred our own, and therefore can sell cheaper than those who import. Young, fresh horses our specialty. We have a few short horn calves for sale. Visitors always welcome. Correspondence invited.

LUNDQUIST & PETERSON BROS.
GROVE CITY,   **MINNESOTA.**

Litchfield Saturday Review, Dec. 21, 1889

was the reply, "for we are obliged to use every conceivable shade and tint. There was a time when white paint was all the demand, as people then thought if they had a white house with green blinds they were just about right; now very few white houses are wanted, for in our severe climate they are cold looking affairs in winter, and dust and heat render them undesirable for summer. However, white houses there still are and always will be. Some have their houses painted in delicate green or cream tints, and the cornice, ornaments and sash touched up with vermillion; this is very pretty and effective. Pink is by no means a bad looking color for the whole house. Others wish for all colors of the rainbow. . . . But we notice, as a rule, people of the most substantial tastes call for some fine dark shade as the predominant color,

"What a good thing Sunday is!"

while the ornaments are finished in white, ecru, or a rich, deep wine color. Some never know what they want till they see the house complete, and then it is all wrong, and we have to go over it again. Why, sir, we painted the same house, last summer, five times, before the whimsical owner was satisfied."
Minneapolis Tribune, March 18, 1883

→►•◄←

"Dude" is the new word given to American youth who puff the cigarette.
Stillwater Gazette, April 4, 1883

→►•◄←

Yesterday evening, while passing Mr. O'Brien's hardware store, a little girl dropped a ten-cent piece, which rolled through a hole in the sidewalk. The child was in deep trouble, which Mr. O'Brien removed by handing her another ten cent piece, saying, "We'll find it to-morrow." He is not a bad man who enjoys a kindly feeling for the little ones, therefore we allude to this circumstance of yesterday which came under our own observation.
Preston National Republican, May 16, 1883

→►•◄←

Record of Crime. Rose Creek is very much excited over a case of incest that has just been discovered. Frank Miner is the criminal, and the object of his lustful passions is his own bright daughter of ten years of age. Mrs. Miner, the child's step-mother, overheard the protests of the girl and when directly accused of the crime, the inhuman father confessed it. The girl testifies that this has been going on all summer. Miner has quietly skipped the country, and will not probably dare to show himself in this vicinity again.
Ashby Avalanche, Grant County, Sept. 3, 1883

→►•◄←

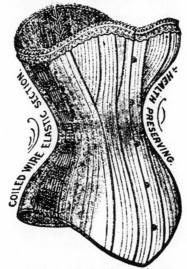
Why Sunday is a "Good Thing." You sleep late on Sunday morning, after the toils of the week; and that is perhaps right. You rise to a day of leisure and enjoyment; and it is proper enough to make Sunday a day of enjoyment. You go to the house of God; and it is very charming to hear the music. You are intellectually fed; and there is great plea-

sure in that. If the discourse is highly adorned, on taking your leisurely walk home, you say: "It was very well put. It was rather an ingenious argument. I do not know as I ever heard those ideas expressed just in that way before. The peroration [recapitulation] was eloquent. We have a minister now that is worth listening to. I enjoy myself in church very much." You sleep through the night, and rise Monday morning feeling, "What a good thing Sunday is!" But you plunge into the world; and there is the same selfishness in it that there was before. "Men are good, bad, and indifferent," you say; "I must attend to myself; I must protect myself against this one; I must overbear that one if he stands in my way." So you go tearing here, hitting there, smiting in every direction, rushing one way and another like a civilized lion among children, leaving destruction behind you, with or without provocation as the case may be."
Douglas County News, Alexandria, Sept. 13, 1883, quoting the Rev. Henry Ward Beecher

→►•◄←

Women's Work Enlarged. When a woman can drive [a team of horses] well, her sphere of usefulness may be very much enlarged. In the country she can do a thousand errands and a large amount of business which otherwise men would have to do. The wife of a farmer of my acquaintance does all of the work which would take him upon the road, except marketing, and she does a considerable amount of this as the marketing consists in simply delivering things at the railroad station. They are prepared for shipment at home and loaded by the men and unloaded by the same sort of help at the depot. Some one may say, "How can a woman do her husband's riding around and her own work at the

"Hang your walls with pictures, scenes from the good old fairy stories that go down from generation to generation."

same time?" Here the ledger may be balanced. The time of the man is worth twice as much as the woman's, on the basis of wages, and more too in this case, as the man is taken away from home and the oversight of the farm and other men. After this column is footed, then add up the benefit of the wife and daughter in getting a change of fresh air, and growing up to be able to help herself instead of being the helpless thing a woman too often is. Give the wife and daughter this change and a chance, and hire some one to take the kitchen. This is good sense.

Glenwood Messenger, Sept. 14, 1883, reprinted from the Rural New Yorker

->-<-

Mr. Wm. Nelson, living a mile south of town, brought in the head and skin of a prairie wolf on Monday and received a bounty of three dollars. He used cold poison in capturing the animal. Another wolf that is prowling about will be served in the same way.

Douglas County News, Alexandria, Sept. 27, 1883

->-<-

How to Amuse Your Children.
You cannot over-estimate the importance of surroundings upon the physical and mental condition of your children. So I urge you to choose for them a large sunny room, well lighted, and in winter well warmed; here collect the treasures that delight children; and hang your walls with pictures, scenes from the good old fairy stories that go down from generation to generation. Try to get games that mean something; animals to take to pieces and put together again, horses to be harnessed into carts, etc. Have it laid down as a nursery axiom that broken things do not mend themselves, and that willful destruction of property is followed by going without. In this way you can check restlessness. . . .

Make your children pick up their toys, and wait on themselves when possible; and absolutely forbid their making their nurse a slave. In this way they will learn to be self helpful and self-reliant.

Win your children's confidence by proving yourself a sympathizer in every joy and sorrow. So few of us older ones realize how all-absorbing the affairs of the present are to our little ones, and how easily the tender feelings are wounded, by even the implied suggestion that you don't care.

Lake City Graphic, Sept. 25, 1883

->-<-

A new discovery has been made. Gas can be made from sawdust.

Stillwater Gazette, Oct. 17, 1883

->-<-

When you give the facts of any case to a newspaper reporter, don't exaggerate a particle. The newspaper man, with the chief facts in his possession, knows how much coloring and how much light and shade is necessary for his readers and he can put on all the nice, delicate touches that are needed. It is very wrong for a citizen to lie to a reporter, for the conscientious newspaperman never means to misinform or mislead his readers. True, there are shysters in the profession who besides being shysters, are unfit for any branch of the profession, and such as these will be enough themselves without any outside aid. But even to these the citizens should always be truthful.

Ashby Avalanche, Dec. 14, 1883

->-<-

Princeton.
Special Correspondence.
Twenty-seven degrees below zero Wednesday morning last.

Manney Cowls, who has been quite ill for the past few weeks, is getting no better.

A.G. Plummer had the misfor-

FREAKS OF NATURE

A freak of nature is on exhibition at the residence of J.W. Wheeler [of Stillwater] in the shape of a young calf without a speck of hair. The skin is as heavy as that of a rhinoceros.
Minneapolis Tribune, March 27, 1884

->-<-

Considerable of a Pig. Albert Lea — P. Creigan, of Newry township, in this county, has a spring pig that has six feet, four in front and two behind, and walks on five of them.
Minneapolis Tribune, Nov. 11, 1885

->-<-

A child was born to Mrs.

Reese [of Rochester] Monday night that had no head. The face was attached to the neck and looked straight up. It was dead when born, and was of unusual size.
Minneapolis Tribune, March 24, 1882

"Santa Claus, in this neighborhood, was but poorly provided with presents, owing, we suppose, to the non-credit system lately adopted by our dealers."

---

tune to freeze his face and hand one day last week.

About eight inches more of snow fell on Saturday last, making now good sleighing.

Our village school will commence about January 20, with Mr. Ewing as principal; Misses Delaney and Pratt will officiate in the lower departments.

Santa Claus, in this neighborhood, was but poorly provided with presents, owing, we suppose, to the non-credit system lately adopted by our dealers.

The masonic lodge, of Princeton, gave a grand dress party after the installation of their officers, Tuesday evening. Sidewells Bana furnished the music.

Notwithstanding the great cry of "no lumbering this winter," a large number of camps are being put up in the woods, and men are being hired at starvation prices: $12 and $15 per month.

Pine County Record, Pine City, Dec. 29, 1883

→✦←

Oatmeal Drink, For Summer or Winter. The proportions are one-fourth pound of oatmeal to two or three quarts of water, according to the heat of the day and the work and thirst. It should be well boiled, and then an ounce or an ounce and a half of brown sugar added. If you find it thicker than you like, add three quarts of water. Before drinking it, shake up the oatmeal well through the liquid. In summer, drink this cold; in winter, hot. You will find it not only quenches thirst, but will give you more strength and endurance than any other drink. If you cannot boil it, you can take a little oatmeal mixed with cold water and sugar; but this is not so good; always boil it, if you can. If at any time you have to make a very long day, as in harvest, and cannot stop for meals, increase the oatmeal to half a pound, or even

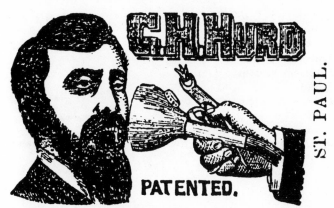

C.H. HURD

ST. PAUL.

PATENTED.

24 East Third street.

Largest and most thoroughly equipped dental establishment west of New York. We extract from 1 to 30 teeth in three minutes without pain or danger. We do the best dental work at lowest prices, and extract and make more teeth than all of the dentists in the city combined. "OPEN EVENINGS." Dr. Hurd **24 E. Third st., near Wabasha.**

Western Appeal, Nov. 5, 1887

three-fourths of a pound, and the water to three quarts, if you are likely to be very thirsty. If you cannot get oatmeal, wheat flour will do, but not quite so well. Cold tea and skim-milk are also found to be good, but not equal to the oatmeal drink.

Pine County Record, Pine City, Jan. 26, 1884, quoting Popular Science News

→✦←

Anoka barber shops close on Sunday, and as a consequence, last Sunday, about one hundred of her citizens chartered a special train and went to St. Cloud to get shaved.

Minneapolis Tribune, Feb. 16, 1884

→✦←

The report on our [Rochester] streets Monday that several of our citizens had been poisoned by eating pressed corn beef purchased at Rommel's market, caused quite a commotion. It seems that in cooking their beef, the Messrs. Rommel put in a double dose of saltpetre; they also put a tight cover on the kettle, which left no chance for the gas to escape, and after the meat had been put into bags it fermented. There were as near as we can learn twenty-seven persons poisoned by eating the meat, but they all recovered in a few hours. The patients were first taken with a severe pain in the stomach, and terrible vomiting and purging ensued. As soon as Messrs. Rommel learned the cause of the sickness,

"As soon as Messrs. Rommel learned the cause of the sickness, they had the meat examined by Dr. Mayo."

they had the meat examined by Dr. Mayo, who reported substantially as stated above, after which the meat was thrown away. No one regrets this occurrence more than Rommel Bros., who usually have one of the neatest markets in the city.

Freeborn County Standard, Albert Lea, Aug. 13, 1884, reprinted from the Rochester Post

-> - <-

THE REPUBLICAN

Chicago & North-Western Railway.

Passenger Trains leave La Crosse for Chicago and the East at 5.59 p. m.

W. S. CASE, Agent.

CHICAGO, MILWAUKEE & ST. PAUL R'Y.

SOUTHERN MINN. DIVISION.

TIME TABLE.

TRAINS GOING WEST.		TRAINS GOING EAST.	
Will Leave		**Will Leave**	
La Crosse ...	8.05 a. m.	Flandreau....	3 10 p m
Lanesboro...	10.28 a. m.	Jackson.....	7.20 p. m.
Isinours.....	10.45 a. m.	Albert Lea..	11.52 p. m.
Fountain....	11.05 a. m	Ramsey.....	12.45 p. m.
Ramsey.....	11.00 a. m.	Fountain....	3.00 p. m.
Albert Lea.	2.30 p. m.	Isinours.....	3.15 p. m.
Jackson.......	7.10 p. m.	Lanesboro...	3.30 p. m.
Arrive at		**Arrive at**	
Flandreau....	11 :25 m.	La Crosse....	6.00 p. m.

F. D. UNDERWOOD, Superintendent.

CALEDONIA, MISSISSIPPI & WESTERN R. R.

TIME TABLE NO. 5.

Took Effect January 18, 1880, at 4 o'clock a. m.

Trains Moving East.		Trains Moving West.	
- Will Leave -		**- Will Leave -**	
Preston	6 25 a m	Caledonia Jun.	4 45 p m
Harmony.....	7 10 a m	Caledonia......	5 30 p m
Canton.......	7 50 a m	Spring Grove..	6 10 p m
Mabel.........	8 10 a m	Newhouse.....	6 30 p m
Newhouse....	8 25 a m	Monroe........	6 45 p m
Spring Grove.	8 45 a m	Canton	6 45 p m
Caledonia....	9 25 a m	Harmony......	7 45 p m
Arrive at		**Arrive at**	
Caledonia Jun.	1010 a m	Preston........	8 25 p m

Passenger Trains make close connections with C. C. D. & M Passenger Trains both North and South

E. P LYMAN,   J. H. JENKINS,
Assistant Supt.   General Supt.

Rochester Record and Union, March 9, 1882

1880s

–>•<–

Minneapolis Working Girls

---

*By the late 1880s, large numbers of Minnesota women were
employed in factories and stores. Many were poorly paid and
suffered from bad working conditions. Eva McDonald was 21 years
old when the St. Paul Globe hired her as an investigative reporter.
Under the pen name of Eva Gay, she wrote a series of 15 articles
about the home life and shop life of the working women of
Minneapolis. She was hired in several factories by employers who
had no idea she was a writer: "I wore old clothes . . . and I had my
hair cut very short like a boy. . . . No employer ever discovered me
. . . because they were looking for a tall, grimly efficient spinster."
Here is her first report.*

Working girls and their lives.

How little the outside world knows of them.

And yet there are thousands in the city of Minneapolis.

On her lecture to the socialists at Turner hall last year, Mrs. Marx-Aveling took occasion to refer to the working girls of Minneapolis and to denounce in the roundest terms the hard work and small wages they received. It is an interesting and a vital subject, but it is a difficult one to handle. The Commissioner of labor, John Lamb, can tell at what pains and trouble he obtained the statistics required by the duties of his office. Many of the shops and factories are guarded for the one purpose of preventing the outflow of information, while the foremen are made spies as well as taskmasters. Fear of discharge prevents the girls themselves from giving any information, which, alas! for it, there have been cases where very shame for it has prevented these girls from describing the meager pittance they earn. This I know by actual word of mouth, and I propose to carry Globe readers with me through a series of articles and show the life, home life and shop life of the working girls and women of Minneapolis.

Every morning the street cars and thoroughfares of the city are thronged with busy crowds of breadwinners. Even a careless observer will note that a large proportion of the crowd are women. Some of them comfortably dressed, showing in their faces no signs of hardship; others hurrying along, their scanty dress, stooping shoulders and pale faces showing that for them the struggle for a living is a hard fight.

Going to town in a car the other morning, and hearing several girls who sewed in factories talking about their work, I concluded to visit these factories, and find out by observation the condition of this class of wage earners.

There are three factories in Minneapolis where pants, overalls, jumpers, shirts, and other articles of working men's cheap clothing are made. These factories, making goods for the wholesale dry goods houses, with which they are connected, do an immense business, and in them many women are employed.

Sewing machines, run by electricity or steam, are used. They are fastened in a double row on either side of tables running the length of the room. Before each machine sits a girl, who receives her work from the cutter's hands, and it goes from her machine ready for sale at a remarkably low price. A row of lamps, directly over the machines, furnishes a good light when daylight is insufficient.

Mounting a single flight of stairs, on my first visit, I found myself in a large and crowded workshop. The brick walls and bare rafters overhead giving a decidedly picturesque, but very dirty aspect.

"Others resting their aching heads on the tables, trying to catch a short nap in the midst of the confusion."

It was just noon, in that room and in a similar one on the floor above, were gathered about 200 girls, some groups busy with their noonday lunch, others discussing in merry tones various plans for evening amusement, a few reading stories papers and novels. . . . Others resting their aching heads on the tables, trying to catch a short nap in the midst of the confusion. All were so busy that I did not venture many questions. I found they worked an average of ten hours a day, work being performed by the piece [they were paid solely on the basis of how many items they produced]. Sometimes they only worked for a few hours of the day, as the work was not ready for the machines. Wages did not seem a pleasant topic, questions in that direction being met by a shrug of the shoulders and a remark to the effect that wages had been cut so much during the past year that only experienced hands could make living wages. In a shop which I visited later, I obtained the exact rate of wages, and there seemed to be but little difference in the scale of prices for the three factories.

My next visit was to a small factory, located in an old store building 20 x 40. There seemed to be absolutely no ventilation. About twenty girls were employed, whose situation did not differ materially from those just mentioned.

Taking, not the passenger elevator, but a tough, iron-railed one, such as is used in handling merchandise, I was next landed at the top story of a large block. This workshop was neatly finished and painted. Here I found about 225 women of all ages working so busily that they hardly lift their eyes to notice a visitor.

Standing near the elevator door listening to and watching the busy scene before me, I found myself breathing an atmosphere whose distinguishing characteristics were a smell of new cloth, dust, heat and sewer gas. It was stifling. There was a row of large windows along two sides of the room. Noticing several girls with bandaged heads and complaining of headache, I asked why they didn't open the windows and get some fresh air? One said: "We can't stand it to have open the windows in this weather, we get such colds and rheumatiz from the draught."

"Where does the sewer gas come from?" I asked, as an extra strong whiff made me feel faint. The girl pointed to a row of closets [water closets; bathrooms] a little farther down on one side of the room. I walked down and saw that they were ventilated by transoms over the doors opening into the work room.

"How do you work in such bad air?" I asked of a stout German girl near by.

"Oh, we get used to it after a while; 'tisn't very

bad now," she said, "but most every day the water isn't running in the closets for an hour or so at a time, but of course they are used just the same. The smell is awful then; some of the girls get sick almost every day, and have to get a pass from the foreman and go out of the shop."

"Can't you go out without a pass?"

"No, we can't."

"Why?"

"Don't know. What do you want to know for anyhow?" she added with a quick glance from under her brows.

Walking on a little farther I saw a pleasant looking girl working for dear life at a pile of calico shirts.

"How many shirts can you make in a day?" I asked.

"About twelve."

"You do all the sewing?"

"Yes. We get them cut and do all the sewing except the buttons and buttonholes."

"How much are you paid for each shirt?"

"Three and a half cents each."

"Three and a half cents!" I repeated. "Is that possible?"

COOPER, JACKSON & COMPANY'S
NEW GIGANTIC SHOW!!
WILL EXHIBIT AT
Preston, Friday, July 28th!

MATES, BUFFALO

ONE HUNDRED STRONG.

NEW, NOVEL, NOTABLE!

WHICH COMBINES IN ITS ORGANIZATION
A Great Moral Circus and Menagerie!

Introducing the Stars of all Nations! New, Novel, Notable! And a refreshing radical reform. In fact an entirely new departure in Arenic Amusements. The Company 100 Strong, is unequaled in number and excels in ability that of any organization now before the public!

The Bravest Woman that Breathes! The Beautiful, Danger-Defying ZAZEL, of London Royal Aquarium

SOMETHING FOR NOTHING

At 10 o'clock a. m. will occur a Grand Demonstration making the Entree of

Cooper, Jackson & Co.'s New Gigantic Railroad Show.

WOMBELL'S ENGLISH MENAGERIE,

And Orsini's Oriental Circus and Hippodrome.

Martial Bands of Music fill the Air.

JUBILEE - SINGERS - AND
CAMP MEETING SHOUTERS.

Equally unique is the cry of the peculiar instruments manipulated by the BAND of SCOTTISH BAGPIPERS Outside and gold Mounted Tableau Cars and elaborate Chariots of rich design lend variety to a Pageant. A LONG LIST OF DENS and CAGES containing the Wonders of the Zoological Kingdom, BOLIVAR, the Mighty War Elephant!

The Largest Elephant on Exhibition.
Borne High Aloft in the midst of the procession, rides QUEEN OF BEAUTY the $10,000 PREMIUM LADY Miss Ida V. Reed, Pronounced the loveliest Lady in the land.

Rochester Record and Union, July 20, 1882

"I wondered how girls that earned $1.50 a week made ends meet."

"Yes. When the work is finished, three bosses overlook it. If the shirts are not well made, we rip them and sew them over again."

"Then you earn about 40 cents a day, or $2.40 a week," I queried.

"I earned only $1.75 last week."

"But you are a new hand, I suppose?"

"I suppose. I've worked here only two years and a half," she said quickly, "and you'll find some of the new hands can only earn 10 cents a day."

Thinking her story rather highly colored, I passed down the shop chatting to the girls here and there, but her story seemed to be true.

"Why," said one, "I can only make twelve pairs of overalls, by hard work, at 7 cents each; we used to get 12 cents and thought it bad enough, but we're glad to take 'em for 7 cents now."

At another table jean pants were finished complete at 8 and 10 cents per pair. The girls here were not talkative, so I sauntered along to the farther end of the room.

A girl working on Mackinaw-lined duck coats told me she could finish four at 33 cents each, a day. She had been sewing for four years.

"How much do you earn a week?"

"About $7 or $8."

"Then you earn pretty fair wages?"

"Yes, but our foreman says we girls wear too many feathers and fine clothes and threatens he'll cut our wages, so we'll be glad to wear plain clothes by next spring."

"Yes, and when he meets one of the girls on the street who is well dressed he'll ask her where she got her fine feathers and dress, and tell her she didn't buy them out of the wages she earns here."

"He says we act as if we thought ourselves ladies."

"I hear he gets 20 per cent of every cut in wages he forces on us," chipped in various voices.

"If your foreman insults you, why don't you complain to the proprietors?"

"What's the use? If we don't want to put up with the way we're treated, we are told we can leave. They can find plenty, glad to get a chance to work for any wages."

The scale of wages in the other shops were about the same as in this.

Many of the employes were married women, who had a home to help keep, or young girls, who lived at home, having no board to pay and regarding what they earned in the shop as merely a help towards their support.

A general inquiry showed that the majority of the girls had to support themselves, paying from $2 to $3 a week for board and lodging, having of course to make what was left after that do for dress

Lake Park Hotel, Lake Minnetonka, Minn.
Minneapolis Tribune, Sept. 3, 1880

and other expenses.

Speaking of dress, one girl said that if the firm would sell the employes calico and sheeting by the bolt at wholesale prices, it would help out. They refused this to the girls, although I, an outsider, could have obtained a bolt of calico at a reduction if I wished.

One girl, who could barely manage to earn $4 a week by hard labor, told me she had a widowed mother and small brother depending on her for support. I wondered how girls that earned $1.50 a week made ends meet.

Many girls refused to say anything, saying that talking and singing were forbidden in working hours. If such was the case, the rule was not always honored.

Despite the complaints of hard work, low wages, etc., they were a lively, intelligent lot of girls. They seemed determined to make the best of their lot and have a good time anyhow.

St. Paul Globe, Minneapolis edition, March 25, 1888

[For a biography of journalist Eva McDonald and other interesting characters, see "Women of Minnesota," edited by Barbara Stubler and Gretchen Kreuter, published in 1977 by the Minnesota Historical Society Press.]

"I never saw such reckless driving in any part of the world as in Minneapolis."

All Hallow Eve last night was appropriately observed in a number of circles. Numerous parties were held about the city, at which the practices and games peculiar to the time were carried out. The mischievous boy was also heard with no small sound, he taking advantage of the latitude granted by Halloween to gather about him a band of congenial companions and commit sundry petty pranks and depredations. Gates and signs were unhung and carried to near and distant points, as fancy prompted; door bells rung from far away points by long strings, and divers other freaks perpetrated on unsuspecting adults.
Minneapolis Tribune, Nov. 1, 1884

—>•<—

Miss Nellie Martell entertained her friends last Friday evening. Cards and various games were indulged in by the merry guests until constrained to desist by the appearance of fragrant coffee and tempting refreshments. This deviation was followed by an animated game with "bean bags," in which the ladies fully sustained their reputations as good marksmen; the gentlemen made marvelous scores. Not until a late hour was the young hostess wished good night.
Rush City Post, Feb. 6, 1885

—>•<—

An Association known as the Anti-Deists has just been established in Paris. Its object is to suppress the word God, or its equivalent, in all the languages of the world, on the ground that the Being so designated is a mere fiction and the word, therefore, is senseless and irrational. They are not any more likely to succeed than are the well-intentioned but impracticable people who go to the other extreme and insist that the word God shall have legal recognition by its insertion in the

Constitution and laws under the impression that this merely formal recognition would cure a multitude of evils.
Rush City Post, March 6, 1885

—>•<—

Careless Driving. To the Editor of the Tribune. A newspaper man from the east, who does not wish to be conspicuous, begs you will warn people here against fast driving. I saw a lady with a little boy at her side very near being killed yesterday. I never saw such reckless driving in any part of the world as in Minneapolis.
Minneapolis Tribune, May 31, 1885

—>•<—

Astronomers say that the planet Neptune is so far from the earth that if Adam and Eve had from the first day of their existence started on a railroad train and traveled steadily, day and night, at the rate of thirty miles an hour, toward Neptune, they would by this time have traversed only a little more than half the distance to the vaporous orb. The human race is, therefore, to be congratulated, upon the fact that Adam and Eve did not undertake any such foolish trip.
Rush City Post, July 17, 1885

"The well-dressed woman . . . knows not only what to wear, but when to wear it."

—∘—

The white flag with a black square center, raised over Mr. C.T. Leonard's store yesterday afternoon, signifies a cold wave. Hereafter Mr. Leonard will re-

FASHION

Demands of Dress. Perhaps even more women might rise to positions of distinction in many occupations suitable for them were it not for the tax on their time and strength consequent on the demands of dress and fashion. With many women, dress in all its details and necessities of shopping, fitting, etc., is a business requiring an average of three or four hours daily. Subtract this from the hours of a working day and it involves a great loss of valuable time and strength. A woman thoroughly devoted to any art cannot dress after the regulation style and pattern. If the man desires to step out on the street for any purpose he puts on his coat and goes. If the woman so goes out it involves an outlay of at least fifteen or twenty minutes' time to "fix up." There are exceptions, but this is the rule. Dress and the requirements and encumbrances of fashion prove a constant draught, impediment and encumbrance on a woman's time and strength — the young and pretty women being here referred to. In this age of competition, success in any occupation must be gained at the cost of constant, unintermitting attention and perseverance. The working editor, merchant, lawyer or artist cannot go with gloved hands, and he often gains time at the expense of a well worn coat in the public thoroughfare. Almost without being aware of the motive, man's garb has, during the last hundred years, more and more adapted itself to the practiced needs of business. Even the dandy of to-day copies the general style of the worker. How much business of any description would a man now accomplish if clad in the ribbons, frills and ruffles of the Court popinjays [people who chatter, wear bright colors and otherwise resemble the parrots named popinjays] of Charles the Second's time? Yet, relative to her own peculiar fashion, the woman retains all the encumbrances of that era.
Saturday Evening Spectator, Minneapolis, Aug. 19, 1882

—∘—

The Rise of the Flannel Shirt. Within the last two years, signs of a movement have been noticed which seems likely to cause a complete revolution in the matter of summer attire for men, and during the present season it has gathered so much strength and volume that its importance cannot with justice be any longer ignored. The introduction of the flannel shirt as a substitute for the rigid-bosomed cotton and linen abomination, which has hitherto been regarded as the test of respectability, has already met with considerable favor, and gained a large measure of that popularity which it assuredly deserves. It is singular that residents in this climate of intense summer heats have not long ago seen that a radical change in their attire was necessary, and, that, as far as all occasions of business or pleasure at this season of the year are concerned, the starched shirt might with good reason be packed away in the same chest which contains the winter overcoat and furs.
Stillwater Gazette, Oct. 10, 1883

—∘—

The Well-Dressed Woman. The well-dressed woman again knows not only what to wear, but when to wear it. In the summer forenoon you will see her in the simplest of cottons, a dress absolutely plain and without ornament, without laces, fringes, decoration of any kind. In the winter at the same time she is equally plainly dressed in cloth. Later in the day she changes to smarter clothes for more ceremonious duties, visits, afternoon parties, and teas — velvets and silks combined in winter, in summer rich gauzes and costly laces. In the evening, for dinner or ball, the most choice and splendid masterpieces of the dress maker's art are reserved; the richest stuff set off with the most elaborate embroideries and the rarest jewels.
Rush City Post, Jan. 23, 1885

"The general complaint is the inability to find work."

Rochester Record and Union, Sept. 14, 1888

ceive regular telegrams from the United States signal service and signals will be displayed to designate the change of weather for each ensuing 24 hours.
Minneapolis Tribune, Dec. 5, 1885

→‑‑←

The superintendent of the poor reports a great many calls for aid, there being over 40 yesterday. The general complaint is the inability to find work. There is also said to be considerable sickness.
Minneapolis Tribune, Jan. 6, 1886

→‑‑←

The tall Lumber Exchange building, on Hennepin and Fifth street, was in a blaze of glory last night. Eight stories were brilliantly lighted with many gas jets, which cast a yellow glare through the curtainless windows, filling the street below with light. Hundreds of people gathered to see the sight.
Minneapolis Tribune, June 6, 1886

→‑‑←

A highflyer on the fifth floor of the West [Hotel] celebrated his birthday, or some other funny event, last evening, by emptying sundry pitchers of water on the heads of passers-by on Hennepin avenue. The pitcher went once too often to the window. He moistened a lawyer, who will swear out a warrant against the offender on Monday morning. Other individuals who were baptized similarly are requested to complain at police headquarters.
Minneapolis Tribune, June 6, 1886

→‑‑←

Card of Thanks. We feel very grateful to all of the citizens of Madelia who sympathized with us when we were visited so suddenly by affliction, and rendered such valuable assistance in taking the remains of our son from the river and helping us afterwards. Such kindness tends to alleviate our sorrow and we hope these friends may ever be blessed.

Mr. and Mrs. N.P. Nelson.
Madelia Times, July 30, 1886

→‑‑←

Residents of Lake Calhoun were much interested yesterday over the baptism of several persons by a party of emigrants going west by wagon. The party halted near the Lurline Boat Club house, went into camp and in the afternoon baptized a young girl, an old woman, and three men in

133

*"We advise our readers who are affected with rheumatism
to give this simple but effective remedy a trial."*

the lake. None of them could speak English. The journey was resumed late in the afternoon.
Minneapolis Tribune, Nov. 10, 1886

—>·<—

A Ten Pin Contest. A rolling match was held last night in the bowling alley, No. 99 Washington Avenue south, between Charles L. Smith, the champion ten pin roller of New York, and a member of the Mutual Club, who is at present employed in building boats for the Lurline Boat Club, and Wm. Schmidt, a local roller of some reputation. Three games were played and were each won by Smith, with the following score: First game, Smith, 268; Schmidt, 224; second game, Smith, 222; Schmidt, 204; and third game, Smith, 217; Schmidt, 208.
Minneapolis Tribune, Dec. 1, 1886

—>·<—

Wenel Polkerbeck, a farmer living north of Hutchinson, upon returning home on Wednesday evening, was thrown from his sleigh by his team running away, and lay in the snow until 10 o'clock Thursday morning. He is alive at the present writing, but is likely to lose both arms and legs. Upon opening his hands by force, his fingers broke off, being so badly frozen.
Minneapolis Tribune, Jan. 9, 1887

—>·<—

For the benefit of a large number who are suffering from rheumatism we publish a cure as related to us by a gentleman who was so ill with this disease that his life was despaired of. He was confined to his bed and so acute was the pain that if a person walked across the room it caused him to cry out in distress. His wife heard that potatoes were good, and as a last resort she put a half-peck in an iron kettle over the stove and let them boil all to

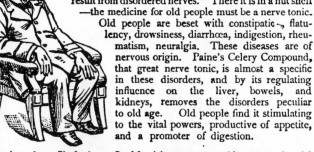
pieces. She then by dint of much labor and extreme pain on the part of her husband, got him up and put his feet to soak in the water, and the pain was relieved as if by magic. Cloths dipped into the hot water were then applied to his knees and other portions affected. His recovery was speedy, and he has not had a severe attack of rheumatism since. We advise our readers who are affected with rheumatism to give this simple but effective remedy a trial. Many have tried it and in every instance it has proved successful.
Madelia Times, Feb. 4, 1887

—>·<—

Married. Almeter-Heber

At the German Catholic church in Belvidere, Tuesday evening, February 1, 1887, at 10 a.m., by the Rev. Father Schmidt, Nick Almeter, of Mazeppa, to Miss Maggie Heber, of Belle Chester.

After the services were over the many friends of the young couple repaired to the home of the bride where a fine dinner was served. The afternoon was devot-

ed to different amusements, smoking and a general good time. At about 4 o'clock they commenced to dance. Some indulged in this amusement, others played cards and some listened to speeches, among which was a deaf and dumb speech by Prof. M. Jungers, which was enjoyed by all who witnessed it. Selling the slipper, waltzing with the bride and all of the old time sports and games were enjoyed. Dancing continued until about 7 o'clock the next morning. Everything was free; no one was allowed to pay for anything; eat, drink, smoke, dance, sing and be merry was the order of the occasion. There were a great many valuable presents given the young couple. All who went claim there was about 200 of the happiest beings present they ever saw. Not a harsh thought or word was indulged in by any one. The bride and groom came down here Wednesday and started at once to keeping house. We join with their many friends in wishing them much joy.
Mazeppa Tribune, Feb. 4, 1887

"With a shrill whistle [the train engineer] started his iron servant at full speed for the drift."

GREAT NORTHWESTERN EXPOSITION!!!

The Grandest Exhibit of the Productions of the Great Northwest ever opened to the Public.
Minneapolis, Sept. 6th, 7th, 8th, 9th, 10th and 11th.

AGRICULTURE, LIVE STOCK, MECHANICS, COMMERCE AND ART!
A Week of Pleasure, Rest and Recreation after the magnificent and golden Harvest of 1880. In addition to the unequaled display in the Departments named,

THE GREAT RACING MEETING OF THE YEAR
WILL BE GIVEN BY THE ASSOCIATION.

THE GREATEST EQUESTRIENNE CONTEST OF THE WORLD!
Miss BELLE COOK, of California, and Miss EMMA JEWETT, of Minnesota, in their Great TWENTY MILE RACE for $5,000.
ST. JULIEN, SORREL DAN, DARBY AND HOPEFUL ARE COMING!
Together with such wonderful turf performers as VOLTAIRE, WEDGEWOOD, HANNIS, MONROE CHIEF, HAMBLETONIAN BASHAW, And a Splendid galaxy of lesser turf lights of the year.

Railway Trains from both ST. PAUL and MINNEAPOLIS will run directly to the main entrance of the grounds, offering equal facilities for reaching the Exposition from either city. The crowds in attendance will be accommodated at the usual rates at the hotels and boarding-houses of both St. Paul and Minneapolis, and parties from a distance need have no fears of a lack of accommodations.

Minneapolis Tribune, Aug. 8, 1880

A Nervy Engineer. Engineer W.H. Blake, of engine No. 2, Duluth & Iron Range railroad, is a good engineer, very watchful and careful, and very "gritty' into the bargain. Yesterday on nearing Knife river "cut" he was signalled to stop, and was informed that the cut was bank full of drifted snow. "All right," said Blake, "keep out of my way," and he backed his train about half a mile, and then with a shrill whistle started his iron servant at full speed for the drift. The shackle-jointed rumble of the train gave place to a continuous t-clack! t-clack! and Blake still urged his machine to further efforts, until with a roar not unlike a gigantic sigh it dashed into the mass of

"A well-dressed woman, whose feet were clad in shoes fit only for a ball room, came to grief while crossing Superior street yesterday."

MRS. LYDIA E. PINKHAM, OF LYNN, MASS.,

Woman can Sympathize with Woman.

Health of Woman is the Hope of the Race.

Yours for Health

Lydia E. Pinkham

LYDIA E. PINKHAM'S
VEGETABLE COMPOUND.

Is a Positive Cure

for all those Painful Complaints and Weaknesses so common to our best female population.

It will cure entirely the worst form of Female Complaints, all ovarian troubles, Inflammation and Ulceration, Falling and Displacements, and the consequent Spinal Weakness, and is particularly adapted to the Change of Life.

It will dissolve and expel tumors from the uterus in an early stage of development. The tendency to cancerous humors there is checked very speedily by its use.

It removes faintness, flatulency, destroys all craving for stimulants, and relieves weakness of the stomach. It cures Bloating, Headaches, Nervous Prostration, General Debility, Sleeplessness, Depression and Indigestion.

That feeling of bearing down, causing pain, weight and backache, is always permanently cured by its use.

It will at all times and under all circumstances act in harmony with the laws that govern the female system.

For the cure of Kidney Complaints of either sex this Compound is unsurpassed.

LYDIA E. PINKHAM'S VEGETABLE COMPOUND is prepared at 233 and 235 Western Avenue, Lynn, Mass. Price $1. Six bottles for $5. Sent by mail in the form of pills, also in the form of lozenges, on receipt of price, $1 per box for either. Mrs. Pinkham freely answers all letters of inquiry. Send for pamphlet. Address as above. *Mention this Paper.*

Red River Valley News, June 23, 1881

---

fleecy whiteness before it. A crowd of section men about sixty feet from the track were partially buried in the billowy waves that fell back from the terrific onslaught. The locomotive and train were completely hid from sight, but Blake "opened her up another notch" and emerged from his 300 feet of snow drifts a trifle disfigured but "still in the ring." Upon reaching a clear spot beyond the cut Blake stopped his engine and proceeded to dig himself out of the snow. Upon entering the drift the headlight was smashed by the masses of snow which were hurled against it, and a little further on the front of the engine cab was dashed in and the snow poured in upon the two men, but Blake "never let up" and on emerging from the

drift was buried up to his waist in tightly packed snow, mingled with bits of broken glass. As a result of his management the train reached Two Harbors, nearly on time, when in the hands of less nervy men it would have been "stalled" and some hours of hard digging would have been necessary to release it.

Lake Superior News, Duluth, Feb. 12, 1887

→·←

A Street Incident. A well dressed woman, whose feet were clad in shoes fit only for a ball room, came to grief while crossing [Duluth's] Superior street yesterday. With elevated skirts she went tip-toeing daintily along, progressing finely until near the

middle of the street, where one shoe stuck fast and was pulled off. Before she could stop, the other met the same fate, and the shock caused by the sudden contact with the cold mud made her lose her balance and step clear off the cross walk into the mortar-like mud of unknown depth with which our principal thoroughfare is paved. Here she remained, unable to move until two gallant gentlemen hastened to her rescue, bore the bedraggled madam to a place of safety, and then bravely went back after the shoes. She was mad but no one can blame her for that. She entered a store near by, and when she appeared again her hosiery was of a different color, but the shoes were still covered with yellow mud. Moral No. 1: Wear rubber

"The blueberries are beginning to ripen."

---

boots. Moral No. 2: Pave the streets.
Lake Superior News, Duluth, April 16, 1887

⇥•⇤

The Blueberry Crop. The blueberries are beginning to ripen, and those who engage in handling this crop are making preparations. The picking is done mostly by Indians, but a great many pale-faces also indulge in this pastime. The prospects are that there will be a large crop where the fires have not run, but the drouths have injured them considerably and there will probably not be an over supply. Brainerd is the principal shipping center of this fruit, and thousands of bushels will be handled by our merchants. J.H. Hallett will send out four or five men to different districts, who buy from the pickers and send them to him by teams. He is now manufacturing crates at the rate of 400 per day, and expects to receive about 5000 crates or 2500 bushels during the summer. The fruit is shipped to all points west and south, and finds ready sale in all the towns, as they are a cheap, wholesome berry, and ripen at a time when other fruits are scarce.
Brainerd Daily News, June 16, 1887

⇥•⇤

As to Immigration. . . . The question of immigration to this country is rapidly becoming one of the most serious and difficult with which the nation's lawmakers have to deal. It is daily becoming more apparent that immigration is entirely too free. Foreign countries regard America as the dumping ground for their human refuse, and taking advantage of the unhampered opportunities which the generous laws of this country give them have for years been pouring into the United States people who in their own lands were a burden on the

CAUTION!
Beware of Imitations!
Send For Price List and Sample Cards.

Western Appeal, March 5, 1887

state or who were a constant menace to law and order. Such persons this country does not want, and such persons should be prevented by force, if necessary, from landing on our shores.

In consequence of the reckless freedom with which they have been permitted to establish themselves in this country, the almshouses and other beneficiary institutions of all large cities have been filled to overflowing, the ranks of the working people have been uncomfortably crowded, and the dangerous class of idle, worthless agitators existing in every city has been considera-

bly augmented. While America is glad to offer the opportunity of securing a comfortable home and more satisfactory living to all who come with the intention of becoming good citizens, who have the ability to support themselves and who possess every willingness to conform to American institutions, she does not want those who come to America solely that they may be supported in idleness by the labor of others, nor those who are constantly decrying the government which affords them protection.
New Richland North Star, July 14, 1887

"Asa Leopold, of Duluth, has a 'musical chair.'"

The Churches. Methodist. — Rev. Thomas McCleary will preach, morning and evening, at the Methodist church. Morning subject, "Why Christians are not more in earnest." Evening subject, "Doubt, Scepticism and Infidelity are Utterly Without Excuse."

Swedish Baptist. — Morning service, 10:30 a.m., sermons by the Rev. J. Fogelstrom of Nebraska. Evening service at 8 o'clock p.m., — subject: "Life insurance for time and eternity" — 1 Tim. 5:8, by the pastor, Rev. Bergstrom. Sunday school at this church immediately after morning service. All Scandinavians will be heartily welcomed. Seats free.

Brainerd Daily News, July 31, 1887

—>•<—

It is reported that the band boys have treated themselves to some brand new stiff white hats and will blossom out in a few days in a style that will astonish the natives. No one has a better right or would look more nobly than the members of the Brainerd City band in such regalia, and their friends will all be glad to see them turn out in fine form with tasty summer headgear. The only trouble is that it is a little late in the season, as the chances seem to be that they will not appear in public many times more before cold breezes begin to blow, when white hats will look rather out of place, who knows but what this is just what is nec-

essary to make some large-hearted and liberal-minded citizens start a fund for some open air concerts for the benefit of those who are not so fortunate as to be able to enjoy the orchestra at Lake View. The boys ought to get up a little parade of their own on the strength of this venture and such a demonstration would be highly appreciated by the citizens.

Brainerd Daily News, July 31, 1887

—>•<—

Superstitions About Funerals.
It is bad luck to whistle or hum the air that a band plays at a funeral.

If two persons think and express the same thought at the same time, one of them will die

INVENTIONS

—>•<—

The Great Invention of the Age. Ola Rosendahl of this city has invented a water shoe which enables him to walk on water. This valuable contrivance he desires to introduce for the following purposes:

First — For fishing purposes.

Second — For walking on water.

Third — For a life-preserver.

On Monday at 3 P.M. he will give an exhibition at Lake Harriet, and at 7:30 P.M. at Lake Calhoun.

Minneapolis Tribune, July 3, 1880

—>•<—

An individual with a patent washing machine, warranted to wash anything from a cambric handkerchief to a baby, attracted a crowd on Washington avenue last evening.

Minneapolis Tribune, Aug. 20, 1880

A Valuable Device. Mr. John Lee has invented and patented a new device in the way of door handles, to take the place of knobs. He has put them on all the large doors in the Davidson Block, corner of Fourth and Jackson streets, and they work admirably and are giving entire satisfaction.

St. Paul Globe, March 6, 1881

—>•<—

William Woodside, a prominent lumber dealer of Duluth, has invented a cheap, portable house, which can be put on the [railroad] cars, or loaded on a wagon, and transported to any point desired. This invention will be of incalculable advantage to the treeless prairies. Three houses can be put up and made ready for use in half a day. They are to be manufactured in Duluth in large numbers, and all that can be made

can be readily sold. They are put up without nails, and they are so arranged that two or more can be combined, and make a house of larger dimensions when desired.

St. Paul Globe, March 23, 1882

—>•<—

Asa Leopold, of Duluth, has a "musical chair," only five of which are in the country. When sat in, the weight of the person operates a music box concealed beneath the cushion.

Minneapolis Tribune, Oct. 31, 1884

—>•<—

H.C. Waldecker [of Austin] has sold to Remington, the gun maker, for $1,000, an interest in his recent invention for preventing the gun from going off until the sportsman is ready.

Minneapolis Tribune, May 31, 1885

" 'Do you love me?' asked Nicholas Finnara."

before the year passes.

If two young girls are combing the hair of a third at the same time, it may be taken for granted that the youngest of the three will soon die.

If at the cemetery there be any unusual delay in burying the dead, caused by any unlooked-for circumstances, such as the tomb being too small to hold the coffin, it is a sign that the deceased is selecting a companion from among those present, and one of the mourners must soon die.

New Richland North Star, Aug. 18, 1887

–>-<–

Shot His Wife. St. Paul, Aug. 23.

"Do you love me?" asked Nicholas Finnara of his wandering wife to-night. Mrs. Finnara had just been brought back from Brainerd, to which place she eloped some days ago with John Priest and $250 of her husband's money. Mrs. Finnara admitted that she entertained some such sentiments. "Do you love me as well as you love Priest?" Mrs. Finnara said "No," and was immediately shot under the right eye, the ball coming out under her ear. She will recover. Her husband escaped.

Brainerd Daily News, Aug. 24, 1887

–>-<–

At a meeting of the [school] board yesterday, it was decided to exclude, from school, all children under six years of age. The principal reason for this decision, is the crowded condition of the Primary department. A child of that age should be kept at home, there is ample time for an education after it has reached the age of eight.

New Richland North Star, Feb. 16, 1888

–>-<–

The Celebrated Picture
"The Horse Fair,"

By Rosa Bonheur, 34 inches long by 20 inches wide sent free to every person sending 50 cents for 6 months subscription to the weekly Pioneer Press. Address the Pioneer Press Co., St. Paul.

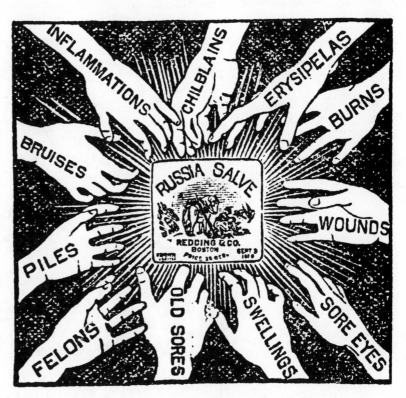

Rochester Record and Union, Jan. 4, 1889

Last Tuesday, W. Kinney was seen on the street all dressed up in a brand spanking new suit of clothes, and as this was something out of the usual routine of his habits, we hastened to learn the cause of this great change, and was informed he had quit the farm and was going back to his profession. He took the train this afternoon for Lake City, where he will open a Law Office, and we know his old friends will give him a hearty welcome back among them. He will be here every Saturday, at the Bank, where he can be counseled and will be glad to see all of his old patrons.

Mazeppa Tribune, May 2, 1888

–>-<–

Busy Bummer Bumming.

This has been a busy week in police courts. Pat Egan paid a second fine of $5 and costs.

D. O'Connell, after promising solemnly for the teenth time not to do so any more, got as full as

THIS NEW AND CORRECT MAP

Proves beyond any reasonable question that the

Chicago & North-Western Railway

Is by all odds the best road for you to take when traveling in either direction between

Chicago and all of the Principal Points in the West, North and Northwest.

Carefully examine this Map. The principal Cities of the West and Northwest are Stations on this road. Its through trains make close connection with the trains of all railroads at junction point.

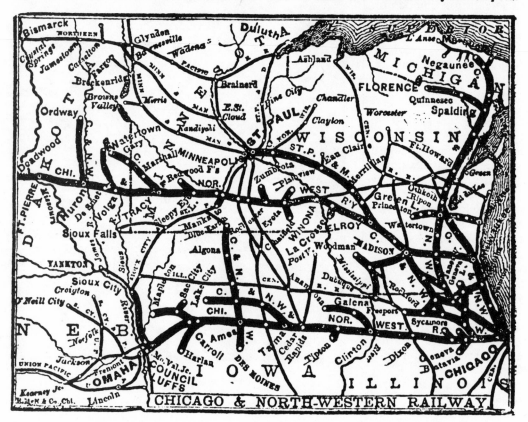

THE CHICAGO & NORTHWESTERN RAILWAY,

Over all of its principal lines, runs each way daily from two to four or more Fast Express Trains. It is the only road West, North or Northwest of Chicago that uses the

IMPERIAL PALACE DINING CARS.

It is the only road that runs Pullman Sleeping Cars North or North or Northwest of Chicago. It has over 3,000 MILES OF ROAD. It forms, amongst othres, the following Trunk Lines : "Council Bluffs, Denver & California Line." "Winona, Minnesota & Central Dakota Line." "Sioux City, Nor. Nebraska & Yankton Line.," "Chicago, St. Paul & Minneapolis Line." "Northern Illinois, Freeport & Dubuque Line." "Milwaukee, Green Bay & Lake Superior Line.'

Tickets over this road are sold by all Coupon Ticket Agents in the United States and Canadas Remember to ask for Tickets via this road, be sure they read it over, and take no other.

J. D. LAYNG, Gen'l Manager, Chicago   W. H. STENNETT, Gen'l Pass. Agt, Chicago.

Rochester Record and Union, May 25, 1882

"The person that isn't satisfied that Caledonia is growing will never be satisfied in heaven."

the moon and disrobing in front of the temple of justice sought a couch on the sidewalk. Judge Evans prescribed thirty days on bread and water.

Thos. Kenny was permitted to go hence.

Wm. Ryan and Jas. McClosky paid $4.50 each for drunks, while Wm. Wood, who should have been wiser, flourished a revolver and paid fifty cents more.

M. Regan, after a fight on Monday with Dan'l O'Brien, which left his face looking like a patch-work quilt, paid Justice Wire $4.50. He then paid $14.50 to secure the release of his friend Egan, and to show his entire approval of such a generous act, filled up again at an expense Tuesday morning of another $4.50.

Dan'l O'Brien for his circus paid $4.50.

Jno. St. Clair and Jno. Carroll, who had interviewed each other's faces with their fists, were fined $4.50 each. Carroll paid up and St. Clair is a boarder.

Two brakemen, Conley and Cloakly, pounded each other very effectually on Sunday, but escaped justice because neither would complain except of his bad luck.

Frank Kelly was peddling clothing at figures which indicated that he had stolen the goods. He was arrested for not having a license. It was suspected that the clothes were from Brainerd and Chief of Police E. Caffrey, of that city, came down, but failed to identify them. Kelly stood his trial yesterday before Judge Wire, Capt. Taylor defending, and was found not guilty.

St. Cloud Journal-Press, Aug. 23, 1888

->-<-

The person that isn't satisfied that Caledonia is growing will never be satisfied in heaven. We have a town that our citizens should be proud of, and that out-

Red River Valley News, Sept. 29, 1885

siders may know the size of our city, we give a list of the manufacturing establishments, dry-goods stores, etc. We have: Ten dry-goods stores, two clothing stores, four restaurants, two jewelry stores, two drug stores, four hardware stores, two tin-shops, three shoe stores, two weekly papers, two job offices, three wagon factories, four blacksmith shops, six hotels, one abstract office, four law offices, one bank, three physicians, one dentist, one opera house, two public halls, two harness shops, two barber shops, two meat markets, two livery stables, one lumber yard, a pop factory and three saloons. Caledonia has a population of about 1,500.

Caledonia Argus, Dec. 8, 1888

->-<-

An Eiffel Tower in Minneapolis. Recently there has been a lot of talk about building an Eiffel Tower in Minneapolis, or rather midway between the twin cities. An architect here in the city has proposed such a project. He has already completed the drafting of

the plans for this "tower of Babel," which is intended to have a height of 2-3,000 feet. Elevators and drive-way enabling the visitors to make use of horse carriages in inspecting it, as well as restaurants and amusement establishments along the road, are included in the elaborate plans. The proponent is convinced that a tower of this kind would attract the majority of the visitors at the Chicago World's Fair to Minneapolis and St. Paul and thus our city would gain world fame. The project and the plans have been completed in detail, but to raise the needed capital will perhaps prove a greater obstacle.

Svenska Amerikanska Posten, a Swedish-language newspaper, Minneapolis, Nov. 5, 1889, translated by the Works Progress Administration

->-<-

"[Minneapolis] can never hope to rival St. Paul in either wealth or greatness."

TWIN CITIES RIVALRY

There is room for only one great city in the Northwest. Past history proves that the city that secures the railroads and the wholesale trade of a section first, is bound to retain them forever. Minneapolis may struggle as hard as she will, but she cannot grasp the trade that has already been secured by St. Paul. The tide in her affairs has already passed; her opportunities have been neglected, and, however unpleasant it may be, however humiliating for her pride, she must be content to take second place. She can, no doubt, become a large city, but she can never hope to rival St. Paul in either wealth or greatness. This is the inevitable, and must be submitted to.

St. Paul Globe, Jan. 7, 1880

–>•<–

The Pioneer Press gets right up and swears that St. Paul has more minors than Minneapolis. Well, why shouldn't she have? The census shows that St. Paul is a minor town, any way.

Minneapolis Tribune, July 22, 1880

–>•<–

It is a well-known fact, and admitted by all truth-loving people in Minneapolis, that there isn't a restaurant in that city where a person can get a decent meal. A lady who recently visited that place . . . was recounting the "hard trials and great tribulations" she and her friends had in procuring dinner. A man who had been listening to her tale of woe spoke up promptly, remarking that, whenever he was in Minneapolis, and felt a yearning for a square meal he always jumped on the train and went down to St. Paul. "Yes," remarked a bystander, "that's about the only way to get a meal in Minneapolis."

Stillwater Gazette, Dec. 27, 1882

–>•<–

The papers down at St. Paul are fond of boasting of the magnitude of the two cities of Minneapolis and St. Paul *as a whole*. It reminds us of the ancient gentleman who bragged of the wealth he and his brother possessed. "Brother and I own 5,000 head of cattle," said he; "I own ten."

Minneapolis Tribune, Jan. 5, 1885

–>•<–

One of Barnum's female "stars," who condescended to express her opinion of Minneapolis said: "Minneapolis is the prettier of the two, and see the differences in our audiences. The St. Paul audience was unusually cold and undemonstrative, while here the audience was warm with applause." Minneapolis is always warm toward the ladies, and when the charming damsels, clad in pink tights and sweet smiles, "sail through the air with the greatest of ease" the temperature of the usually cool and pleasant city reaches a white heat.

Minneapolis Tribune, Sept. 5, 1886

–>•<–

→ HOTEL ST. LOUIS, ←

NORTHOME, ON BAY ST. LOUIS, LAKE MINNETONKA.

Now open for the season of 1889.

Situated on the highest ground on the shores of Lake Minnetonka and commands extensive views of almost the entire lake and surrounding country. The Hotel has spacious Verandas on each floor. Thorough ventilation, perfect drainage and sewerage systems, and is furnished with all modern conveniences. It also has a mineral spring which furnishes an abundant supply of fresh water. The C., M. & St. P. Railway runs frequent fast trains direct to the Hotel.

For Rates, etc., address

WALLACE W. WAIT, Manager,
NORTHOME P. O., MINN.

1890s

St. Paul Dispatch, Sept. 8, 1894

Minneapolis was the biggest lumber market in the world and the world's flour-milling center. However, the financial panic of 1893 checked rapid growth of those industries in Minnesota, as well as railroad expansion and settlement. Forest fires in 1894 wiped out the towns of Hinckley and Sandstone and killed more than 400 people. Immigration swelled, especially from Germany, Sweden, Norway and Denmark. Czechs and Slovaks came to work in the mines.

1890s
–>•<–

Hinckley Forest Fire

"A cyclone of wind and fire," as the Minneapolis Tribune called the forest fire in a banner headline, roared through western Pine County on Sept. 1, 1894, near the end of an extremely dry summer. One of the most devastating fires in history, it spread over parts of five counties in east-central Minnesota and killed about 415 people — nearly half of them in Hinckley, then a town of 1,200. This story from the St. Paul Dispatch was one of the first detailed newspaper accounts, two days later.

PINE CITY, MINN., Sept. 3. — After the deluge what? The reaction has come at Hinckley. The excitement which has buoyed up so many of the survivors, even in the face of the fact that so many friends and relatives had perished in the fiery flood, has passed away, and dull, lethargic grief has taken its place. The uninjured refugees at Pine City, and there are several hundred of them, stand about the street corners in little knots and discuss the incidents of the catastrophe which struck the town. The probable death of this one or this family, and the news of the escape of another, who was at first supposed to have perished, are all discussed with the same benumbed air, expressing neither sorrow and despair in the one case, nor elation or joy in the other. The night was a gloomy one. The hospital patients demanded the attention of the physicians all night, and the only druggist in Pine City was kept busy until daylight filling prescriptions and supplying lotions, for most of the injuries were burns, more or less serious. By morning all were in a state of comparative comfort, and there were none whose hurts were deemed fatal.

Pine City Samaritans.

Among the good citizens of Pine City who had opened their hearts, their homes and their public buildings to their stricken neighbors, all was bustle and activity. The town hall was kept open all night, and coffee and plain fare served to all comers. The court house, the school house and many a private home was thrown open. Every blanket in town was called into service. The women and children were given the better quarters, and the men stretched out in rows on the floors of the two public buildings named. Before daylight the town was astir. The arrangements for the relief of the destitute further up the line, where hundreds of men, women and children are not only homeless, but absolutely without a scrap of food or bedding or extra clothing, were taken up where they were dropped at midnight. The appointed committees met and got their work well in hand. Before 7 o'clock in the morning the construction train, loaded with bridge material for the repair of the bridge across the Grindstone river at Hinckley, came up from Rush City.

Supplies for the Suffering.

A couple of hundred loaves of bread and other light provisions were placed on board in charge of Judge J.C. Nethaway, of Stillwater, representing the relief committee. A party of laborers to dig graves and inter the bodies was collected, and the train proceeded into the burned country. At Hinckley the provisions were loaded on to a handcar manned by Judge Nethaway and a volunteer crew, and a start was made across the shaky bridge to Miller, nine miles further north, where are reported a dozen or more dead and three or four times as many hungry and homeless. From Miller they expect to work east to Sandstone, about five miles across the

"In an indiscriminate heap lay more than ninety corpses, men, women and little children."

country on the Eastern Minnesota railroad, where there are between forty and fifty dead and a couple of hundred living who were saved in the Kettle river and in the great sandstone quarries. About 11 o'clock the bridge was sufficiently repaired to admit the passage of a train, and an engine, freight car and caboose, with a plentiful supply of food and a meager store of coffins in charge of Undertaker O'Halloran, of St. Paul, was sent north.

Situation at Hinckley.

At Hinckley the visible situation had not materially improved over night. The thirty or forty caskets and boxes with their gruesome contents still lay alongside the track, where they were placed last night. No attempt had been made to dress or embalm the bodies, and they were already growing very offensive. Fortunately the day was cool and cloudy, and grateful showers fell at intervals during the forenoon. The remains of the dead, however, were in such horribly blistered and burned condition that decomposition rapidly set in. Undertaker J.G. Donnelly, of St. Paul, was on the ground, and he advised that the bodies be put under Mother Earth as rapidly as possible. Every attempt at identification had been exhausted. From these bodies by the track the officers of the Duluth road had removed and carefully preserved every trinket and article of jewelry, and even shoes and scraps of clothing, placing those from each body in a receptacle numbered identically with the casket, so that possibly when the refugees return they may recognize them and know whether their friends have been interred.

At the Cemetery.

Out in the little cemetery, a mile east of town, was a scene which words are absolutely powerless to describe. At best the little spot would be as dreary as could well be imagined. It is on top of a rough sandy knoll, where nature is seen at her worst, and absolutely no attempt toward artificial embellishment has ever been made.

There were only a few little sandy, unsodded mounds before. Now, with the blackened, fire-scarred stumps and fallen trunks of trees all about, it presented an appearance of desolation hard to describe. But in the center of the open was the crowning horror. In an indiscriminate heap lay more than ninety corpses, men, women and little children. Some burned crisp, others only browned by the heat, and none with a fragment of clothing larger than a man's hand to conceal their awful nakedness. Some were mere trunks, the extremities having been burned off. Some were bloated until the abdomen had cracked open and intestines were protruding, skulls were burned open and brains escaping, all were twisted and cramped in agony of death that had overtaken them.

Burying Loved Ones.

A force of men were quickly at work digging a shallow trench along the south end of the cemetery. The sandy soil was hard as flint. It had been baked to a crust by weeks of drought and almost solidified by the fire. The work progressed slowly. Off in the corner of the clearing two smaller graves were being dug. One was for Mrs. William Gri-

HINCKLEY BEFORE THE FIRE.

"And of this whole family of three generations only the sorrowing grave digger and his wife and child . . . are left."

singer and her two baby girls, Caroline, aged 6, and Mabel, aged 3. The husband and father had recognized them in the grisly heap, and was hard at work preparing for them a final resting place apart from the trench designed for the unidentified, his labors dulling, for the time, the acuteness of his anguish. The other grave was for the Best family, whose numbers make their destruction notable even in this time of death.

The Best Family.

John Best, Jr., was digging the pit with the friendly assistance of two neighbors. Laid in a row, decently covered, were the bodies of John Best, Sr., Mrs. Best, Fred Best, aged 23, Bertha, aged 17, Mrs. Annie Wigel, a married daughter, and her 3-year-old daughter Minnie, Miss Annie Truttman, of Diamond Bluff, Wis., a visitor, aged 26, and Victor Best, aged 8. Two other sons, George, aged 25, and Willie, aged 21, are missing, and are certainly dead. And of this whole family of three generations only the sorrowing grave digger and his wife and child, who took refuge in a dug-out, are left. They all lived together about two miles southeast of Hinckley. The only others of those ninety odd, who were recognized, were Charles Anderson, cashier of the bank; Mrs. William Ginder and her daughter Winifred, aged 6. One or two others were imperfectly identified, but it was largely guesswork. Enough rude boxes were knocked together from rough boards to contain most of these bodies, and they were rapidly laid away under the sand, but not before other bodies began to come in. In the swamp across the Grindstone, where these corpses were found yesterday, were about thirty-five others, which were brought in this morning, making a total of upwards of 130 dead in this little space of four or five acres.

Brave Operator Dunn.

Down near the river was found the body of Thomas Dunn, the Duluth [telegraph] operator at Hinckley. Dunn was born and raised here and was a universal favorite. He stuck to his key until the depot was burning above his head. The delay in locating his body led his friends to hope that he might have escaped, but this morning the finding of his blackened corpse put an end to all uncertainty. . . .

Improvised Telegraph Office.

The busiest point at Hinckley at noon was the Associated Press telegraph office. It is not much of an office, but it served the public with the Associat-

SCENES OF THE GREATEST DISASTER THAT EVER SHOCKED MINNESOTA.

St. Paul Dispatch, Sept. 8, 1894

ed Press report, the only press report sent out of Hinckley today. The wires were brought down to a burned stump of a pole. A dry goods box near by furnished the operator with a desk. A cracker box made him a comfortable seat. A burned railroad spike held down the copy in the brisk breeze. A rough board, one end resting on the operator's table and the other on a milk can, furnished the Associated Press correspondent his desk, and his seat was a beer keg — empty. . . .

One House Left Standing.

The Associated Press correspondent took a five-mile tramp out through the woods to the north of town this morning, through a scene of desolation which rarely falls beneath the eye of man. The country is absolutely swept clean. There is but one settler's house standing within an unknown radius of miles. It is that of Mike Dean, on the edge of the river, three miles east of town. It was a new house and very substantial. Dean and a neighbor fought the fire until they had to abandon hope. They got the women and children into the water. Covering their heads with cloths kept wet by dashing water over them, and when the fire had passed, they came out unhurt and were much surprised to find their buildings standing, and this morning when the Associated Press correspondent entered the clearing, the house dog barked as savagely and the rooster

"I have known plenty of business men whose disrespectful treatment of correspondents has been bitterly remembered and repaid with compound interest."

crowed as lustily as if they had not come within an ace of death.

Victims Identified.

The handcar party which went north this morning has just returned. It met the Duluth construction train about eight miles up the track with word that the City of Duluth had furnished the necessary relief at Sandstone and Miller. They accordingly turned back and on the way in located eleven bodies. . . .

Useless Loss of Life.

Above Skunk Lake the work train reported twelve bodies on the right of way, presumably settlers. In retrospection, the most sorrowful feature of the terrible fatality at Hinckley is the thought that had the situation been realized in time not a single life among the residents of the town need have been lost. The Great Northern gravel pit, where only a hundred sought safety, is about ten acres in extent, broad enough and long enough and deep enough to have sheltered every soul in Hinckley, with all their domestic animals. There is a pool of water of considerable depth. The banks are bare of grass or shrubbery, and there was no inflammable material near the brink on the side from which the fire came. Those who did seek this haven passed the hours of their enforced imprisonment in comparative comfort.

This morning a detail of twenty regulars from Fort Snelling, under command of Capt. Hale and Lieut. McCoy, and an army surgeon came in from St. Paul. They brought some tents, but, finding that Adjt. Gen. Muehlberg had sent up 180 state tents, the regulars turned in and put up fifty of them for the refugees with regular army expedition. The local physician was about played out, and there was an abundance of work for the army surgeon. A portion of the tents will be put up at Hinckley.
St. Paul Dispatch, Sept. 3, 1894

–>·<–

[Grace Stageberg Swenson tells the story of the Hinckley fire in her book, "From the Ashes," published in 1979 by the Croixside Press. She reports that the fire hastened the demise of the lumber industry; the people who resettled were farmers. In the first issue of the Hinckley Enterprise after the fire, the editor wrote optimistically, "The fire . . . did in 15 minutes what it would have taken the husbandman 15 years to accomplish. All nature is with us; it seemingly knew our needs, and came to clear the land."]

–>·<–

Local News. Ira Wheeklock drove over from Ada last Thursday, remaining in town an hour or two.

W.M. Tomlin, state inspector of steam boilers, has been in the city several days this week.

The ladies of Rev. Ofsedal's church are holding an auction sale and festival in Nelson's hall today.

The new school house is rapidly approaching completion. The plastering was finished Tuesday.

Miss Eva La Due gave a birthday party to some of her young friends and schoolmates Tuesday evening.

Mr. and Mrs. C.R. Snyder entertained a few friends on Tuesday evening, the occasion being Mr. Snyder's birthday.
Fertile Journal, Nov. 20, 1890

Great rejoicing. The inhabitants of St. Paul, and most especially the feminine inhabitants, are rejoicing over the completion of the long heralded street-car line between St. Paul and Minneapolis. They will now be able to easily travel to Minneapolis, where everything can be purchased at much lower prices than in St. Paul. They are not slow in taking advantage of this, either. For 10 cents one can travel from any place in St. Paul to any place in Minneapolis.
Svenska Amerikanska Posten, a Swedish-language newspaper, Minneapolis, Dec. 16, 1890, translated by the Works Progress Administration

–>·<–

R.S.V.P. "I always make it a point," remarked a manufacturer . . ., "to reply to every communication of a business nature addressed to me. It doesn't matter what it is about, provided only that it is couched in civil language. I do this because courtesy requires that I should; but aside from that, I find also that it is good policy. Time and again in my life I have been reminded by newly secured customers that I was remembered through correspondence opened with me years before, and many orders have come to me through this passing and friendly acquaintance with people. On the other hand, I have known plenty of business men whose disrespectful treatment of correspondents has been bitterly remembered and repaid with compound interest. Silence is the meanest and most contemptuous way of treating anybody who wishes to be heard and to hear, and resentment is its an-

*"The parties . . . had lived together in peaceful harmony,
and had shared the joys and sorrows of each other for half a century."*

swer every time."
Willmar Argus, Jan. 1, 1891

→·<·

Eloped. James J. Wilcox, of the town of Liberty, and Miss Lettie La Fave, of this place, were married at Crookston yesterday. The couple attended a dance at the residence of P.J. Carey in the town of Reis Tuesday night. During the evening they decided that there was a happier state to be secured, and suiting the action to the thought, they drove to Beltrami and took the morning train to Crookston to seek connubial bliss. The knot was duly tied, and last evening they returned home for the parental blessings.
Fertile Journal, Jan. 8, 1891

→·<·

Golden Wedding. A golden wedding occurred last Friday about three miles east of Willmar. The parties who had lived together in peaceful harmony, and had shared the joys and sorrows of each other for half a century were Mr. and Mrs. Andrew Aslackson. Their lives had been blessed with children who were

St. Peter Herald, April 10, 1891

"Each one added to the happiness of the occasion by bringing a good basket of eatables."

present to witness the occasion and return the blessing to their aged parents, and they brought with them their children to help grandpapa and grandmamma celebrate. Mr. Aslackson has reached the good old age of 78 years, and his wife, his faithful helpmate, the 74th mile stone. The meeting of three generations is of course something unusual, but when we take into consideration that the mother of the bride who was celebrating her golden wedding was present and assisted in the festivities is something more than usual, and probably does not occur once in the celebrating of a hundred golden weddings or perhaps a thousand. The old lady now in her hundred and first year can look back to the time when her daughter, who celebrated her golden wedding, was married, for she at that time lost her husband and has remained a widow ever since. There were present at the golden wedding over 100 people, and each one added to the happiness of the occasion by bringing a good basket of eatables. The presents were numerous, amounting to nearly fifty dollars. It is to be hoped that Mr. and Mrs. Aslackson will celebrate their diamond wedding and be as healthy and prosperous as at present.

Willmar Argus, Feb. 5, 1891

→•←

To keep glassware bright wipe directly from the hot suds. Tumblers used for milk should be thoroughly rinsed in cold water before being immersed in hot suds, as hot water seems to drive the milk into the glass and give them a dingy appearance.

Renville Times, Olivia, Feb. 12, 1891

→•←

The Burden of Big Houses. An ideal of earthly comfort, so common that every reader must have seen it, is to get a house so big

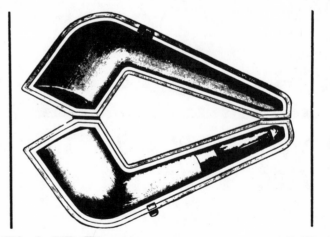

"He had been snubbed several times in his affectionate suit, but still persevered."

---

that it is burdensome to maintain, and fill it up so full of jim-cracks that it is a constant occupation to keep it in order. Then, when the expense of living in it is so great that you cannot afford to go away and rest from the burden of it, the situation is complete, and boarding houses and cemeteries begin to yawn for you. How many Americans, do you suppose, out of the droves that flock annually to Europe, are running away from oppressive houses? When nature undertakes to provide a house, it fits the occupant. Animals who build by instinct build only what they need, but man's building instinct, if it gets a chance to spread itself at all, is boundless, just as all his instincts are. For it is man's peculiarity that nature has filled him with impulses to do things, and left it to his discretion when to stop. She never tells him when he has finished. And perhaps we ought not to be surprised that in so many cases it happens that he doesn't know, but just goes ahead as long as the materials last.

If another man tries to oppress him, he understands that, and is ready to fight to the death and sacrifice all he has rather than submit, but the tyranny of things is so subtle, so gradual in its approach, and comes so masked with seeming benefits that it has him hopelessly bound before he suspects his fetters.

Renville Times, Olivia, Feb. 12, 1891, reprinted from Scribner's Magazine

–>•<–

He told his son to milk the cows, feed the horses, slop the pigs, hunt the eggs, feed the calves, catch the colt and put it in the stable, cut some wood, split up the kindlings, stir the cream, put fresh water in the creamery after supper and to be sure to study his lessons before he went

to bed. Then he went to the Farmers' club to discuss the question, "How to Keep Boys on the Farm."

Renville Times, Olivia, Feb. 19, 1891, reprinted from "Field and Farm"

–>•<–

A Cokato Revivalist in Trouble. Peter Halgren, an itinerant revival preacher, who formerly lived near Cokato, is in the Hennepin county jail for the attempted murder of Miss Christine Peterson of Minneapolis who last week refused his offer of marriage. Halgren had been dividing his time for several weeks between revival preaching in South Minneapolis and following up a vain courtship with Miss Peterson. He had been snubbed several times in his affectionate suit, but still persevered. Finally giving up all hope, he attempted to shoot both the young lady and himself. Only flesh wounds, however, were inflicted. But, supposing that his sweetheart would die, he hunted up and down the Mississippi to find a hole in the ice and drown him-

"He left on the table in his room a letter stating that he was going to a land where the sun does not rise and the stars do not shine."

self. For the third time, as usual, he failed.

He left on the table in his room a letter stating that he was going to a land where the sun does not rise and the stars do not shine. Later events reveal, however, that after his fruitless hunt for a hole in the ice he set out on foot for Delano, then to Watertown, Lake Mary, Howard Lake, Smith Lake, Crow River, Cokato and Kingston. At a farm house near the latter place, he was arrested this week Tuesday by John Tracy, village marshall of Cokato, and was taken to Minneapolis on the train yesterday afternoon. The .32 caliber revolver which he had used was found on his person. He says that he was making his living and paying his way by preaching and praying. The young lady's wound is rapidly recovering. Halgren was arraigned in the Minneapolis municipal court this morning on a charge of assault with a dangerous weapon. **Howard Lake Herald, Feb. 19, 1891**

→⟩-⟨←

An 11-year-old Danish boy from Copenhagen, who understood not a word of English, but had a tag tied around his neck giving his destination as "G. Peterson, Embarrass River, Minn.,"

PURE WINES AND LIQUORS.
A. M: SMITH'S CALIFORNIA WINE DEPOT,
249 Hennepin Avenue, Minneapolis,

has the largest, finest and best stock of Domestic and Imported Wines, Whiskeys, Brandies, Gins, Rum Punches and everything that belongs to the business. I buy direct from the maker and grower, and can and do sell first-class liquors cheaper than other dealers. My motto is:

Small Profits, Pure Goods, and Honest Dealing.

Here are a few Sample Prices: Rye and Bourbon Whiskies, $2, $2.50 and $3 per gallon, Grape and Cognac Brandies at $2, $2.50 and $3 per gallon; White New England and Jamaica Rums at $2.50 and $3 per gallon; Genuine imported "Norsk Aquavit" at $1.25 per bottle. Danish and Swedish liquors in stock.
A. M. Smith's biography in Danish or Norwegian given away to customers

The North, Dec. 30, 1891

"It was a typical picnic day: cool, squally, and occasionally two-minute showers."

arrived recently hale and hearty at that address.

Svenska Amerikanska Posten, Minneapolis, June 2, 1891

–›–‹–

The M.E. [Methodist Episcopal] Sunday school picnic took place last Saturday pursuant to announcement. It was a typical picnic day: cool, squally, and occasionally two-minute showers varied the program and prevented any dryness in the day's exercises. The squally part is always enjoyed by the children, and the coolness of the atmosphere had a tendency to render the mosquitos too rheumatic for an aggressive campaign. After dinner came the exciting regatta. Two boats entered the contest. The oars of one were plied by Miss Denman assisted by E.M. Tousley; and the other, by Miss Luddington with Glen Smith as ballast and pilot. After a heroic splash for the goal, and the mists had cleared away, it was decided that boat No. 2 had come out behind.

Howard Lake Herald, July 30, 1891

–›–‹–

[Country road repair before the days of automobiles was largely a matter of farmers showing up with tools and beasts to work off their road tax. For some it was drudgery; for others it was a chance to get together with neighbors and spend a day or two working and gossiping. This letter to the editor is a plea for better roads, written by Lucien A. Sweet, a farmer in the Fairmont area.]

I write this to assail a custom — you can hardly call it a system, unless in the sense of a system to accomplish nothing. . . .

The town supervisors divide the town into districts; some may have two or three miles of highway with $25,000 or $30,000 worth of taxable property; others may have five or six miles of road

Northwestern Christian College.

Location Eighteen miles West of Minneapolis, in the Village of Excelsior on the famous Lake Minnetonka.

Departments Kindergarten, Model School, Preparatory, Normal, Collegiate, Biblical, Commercial, Music, Art.

College Extension Where those who cannot attend College may study at home. Same studies, same grading as those in College.

Special Summer Term For non-resident students, those wishing to make more rapid progress, and for review.

Expenses From $125.00 up for board, room and tuition. SUMMER COTTAGES can be rented by clubs during school year.

Advantages Most Healthful Location. Most Attractive Surroundings. Most Economical. Most Rapid Progress. Most Accessible. PARENTS MAY MAKE EXCELSIOR THEIR HOME, obtain a good living, and take care of their children while passing through the studies from the Kindergarten grade to completion of Classical Course. Address the President,

M. H. TIPTON, EXCELSIOR, MINN.

Northwestern Tourist, Excelsior, July 4, 1891

with not much more tax. At the town meeting the self-cheating farmers are on hand to elect an overseer whom they know will let them cheat themselves. Here the matter rests. . . .

Then as June approaches the newly-elected overseer goes around and warns out the people in his district to work. The next day, all the way from 7 to 10 o'clock, you will see all sizes and ages of people assemble. The preacher's son and school master bring along their weapons of slaughter. The Irishman brings his old ox Dime and the colt (a well matched team) but "jist the tame fer to work out the road tax." After a time the plow and scraper are started, begin to rend and tear, fill up one mud hole by making another. The highway is butchered in every conceivable

"I am informed that there was but one article in the house left intact."

---

way but the right way. Care is taken that the ox and colt don't sweat. The sun is closely watched. The other people lean on their shovels while the old men tell stories.

Thus the days and week passes; then the end of the tax and they are all happy; go home congratulating themselves that they have accomplished much. The year's road labor ends, no matter whether it is finished or not.

Farmers, let us stop and think. We have about $200 to expend annually on our roads, suppose we had a good competent man appointed by the supervisors, who understands the system and science of road making and let him use this money to hire men and teams to work on our highways all through the season, from spring until it freezes up. When there is a bad place let it be fixed, as the railroads do. . . .

We are cheating ourselves. Let us stop. Let us cast off this old custom of feudalism and pray our legislature to inaugurate this grand system that has proven so successful in other states.

Freeborn County Standard, Albert Lea, May 11, 1892

-›-‹-

Died, in Olivia, July 10th, 1892, at 4:25 P.M., LOUISE, wife of J.A. Barge, aged 30 years.

A husband and five young children, the youngest being one week old, are left to bear the strain of this sudden and irreparable loss. The heartfelt sympathies of this entire community go out to this bereaved family in their hour of sorest affliction.

The funeral services were held last Tuesday morning, Rev. Kemerer officiating. The remains were escorted to the cemetery west of the village by a large concourse of relatives and sympathizing friends and acquaintances, where they were

I am little, but smart. I can work cheap and live cheap but I am not capable of doing the quality of work or of handling the quantity of business that is done by white labor in that old reliable Minneapolis institution the

CASCADE STEAM LAUNDRY 316 SECOND AVE SO. J.R. PURCHASE PROP.

Northwestern Tourist, Aug. 1, 1891

reverently deposited under that low, green tent whose curtains never outward swing.

Renville Times, Olivia, July 14, 1892

-›-‹-

On the 18th inst. lightning struck the house of Martin Nelson, a farmer living about four miles north of this place [Hector], making a total wreck of the house and everything in it. Even the dishes were completely demolished. I am informed that there was but one article in the house left intact, and that was a motto framed and hung on the wall and read, "In God We Trust." The family, consisting of man and wife and one child, were uninjured.

Renville Times, Olivia, July 21, 1892

-›-‹-

About the Swedes. A man from the southern states recently asked [U.S.] Secretary of State [Walter] Gresham what ought to be done to turn the stream of immigrants toward the South. Gresham asked what kind of immigrants they desired and re-

"Several very tough looking Italian tramps and peddlers put in an appearance near the city."

ceived the answer that all honest, active and industrious persons would be welcome in the southern states.

"Do you know the Swedes?" Gresham continued. "They are an excellent race; honest, industrious, sober, contented and thrifty, and when they settle any place it is usually for good. They would make good pioneers in any state, but it is hard to persuade them to go south, because since the beginning of history immigrants have striven to remain on the latitude on which they were born as far as it is possible. The Swedes are a northern race, for which reason it is not easy to persuade them to go to a country where the climatic conditions are directly opposite to those of their native land. But if you really desire the Swedes in the south, I think it would be a good idea to interest their clergymen in the idea, as the Swedes are a simple and religious people. They look upon their ministers as their leaders, and depend upon them in their sorrows and tribulations. The first thing they do when they settle anywhere is to build a church and next to this they build a residence for their pastor, which as a rule is the handsomest house in the municipality.

"If one can only convince a Swedish clergyman, that one or another place is desirable for his countrymen, then one can easily persuade 50-60 families to come along."
Svenska Amerikanska Posten, Minneapolis, May 23, 1893

→•←

Monday, several very tough looking Italian tramps and peddlers put in an appearance near the city. During the day two of them were complained of and taken before the city authorities, and afterwards were escorted to the limits and told to "skip." They skipped out to Mealey's

" Oh, my ! have you seen the new 'Mather' fastening ? No buttons ! no hooks ! and so convenient. They are for sale by

place where they showed a determination of remaining all night, but received too warm a reception. That same night two attempted to gain entrance to D.S. Gow's and H.W. Plummer's residences, but were not successful. They manoeuvered around all next day and Sheriff Tierney succeeded in holding some of their packs, knowing they would soon come after them. The city has no desire to support such characters, and will make them move on. Tramps are very plentiful this year and are somewhat saucy if the men folks are not around.
Anoka County Union, Anoka, July 19, 1893

→•←

According to the old superstition we shall have twenty-one snow storms this winter because snow fell on the 21st of the month. That ought to keep us clad in a mantle of white, pretty much all winter.
Grand Rapids Magnet, Nov. 28, 1893

→•←

A Warning. As the new year begins many great changes will be brought about in the different departments of the city government. A well-founded rumor has it that the few Swedish workers now employed in these departments are slated for dismissal, unless our Scandinavian aldermen keep their eyes open. Be on your guard therefore Messrs. Aldermen. Attempts will be made to crowd out the Scandinavians and replace them with German and Irish Catholics.
Svenska Amerikanska Posten, Minneapolis, Dec. 26, 1893

→•←

Christmastide.

How it Was Observed by Wadena Citizens. A Christmas praise service was held [at the Congregational Church] Sunday evening. The church had been previ-

"He is said to have been engaged to the notorious 'Finlander Kate.'"

ously decorated with evergreen festoons and an archway over the pulpit, above which was suspended a star with an electric light at the center. Upon either side of the pulpit were the inscriptions in living green: "Peace on earth" — "Good will to Men." A large part of the programme was furnished upon printed slips and consisted of responsive scripture readings and beautiful and appropriate music. The pastor, Rev. E. Cory, led the reading and offered the invocation, and the singing which was excellent, was led by a choir of boys and girls under the direction of Miss Winnie Rathbun. ... Little Germaine Chase and Ouida Winslow gave very pretty recitations entitled "Christmas is Here" and

Rainy River Navigation Company.

The Electric-Lighted Stee Passenger
S. S. KEENORA

Leaves Rat Portage MONDAY, WEDNESDAY and SATURDAY on arrival of C. P. R. trains for

FORT FRANCES,
FOLEY'S,
MINE CENTRE,
SEINE RIVER and
RAINY LAKE CITY.

Staterooms open for Passengers at 8 p. m. night of sailing.
Daylight run on the Lake of the Woods and Rainy River.
Ship your freight care Keenora it will receive careful handling and quick dispatch.

WALTER ROSS,
Gen. Freight and Passenger Agent.
Rat Portage, Ontario.

Rainy Lake Journal, Oct. 21, 1897

"The night after Christmas," to the great delight of all. ... At the close of the exercises the teachers of the classes distributed in a quiet manner among their classes the gifts of the school to their classes, and also gave to each child in the house a bag of candy and nuts.

Wadena County Journal, Wadena, Dec. 28, 1893

—>•<—

MINING

[Iron mining began in Minnesota in 1884. By the early 1890s, it was a big business and immigrants were recruited to work in the mines.]

Joseph Rossio, an Italian, was instantly killed by a fall of ore and rock at the Montana Monday afternoon. His body was crushed out of all resemblance to the human form. Deceased left a wife and child in the Turin district of Italy. Deceased was 30 years of age.

Vermillion Iron Journal, Tower, Oct. 27, 1892

—>•<—

Elias Houtahla, a Finn, was killed at the Minnesota mine Monday night. He was working in a stope and after a blast hastened back to his work before the remaining loose ore and rock was barred down from overhead. He is said to have been engaged to the notorious

"Finlander Kate."

Vermillion Iron Journal, Tower, Dec. 1, 1892

—>•<—

John Mihelich, an Austrian, was instantly killed at No. 3 shaft at the Chandler Monday night. The deceased and his son were pushing a car of oar in the 6th level and on arriving near the gates the gate tender called to them to stop, as the cage had just started for the surface. For some reason the men could not stop the car and it went into the shaft falling a distance of 150 feet. Mihelich, in his effort to hold back the car, was jerked headlong down the shaft.

Vermillion Iron Journal, Tower, July 6, 1893

—>•<—

If there was ever any doubt with the Minnesota people as

to the practicability of crushing their ores, it has doubtless been wholly dispelled. The 65-ton crusher at No. 8 stockpile is in successful operation. It chaws up great blocks of hard Bessemer ore as easily as the average small boy munches peanuts, while the sound is not unlike that of an old cow eating corn from the cob. Blocks weighing 600 and 800 pounds are broken without any apparent effort — much to the surprise of envious Finn laborers working on the stockpiles with sledges. The 22-ton crusher in No. 3 pocket for the past four weeks has been crushing 200 tons every ten hours, and it is expected that the large crushers will crush between 400 and 500 tons.

Vermillion Iron Journal, Tower, June 22, 1893

Coffee Made Her Insane

The source of Johanna Lindberg's problems was not questioned at the time. "Coffee Made Her Insane" was the headline in the St. Paul newspaper. Physicians and sheriff's officers agreed that she was a "coffee drunkard." We can guess otherwise today.

Mrs. Johanna Lindberg Committed to Rochester

For Some Time She Is Said to Have Drunk Twenty Quarts of Coffee a Day — She Drank It as Strong as It Could Be Made, and Kept the Pot Boiling All the Time — Threatened Her Husband's Life and Was Arrested — One of the Most Extraordinary Cases Ever Heard Of.

Mrs. Johanna Lindberg, of 406 Arundel street, was committed to the Rochester insane asylum yesterday by Judge Willrich, of the probate court. The case is very peculiar, possibly the most extraordinary that has ever been brought to the attention of the local authorities. Mrs. Lindberg is violently insane, and the cause is alleged to be the excessive use of coffee: in fact, she might be called "a coffee drunkard."

It was stated yesterday that symptoms of insanity had manifested themselves during the past three months, and that recently she became so violently insane as to threaten her husband's life. The threat and its attempted execution caused the interference of the officers, and the whole story was told yesterday in probate court. Mrs. Lindberg, who is about forty-five years of age and has three children, is said to have been so inordinately fond of coffee that she consumed vast quantities daily. The habit is of long standing, and has grown beyond all bounds. No victim of the liquor habit could be more completely wedded to his destroyer, so it is said, than is Mrs. Lindberg to her favorite beverage. She was miserable when deprived of coffee, and coffee of the strongest kind. Her desire is so intense that she is said to have kept the pot boiling constantly in order to lose no time in preparing the beverage.

For weeks and months, she is said to have drunk from thirty to forty pints of the blackest coffee daily. The unusual strength was not sufficient to appease the longing for the effects of the drink, so expedients were resorted to that extracted the last vestige of color from the roasted and pulverized berry. And the cups generally used on breakfast tables were discarded as being too small and insignificant, so a large sized tin cup was substituted.

Mrs. Lindberg is described as being above the average size and possessed of unusual muscular strength in spite of her peculiar dissipation. When Deputy Sheriff McKenny attempted to induce her to accompany him to the probate court, she resisted vigorously, and it was with some difficulty that she was overpowered, since the officer was loath to hurt her in any way. Deputy McKenny took her to Rochester yesterday afternoon.

-≻•≺-

[The next day's news was more hopeful. The headline read: ALL VIOLENCE SUBSIDED. MRS. LINDBERG WILL PROBABLY RECOVER HER REASON. The article gave this additional information, correcting the spelling of the officer's name along the way.]

Mrs. Johanna Lindberg, who was so violent when she was arrested by Deputy Sheriff F.W. Kenney at her home . . . that it was with the greatest difficulty that he was able to put sufficient clothing on her to make her presentable in the probate court where was examined later in the day, was taken to the Rochester insane asylum without any difficulty at all. Her violence had entirely subsided, and she meekly obeyed all the orders of the matron who attended her, making it entirely unnecessary for Kenney to use force during her transportation to Rochester.

. . .Those who are familiar with the subject of

"Caffeine is a poison which acts on the nervous center and finally destroys the mind."

insanity . . . say there has not been a similar case in this state. In fact many doctors say that no similar case is known to the profession.

. . . Her youngest child, a boy, is only five years old, and Dr. Lee of this city who was called to attend her last Saturday, says that ever since the birth of that child she is said to have been suffering from minor ailments. Her husband told Dr. Lee that his wife began at that time to drink coffee as a cure for headaches. There is nothing peculiar in that, as coffee is a favorite beverage among the Swedes, perhaps to a greater extent than among other nationalities, and her husband says he never thought it would hurt his wife to drink good coffee. As the years rolled by she gradually increased the number of times she drank for headaches, until about two years ago she would drink the coffee without any cream and sugar to dilute it. She became subject to insomnia, and Dr. Hanley was called upon one occasion about that time to visit her.

Dr. Hanley says he cannot remember who called him, but he does remember that it was intimated to him at the time that the woman was not mentally sound. He went to the house but was told that neither Mrs. Lindberg nor her husband desired that he should make any investigation. They insisted that there was nothing for a doctor to do, and he finally drove away.

From that time Mrs. Lindberg, her husband tells Dr. Lee, has become more and more addicted to the coffee or "caffeine" habit. The doses of this stimulant have become stronger and have been administered more frequently until at last she drank from thirty to forty large cups of coffee a day. During the past six months her husband states that she would do nothing in the way of caring for her children and for home. She did not seem to have lost her affection for her family, but it was only secondary to that all-absorbing love for her favorite beverage.

It has become rumored in the neighborhood of late that Mrs. Lindberg was not entirely sane; that she was "a little flighty." The "mischievous small boys" took advantage of this fact to tease and trouble her whenever she came out of the house, which she never did except to go to the pump for water with which to supply her coffee pot. A few days ago it is claimed that she seized a stone, while in a rage at the boys, and attempted to strike one of these boys. That act led to calling Dr. Lee and later to her arrest and commitment to the asylum.

Will Probably Recover. "If coffee drinking is the original cause of her insanity," said Dr. Lee to a Pioneer Press reporter yesterday, "she will no doubt recover and leave the hospital a well and sane woman. Caffeine is a poison which acts on the nervous center and finally destroys the mind, but when the poison is taken away the person afflicted will recover. It will be a hard fight, no doubt, for the passion for this form of poison is as strong as the craving, will-destroying passion for opium. If she recovers she will always be in danger of falling back into the habit, just as a reformed opium eater or drinker of alcoholic beverages is always liable to become again addicted to the use of his favorite poison. The demand for the poison is always in the system and if it is quickened by any indulgence, no matter how small, the person afflicted stands in immediate danger of being overcome with the burning desire to satisfy cravings for the poison with which his system is filled. Mrs. Lindberg will have to abstain entirely from the use of coffee when she comes from the hospital.

"Tea has the same action upon the human body, when taken in excess. This we find to be true with the tea-tasters, who break down physically from introducing too great quantities of the tea-poison into their bodies. It would be just as natural for a person to become a 'tea drunkard' as a 'coffee drunkard.' I do not think there is any danger of cutting off a person thus addicted from the poison under the influence of which they are living. Mrs. Lindberg will no doubt be deprived of her coffee at the asylum; but, if she is watched, she will not be in any danger. It is certainly a very interesting and extraordinary case, and I am going to watch it as closely as I can.

"I do not think that the effect of caffeine upon the human system, when taken in excessive quantities, has ever been demonstrated," said Dr. Hanley, in talking of this matter yesterday. "The text writers have touched upon the matter, but only in a theoretical way. Prof. Bartolow, in his Materia Medica and Therapeutics, says:

" 'Caffeine in a small quantity acts as a stomachic tonic, and rather improves than lessens the appetite when administered in diseased states. It is feebly laxative. . . .

" 'As regards the action of caffeine on the brain, it may be stated that, at first, drowsiness occurs; this is followed by wakefulness, excitement, muscular trembling, confusion of the mind, hallucination and delirium. The cerebral effects terminate in deep torpor, but this probably is the result of exhaustion. Rise of temperature, convulsions and general paralysis occur when toxic doses are administered to animals; but the temperature declines when paralysis supervenes.' "

Dr. Hanley further stated that he had never known of a person who was addicted to the habit of drinking coffee to excess. He said he could readily see how a person could get into such a habit by

"Mrs. Lindberg's name will no doubt figure prominently in essays and books."

using coffee, strong coffee, for headaches, as a good many people do. He also admitted that the habit would be very serious, if not as serious as the opium habit, though it would be very different from the latter.

The outcome of this case will be watched with much interest by all the physicians of the city and state, and Mrs. Lindberg's name will no doubt figure prominently in essays and books written upon medical subjects, as one of the first "coffee-drunkards" known to the profession.

St. Paul Pioneer Press, July 9 and 10, 1895

-><-

[Johanna Lindberg did not recover. She died terribly insane at Rochester State Hospital in 1905, more than 10 years after she was committed. Hospital records show that sometimes she was "very disturbed" and "violent;" at other times she would not speak and took "no notice of anything."

[In hindsight, it is clear that coffee did not make her insane. Rather, her excessive coffee drinking was brought about by her psychosis. To say that coffee made her insane is like saying that water causes the insanity of a compulsive hand-washer.

[Caffeine probably aggravated Mrs. Lindberg's condition. Although hospital authorities refused to let her have caffeine, she longed for it. One day, after being in the hospital for four years, she "became troublesome in dining room, taking tea and coffee from other patients. Obliged to eat from tray on ward."

[She received little or no treatment. The records say only that she was encouraged to exercise outdoors, and she rebelled against that in her later years. She lived half a century before drugs existed to help treat mental illness, and psychoanalysis was just in its infancy.

[Admission records from Rochester State Hospital show that the same summer Johanna Lindberg was committed, there were many other tragic cases. Among them: a 53-year-old housewife from Steele County institutionalized for "change of life;" a 32-year-old Wabasha County woman for "domestic trouble;" a 43-year-old St. Louis County physician for "excessive use of morphine;" a 40-year-old Ramsey County woman for "spiritualism;" a 28-year-old Washington County housewife "following

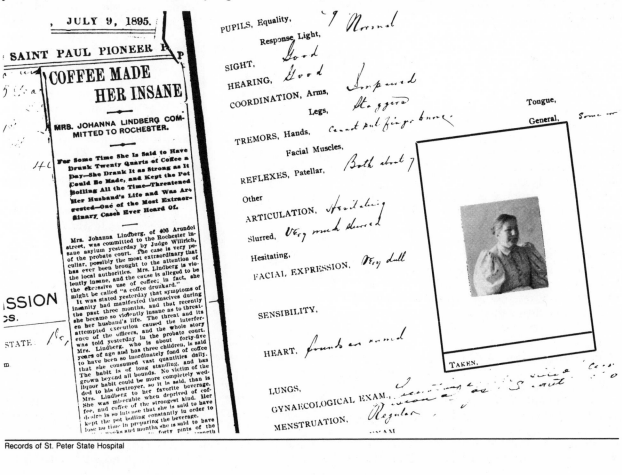

Records of St. Peter State Hospital

"One of the ways of telling whether a man is a married man or not is to examine his pockets."

childbirth;" and a 26-year-old Ramsey County man for "masturbation," presumably public masturbation. "Excessive drinking" seems to be the most common reason for admission.

[Census records and St. Paul city directories show that Mrs. Lindberg's husband, Peter, a carpenter, remained in St. Paul and lived for years with their three sons, Harold, Oscar and Charles. Records of other patients tell of visits from their families; her records have no such comment.]

→•←

The belief that antique furniture is necessarily better than well-made new furniture must be accepted with caution, as any honest repairer of antiques will admit. Cabinetmakers of the last century used excellent wood and did good work, but they manufactured for houses not heated with steam, but by means of hearth fires. It was safe, therefore, to make the larger slabs of sideboards and the like of cheap wood veneered with mahogany. When furniture thus constructed is exposed to steam heat in modern houses it soon warps and becomes unsightly. The best repairers of antiques replace veneered slabs with solid mahogany taken from old and seasoned furniture.
Fergus Falls Journal, Jan. 24, 1894

→›•‹←

Druggist L.M. Kaplan received a very handsome and expensive soda fountain this week, and is placing it in position in the front end of the Palace drug store. The fountain is six feet high, made of the finest marble, with a plate glass mirror and electric light fixtures, and is truly a thing of beauty. The Palace has been rapidly forging to the front during the past two years, until it is now the finest equipped and handsomest drug store in Southwestern Minnesota, and a credit to our city.
Adrian Guardian, Feb. 16, 1894

→›•‹←

Underwood. Theo. Sjordal is loading up a car of cows today to ship to Michigan and farmers are bringing them in. He pays from $18 to $22 for them.

Miss Hannah Moen and Miss Bessie Sande came up from Fergus Saturday evening to attend the entertainment and dance, and remained till Monday morning.

Jno. Anker has bought up the J.O. Kolstad farm for $2,600 and will move to it in April. The farm is one mile north of Underwood.

The entertainment took in about $15. There were two other dances the same night which took away some of the young folks.

W. L. DOUGLAS
$3 SHOE FOR GENTLEMEN.

$5.00 Genuine Hand-sewed, an elegant and stylish dress Shoe which commends itself.
$4.00 Hand-sewed Welt. A fine calf Shoe unequaled for style and durability.
$3.50 Goodyear Welt is the standard dress Shoe, at a popular price.
$3.50 Policeman's Shoe is especially adapted for railroad men, farmers, etc.
All made in Congress, Button and Lace.
$3.00 for Ladies, is the only hand-sewed shoe sold at this popular price.
$2.50 Dongola Shoe for Ladies, is a new departure and promises to become very popular.
$2.00 Shoe for Ladies, and $1.75 for Misses still retain their excellence for style, etc.
All goods warranted and stamped with name on bottom. If advertised local agent cannot supply you, send direct to factory enclosing advertised price or a postal for order blanks.
W. L. DOUGLAS, Brockton, Mass.
WANTED.—Shoe dealer in every city and town not occupied, to take exclusive agency. All agents advertise in local paper. Send for illustrated catalogue.
☞ NAME THIS PAPER every time you write.

Litchfield Saturday Review, March 21, 1891

Mr. and Mrs. G.H. Woldy have a daughter.
Fergus Falls Journal, March 26, 1894

→›•‹←

Mr. Millett, an old gentleman of 90 summers, who resides a few miles from Belle Plaine, made the trip to this city last Thursday on foot. He was enroute to Shakopee, and was persuaded to take the train from here after a ticket had been purchased. He is one of the prosperous farmers of his section, and in days of yore used to do a great amount of trading in Jordan. The old man seemed to be in very good spirits after his 12 mile walk.
Jordan Independent, March 22, 1894

→›•‹←

A Difference in Pockets. One of the ways of telling whether a man is a married man or not is to examine his pockets. In the pocket of a bachelor you will find:

Half a dozen letters from girls.

A tailor's bill.

Three or four old checks for theater seats.

Bills for supper.

Theatrical-looking photographs.

A lot of invitations for dances, dinners and receptions.

A tiny glove scented with violet.

But the married man's pocket will contain:

An old bill.

A couple of unposted letters which were given to him to post a week past.

A sample of an impossible shade which he must match.

"Nothing is pleasanter to use as a cure for rough and sunburnt skin than plain slices of cucumber."

A newspaper clipping telling a sure cure for croup.

A shopping list, ranging from a box of blacking to three yards of lace.

Bills.

More bills!

Jordan Independent, Aug. 23, 1894

→•←

Nothing is pleasanter to use as a cure for rough and sunburnt skin than plain slices of cucumber, says an exchange. The way to use it is to cut off a slice and rub the skin well with it, drying afterward with a soft towel. This remedy is said to be quite as efficacious as any of the nostrums in vogue for the purpose, and has the advantage of being a great deal cheaper.

Jordan Independent, Aug. 30, 1894

→•←

Monday afternoon a stranger claiming to hail from Lake Park, Iowa, came to Worthington for the purpose of purchasing a bicycle. He negotiated with Jud Mattison, an employe of the roller mills, and asked the privilege of trying it before closing the deal, which was given him. He rode awkwardly up the street, but no sooner had he turned the first corner than he "lit out" as though pursued by the evil one. A dozen or more of Worthington's expert wheelmen gave chase in a very short time, and although they stayed out until dark, some of them going as far as fifty miles, no trace could be found of the daring thief. It is reported that a wheel was stolen at Sheldon a few days since under similar circumstances, and it would be well for wheelmen everywhere to be careful about letting strangers mount their wheels for any purpose whatever.

Adrian Guardian, July 25, 1895

→•←

Referring to the fact that cler-

gymen are wasting valuable time by preaching against bicycle riding on Sunday, H.P. Hall suggests a better method of enlisting that very large element of our population by holding union religious services Sunday afternoons especially for wheelmen and wheelwomen. Select an outdoor site, six or eight miles distant in the country, adjacent to some good cycling road. Make the distance just great enough so that the bicyclers will want to take a half

"He has come to stay until he sees Adrian properly lighted with electricity."

---

hour's rest when they reach the chosen spot. They are bound to ride on Sunday and this will give them a trip with an object.
Mankato Review, April 28, 1896

⇥•⇤

How to Treat a Wife. First, get a wife; second, be patient. You may have great trials and perplexities in your business, but do not therefore carry to your home a cloudy or contracted brow. Your wife may have trials, which, though of less magnitude, may be hard for her to bear. A kind word, a tender look, will do wonders in chasing from her brow all clouds of gloom. To this we would add, always keep a bottle of Chamberlain's Cough Remedy in the house. It is the best and is sure to be needed sooner or later. Your wife will then know that you really care for her and wish to protect her health. For sale at J.C. Thro's drug store.
Mankato Review, May 6, 1896

⇥•⇤

C.J. Busch, of Owatonna, was down [from Medford] last Monday evening entertaining and getting acquainted, with our citizens

The North, March 30, 1892

in the K. of P. [Knights of Pythias] Dining Hall. He brought apples and cigars. Card tables were in abundance. There were about sixty present and a very enjoyable evening was passed until about 10:30, when everybody adjourned to their respective homes.
Owatonna Chronicle, Oct. 14, 1897

⇥•⇤

How to Escape Colds ... Let the body be hardened by a cold sponge bath or even a cold plunge, followed by brisk rubbing with a "scratchy" towel, every morning. Let the clothing be adapted to the season, though always as light as possible, but keep the neck uncovered — no turned up coat collar, no muffler, no boa. Never let the temperature in the house rise above 70 degrees in the winter. Air every room systematically every day, no matter what the outdoor temperature may be. Always have fresh air in the bedroom. There is nothing poisonous in "night air," popular belief to the contrary notwithstanding.

INVENTIONS

⇥•⇤

J.D. Wallace, superintendent of our waterworks and electric light plant, who spent several months here this summer, is with us again. ... He is looking and feeling well, and says he has come to stay until he sees Adrian properly lighted with electricity. The waterworks are a success and we have every reason to believe the lights will be, as both were under his skillful care, and he never does things by halves.
Adrian Guardian, Dec. 6, 1894

⇥•⇤

A new invention has been made by a Swede, by name Per O. Elliot, 905 Washington Ave. So. It is a simple little apparatus designed to aid in attaching the postage stamp to a letter thus making it unnecessary to fumble around with big and clumsy fingers in an attempt to afix it. As soon as the inventor receives the patent papers he will sell his invention, preferably to a Swede.
Svenska Amerikanska Posten, Minneapolis, May 21, 1895

⇥•⇤

W. Sargeant has just received an apparatus for taking photographs by flash light, which enables him to do excellent work without the aid of a gallery, and at almost any time or place. Family groups, and interiors can now be taken most satisfactorily and with completeness of detail. The trials he has made have been very gratifying.
Wadena County Journal, Wadena, May 24, 1895

SPECIAL  PRICES

FOR THANKSGIVING WEEK.

Having placed our order early in the season for a HUGE STOCK OF FINE TABLE CUTLERY AND PLATED WARE for the Holidays, we have decided to give our customers some special inducements in prices to help us convert the goods into cash, even though the times are close.

CARVERS { Worth $.75 per pair for......$ .50
Worth 1.50 per pair for...... 1.00
Worth 2.50 per set for........ 1.75 }

A large variety of Elegant CARVERS cheap.

CARVERS { Worth $3.00 per set for ...$2.00
Worth 4.00 per set for ... 2.50
Worth 6.00 per set for ... 4.50 }

Warranted Triple Silver Plated Knives and Forks, extra plate on wearing points, worth $4.50, for $2.85 per set.

We have a cheaper quality, worth $2.50, for $1.50 per set.

KLAUSS BREAD KNIVES, sets of three, usually sold at 75 cents; our price this week, 50 cents per set.

WAFFLE IRONS,
The very best at 50 cents each.

We have just received a large stock of

5 O'Clock Teas.

All the latest designs.

Remember our Special Sale of

JEWEL STOVES.

Northwestern Hardware Co.,

417 and 419 Wabasha Street.

St. Paul Pioneer Press, Nov. 26, 1893

"Local players put . . . up a surprisingly good game considering that they had to learn their signals and plan their plays while on the train."

In a word, don't be always afraid of catching cold, don't coddle, but meet cold and wet and changes of temperature like a man, or rather like a horse, and you will then run a better chance of being as strong as a horse.
Renville Times, Olivia, Oct. 21, 1897

→‑←

Played Football at Winona. An Owatonna Football Team Meets Defeat at Winona on Thanksgiving Day — A Good Game, However.

An Owatonna aggregation of football players went to Winona Thanksgiving day and took part in an interesting game with the high school team of that city. The game was originally scheduled for the Pillsbury academy eleven, but at the last moment circumstances arose which made it impossible for them to go. So a team was hastily gotten up, consisting mostly of the ex-collegiate players of the city, and, with the consent of the Winona team, filled the date. The game was a good one, the local players putting up a surprisingly good game considering that they had to learn their signals and plan their plays while on the train. The first half was stubbornly contested, the Winona team succeeding in scoring only at the very end of the half. Towards the last of the game the fact that many of the Owatonna boys were out of training and practice began to tell on their strength and snap in playing, and as a result Winona secured three more touchdowns, which, with the goals obtained, made the score stand 22 to 0. Though this seems like a bad defeat, those who were present do not consider it so, taking into account the lack of practice and condition of the Owatonna team, who while they were fresh, demonstrated themselves the equals of the home team. The game was a clean one and greatly enjoyed

A TRIUMPH OF MODERN BREWING IS THE

Gilt Edge Beer

$3.00

TAKES A CASE OF 24 QUARTS OR 36 PINTS IF CASE AND BOTTLES ARE RETURNED.

Minneapolis Brewing Co.,
Minneapolis, Minn.

Orders Promptly Filled by
A. PRIEBE, Agent,
SAUK CENTRE, : : MINN.

Long Prairie Leader, April 26, 1895

by both players and spectators, there being of the latter a large assemblage. The gate receipts amounted to two hundred dollars. A band was present to add music to the pleasure of the afternoon. Following the game the Owatonna players were tendered a reception by the junior class of the high school. . . . The line up of the local team was as follows: l.e., C.C. Chadwick; l.t., Geo. Pratt; l.g., E. Oppliger; c., J. Jensen; r.g., Geo. Holmes; r.t., G.B. Bennett; r.e., E. Chadwick; q.b., J. Dye; l.h., P.H. Evans; r.h., A. Kasper; f.b., W.C.V. Nelson.
Owatonna Chronicle, Dec. 2, 1897

→‑←

On last Monday afternoon Dr. Will Mayo, of Rochester, and Dr. B.M.J. Conlin of this city performed a difficult and dangerous operation for strangulated hernia, upon Mrs. James Clark. Owing to the advanced age of Mrs. Clark few hopes were entertained of her recovery, but she has since gained slowly and it is now thought that there is a chance for her surviving the operation.
Owatonna Chronicle, Dec. 30, 1897

→‑←

No sensible woman expects a man to take off his hat and keep it off because she happens to enter an elevator. It is a foolish thing to do. It means nothing in the way of deference, and it is extremely dangerous to health. There are more draughts in one elevator than in twenty street cars — more grip, more bronchitis, more pneumonia. An elevator is not a drawing room. It is a vehicle, and we know of none in which it more behooves one to be careful.
New Ulm News, Jan. 1, 1898

→‑←

The St. Paul Pioneer Press, in the exuberance of its imagination, referred to the closed year of 1897 as having witnessed the return of prosperity by "leaps and bounds." Possibly this may have had a double meaning, for, looking over this State, while there may have been some leaps forward there were many bounds backward. In Mankato alone there were nearly all bounds backward and but few leaps forward. The failure of R.D. Hubbard, the large glass block clothing firm, J.A. Willard, M.D. Willard and R.E. Brett, represented millions of dollars, and the closing of the linseed oil mill, the meat packing house, the knit-

"It was clearly demonstrated that there is no need hereafter to send off for professional performers."

ting works and the fiber ware factory, must have thrown several hundred men and girls out of employment. Some other localities fared better, and some were not struck so hard, but outside of the tariff-protected lumber interest . . . and flour mills, the profits of which have been increased through the misfortunes of Europe, it has been difficult to discover any great leaps of prosperity.

New Ulm News, Jan. 15, 1898

→·←

Tracy Artists Meet. Mr. and Mrs. Homer Whiting were "at home" to numerous friends on Monday evening. Special pains had been made in the arranging of the literary program of the evening to bring to the surface various stars in their particular lines. It was astonishing and a source of profound gratification to all present to learn that so much latent talent in various lines existed here among home people. On hearing the various numbers, it was clearly demonstrated that there is no need hereafter to send off for professional performers. Take, for instance, Prof. Jahonas Sylvanius Priceus — in other words, Conductor J.S. Price — on his celebrated, imported German harmoniphone — a perfect wonder. Then that quartet of good fellows, whose voices have been heard in season and out of season in all time and out of time, whose harmony, whether in rollicking laughter or in dismal wail, was simply phenomenal, the Messrs. Whiting, Sieter, Blakesley and Patrridge (O.L.). Then that prima donna, Mademoiselle Segur, in her elegant rendering of that beautiful opera, "Rock-a-by Baby." And need we mention the world-renowned pianist whose gyratory motions, stool and all, are the envy of an admiring public — Paderewski — commonly known as Dr.

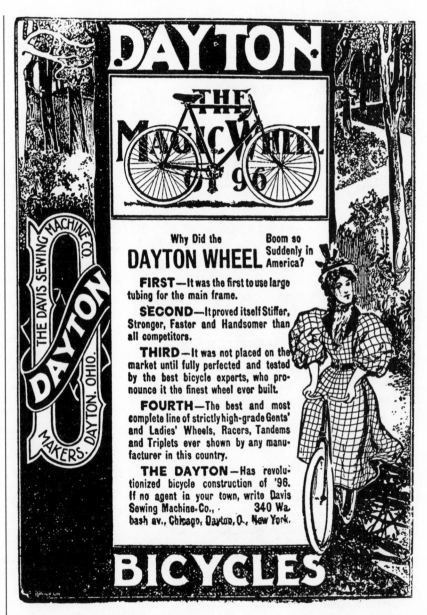

Rainy Lake Journal, Nov. 26, 1896

James. . . . Not until Monday evening was it suspected that we had in Tracy an Ella Wheeler Wilcox, but the gems of rhythmical cadences as they fell upon the tympanums of those present revealing a composition at once beautiful and impressive, showed that the spirit of the muse had fallen upon Mrs. Newton, the poetess of the evening. She it was who told in rhymical rhyme that

the time to go home was before the lights went out. In addition to the pleasure of listening to the foregoing named musical and literary artists in their initial performance, the company was entertained with late social games and closing with light refreshments, which included strawberries and ice cream. As entertainers Mr. and Mrs. Whiting are experts.

Tracy Republican, Feb. 25, 1898

1890s
-›•‹-

Murder of Kitty Ging

Kitty Ging was a 29-year-old, unmarried dressmaker in Minneapolis's fast lane in 1894. Described as a large, good-looking woman, she lived at the fashionable Ozark Flats at Hennepin Av. and 13th St.; the red brick building still stands and is now the Bellevue Condominiums. Her murder, on the edge of a tamarack swamp on the north shore of Lake Calhoun, created quite a stir.

FOUL MURDER!

The Body of Catherine Ging Is Found Near Lake Calhoun.

A Bullet Hole in the Head Tells the Awful Story.

Other Wounds Show that Her Companion Did the Deed.

Harvey Axford Called into Close Conference with the Police.

Harry Haywood Tells About the Dead Woman's Business Affairs.

Murder has been done.

A pedestrian on a lonely, dark road finds the ghastly corpse of a fair woman. By whose hand came it there and in that condition?

That is the question to the solution of which the police are devoting every energy. At the morgue the battered remains of beautiful Catherine Ging lie — terrible evidence of an assassin's dastardly work.

Just why the murderer should have selected her as his victim is not entirely apparent up to this time. It is learned today that she has within a week had at least $7,000 in the safety vaults of the Minnesota Loan and Trust Company, on Nicollet avenue. Robbery may have been the motive but there are other facts in the case which tend to throw discredit upon this theory.

One of the last acts of the dead girl was to engage a single rig at Goosman's West hotel office. [The West was a huge and elegant hotel, known especially for its Grand Stairway, made of white marble.] She drove away alone into the dark. It is known that she had lately been receiving attentions from a certain man, but seems to have exerted herself to having kept her acquaintance with this man from the knowledge of her friends. Undoubtedly this was the man who accompanied Miss Ging on her last ride. Young ladies do not take long drives at night on winter evenings alone. The supposition is that her gentleman friend was picked up soon after she drove away from the West hotel.

The police are now looking for that man.

The body itself tells an awful story. The bullet entered under the right ear, traversing the head diagonally and coming out of the left eye. The nose is broken, the blow causing the fracture having been administered from the right hand side of the face. There is a bad cut just below the mouth, evidently the result of a heavy blow which drove the lip against the teeth. This cut pierced the lip and it is a significant fact that it also is on the right hand side of the face.

When found the body was lying in the road upon a buggy robe. This robe was saturated with blood. The girl's hair was disheveled, a fact in itself which tells of a terrible struggle, inasmuch as Miss Ging was always remarkably neat about her coif-

---

"How intimate the relationship between the two was, remains to be seen, but there must have been a quarrel between them."

---

fure. The buggy, brought back to the livery stable by an intelligent horse, driverless, contained a pool of clotted blood and brains.

These are the facts which the police have to work on, and here are the probable circumstances leading up to the murder and of the deed itself.

In the morning Miss Ging received a note, which, after reading, she tore into small bits, apparently greatly agitated. The boy who brought the note cannot be located today, but Eddie Egan, messenger "47" of the A.D.T., states that he has carried at least 15 or 20 notes to Miss Ging from a man who always telephoned for him from the Nicollet house. This man was about 5 feet 7 inches in height, had a complexion which bespoke high living, gray hair and a light mustache. This man always refused to sign the delivery ticket, and would pay the boy extra for not insisting upon that point. The boy, also, was always instructed never to let anybody see the notes, which were to be delivered personally to Miss Ging.

Last night Miss Ging, in accordance with an arrangement by the note received yesterday morning, proceeded to the West hotel, where she was furnished with a rig by Goosman. She proceeded up Fifth street to First avenue N., where she was met by her friend, according to the appointment. This was about 7:10 p.m. How intimate the relationship between the two was, remains to be seen, but there must have been a quarrel between them.

At 8 o'clock the fatal shot was heard by a woman who lived about 15 rods from the place where the body was found. The buggy containing Miss Ging and her friend must, then, have proceeded almost directly from the West hotel to the spot at which the murder took place. Sergt. Getchell states that he passed the buggy earlier in the evening, at Chicago avenue and Lake street, and that the occupants were quarreling.

The location of all the wounds on the body points to the conclusion that, as the two were driving along, quarreling, the man, who held the reins and consequently sat on the right side of the buggy, threw his left arm over Miss Ging's shoulder, grasping her by the back of the neck, throwing her head forward so that her head hung over the side of the buggy, away from him. The shot must have been fired when the woman was in this position, as shown by the position of the wounds of ingress and egress. The blood and brains in the buggy show that, after the woman was shot in the head, a frightful struggle ensued in the vehicle, during which these awful stains were made.

The broken nose and mutilated lips of the corpse are doubtless marks made by the butt of the revolver, desperately wielded to finish the dark

MISS CATHERINE GING.
(From a Photograph by Haynes)

deed. Finally, the woman becoming unconscious, the murderer, with fiendish deliberation, drove a little to one side of the road, and, taking out the fur robe, spread it upon the ground and laid the bleeding, unconscious body of his victim upon it.

The seemingly insignificant fact that the body was laid upon this robe shows that the murderer must have had some regard for the fair girl whose life was even then fast ebbing away, as the result of his own recklessness. He probably supposed her dead at that time, but the fact that the robe was saturated with blood underneath her wounds when the body was found, shows that she could not have died until some time afterward.

In their search this morning, the police were greatly aided in their work by Messenger Boy "47," who, when several photographs found among the dead woman's effects, were shown him, without hesitation pointed out the photograph of the man who had given him the notes to carry to Miss Ging. It was then the matter of a short time to ascertain the man's name, and the chances are he will be arrested in short order.

"It was evident that Miss Ging had been shot from behind, as shooting herself behind the ear would have been a most difficult feat."

HOW THE BODY WAS FOUND

It Lay Beside the Road on a Robe and Was Yet Warm.

The body was found last night on the Excelsior road, near Thirty-first street.

The condition of the body and the circumstances under which it was found indicate murder. The dead woman was discovered by William Erhart, a baggageman on the Minneapolis, St. Paul & Sault Ste. Marie railway.

When found the body was still warm. It lay face upwards on a buggy robe. A ragged bullet hole showed behind the right ear, and another wound in

Harry Hayward.

the face, just below the left eye, showed where the missile had found egress. The woman's face and hair was bathed in blood, and the robe on which she lay was saturated with it.

Erhart, the man who discovered the body, lives on the Excelsior road. He left the St. Louis car at Thirty-first street, and when a short distance from that point, was passed by a runaway horse attached to a buggy. Fifty yards further on, Erhart found the remains of Miss Ging. He recognized at once that a doctor must be summoned, and at once ran to the nearest drug store, 3001 Hennepin avenue. From this point the case was given over to the police authorities by telephone. The search for a medical man brought Dr. William Russell to the scene. The doctor was accompanied by his son, Jay Russell, and a friend. The patrol wagon caught up with the medical party and carried them to the place indicated by Erhart. Dr. Russell at once decided that the woman was dead. A careful search revealed nothing that could throw light on the case. It was evident that Miss Ging had been shot from behind, as shooting herself behind the ear would have been a most difficult feat.

The body was removed to the morgue, and Coroner Spring summoned. A post mortem examination of the body was made, but nothing in its appearance indicated other violence than the shooting. Miss Ging had been attired in a closely fitting black cloth dress, seal skin sack and a toque hat. The clothing was not disarranged — there was no sign of a struggle. The identification was made by plain markings on the underclothing.

The buggy belonged to Goosman's livery stable. At the stable nothing was known except that Miss Ging engaged the rig last evening at 7 o'clock and went driving alone. The young woman had engaged rigs in a similar manner and had gone out alone three times during the past week. On one occasion she called for the rig and another time she telephoned for it from the West hotel.

Last night at 9:30 the horse entered the barn dragging the empty buggy. The lines were tied about the whip in a manner that made it plain that the buggy had recently been occupied. The stable people point out that the lines would not have remained tied round the whip had there been a runaway, and a belief exists that some one drove the rig down town and turned it loose near the barn.

A large clot of blood and brains was found on the buggy top, inside. No notice was taken of this, the stable men thinking Miss Ging had taken up some one who was injured, and that while she was attending to them the horse had run away. Goosman waited a reasonable length of time and then went to Miss Ging's residence in the Ozark flats. People there knew nothing of her whereabouts, having seen nothing of her since she left the house.

A short time later Lieut. Coskran, of the police department, with Detectives Morrissey and Courtney, visited the rooms at the flats. Miss Ging roomed with her niece, a Miss Ireland, and they were tenants of a family named Murray. Miss Ging's relatives live at Auburn, N.Y. Miss Murray was aroused by the officers and told of the murder. She absolutely refused to credit the story at first, but later understood that it was true. Miss Ireland, the niece, a girl of 17, was then aroused. She was heartbroken, and could not be consoled. Nothing could be learned from her as to Miss Ging's actions during the earlier part of the evening. She did not know who Miss Ging's company was to have been that evening.

The niece, Miss Ireland, furnished a faint clew

in the statement that Miss Ging received a note while at the store yesterday morning. It was brought by a messenger boy. After reading it, Miss Ging tore the note up with every appearance of anger. As to whom the note came from, Miss Ireland had no idea.

Sergt. Henry Getchell, of the Fifth police precinct, made a careful search of the vicinity of the murder after the body had been removed. He found where the buggy had been turned around 50 feet beyond where the body lay. There were also marks of a man's feet. The imprint was that of a sharp-toed shoe. Sergt. Getchell passed the rig on Lake street at about 8:30. He noticed it because the man and woman in it were evidently quarreling. He is certain that it is the same rig in which the murder was committed.

HARVEY AXFORD'S STORY

His Picture Found in Miss Ging's Boudoir.

When Eddie Egan, A.D.T. messenger 47, identified the photograph found on Miss Ging's dresser as the man who had given him notes to carry to her, a search was immediately begun to locate the original. It did not take long for the detectives to identify the picture as that of Harvey Axford, formerly traveling salesman for Patterson & Stevenson and at present local manager for Marx & Haas, a clothing manufacturing house in St. Louis. In the meantime The Journal, without having seen the photograph and without any tip from the officers, had followed another clew which led to Mr. Axford's office, and when the detectives arrived an interview had already been procured by a Journal man. Mr. Axford was first approached on a matter of business and a newspaper lying on a desk afforded sufficient excuse for referring to the tragedy.

"That was an awful murder," said the newspaper man.

"Awful! Awful!" said Mr. Axford excitedly. "I was just reading the noon edition to see if they had any trace of the murderer yet."

"You knew Miss Ging?"

"Know her," replied Axford. "I should say I did. I've known her for six or seven years. We used to board together at the Linden — that is, my wife and I and Miss Ging. Two years ago she went to Chicago with us. She used to visit at the house often and was a great friend of my wife. She was a girl in a thousand. Somebody asked me this morning if I had heard of the murder, and I couldn't believe it. I told my wife to go over and see if she could do anything for the niece."

"As a friend of hers have you any idea what motive there could have been for the murder?"

NOT THE RIGHT WAY

bnt any way to get the work done is the method of some laundries. Ours are different. We look upon your linens, curtains, etc., as something to be carefully and skilfully laundered and returned in a condition as perfect as when it left your house.

TWO HARBORS STEAM LAUNDRY,

T. A. BURY, Manager.

Iron Trade Journal, Two Harbors, June 9, 1898

"No, I haven't, unless some fellow wanted her money. She always had money. Was anything found on the body?"

"Yes, a diamond ring and a gold medal in a chamois skin bag, pinned to her corset."

"Was any ring found on her finger?"

"No."

"Then that ring [in the bag] must have been the one given her by Reed."

"Did you ever go out with Miss Ging?" he was asked.

"Yes, once in a while, but not to amount to anything."

"Did you ever write to her?"

"I believe I have."

"And sent the notes by messenger?"

Real Furniture Bargains!

Judge for yourselves by looking them over in our large window. In connection with our Duluth house we have closed out a large lot of medium-priced Chamber Suits and Tables at a very low cost, from a factory that is going out of business. We own them so cheap that we can well afford to sell them at what other dealers call **Half Price.**

NOTE THIS BARGAIN!
It is a Real Bargain— not Elm or Ash—but SOLID OAK, well finished and carved, for only

$11.75.

Think
—OF—
FRESH,
NEW
GOODS
At these Prices!

	Former Price.	Now.
No. 8—Center Table	$2.50	$1.50
No. 12—Center Table	6.00	3.50
No. 593—Center Table	8.00	6.30
4 Drawer Oak Bureau	13.50	8.90
No. 257—2-piece Chamber Suit	12.50	7.48
No. 59—2-piece Chamber Suit	15.00	9.35

No. 576—Very Heavy 3-piece Chamber Suit, nicely carved, with Bevel Plate Mirror, 24x30...$25 Former Price. / $15.65 Now.

And Last, but Not Least—

No.357--Polished Oak Bookcase and Writing Desk $10 4.85

Customers Out of Town Must Send in Orders Early As These Goods Cannot Last Long! Send for Catalogue, But if these Special Goods Are Wanted, Send for Them At Once, and Mention this Advertisement.

Smith & Farwell Company
409 and 411 Jackson St.

St. Paul Pioneer Press, Dec. 3, 1893

"I never was very intimate with her; only had a passing acquaintance with her, brought about by our business relations."

"Yes."

"How many times?"

"Quite a number."

"When did you write to her last?"

"About a month ago, when I was in Des Moines."

"But when did you write to her when you were in the city?"

Mr. Axford studied a moment and answered: "About three weeks ago, I guess."

"Did you write to her last Saturday?"

"No."

"Do you remember the boy who carried the notes?"

"Yes."

"Did he have red hair?" (Eddie Egan has red hair.)

"No."

"Did Miss Ging have one of your pictures?"

"Yes, and I had one of her."

At this point Detectives Morrissey and Courtney, who had been working all night on the case, entered the room, and broke up the conversation. Mr. Axford was asked to accompany them to police headquarters, where a thorough investigation of his whereabouts last night was conducted.

Mr. and Mrs. Axford room at 1360 Nicollet avenue. Mrs. Axford was not at home this afternoon. The people in the house say that the two went out to dinner last night and returned early and were heard talking in their room all the evening. No one appears to have actually seen them.

HARRY HAYWOOD'S STORY

He accounts for his Whereabouts —
Miss Ging's Finances.

This morning Harry Haywood was seen and was willing to talk on the relations which he sustained toward the murdered woman. It was evident that the unpleasant position in which he was placed by the circumstances of the case was telling on him, as he looked worried and worn out. He was asked to make a statement as to his whereabouts last evening, and without hesitation he said:

"I was at the Ozark until about 7:30, when I left there and went over to take Miss Bartleson, a friend of mine, to the theater. We went together to the Grand Opera House and afterwards I accompanied the young lady to her home and left her after 11 o'clock. The last time I saw Miss Ging was yesterday morning, shortly before 12 o'clock. I did not have any conversation with her, and that was the last time I looked upon her alive. I am thankful that I can account for every moment of my time last night."

Mr. Haywood was next asked what his relations were with the murdered young woman and how long he had been acquainted with her.

"I rented the rooms to her about three weeks ago," he said, "although I have known her for some time previous to that, both in a social and business way. Last summer I used to take her driving, but it has been some time since I have been out with her; it has been at least two months. I never was very intimate with her; only had a passing acquaintance with her, brought about by our business relations. I supposed you wish to know what my business relations were with her. I loaned her at different times large sums of money. I have her notes for different amounts which she got from me during the past summer. I have two for $2,000 and another one for $1,000, which she gave me during August and July. The past week she got about $7,000 from me to start in business, and as security she was to give me a chattel mortgage upon her stock. She was in business in the Syndicate block before, but she desired to extend her business. She was going to rent a store opposite to the Syndicate block to go into the millinery business, and I am not sure but that she

"She always seemed to be a good business woman and knew how to take care of her money."

rented the store last Saturday. Beside the chattel mortgage that I was to hold, she made over to me a $10,000 policy, in the Travelers' Life Insurance Company, to secure the other notes that I had cashed for her. She always seemed to be a good business woman and knew how to take care of her money."

"Did you give this $7,000 to her in money or in the form of a check?" was asked.

"I paid the amount to her in cash, and for some time she seemed desirous to turn all she had into cash. I do not know why she wanted to do it."

"Do you know where she placed the money?"

"She put it in a box which she had rented in one of the trust companies in the city, and I suppose it is there yet, unless she withdrew it lately. I have not heard from the company, and I do not know how we shall find out about it, as I believe the company will refuse to allow any one to look without orders from higher powers."

"Did she have any other place of putting her money that you know of?" was next asked Mr. Haywood.

"She used to have an account with Jones & Sons, I think, but she told me, I am certain, that she had taken everything out of their hands, and I am positive that the trust company was the only place where she kept her money and papers."

After Mr. Haywood told these things about her finances and seemed to know nothing more about them, he was asked whether any suspicion rested upon any one.

"Lately she was very careful that I should not know where she went evenings, telling people that they should not tell me. When she went driving in the evenings, as has been stated before, she was always very careful that I should not find out who she went with. She was acquainted with a man named Reed, of St. Paul, and had gone down there to meet him in various restaurants. This man used to come to Minneapolis also, but lately she gave me the impression that she had given him up, but I have learned that she had received notes from him. This man, perhaps, would know something about her whereabouts last night."

REED OF ST. PAUL

A Former Minneapolitan Gives an Account of Himself.

The theory that a man named Reed, living in St. Paul, was responsible for the death of Catherine Ging is no longer tenable. The only Reed in St. Paul who knew Miss Ging was Frederick I. Reed, manager of the Golden Rule department store, and one of the firm of Reed & Lennon, in South Minne-

THE SWEETS OF LIFE.

"Sweets to the Sweet" is a soulful motto. Who would be guilty of mixing bitter with the sweets offered to such charming creatures? Yet that is just what dishonest confectioners do. Their adulterations are deleterious. Christian Nelson makes a speciality of the very best candies and sells sweets that are at once wholesome and palatable.

Litchfield Saturday Review, Oct. 24, 1891

apolis. This gentleman was formerly for 17 years buyer for Segelbaum Bros., in Minneapolis, and he is a man of well-established reputation. Mr. Reed was called on by a Journal man this morning and

"To what cause do you ascribe the murder?"

asked what he knew of the young woman who was murdered last night. "A good while ago," he said, "I boarded at Mrs. Hemstock's place, the Linden. We were very good friends and went about together a great deal. I have frequently taken her driving and to places of amusement. My belief is that she had no questionable associates whatever, and I knew her as a particularly strong-minded girl, and I am sure that she did not commit suicide. To my mind it is evident that she was murdered for her money. She certainly had saved a considerable sum. I never knew Miss Ging to drink anything. She never drank in my company. I do not know Mr. Haywood, of the Ozark flats."

"To what cause do you ascribe the murder?"

"Perhaps robbery, perhaps a love affair. Miss Ging had a lover in the East whose name I do not know. She told me once that this man was very persistent in his desire to marry her. I do not know whether she cared for him or not. I have not seen Miss Ging for months and knew nothing of her death until I read the papers this morning. Last night I worked here in the store from 7 to 11 o'clock."

The Post Mortem.

A post mortem examination was conducted this morning on Miss Ging's body and revealed that fact that there was another fracture of the skull than that caused by the fatal shot. No other circumstances of significance were noted.

Minneapolis Journal, Dec. 4, 1894

-›-•-‹-

[Want to know who did it?

[Okay, the man responsible for the murder was Harry Hayward, the 29-year-old professional gambler and ne'er-do-well who had courted Kitty Ging. Hayward — incorrectly called Haywood in this and other early newspaper stories — hired someone to do the dirty work.

[Kitty Ging, it turns out, had a reputation for being less than scrupulous. It is impossible to know now if she was Hayward's mistress, but it is clear she liked his money and underworld connections. He had been more interested in her romantically than she in him.

[Hayward hired Claus Blixt, a janitor in his father's apartment building, to take Ging for a buggy ride and do her in. Hayward denied everything, but a jury, after hearing 136 witnesses over 46 days, found him guilty. The court sentenced him "to be hanged by the neck until you are dead." He walked to the gallows in a fashionable cutaway

coat and pinstriped suit. Death came with difficulty; his neck did not break and he thrashed on the rope until he strangled. Claus Blixt pleaded guilty and spent 30 years in prison, becoming quite insane before he died there.

[For an account of the Ging murder and other fascinating cases, see "Murder in Minnesota" by Walter N. Trenery, published in 1985 by the Minnesota Historical Society Press.]

173

"He earns his money like a horse, and too often spends it like an ass."

[This was written during the Spanish-American War, which reflected, in part, American sympathy for the oppressed people of Cuba.]

The St. Paul papers last week related the death by starvation of a six year old child in that city. The little girl was a child of a German family, Mr. and Mrs. John Last. They either did not know enough to make their condition known or were too proud to beg. When Dr. Artz was called the child was beyond recovery. The family have three other children, who had nothing to eat for several days, and their only nourishment was black coffee. The family has since been cared for by the city. The condition of this family is the condition of thousands of families scattered in the larger cities of the country. It is probably not too much to say that there are in the United States as many hungry and starving people as there are in Cuba, but they are not massed, and neither city, State nor Congress has awakened the sympathy of the country in their behalf. It is worse than a mockery; it is a crime, to permit our own people to starve while plunging the country into a gigantic war under the pretense of relieving suffering Cubans. But there would not be a chance to make political capital out of quietly distributed home charity, nor to make millionaires of army and navy contractors. This is a big country, and we do things on a large scale, leaving the little affairs to take care of themselves.

New Ulm News, May 30, 1898

—>-<—

LUMBERING

[A lumberjack from Grand Rapids wrote this essay for his hometown newspaper "in the cheerful accompaniment of the howling of apparently every wolf in Itasca county." He was identified only as L.J.]

No one knows till he has tried it, how thoroughly cut off from the world the denizens of a lumber camp are in the winter. No news of the outside world less than two to four weeks old. The "hope long deferred that maketh the heart sick" of getting a letter from your best girl "next time the tote team gets in," and the almost certainty that the best girl aforesaid is making the best use of her time, and has another fellow on the string. The growing familiarity of the ... bedbug, familiarity by the way that breeds contempt — and misery — in very short order. The hard work of the woods, the generally poorly ventilated camps wherein a man of good sense of smell, may readily locate every sleeper who has supped — "not wisely but too well" on the succulent bean. The frozen heels, noses and ears which agreeably vary the monotony of camp life; ... these and many other causes combine to make the life of the Lumber Jack ... rather more full of variety than pleasure.

Yet in spite of all its drawbacks, the Lumber Jack's life has a fascination quite equal to that the briny wave has for Tarry Jack. To be sure he earns his money like a horse, and too often spends it like an ass. ...

The Lumber Jack is a man whose faults are those of a strong manly nature. He never turns his back on friend or foe. He will share his last dollar with a friend, and thrash any man who offers insult or injury to woman or child in his presence. He is never an anarchist or encourager of such like lunacy. He is honest, courageous, and in short as good a citizen as they make. Above all he has the true American independence, and would shake hands with the Czar of Russia on his throne, aye, and call him "Nick old boy" and ask him out to have a drink as soon as look at him.

Grand Rapids Magnet, Dec. 10, 1891

—>-<—

Not a single sawmill in Minneapolis has been able to start up yet because of low water-level and the resulting lack of timber. The lumber industry of Minneapolis is as everyone knows the most extensive in the world. About 6,000 workers are employed at the local sawmills, when they are running and all these workmen are now praying for rain every passing day. May their prayers be heard soon, as this has been a hard winter for many. This has been the most beautiful spring anyone can remember, but rain, a great deal of rain, is now needed in order for the crops to grow.

Svenska Amerikanska Posten, Minneapolis, April 30, 1895

"Deceased's lot in life was not as a path strewn with roses."

The Final Summons. Mrs. Mary Williams, wife of Oliver Williams, died at her home in this village Monday forenoon of diabetes. She was about 70 years of age and had been ill for some time. Deceased suffered a partial loss of sight and hearing in addition to failure of health, and her environments were such that she was the object of much pity and sympathy. She suffered great agony before being relieved from pain by death's cold embrace.

Deceased's lot in life was not as a path strewn with roses. Her days of sunshine and happy contentment were limited, and many of the comforts and blessings of life denied to her. The things of this world do not stand equipoise; in this life there are many incongruities and inconsistencies; our scales of justice do not balance, measure and deal out equality. But death is the great leveler that evens up all of the inequalities of this world, and it is a blessed thought that when we are done with the things of time the final judgment which carries us through the ceaseless ages of eternity will be a just one.

The funeral was held yesterday, services being conducted at the house by Rev. James Godward, who based his remarks upon the words of the scripture as found in Ecclesiastes third chapter and second verse: "A time to be born, and a time to die; a time to plant, and a time to pluck up that which is planted."

The body was interred in Union cemetery east of town, Messrs. Ole O. Canestorp, P.H. Clague, K.O. Laastuen, Lars Lynne, H.T. Fikkan and M. Warfield acting as pall-bearers.
Grant County Herald, Elbow Lake, Feb. 2, 1899

—>-<—

Wanted — A bar-tender, must possess superior intelligence and be a strictly "total abstainer." . . . Only a clear head can be capable of the quickness and alertness required to mix the three hundred standard drinks, as well as the new ones constantly coming into use.
Annandale Advocate-Post, June 29, 1899

—>-<—

On Monday the McCalla house, occupied by Mr. Steele and relatives, caught fire and the roof was destroyed before the fire could be stopped. There were some exciting events. One man

☞ DONALDSON'S ☜
GLASS BLOCK!

The daily crowded condition of our big store makes advertising seem almost superfluous, It is freely admitted that we do not only the largest business in this section, but one of the

Biggest in the Country.

The Following Important Bargains Offered for All This Week:

Dress Goods Dep.

18 1-2c, worth 35c.

Forty pieces, the balance of our rich Tweed Bourette Suitings, full 36 inches wide, elegant colorings; 35c is a low price, To clean them up quickly we say 18 1-2c yard.

39c, worth 69c.

Strictly all wool Scotch Tweeds Alsatain and Golden Rod Suitings, 38 and 42 inches wide, beautiful styles and colorings, some have been 50c and some 69c, now all in one immense lot to close out quickly at **39c** a yard.

Brilliantines.

59c, worth $1.

Blacks and all the new rich colors in beautiful lustre brilliantines, 40 and 42-in. wide goods, 89c and $1 qualities, 125 pieces. To clean up quickly we say 59c per yard.

Silk Department.

Ten pieces of 27-inch black Japanese silk, French dye, splendid value for $1.00 per yard.

Special 75c per yd.

Wash Silks, Twilled Indias, new designs, changeable surahs, all new and desirable, worth $1.00 per yard.

Special price 69c.

Upholstery Dep.

Rope Portiers.

$6.98 each.

17 strand --- all the newest colorings, peach and blue, ecru and peach, sage and peach, worth $8.50; while they last, $6.98 each.

Dotted Muslins

25c yard.

Finest of Scotch weave Mahogany, blue, Nile yellow, shrimp or white dots on fine muslin ground, worth 30c, special 25c yard.

Printed Draperies

6 1-2c yard.

32 and 36 inches wide, in a big line of colorings and patterns, bargains at 10c, special 6 1-2c yard.

Nottingham Lace Curtains

75c pair.

Heavy side borders, taped edges, excellent quality of lace, 42 inches wide and 3 yards long, a grand bargain at $1.00, special 75c pair.

Chenile Covers

59c each.

4-4 size, mottled effects; fringed all around, a bargain at 75c, special 59c each.

Hosiery -:- Dep.

Ladies' full regular made hose in fancy boot patterns in tan, mode and slate colors, splendid value at 19c. Our price **15c.**

Ladies' full regular made fast black 40 gauge cotton hose, made with double soles and high spliced heels. Our famous Glass Block Special. Cannot be duplicated for less than 40c. Our price **25c.**

Childrens' heavy cotton hose, Derby and Rich elieu ribbed, made with double knees, soles and toes, sizes 6 to 10 inches. Our price **25c** all sizes.

Underwear.

Ladies' genuine French lisle thread vests, low neck sleeveless, silk ribbon on neck and arms; imported Swiss garments, our price **50c.**

Ladies' lisle combination suits, in ecru only; in low neck, high neck short sleeves, high neck long sleeves, our prices **89c, $1, $1.19** per suit. Value $1, $1.25, $1.50.

Ladies' pure China silk thread vests. The handsomest garment made, in black and colors, our staple $4.98 garment; our special price **$2.75** all sizes.

Wash Goods Dep.

Bargains Extraordinary.

Scotch Ginghams, 20c and 25c qualities; French printed novelties, have sold at 25c and 35c; our special price **12 1-2c** per yard.

Scotch Zephyrs.

All new weaves. Bedford cords, crepons, Paisley spots, silk stripes, elegant styles, have sold at 50 and 60c. Your choice **39c** per yard.

Satin Broche.

The latest printed fabric, black grounds, with colored figures, the finest lot of designs we have shown. Actual value 50c and 60c per yard. Special price **39c** per yard.

10,000 yards of fancy ginghams, always sold at 10c; 2 cases 10 counting flannels; special price 5c per yard. Limit 20 yards to a customer.

Decoration Bunting

In Any Quality at Special Prices. See Our Window Display.

The sale of decoration bunting is unprecedentedly large. You'd better get what you want at once while our assortment is complete.

DONALDSON'S   GLASS   BLOCK   STORE.

The North, May 25, 1891

"The splendid complexions and color of English women are due largely to their judicious outdoor life."

carried a flat iron across the street where it would not catch fire, handling it like a basket of eggs. Another carried a bucket of water three blocks and tried to throw it on the roof. Another one threw a hand-grenade which went through the roof, out of the window and narrowly missed killing some of the fire company. The occupants lost nothing, thanks to neighborly assistance, and desire us to express their thanks to the public, and particularly the fire company.
Annandale Advocate-Post, Aug. 3, 1899

–>-<–

The State Fair is one of the annual events that every farmer ought to take in. It represents largely the very interests which he cares most for; in fact there is nothing outside of the amusement features that he is not familiar with. He can take the boys and girls to enjoy them with him. He can be assured that they will be entertaining, exciting and at the same time worthy of the state and the occasion. There will not be a single department at the fair which will not well repay a day's study and the amusement will fill up the evenings agreeably.
Annandale Advocate-Post, Aug. 24, 1899

–>-<–

How to be Beautiful. Keep the body in a condition of exquisite cleanliness, avoid impure and strongly scented soaps and be careful in the choice of cosmetics.

Put on sensible shoes, and in comfortably fitting garments take brisk walks in the open air.

Be careful to eat simple food and keep the internal mechanism in order.

Keep regular and early hours. Get plenty of sleep.

Avoid worry and fretting over trifles, which will give a strained,

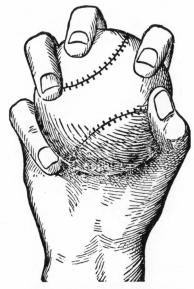

Judgment !

From every tobacco chewer is wanted as to the merits of

LORILLARD'S

Climax

PLUG.

All good judges of chewing tobacco have thus far been unanimous in pronouncing it the best in quality, the most delicious in flavor, the best in every way. It's Lorillard's.
Ask the dealer for it.

Long Prairie Leader, May 6, 1895

tired look and eventually wrinkles.

Women who want color in their faces — that is, natural color — must take plenty of exercise and enjoy fresh air. To stay in a room which is not well ventilated after having been out for a walk is as bad as having no walk at all. The splendid complexions and color of English women are due largely to their judicious outdoor life. The cause of sallow skins in young people is, as a rule, lack of exercise. It is foolish to think that

because one is active indoors, nature is satisfied. Never was there a greater mistake. As surely as a plant needs fresh air and sunshine, so does the human being. If possible, it is not too much to spend two hours daily in the open air, going for a brisk walk of four miles if you can stand it. If this is continued, the clearness and texture of the skin will improve. Besides this, the feeling of elasticity and good humor which it will impart will make it well worth all the trouble. Nothing makes one so dull, morbid and heavy looking as constant indoor life. No matter how active may be the demands of that life, nothing can compensate for the loss of outdoor exercise. The exercise is better for being taken in the early hours of the morning, for then the air is purer and the body in better condition. Fresh air should enter the living as well as the sleeping rooms. The state of the skin of course varies with the state of the atmosphere. A dry climate is hard on the best skin.
Grant County Herald, Elbow Lake, Sept. 21, 1899

–>-<–

How to Become Muscular. Walk a great deal, carrying something always in the hands. This develops the arms. To roll a hoop might be good if one were brave enough to do so in public. Practice lifting a little every day. Never strain or tire yourself. Eat meat, drink milk and practice bending backward, forward and sideways every day. At night rub about a tablespoonful of brandy or rum into your skin on the under and tender part of the arms.
Grant County Herald, Elbow Lake, Oct. 12, 1899

–>-<–

1900s

In 1900, 43 percent of Minnesota farm land was in wheat. A new tide of immigration centered in the northern and western parts of Minnesota. Lumbering was at its peak in 1905; 300 mills were operating in the state. The automobile age began; 7,000 cars were licensed in the state by 1909.

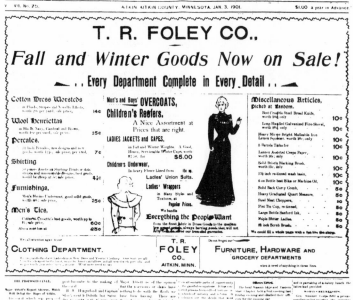

1900s

–>•<–

A New Century

The advent of the 20th century was heralded — not when one might think, at the end of 1899, but at the end of 1900. Think about it. The first year was the year 1, right? Right. So the first 1900 years were over at the end of 1900 A.D., making Jan. 1, 1901, the first day of the 20th century. So the hoopla was in 1901.

THE NEW YEAR.

The old year passed away at the stroke of twelve on Monday night and a new one as well as a new century was born. We are sometimes told by the pessimist that the world is getting worse instead of better, but a comparison of the world today with what it was a century ago in every domain must lead to the inevitable conclusion that the people whose privilege it has been to greet the dawn of the new century are living in the blessedness of a light never dreamed of by the forefathers.

The science of the Nineteenth Century has emancipated thought from the yoke of ancient superstition. It has radically changed our concepts of the genesis of life in plants and animals and man, of the earth and of the universe, of society and government. . . . It has revolutionized the methods of education, of dealing with insanity, pauperism and crime. It has purified and energized the philanthropy of the world. It has transformed medicine from an empirical mystery to a science, armed it with the power to prevent or cure a multitude of devastating diseases which had baffled the physicians of an earlier day, and raised sanitation to an essential department of domestic and municipal economy. It has banished pain from the operations of surgery. In demonstrating the certainty that the universe is governed by unchangeable laws, it has so modified old beliefs that religion, which formerly resented its profane intrusion into its sanctuaries of dogma and tradition, now goes hand and hand with it in proclaiming the fatherhood of God and the brotherhood of man. It has abolished the slavery of body and mind. It has made the education of the masses the chief concern of every enlightened state. It has emancipated women from the thralldom of old conventions and opened to them all suitable paths of opportunity in the gainful occupations. It has converted prisons from cells of torture into schools of industry and reform. It has driven out the devils that were supposed to possess the insane, and in every state has established hospitals for the humane and rational treatment of these victims of cerebral disease. It has established schools for the deaf and dumb and feeble-minded. It has done away with piracy and privateering, and in many ways mitigated the horrors of war. In cheapening and multiplying the productions of the press it has immensely increased its power and has brought the government of all lands more and more under the sway of the enlightened public opinion of the world. It has liberalized thought, assuaged the animosities of sects and made universal toleration a tacit canon of all creeds and of all the codes of morals and manners. There is no pause in the persistence of force or in the operation of the great law of development. All the achievements of the past are but the elementary beginnings of the great work on which science and invention have entered — the stepping stones to higher things. They are pregnant with the promise and the potency of a richer and nobler fruitage in the century whose opening gates we have entered. Luminous as has been the era marked off in historic chronology as the Nineteenth Century, its light has penetrated only the fringe of the dark mass of barbarism, of ignorance, of poverty, which still darkens a large part of the world and the under strata of society even in civilized states. Stupendous as seems the progress the world has made even in our day, it has brought us only to the foothills of the vast ascent whose far-off summits, rising with the centuries,

*"The palace-like residence of Mr. and Mrs. Hill on Summit avenue
was the scene of the wedding."*

will be crowned with the glory of that new day when wars shall cease and poverty and crime shall be no more and the parliament of man shall proclaim the reign of righteousness and peace throughout the federation of the world.

Aitkin Republican, Jan. 3, 1901, reprinted in part from the St. Paul Pioneer Press

—⇥•⇤—

[Charlotte Hill was the first of the children of railroad magnate James J. Hill to be married in the family's new mansion on St. Paul's Summit Avenue. Described as quiet and not particularly sociable, Charlotte chose a "simple" wedding.]

At high noon today the third daughter of Mr. and Mrs. James J. Hill was wedded to a young man from the East.

The Hill-Slade nuptials have been the chief topic of conversation and speculation for weeks, not alone in St. Paul's exclusive set, but in New York and Philadelphia as well. The Slades have a wide connection in the East, and as the Hill family is coming to be as well known in New York city as in St. Paul, the interest in the wedding has been even greater than might have been expected from the mere prominence of the bride's family.

The palace-like residence of Mr. and Mrs. Hill on Summit avenue was the scene of the wedding.

The interior, with its richly hung walls, its stately rooms, its splendid gallery of pictures, and its wide reception hall, was made even more beautiful by a magnificent arrangement of flowers. These were largely from the Hills' own conservatories, as were also the palms, vines and other foliage employed in the decoration.

During the ceremony the place was a veritable "Dream of Fair Women." By far the greater number of the guests were women. Miss Hill has been much abroad and absent at boarding school, and her intimate friends in St. Paul are therefore confined chiefly to the young women she knew at the Visitation convent and the daughters of her mother's more intimate friends. A few men were in the company, but these were relatives of either the bride or the groom.

It was feared until last evening that Archbishop John Ireland would not be in the city to officiate at the nuptials. He arrived, however, late yesterday, and was able to gratify the wish of his old friends in officiating at their daughter's wedding. [Mrs. Hill was Catholic; her husband was not. The archbishop was a friend of theirs.]

The guests began arriving a few minutes before the noon hour. By 12 o'clock half a hundred carriages were waiting at the door to unload their freight of handsomely gowned women. It was but a little after the moment of high meridian when the organ pealed out its nuptial summons, and the bridal procession swept down the stairs. Five minutes later George Theron Slade and Charlotte Elizabeth Hill were pronounced man and wife.

The archbishop was assisted in the service by the aged Msgr. A. Oster, the priest who officiated at

Ely Miner, Dec. 11, 1901

"The service was extremely simple."

Albert Lea Evening Tribune, Nov. 24, 1908

Mr. and Mrs. Hill's marriage, more than thirty years ago.

Rev. Fr. Patrick Heffron, of St. Paul's seminary, was also present to take part in the ceremony.

The service was extremely simple, notwithstanding the presence of the three distinguished prelates.

All the guests were assembled in the white drawing room, which overlooks the river. The three great windows at the end were hung with heavy garlands of white asters. The white festoons extended far over the walls at either side.

Just before the windows stood the three clergymen in canonical robes.

There was no altar, but a pre dieu pillow of white satin marked the place to be occupied by the bride and groom.

The music room is just opposite the white room,

*"She wore a tulle veil and carried a large bouquet of lilies of the valley
tied with a white gauze ribbon."*

and there Mr. Danz's orchestra was stationed, and there G.H. Fairclough was seated at the pipe organ.

As they began the wedding march, the two children of Mr. and Mrs. Samuel Hill, niece and nephew of the bride, entered the room and stretched white ribbons at either side of a central aisle. [The children's mother was James J. Hill's eldest daughter, Mary Frances. She had married Samuel Hill, a Minneapolis attorney and not a blood relative.]

The ushers, Brinkerhoff Thorne and Mr. Loomis, of New York city, caught the ribbons and held them at the door.

First in the bridal procession came Mrs. James J. Hill, with Mr. Hill, her brother-in-law, with Mr. and Mrs. Samuel Hill and Mr. and Mrs. Louis Hill following. These, the bride's near relatives, took their places at the left and near the clergymen.

Mr. Slade, with James N. Hill [the bride's brother], his best man, entered next and stood at the right.

The Misses Clara and Rachel Hill came next, and, following them, the eldest daughter of Mr. and Mrs. Samuel Hill, with Gertrude Hill, the bride's youngest sister.

Mr. and Mrs. George P. Slade, the groom's parents, with his aunts and sisters, entered and stood at the right of the clergymen.

Miss Ruth Hill was the only bridesmaid, and she, walking alone, preceded her father and the bride.

The bride was dressed in an exquisite plain white satin gown, with thin yokes at both front and back from which fell a deep ruffle of point lace. She wore a tulle veil and carried a large bouquet of lilies of the valley tied with a white gauze ribbon.

Miss Ruth Hill wore pink chiffon and satin and carried pink roses.

The other girls in the bridal party wore simple gowns of white chiffon.

Mrs. James J. Hill wore a handsome costume of white brocaded crepe.

Mower County Transcript, Austin, Aug. 24, 1905

Mrs. Slade was in black and white silk.

Mrs. Louis Hill wore her wedding gown of white satin, point lace and gardenias with green leaves in her hair.

Mrs. Samuel Hill's costume was of light tan silk.

After the ceremony, Mr. and Mrs. George Theron Slade, the newly-wedded pair, stood for a few minutes to receive the guests.

Mr. and Mrs. James J. Hill and Mrs. Louis Hill stood in line with them.

A wedding breakfast was served on small tables in the dining room, fifty guests being seated at once.

The tables were decorated with maiden hair ferns, with clusters of lilies of the valley and American beauty roses.

The hall and staircase were decorated with palms, with large bunches of yellow chrysanthemums surmounting the newel posts.

The guests were given an opportunity to see the many handsome gifts. Some of these were superb. Especially noticeable was a case of beautiful silver, comprising an entire table service, from the bride's parents, and a dozen gold plates. Another beautiful gift was a Russian enamel bowl, which was distinguished by connoisseurs from among the Russian exhibits at the world's fair. This was the gift of James N. Hill.

There was an exquisite pearl ring for the bride, a carved wedding chest and a silver bowl.

Nearly 300 guests were present. . . .

The bride and groom have not revealed to their friends the destination of their wedding journey. They will leave in Mr. Hill's private [railroad] car this evening and after Christmas will go to housekeeping in New York city.

Miss Hill is 22 years of age. She resembles her father and is said to be much like him mentally as well as facially. She is intensely practical, and devoted to a few friends rather than to society at large. She has an athletic figure and is an excellent golf player. She has had excellent musical training and is widely read. Like her sisters, Miss Charlotte Hill

"A bouncing baby boy made his appearance in the home of Mr. and Mrs. Charles Peterson."

MEATS

Have you been at our market recently and seen our stock of Hams, Bacon, Salt Pork, Lard, Beef, Pork and Provisions? Our Meats are the choicest money can buy and we guarantee every pound we sell. Below we quote a few prices:

Boneless Breakfast **Bacon, lb** 12½c	**Pig Pork Roast, lb** 10c
Sugar Cured **Picnic Hams, lb** 9c	**Pig Pork Steak, lb** 10c
Sured Cured **Hams, lb** 12½c	**Round Steak, lb** 10c
Our Pure Dairy Brand **Lard, lb** 10c	**Shoulder Steak, 8 and 10c**
Salt Pork, 12 lbs $1.00	**Shoulder Spare Ribs, lb**
½ barrel Salt Pork at Wholesale Prices	**3c, 10 lbs** 25c
Boiling Beef, lb 4c	
Short Rib Beef, lb 5c	**Hamberger Steak, lb** . . 10c
Roast Beef, lb . . 8c and 10c	**Pork Sausage, 3 lbs** . . . 25c

Cash Paid for Butter and Eggs.

We invite you to call and see the quality of the meat we have to offer at these prices and be convinced that you can save money by trading with us.

HORMEL'S PROVISION MARKET.

Mower County Transcript, May 17, 1905

is an expert needlewoman, and it will be remembered that many of the soldiers in the Philippines and in Cuba have owed comfort to her busy fingers. Mrs. Hill has trained her daughters in all of the household arts and this young St. Paul girl will bring to her husband gifts of far greater worth than the large fortune which she will inherit. Miss Hill is anything but a social butterfly. Indeed the few who know her intimately speak of her as being interested only in those society functions of the quieter and less formal sort.

Miss Charlotte Hill is the fifth in a family of eight children. Those older than she are James and Louis Hill, Mrs. Samuel Hill and Miss Clara Hill.

The Slade family is well known in New York, where it has long been prominent. Mr. Slade is a graduate of Yale, where he was a classmate of Miss Hill's brothers and where he was as closely devoted to his studies as he was to athletics. He already ranks high in the business world and in railroad circles.

St. Paul Dispatch, Oct. 9, 1901

[The Hill mansion now is owned by the Minnesota Historical Society and is open for tours. Have a look and decide how "simple" you think the wedding was.]

→·←

A bouncing baby boy made his appearance in the home of Mr. and Mrs. Charles Peterson on Thursday of last week, and the number of cigars Charley dug up was almost enough to cause a cigar famine.

Kittson County Enterprise, Hallock, Jan. 12, 1900

→·←

*"A calm nature is necessary, too, for a person always in a flutter
either with rage or joy wears himself out."*

Call a girl a chick and she smiles; call a woman a hen and she howls. Call a woman a witch and she is pleased; call an old woman a witch and she is indignant. Call a girl a kitten and she rather likes it; call a woman a cat and she hates you. Women are queer. If you call a man a gay dog it will flatter him; call him a pup, a hound or a cur and he will try to alter the map of your face. He dont mind being called a bull dog or a bear and yet he will object to being mentioned as a calf or a cub. Men are queer, too.

Turtle River Pine Tree, Jan. 18, 1900

→·•·←

People Who Live Long. Those who live long are always small eaters. The enormous task the liver and stomach of a gourmand have daily is too much for any system.

Because one's parents and grandparents lived to be nearly 100 does not make it certain that their descendants will do likewise, for the inheritance of vitality may all be dissipated in 20 years of high living. A small stock of vital force well taken care of may last twice as long.

Usually with long-lived folk the trunk is long and the legs short in proportion. The habit of deep, slow breathing also belongs to this section of the human race. A calm nature is necessary, too, for a person always in a flutter either with rage or joy wears himself out. Easy motions and a light step, with muscular relaxation, are other characteristics.

People who are long lived all have certain physical traits that are not noticeable. In the first place they have straight backs. The majority of folk have curvature of the spine in some degree, unnoticeable it may be, but it is there. The man who will live to be old has a straight back, holds his head up and had a broad, deep chest. This means that the vital or-

gans are not crowded and perform their functions unimpeded.
Worthington Gazette, March 2, 1900

→·•·←

[Today's rules of free press/

fair trial would not permit this kind of writing.]

L.N. Bailey, of Bemidji, was in the city last week. Mr. Bailey is attorney for Rus Whipple, the man that murdered Bennie

"My wife pitied me and petted me and made so much of me that the toothache disappeared!"

Moore last week in Bemidji, and was here endeavoring to ascertain what he could of the former character of his client. Whipple is not spoken well of by people of this city who used to know him.
Thief River Falls News, Feb. 15, 1900

→•←

The Markets. Our markets of the week are as follows: Young men — unsteady; girls — lively, in demand; coffee — considerably mixed; fresh fish — active and slippery; wheat — a grain better than barley; eggs — quiet, but will probably open in a few days; whiskey — steadily going down; onions — strong and rising; breadstuffs — heavy; boots and shoes — those in market "soled," and steadily going up and down; hats and caps — not as high as last fall . . .; tobacco — very slow and has downward tendency; money — close, but not close enough to get hold of; feathers — light and going up; iron — very firm; butter — growing stronger; opium — a drug in the market; advice — good, but no demand.
Thief River Falls News, July 26, 1900

→•←

A Natural Conclusion. There is a small boy in this town who has a father noted for his business ability, but who occasionally makes the air blue when things do not suit him. The other day while the small youth was playing, his mother heard some words that filled her with consternation. She promptly punished the small offender in a most summary manner, and when she discovered him thinking deeply a short time afterward, she hoped her lesson was "doing him good." At night, when the father returned, his son climbed into his lap, and in a most confidential tone he said, "Say papa, we've got to be more careful. Mamma hears a d—n sight more

Flood it with sunlight
whenever you can—that's all the renovating needed by
THE STEARNS & FOSTER
Look for our name **MATTRESS** on every Mattress

The "Webbing Process," employed exclusively in all Stearns & Foster Mattresses, makes them the most **Comfortable**—most **Enduring** that can possibly be made.

The Stearns & Foster Mattress is the product of the largest mattress factory in the **World**. This means something to you. It means that these mattresses are produced at the **minimum** of cost, which enables **you** to buy at the **lowest possible prices** consistent with **honest, well-made** mattresses.

Open   Closed
This device on every Mattress

Come in to-day • let us show you The Stearns & Foster Mattress. Several styles to choose from. Better mattresses **could not** be made or sold for less money.

Sold by **PALACE FURNITURE COMPANY** ALBERT LEA MINN.

Albert Lea Evening Tribune, Oct. 29, 1908

than we give her credit for."
Morris Sun, Nov. 15, 1900

→•←

His Remedy. An exchange [newspaper] tells of a man suffering from toothache, who met a friend and told him his woes, when the following dialogue occurred: Friend — "Ah, I had just as bad a toothache as you, yester-

day, and I went home, and my wife pitied me and petted me and made so much of me that the toothache disappeared! You take my tip." Sufferer — "Is your wife at home now, do you think?"
Morris Sun, Nov. 22, 1900

→•←

Alex Thompson, of Crookston, was in town Tuesday, look-

"There is no denying the fact that considerable thieving is going on in this village in way of appropriating wood and coal."

---

ing after his business interests here. Mr. Thompson wore the coat he recently won at a church fair in a contest between Conductor Murray and himself for the "handsomest" man in the parish. The coat is a fine coonskin with fine quilted satin lining and Otter collar and cuffs. It brought the handsome sum of $680. Alex says there isn't much in the coat, but the handsome thing of it is knowing that he is "the handsomest man in the parish."
Kittson County Enterprise, Hallock, Nov. 30, 1900

→-←

On Friday evening the Coffee Club will discuss the question, "Who is the greatest person of the century?" Five names have been selected, namely Ruskin, Bismarck, Lincoln, Napoleon and Gladstone, and their respective claims to such distinctive designation will be considered and discussed.
Morris Sun, Dec. 20, 1900

→-←

There is a story of a fugitive murderer caught by a mob of lynchers. "How did you know me?" "We recognized you by your picture in the papers," replied the ringleader. "Do I really look like that?" "Yes." "Then hang me."
Canby News, Jan. 25, 1901

→-←

The four-year-old son of F.W. Farnum, who lives in Hammer, swallowed a common barb wire fence staple last Thursday evening about 6 o'clock, and it did not come away from him until the following Saturday afternoon. The only remedy used to effect this was to feed the child coarse food, bread and butter and the like. Fortunately the staple passed through as the child swallowed it, the smooth or rounded portion first. The boy seems to be

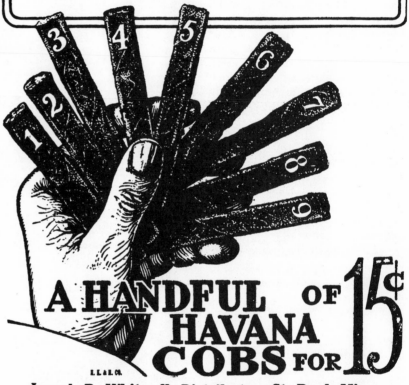
none the worse for his experience, but a great weight of anxiety is lifted from the parents.
Canby News, Feb. 15, 1901

→-←

There is no denying the fact that considerable thieving is going on in this village in way of appropriating wood and coal that is not kept under lock and key. Certain parties are known to do this business and if they persist in loafing around with the expectancy of roasting their shins by the fuel earned by the sweat of someones else brow, it is only a question of little time when they will be brought up with a short turn. A man who will himself engage in this nefarious business and even allow his children to steal for him needs mighty close watching.
Canby News, March 22, 1901

"Religion seems to be the cause of her insanity."

Last Monday Mrs. Ole Johnson living a short distance south of this place, was brought in for examination before the board of insanity. She was adjudged insane and was taken to the asylum in the afternoon by Sheriff Anderson. Mrs. Johnson had been mentally deranged for some time, but only in a mild form, until lately, when she had rapidly grown worse. Religion seems to be the cause of her insanity.

Kittson County Enterprise, Hallock, April 25, 1901

→-<-

The cost of the average boy who is depending upon his parents until he reaches the age twenty-one years for a livelihood has been figured out by an interested party to be $4,000, and an eastern paper questions whether it pays to raise boys at this price, especially when the boy turns out to be a cigarette fiend with a breath like a turkey buzzard and untrammeled and an unconquerable desire to avoid work. Not all boys, nor any great majority of them, are of the class above mentioned and there are many people in this world of ours who would give many times the amount for two strong arms to lean upon in their declining years. There are boys and boys.

Brainerd Dispatch, July 5, 1901

→-<-

Rest rooms are now quite generally advocated by the local press and progressive citizens throughout the country. The Canby Herald says on the subject: We see from some of our exchanges that various towns have provided free rest rooms for the accommodation of women and small children from the country. Such a move it seems to us is decidedly practicable, and no doubt highly appreciated by those who have ridden a long distance and become weary, especially by those who have little children with

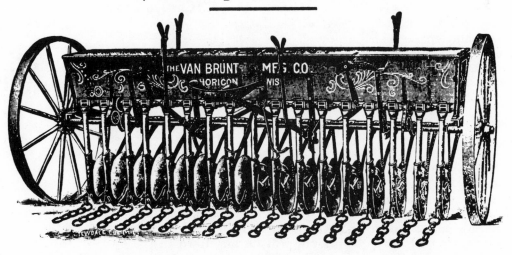
Bellingham Times, Dec. 29, 1904

"We heard of a man the other day who said that tobacco was what saved his life."

them to care for. We know of nothing that could be established here in Canby, at a small expense, that would be more appreciated by those who come here to trade, than the opening of such a free rest room. We are hardly prepared to say just how the small expense of maintaining the room could be met, but presume it could be done by contributions from the business men whom these people patronize. We think the matter is worth considering.

Minneota Mascot, July 12, 1901

–⟩–⟨–

As we went to press Thursday evening last week it was impossible for us to notice several social functions that took place here that evening. Mrs. N.W.L. Jaeger entertained about twenty ladies at four o'clock coffee; Miss Theresa Sanderson gave a party at which a score of young ladies were present; Mr. and Mrs. J.S. Anderson entertained about fifty friends at a lawn party, and quite a number of young people enjoyed a dance at the G.T. Hall. All this in one evening speaks well for Minneota from a social standpoint. However, our people have always been given credit for being sociable, so it is not at all surprising.

Minneota Mascot, Sept. 6, 1901

–⟩–⟨–

Anton Helleckson was in town this week and informed us that his arm, or rather the stub that is left of what was once an arm, is now nearly healed. Anton has little love for corn shredders and we can't blame him. There should be a law against selling these machines, at least unless the manufacturers furnish a cast iron man to do the feeding.

Minneota Mascot, Dec. 6, 1901

–⟩–⟨–

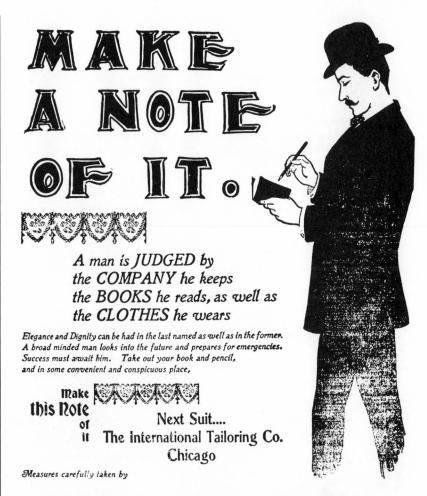
We heard of a man the other day who said that tobacco was what saved his life. The doctors had given him up. He tried everything but still he ran down in flesh. He had become a mere skeleton. As the last resort a doctor prescribed chewing tobacco, just plain, ordinary navy plug. He went to chewing and to-day he weighs 240 pounds, and is as hearty as a buck. He also has tobacco all over his shirt bosom, and some people wonder if he might not just about as well remain sick.

Redwood Gazette, Redwood Falls, Dec. 18, 1901

–⟩–⟨–

Wants a Divorce
Mrs. Cloutier Does Not Love Her Husband.

Caroline Cloutier has asked for a divorce from her husband, who conducts a small store . . . in this city.

Mrs. Cloutier has had troubles

10

Per Cent
Discount
for Cash
will be given
on all
Merchandise
and Millinery
Goods on

Wednesday, Nov 18

OF THIS WEEK

Just think of it, a 10 per cent discount for cash on all brand new selected goods at this time of the year, for

THE OPENING DAY ONLY

We will have an Ostrich Plume, which is 6 feet long and valued at $500.00, on exhibition for the Opening.

Remember the Day, the Place and the Discount

SOUVENIRS FOR THE LADIES.   MUSIC FOR ALL.

Selected Music by Clausen's Orchestra.

Lembke Dry Goods Company

Albert Lea, Minnesota

Albert Lea Evening Tribune, Nov. 16, 1908

"She alleges that the present spouse is abusive, calls her names which would not look well in print, plays handball with the dishes, and is very jealous."

of her own until you cannot rest, having been married four times. She lived on a farm north of Crookston with her first husband and found, after several years, that he had a wife living from whom he had never been divorced. He died, however, before separation was brought about. She then married No. 2, but was speedily divorced from him. Cupid served her a queer trick next time and she succumbed to the smiles of an Indian named of Deszelart. Mr. and Mrs. Deszelart were very happy until the bride discovered that her husband had another wife in Canada.

She sued for a divorce and the day it was granted met and loved the present incumbent of the chair at the head of her table.

She alleges that the present spouse is abusive, calls her names which would not look well in print, plays handball with the dishes, and is very jealous. She will therefore sue the court that absolute divorce be granted her. Cloutier is said to be quite rich having several farms and a valuable piece of property in Thief River Falls.

Thief River Falls News, Dec. 19, 1901

→•←

Died. — On Tuesday June 17th, the two-year-old son of Mr. and Mrs. Oscar Olson of Bismark. He had been sick from mumps a few days and contracted a cold and inflammation from which he died. The funeral was held Friday from the Swedish Lutheran Church, Rev. Sard of Lafayette officiating in the absence of Rev. Bergstrom. The remains were interred in the Winthrop cemetery.

Winthrop News, June 19, 1902

→•←

The people of Winthrop have made a Christmas present to an unfortunate woman in that city which will have its influence with the great St. Peter at the

"Charity of that kind comes from a neighborhood where it must be a pleasure to live."

gate, if such a thing is possible. Last spring the husband of Mrs. Peterson was killed in a threshing machine accident and she was left destitute with several small children to care for. Kind hearted people set to work and soon raised sufficient money to buy a lot and build a house for her, and it is to be ready for her Christmas. The list of those who have contributed includes about all who are in the city and the amounts are not higher than $5 and many of them for 25 cents, so the good work has been well distributed. Charity of that kind comes from a neighborhood where it must be a pleasure to live.

Winthrop News, Dec. 11, 1902, reprinted from the New Ulm Review

—>•<—

The attorney general gets a raise of salary, the superintendent of public instruction has a bill raising his salary making rapid progress through the legislature, and now the railroad commissioners come in and ask for a raise of from $3,000 to $3,600. When will this persistent plugging for increased salaries cease? Certainly not until the members of the legislature rise to the occasion and say "no more, gentlemen, no more; you were anxious to get the office at the present salary, and if you don't want it now, resign, there are plenty of others who would be glad to have it."

Redwood Gazette, Redwood Falls, March 25, 1903

—>•<—

Paving Sibley Avenue. A meeting was called for last Tuesday evening to discuss the question of paving the main street for a couple of blocks in the business section. About a dozen property owners along the street came out, but when it was stated that two blocks of brick paving would

Ely Miner, Jan. 25, 1901

cost ten or twelve thousand dollars, there was but little demand that the improvement be undertaken. It was voted as the sense of the meeting that the council fix the street by lowering the gutters and giving the street a good coating of gravel. A brick pavement, if the expense is to be borne entirely by the owner of the abutting property, would cost about $200 for each 25 ft lot. Pav-

"[The trip] has sadly shaken the confidence of the above gentlemen in the automobile as a reliable medium of transportation."

AUTOMOBILES

[Horseless carriages appeared at a bicycle show in Minneapolis in 1896. That same year, they began to appear on Twin Cities' streets. Swan J. Turnblad, publisher of the Svenska Amerikanska Posten, a Swedish-language newspaper published in Minneapolis, was one of the first owners. Minneapolis banker Edmund J. Phelps was another. By 1902 auto owners got together at the Hotel Radisson to form an automobile club. There were said to be about 125 automobiles in Minneapolis alone, and the number in St. Paul and the rest of the state could not even be guessed at.]

When Frank T. Heffelfinger and George Peavey of the Peavey Grain company started for Minneapolis in their automobile early last Saturday, they little thought what trials and tribulations were ahead of them. What was undertaken as a pleasure excursion became a "pleasure exertion," which has sadly shaken the confidence of the above gentlemen in the automobile as a reliable medium of transportation.

They were "eating up" a stretch of road cityward from Minnetonka Mills at 8 o'clock, when the machine suddenly commenced snorting and bucking like a bronco. Then, with a convulsive shudder, which nearly unhorsed its occupants, the works ran down completely and left the tourists stranded in an inhospitable clime. To add to their discomfort, large, chilling rain drops began to descend steadily.

Being long and lithe of limb, Mr. Heffelfinger volunteered to walk to the Peavey elevator at St. Louis Park, whence he could telephone for the hired man to drive the old, reliable family team [of horses] out to the stranded wreck and tow the same to port.

"I won't be long," he called to Mr. Peavey, and with this comforting assurance he trudged six miles through the rain and mud to the park, where he made by 'phone the necessary arrangements. Thinking no more of the occurrence, Mr. Heffelfinger went to his office and resumed business.

Three hours later a telephone message from his man at St. Louis Park informed him that neither George Peavey nor the auto were anywhere to be found. Heffelfinger used a slang phrase, and, giving the driver more explicit directions, urged him to try again. Long after noon, unable to report progress or any trace of the castaway, the searching party gave up the hunt and returned to town for the second time.

In the interim, though inwardly cursing his fate, Mr. Peavey tried to make himself as comfortable as possible, by buttoning his rain coat close about him and camping under the tarpaulins. He would have been resigned, as the long hours wore on, but for the fact that, while he had plenty of tobacco, a minute examination of his apparel failed to disclose a match.

At 4 p.m., thoroughly chilled, after eight hours in the saddle, at war with all the elements and a pronounced enemy of society in general, he struck out for town himself. By this time the road was one long drawn out mire, and it was far from easy going. Mr. Peavey's heart bounded with delight when a farmer's wagon overtook him.

"Give you $5 for a ride into town," offered the pedestrian.

"No strangers kin ride with me," replied Reuben, suspiciously. "Giddap!"

Mr. Peavey thought of "man's inhumanity to man," and kept moving as best he could toward St. Louis Park, which he finally reached, bespattered with mud from head to foot.

Minneapolis Journal, Oct. 28, 1902

→·←

The Prejudice Against Automobiles. [Editorial] The automobile is exciting prejudice similar to that formerly directed against the bicycle, and for similar reasons. With the passing of the bicycle "scorcher" [speeder], public sentiment changed, and today one takes the bicycle as a matter of course, and it finds its proper place as one of the conveniences, and even necessities, of modern life. The same foolish and apparently uncontrollable desire for a high rate of speed, no matter at what risk to the life and limb of others, that characterized the pioneer wheelmen, has reappeared with the automobile craze, and in proportion as the danger to the public is greater, public resentment naturally increases.

In New York city there have been numerous assaults upon automobile parties by boys and young men living in the unsavory parts of town. Several women and children have been fatally injured by flying sticks and stones. Machines have

"When you get a good minister you ought to stand by him."

AUTOMOBILES

been wrecked by the score, until finally they are no longer driven thru certain sections of the city. . . . Boston also furnishes several illustrations of popular disapproval of the way in which reckless drivers handle this newest toy of the rich and the well-to-do. . . .

The remedy lies with the automobilists themselves. A little more thought for others, a little more willingness to divide the "right of the road" with slower vehicles and pedestrians, and a little less of the mad desire to violate all the laws regulating speed, will solve the problem. It can never be solved by nominal fines for violations of the speed law. . . . Minneapolis has been rather more fortunate than some other cities farther east, but it is because her automobile owners have of their own accord evinced a keener sense of fair play.

Minneapolis Journal, July 21, 1904

–>–<–

A new fad among young men is that of naming the make of an approaching automobile. The special knowledge, as well as keenness of eye to do this successfully is considerable, and, singularly enough, those who have most skill in it, are not people who own automobiles, but those who would very much like to, but cannot afford to.

The distinguishing characteristics of many makes of machines are of a minute and apparently unimportant character. But there are some, it is said, who are absolutely familiar with them all, being able even to name the season of the model to which they may refer. The peculiar noise made by the engines of so many makes, is perhaps one of the simplest ways to distinguish between them, and it is possible to tell the make of a passing machine without looking at it.

Duluth News Tribune, May 5, 1907

---

ing the front of the alleys and at the street intersections would cost the village a couple of thousand dollars more, and in view of the fact that the soil here is of such a nature that a fairly good street can be maintained with the material at hand, it was thought advisable to take the conservative course.

Litchfield Independent, April 21, 1903

–>–<–

Don't worry clubs are badly needed in Renville county. Twenty three patients were sent from there to the insane asylum last year, and seven more have been committed during the first three months of 1903.

Redwood Gazette, Redwood Falls, April 29, 1903

–>–<–

When you get a good minister you ought to stand by him. He is only human, and is liable to err in some matters of judgment, and

St. Paul Daily News, Oct. 8, 1909

"The big cities are veritable hell holes of iniquity for entrapping young women."

you ought to overlook the fact, and still insist that he is a good fellow and the right man in the right place. Don't criticize his every act, but rather help him to build up his church, to build up the church property and to build up the town. If you will do that you will be a pretty good fellow yourself, and your chances of reaching the place where all religious paths are presumed to lead, will be a great deal better.

Redwood Gazette, Redwood Falls, May 13, 1903

–>-<–

Ate Mud Pies. Little Eva Tostivan, aged 4 1/2 years, is hovering between life and death. Some days ago she and some of her little playmates made some mud pies that looked so good that Eva ate one of them. Obstruction of the bowels set in and an operation was the only chance for saving the child's life. It was performed on Thursday. She is alive still but very weak.

Wabasha County Herald, Wabasha, Aug. 25, 1904

–>-<–

Stay Away from the Cities, Girls. The Minneapolis papers contain warnings to country girls not to come to the twin cities with the expectation of getting work. . . . Hundreds of girls go to the cities from all parts of the state and adjoining states, hoping to get work as clerks in department stores. Proprietors of these stores report that there are ten applicants for every position. The result is that many girls, who do not usually have any extra money, and not finding the desired employment, fall into evil ways in the city and are ruined. The big cities are veritable hell holes of iniquity for entrapping young women, and strenuous efforts should be made to prevent this lamentable condition of affairs. There is an unlimited demand

Mower County Transcript, Dec. 12, 1906

for girls for domestic service, with good pay and moral safety in most cases, but there is a deep seated aversion on the part of young women to go into this work, and thousands will eke out a miserable existence as a meagerly paid clerk, living poorly in shabby tenement rooms, rather than accept work as a family servant. The reasons for this aversion to housework are several. Taking up housework entails a drop in the social scale, for one thing. Why this is so is not so easily explained, but it seems to exist. Secondly, the work is more continuing, lasting from early in the morning till late at night. There are few hours of liberty. Thirdly, servant girls are in many cases treated by their employers as though a wide social gulf existed between them. This is not so much the case between employers and their hired help in stores or shops.

Litchfield Independent, Dec. 13, 1904

*"A woman with a mission never has accomplished half as much
for the world as a woman with a baby."*

Sit down in disgruntled idleness and the world is a hovel. Get up and sing and work and you will find it a palace.
Norman County Index, Ada, Jan. 5, 1905

—⇁•↼—

Slates are fast disappearing from schools all over the country. In many states the health boards have made regulations forbidding the use of slates in the schools, declaring them unsanitary. No more spitting on slates and then wiping them off with their sleeves for the boys of this generation. No more sponges to throw at each other. All the pleasures of our boyhood seem to be denied to the child of today, who must content himself with paper. Paper tablets are replacing the slates, and last year in the United States about $10,000,000 worth of paper tablets at retail prices were sold. This would make about 160,000,000 tablets.
Norman County Index, Ada, Feb. 9, 1905

—⇁•↼—

Men's Column. Men ought to know that:

A woman with a mission never has accomplished half as much for the world as a woman with a baby.

Girls sometimes shoot their lovers for making love [courting] too coldly, but never because they make love too violently.

If married men treated their wives with half as much consideration as they do their sweethearts, divorce lawyers would starve to death.

A two-headed family is as much of a monstrosity as a two-headed child.
Norman County Index, Ada, July 6, 1905

—⇁•↼—

Ye Country Editor Comes to See Us. Hibbing was honored this

St. Paul Daily News, Oct. 23, 1909

week by the presence of the state editors and their ladies, and the visitors enjoyed exceedingly the brief time given them in the metropolis of the Mesaba iron range. Many of them had never seen an iron mine, and were truly amazed at the sights presented to their wondering view. They had speculated on what to attribute Duluth's sudden commercial importance; now they know. To the mind of the editor of the southern and western portions of the state the Mesaba range has been but a rugged, barren, bleak and uninviting wilderness, dotted here and there with great yawn-

ing holes in the ground out of which comes the ore of iron that is such an important factor in the commercial interests of the world. He never dreamed of the vast wealth required to extract the ore from the bosom of Mother Earth, or the skilled men that must be employed to do the work; and he never dreamed of the advanced civilization and elevating influences to be found in the Minnesota mining camp. That Hibbing is but eleven years old still has a place in his mind with the story of Jonah and the whale. In his mind he pictured a town of "lowly miner's cabins," rough, bearded men, wearing hob-nailed boots, burdened with six-shooters and masticating the seductive "peerless" of commerce [chewing tobacco], and thought it unsafe for Christian people of retiring dispositions to invade the domain of the man with pick and shovel. And of women he expected nothing. But he was surprised. He found our women the most beautiful and charming in the land, and he wanted to camp right here. He found, too, a modern town of every influence of home, church, school and good society, equal to anything he ever rubbed up against; equal to that of the quiet little hamlet nestling in the valleys of golden grain where he wallops a Washington hand press fifty-one weeks every year. When he gets settled down to his fried liver and boiled potatoes after the trip down the lakes, he will take his mighty pen in hand and tell his readers that the "iron country" is the garden spot of the Bread and Butter state, that its people wear just as high collars, as loud socks, as many diamonds, worship at their fine churches just as often, have just as good schools and base ball teams as any community of people anywhere — with the added convenience that one does not have to

"The best way to keep the boy on the farm is to offer him some inducement to remain there."

go too far to get a drink. He will tell of a people that are good to meet, and when he completes his able article on "Our Trip to the Iron Range," he will arise to his fullest height and lay his hand upon his swelling heart, after the manner of the old Roman in the glory of the empire, and proudly say, "I am a Minnesotaen." The editorial party was greatly pleased with the iron range trip and the one regret was that more time was not given to see the mines and become more familiar with the methods of operation. Hibbing will surely profit by the editorial visit.

Mesaba Ore & Hibbing News, Aug. 26, 1905

→•←

Frank J. Hoffman, former window trimmer at the Itasca store [in Hibbing], spent Sunday handshaking with his Hibbing acquaintances. He now makes his home at San Francisco, California, and likes the place good. Mr. Hoffman recently declined a most flattering offer to go to Paris and take charge of the windows of the largest store in the French nation's capital. The position had a salary attachment of $35 a day, but Mr. Hoffman don't like the French people, so he says.

Mesaba Ore & Hibbing News, Sept. 2, 1905

→•←

The best way to keep the boy on the farm is to offer him some inducement to remain there. For many years sociologists have been greatly disturbed at the tendency of the brightest of the country young people, especially of the boys, to hike to towns, where, in their minds, there are greater opportunities for a "good time" or material advancement, as [depending on whether] they are light or serious minded. The close observer, however, may note a vice versa tendency of late.

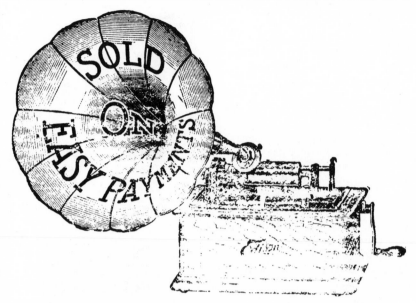

Edison Phonographs, - - - $10 to $50

50 cents per week. $2.00 per month

You cannot understand or appreciate the Edison Phonograph until you examine it or hear it play or sing. We extend an invitation to every one to call and hear them whether you intend to buy or not. We now have on hand the entire catalogue list of Edison Records.

Price 35c. $4.20 per doz.

Henry J. Harm
JEWELER

Telephones--- Northwestern 246-J
Tri-State - - 413-R   211 Broadway

With the hustle for a living in the overcrowded cities, even in good times, becoming so strenuous, and with free mail delivery in the country and the tendency toward better roads, better living, and the drudgery saved measurably by improved machinery, there is steadily more inducement to remain in the country, and to leave the city for the rural districts.

Warren Sheaf, April 23, 1906

→•←

This year's freshman class is having a bad time of it. You see they don't know how to designate themselves, to let the people know that they are (regents willing) to get their diplomas in 1910.

"The clothing of a little girl caught fire from wax candles in the decorations."

Ordinarily one would call them the "class of oney-ought," but this does not sound quite right to their ears, while plain "ten" is too plebeian and "I-owe" is likely to come too near the facts of the case to be agreeable.

Minneapolis Tribune, Oct. 3, 1906

‐>‐<‐

Panic in a Church. During the presentation of a Christmas program at the United Brethren church in LeSueur Center, the clothing of a little girl caught fire from wax candles in the decorations, and before the flames could be extinguished five or six children were badly burned. Grace McCall, aged five years, and Martha Yackle, aged six, were so seriously burned they may not recover. They inhaled the flames and their faces were burned to a blister.

The church was filled to the doors and excitement ran high, women and children screaming and rushing madly for the nearest exits. It is safe to say that wax candles will hereafter be dispensed with in Christmas decorations here.

Montgomery Messenger, Dec. 28, 1906

‐>‐<‐

Stenographers are nowadays being put to many uses, which a few years ago had never even been thought of. The most advanced field which has been opened to them is keeping histories of cases for physicians. A number of local doctors have formed the habit of having girls take notes of their conversations with patients who visit them at their offices. A specialist the other day, in discussing the new plan, said:

"Before I took my stenographer with me I was bothered by mothers calling me up and saying that they had forgotten some of my instructions and asking me to repeat them. All I have to do now in such cases is to turn to my notes and read them to the nurse or anxious mother.

"Of course when I treat a person who is dangerously ill the patient is usually left in the hands of a trained nurse, but in all cases the plan of having stenographic notes on the subject has proven a great help to myself and a number of fellow practitioners, who have inaugurated the same system."

Duluth News Tribune, May 31, 1907

‐>‐<‐

Fred Robertson, a resident of Blackduck, was brought down to the county jail this morning and will live at that institution for forty days as the enforced guest of Sheriff Bailey.

Robertson has, according to the proof adduced in justice

APPENDICITIS

that dreadful fiend that threatens the life of rich and poor, can attack and kill only those whose bowels are not kept thoroughly cleaned out, purified and disinfected the year round. One whose liver is dead, whose bowels and stomach are full of half decayed food, whose whole body is unclean inside, is a quick and ready victim of appendicitis.

If you want to be safe against the scourge, keep in good health all the time, KEEP CLEAN INSIDE! Use the only tonic laxative, that will make your bowels strong and healthy, and keep them pure and clean, protected against appendicitis and ALL EPIDEMIC DISEASES. It's CASCARETS, that will keep and save you. Take them regularly and you will find that all diseases are absolutely

PREVENTED BY

Cascarets

LIVER TONIC

10c. 25c. 50c. ALL DRUGGISTS.

BEST FOR THE BOWELS

NEVER SOLD IN BULK.

Ely Miner, Jan. 25, 1901

"A certain man . . . went in a hardware store in Starbuck and asked to purchase an ax."

court at Blackduck, been absorbed of late in the misguided pastime of beating his wife, which his better half finally resented and made complaint to the authorities, with the result that Robertson was sentenced to serve forty days in the county jail for his exhibition of physical prowess.

Bemidji Pioneer, June 27, 1907

→⸱←

A rather amusing story is going the rounds of the press about a certain man who went in a hardware store in Starbuck and asked to purchase an ax. Being shown the article and being told the price was $1.15 he said, "Why I can get the same article in Chicago for 90 cents." The hardware man said, "All right I will give it to you for the same price provided you will do the same with me as you would do with them." The customer agreed with alacrity thinking he had made quite a bargain. He handed him a dollar bill and the dealer promptly handed him back the ten cents change. "Now," said the dealer, "I want 25 cents more to pay the express charges." This also the customer gave him. "How much did your ax cost you?" "$1.15." "Very good, now give me 5 cents more for the money order fee and postage," which the customer was obliged to hand over. "Now how much did your ax cost you?" "$1.20," said the customer as he reached for his purchase.

"Oh no not yet," said the dealer as he tossed the ax back on the shelf, "call for it in ten days. That will be as soon as you can get it from Chicago and we're doing business on Chicago terms you know."

Bemidji Pioneer, Aug. 11, 1907

→⸱←

John Geyerman met with a peculiar accident last Saturday which has since developed very

---

day. C. B. Steelman, secretary, 825 Railway Bldg., Minneapolis.

HELP WANTED—FEMALE

LADY STENOGRAPHER, SMITH-PREMIER; plenty work, but good prospects; $50.
Stenographer, North Dakota land, $60.
Bookkeeper, stenographer, South Dakota, $40.
Stenographer, Minnesota flour mill, $45.
S. A. Morawetz & Co., 910 Security Bank building.

WANTED — STENOGRAPHER, REASONABLY rapid and accurate, that can spell and punctuate; very light, but interesting work; salary is small; write letter of application, stating salary desired, and deliver to room 9, main floor, Tribune building, between 12 and 1 p.m.

WANTED — GOOD GIRL FOR GENERAL housework where second girl is employed; must be neat and fair cook; good home and wages to right party. Inquire 1768 Bryant av S, one block from Hennepin on Kenwood car line.

WANTED—A GOOD COMPETENT GIRL OR woman for general housework; without washing; one willing to go to Summerville, Minnetonka in summer months; best of wages. 2424 Colfax av S.

WANTED—COMPETENT GERMAN GIRL FOR general housework; best references required; $5 a week paid; nurse and laundress also employed; for small family. Telephone South 2091. J.

WANT LADY AND GENTLEMAN DEPUTIES in every county in Minnesota; fraternal, social and beneficial society. Good contract for hard workers. Mystic Toilers ___ exchange.

HIGH SCHOOL GIRL TO WORK IN BAKERY afternoons and all day Saturday; Scandinavian preferred. Cottage Bakery, 1509 E Franklin av. Telephone T.-S. 7110.

EXPERIENCED LADY CLERK IS WANTED IN a small North Dakota town; a lady of 30 to 35 years is preferred. Address, giving experience, 4197, Journal.

STEADY RELIABLE YOUNG LADY OF 16 OR 17 to do light office work; no experience required; steady place; start at $2.00 a week. Address 4510, Journal.

STENOGRAPHER FOR LAND OFFICE, $90; assistant bookkeeper for grain business, $50 and advancement; both desirable. Peterson & Co., Kasota block.

DRESSMAKING — SPRING SUITS MADE from $6 to $8; separate skirts, $2.50 to $3; silk shirtwaists, $1.50; silk petticoats, $1.50. 907 5th av S.

WANTED—A COMPETENT GIRL FOR GENeral housework; family of three; modern house; good place for the right party. 3321 Park av.

WANTED—HEAD WAITRESS IN LARGE REStaurant in city; must have good recommendations from former employers. Address 4342, Journal.

BRIGHT YOUNG WOMAN CAN PAY LARGE part tuition by office work, one hour daily, in leading business college. Address 4472, Journal.

WANTED—GIRL FOR GENERAL HOUSEwork; family of three; two houses east of Hennepin. 1415 W 31st st. Tel. South 846-J.

WANTED FOR MONDAYS A CAPABLE WOMan for washing and ironing; only experienced need apply. S. L. Sewall 2001 Stevens av.

IMMEDIATELY—LADIES TO TRAVEL; $35 month and expenses; city work; $2.50 per day, call National Hotel, Room 54, 9 to 6.

WANTED—FOUR LADY CANVASSERS; $2.25 daily; money every night. 31 Arcade building, entrance 116 4th st S, third floor.

WANTED—A GIRL FOR GENERAL HOUSEwork; no laundry; none but competent girl need apply. 2018 Humboldt av S.

WANTED — NEAT GIRL FOR GENERAL housework. Small modern house. 2525 W 40th st. Telephone T. C. 7651.

WANTED—A COMPETENT WORKING HOUSEkeeper for out of town; good pay. For particulars call 710 7th st SE.

Minneapolis Journal, March 12, 1908

---

six years' road experience; married; want to get off the road. Address 3247, Journal.

SITUATION WANTED; STATIONARY ENGIneer; have chief license; to take charge of plant, or will work as assistant; married, good reference. C. Perkins, 1611 Clinton av.

YOUNG MAN MUST HAVE POSITION OF some kind; four years' general office and stenographic experience; good references; will leave city. Address 4515, Journal.

POSITION BY FIRST-CLASS ENGINEER; AM 26 years and married; have shop experience; good reasons for leaving last place; best of references. Address 4248, Journal.

A YOUNG MAN ATTENDING COLLEGE DEsires place to work for board mornings, noons, evenings and Saturdays. Phone Twin City 9506. Ask for Thompson.

SITUATION WANTED BY AN ALL AROUND butcher, married and 30 years old; can furnish references if wanted; want work at once. Address 4262, Journal.

A COLLECTOR WITH 15 YEARS' EXPERIence; can collect your accounts either on salary or commission; references furnished. Address 3324, Journal.

YOUNG MAN OF 20, HIGH SCHOOL GRADuate, wants to hear of good position where there is a chance to advance. Address at once 2042, Journal.

YOUNG MAN WISHES TO GO WITH CIVIL engineering or surveying crew; will stay through season; can start at once. Address 3589, Journal.

A FIRST CLASS CHEF WANTS POSITION AT once, in or out of city. Harry W. Morrison, Colorado, 90 12th st S, N. W. phone Main 1204-L2.

WANTED—POSITION AS HOTEL CLERK; 12 years' experience in hotel business; some experience as head waiter. Address 4322, Journal.

POSITION BY GOOD INSIDE WIREMAN AND lineman; good man for electric light plant; can run part of the time. Address 4251, Journal.

WANTED—BOOKKEEPER, STENOGRAPHER and general office man desires position at $40 a month. Address Box 741, Crookston, Minn.

YOUNG MAN WANTS WORK; MUST HAVE it quick; willing to do anything; prefer wholesale or retail store. Address 4290, Journal.

COMPETENT STENOGRAPHER AND GENeral office man, employed during the day, would like work evenings. 8547, Journal.

BY ENERGETIC YOUNG MAN OF GOOD education, best references, office position desired; experienced. Address 3267, Journal.

ELECTRICIAN WITH SEVERAL YEARS EXperience in lighting and power construction, desires position. Address 3306, Journal.

YOUNG MAN WITH TEN YEARS' EXPERIence, wants position in grocery; good references. O. R. M., 1512 Nicollet, flat E.

FIRST-CLASS PAINTER WANTS WORK; CAN do hardwood finish, weathered oak, enameling, frescoing, etc. Address 4500, Journal.

BY CARPENTER WHO CAN PLASTER AND build chimneys; good work, right price by day or job. Address 4302, Journal.

A FIRST-CLASS LADIES' SHOE SALESMAN wants position; city experience and first-class references. Address 4083, Journal.

CARPENTER WANTS REPAIR OR NEW work, and hardwood floors; price right. Address 4147, Journal.

YOUNG MAN WITH $300 WOULD LIKE TO learn some business or get on the road. Address 3458, Journal.

FIRST-CLASS COOK, CHEF, DESIRES POSItion in or out of city. J. M., 1026 5th st S, Minneapolis, Minn.

WANTED — PLASTERING, KALSOMINING, whitewashing, painting. Low prices. Address 4108, Journal.

BAKER, GOOD ALL-AROUND MAN, WANTS position in or out of city. E. Erbach, 26 Western av.

EXPERIENCED CHAUFFEUR WANTS POSItion; can furnish references. Address 3104, Journal.

"He wants to join the navy, but he has the sweetest, dearest, little wife, with whom he could not part."

serious symptoms in the part affected. He was engaged in dressing poultry for the Big Store when one of the fowls scratched him on the face near the eye. Although the wound at first seemed to be of little consequence, it has since become painful, and has assumed a rather alarming appearance, but it is hoped that medical skill will save him from a severe case of blood poisoning.
Worthington Advance, Jan. 10, 1908

-›-‹-

Swan Lofberg, of Argyle, was in town yesterday. The accidental death of his son, Albert, shortly before Christmas, was a severe blow to this old Marshall County pioneer. When driving from town the wagon was upset and the son thrown underneath, receiving injuries from which he died almost instantly. The son had rented the farm, and the father had prepared to live the rest of his days free from care and trouble. But death came and changed his plans.
Warren Sheaf, Jan. 16, 1908

-›-‹-

A Thief River Falls young man wrote the recruiting officer at Minneapolis, asking what kind of quarters were furnished married men on board ship. He wants to join the navy, but he has the sweetest, dearest, little wife, with whom he could not part. He was informed that Thief River Falls was a better place for married men than the navy.
Warren Sheaf, Feb. 27, 1908

Ely Miner, May 31, 1901

"The charity of a country newspaper man is more marked by what he does not print than by what he gives out of his financial means."

The funeral of Abner, the baby boy of Mr. and Mrs. J.O. Sether, was held Sunday afternoon, from the Norwegian Lutheran church. The twin brother died a few weeks ago. This community extends heartfelt sympathy to the bereaved parents. Their children are safe, very safe, on the other shore.
Warren Sheaf, Feb. 27, 1908

–>–<–

Editors First to Learn. An exchange [another newspaper] says: The local editor is always first to hear of any little trouble in the community. There is but little happens in this sphere of activity, no matter how closely the secret may be guarded, but that he knows of it, and most times he knows the real and true history of the transaction, but he does not always publish it to the world, and many times softens the unpleasant parts of the transaction until the true import of the incident is so cleverly concealed that its happening injures the reputation or standing of nobody. The omission from the local paper of the details of a family quarrel, unpleasant gossip concerning a neighbor and the wife of another (even though founded on facts), the factional fight in the church choir, the financial difficulty of a banker or merchant, the elopement of a prominent society lady or the visit of a girl to the maternity home, and a thousand and one other little incidents in everyday life that are constantly happening in any community and which would prove very spicy reading in these times when sensational and yellow newspapers seem so popular: all this is newspaper charity. Yes, the charity of a country newspaper man is more marked by what he does not print than by what he gives out of his financial means, or by the free use of the columns of his paper.
Bemidji Pioneer, April 9, 1908

St. Paul Daily News, Oct. 24, 1909

–>–<–

The cook book published by the Ladies' Guild of the Episcopal church is now out and can be procured from any of the ladies. The book should be in every home in the city. It contains in addition to the complete and selected line of late and practical recipes a large amount of information relative to luncheons and spreads for special occasions that is of special interest to every society woman. This feature alone is worth many times the price of the book, which is only 35c. The edition is limited and if you want one you will have to speak quick.
Worthington Advance, May 29, 1908

–>–<–

A man named Jack Moore, permanent residence in St. Paul, is sojourning for 30 days at the local bastille as a result of trying to persuade the conductor on one of the night trains going east last week that 50 cents was enough to pay his fare from Breckenridge to St. Paul and trying to beat up the conductor when he was informed that it was below the ordinary rate. He was taken off the train here and given 30 days that he might get better posted on railroad fare rates. Mr. Moore possesses a fine voice with which he entertains all those in the vicinity of this hotel at all hours of the day.
Swift County Monitor, Benson, Sept. 18, 1908

–>–<–

Work is progressing rapidly on the new hospital which is being erected at the poor farm exclusively for the benefit of tubercular patients, who will be kept strictly isolated from the other wards of the county at the farm.
Duluth News Tribune, Sept. 13, 1909

–>–<–

Albert Lea Evening Tribune, Dec. 22, 1908

1910s

The Minneapolis Morning Tribune

MINNEAPOLIS, MINN., TUESDAY, NOVEMBER 12, 1918

Truce Terms Crush Militarism of Germany;
Allies Celebrate Victory Over Autocracies

Victory Joy Continues to Sweep City

Germany Faces Famine; American Aid Beseeched

Gerard Urges Extradition of Wilhelm

Foe Divers Called Together to Fight Against Armistice

Beaten Hun Begs Peace Upon Knees

One Kaiserling Reported Shot; One Attempts Suicide

Shell Avalanche Poured Upon Foe In Last Moment

Germany Shorn of Power; Drastic Armistice Terms Presented to Congress

Everything America Fought for Attained in Rigorous Conditions Teutons Must Meet.

Armistice Terms Greatest Drama's Closing Chapter

Peace Parley Preparations to Come Next

British Battleship Torpedoed and Sunk

Drys Lead by 15,482; Wets Claiming Victory

Mass Meeting at Institute Tonight

Armistice Will Not Lower Food Prices, Says Hoover

The War in Brief

Minneapolis Tribune, Nov. 12, 1918

The state's population in 1910 passed the 2 million mark. Milling began its decline in 1915. Prohibition began in 1919. During World War I, anti-German feeling was strong in Minnesota and the Commission of Public Safety was given vast powers to enforce the war effort.

1910s

–>•<–

Wedding Dance

*Not all the newspaper stories that mean the most to people are about
major world events — war, elections, disasters. In many an attic are
stored articles such as the following, a Two Harbors wedding dance
in 1914.*

OLD TIME DANCE
ENJOYED BY ALL

**Mr. and Mrs. A.G. Peterson Received Great Ovation
at Pavilion at Silver Creek on Thursday Evening.**

THE SOCIAL DANCE held in the Silver Creek
pavilion last Thursday evening, which was in
the nature of a wedding reception in honor
of the marriage of Miss Elsie Sonju and Adolph G.
Peterson, proved enjoyable beyond the hopes and
expectations of those who were in charge of arrangements.

The party was arranged on very short notice, by
the many friends of the young couple. Mr. A.J.
Sonju, of Maple, father of the bride, asked Mr.
Thomas J. Brown, of this city, to make arrangements for music and to invite as many Two Harbors
people as he could reach in the limited time. The
number of people from this city who took advantage of the opportunity for an outing is evidence
that Mr. Brown was a very busy man for one day in
his life. Nearly every automobile in this city made
from one to three trips between here and Silver
Creek, and on each trip they were loaded to capacity. At midnight both sides of the county road near
the pavilion were lined with automobiles for a
quarter of a mile. With all lights burning there was
sufficient illumination for a small village, and if
one not familiar with the circumstances should
have chanced to pass along there during the night
they would have been inclined to believe that some
great historic event was being celebrated, and that
it was being attended by all notables from the surrounding country.

The celebration was, indeed, of considerable
moment, but there was lacking the pomp, affecta-

tion and ceremony that is invariably present when
events in history are being commemorated, and instead, there was everywhere evidence of the good
fellowship that has always been attendant upon the
gatherings in the country where there is no artificial social distinctions, where every one is known
to all, and where the sole object is to enjoy life to
the limit. This function was in honor of the first
born of the pioneers of Lake County, and after a
large number had gathered a messenger was dispatched to the residence of the groom's parents
near by, where the young couple were spending
their honeymoon, and they were brought to the pavilion and received the hearty congratulations and
best wishes of the many friends there present.

The pavilion is a large one and the young men
and maidens of the surrounding country had the
interior neatly decorated with evergreens and wild
flowers. It is situated in the midst of a dense grove,
and as the strains of the music and the muffled
shuffling of many feet were heard through the leafy
bower there was brought to the minds of many now
past life's zenith, memories of other days in other
places when they were young and just embarking
on life's journey. Men nearing the end of life's allotted span swung the shy country maiden on the
corner, while the young men of the country tan-
goed and turkey trotted with the sophisticated ladies from the city. It was indeed an occasion that
will mark an epoch in the lives of the young people
in whose honor it was arranged, as well as the many
friends who spent one long evening of unalloyed
pleasure.

A substantial supper was served shortly after
midnight, and after the bride and groom had been
toasted and roasted to a still whisper, they were
presented with a handsome kitchen cabinet, a gift

*"Two or three brainless galoots carrying an overload
of the stuff that made Milwaukee famous..."*

from their many admiring friends. The presentation was made by our fellow-townsman B.F. Fowler, and it is said by those present that he was at his best and far excelled all previous efforts at oratory, wit and humor.

Two Harbors Journal-News, July 23, 1914

→•←

Off to the Cleaner. Many women cast aside a good pair of gloves which have not been worn half a dozen times merely because they are "awfully dirty." For people who cannot afford to spend from $1.50 to two dollars every week in this line this is sinful extravagance. Have you ever looked over your stock of colored gloves when you have pronounced them past worthy? If not, take a spare hour and do so. Sew on missing buttons, tighten those that are loose, mend all the tiny rips, and then take them to a trustworthy place and have them cleaned. If they return home with a disagreeable odor, hang them on a chair-back near an open window for a day or two. If you have all your gloves cleaned at ten cents a pair they will probably not cost you as much as one new pair.

Madison Independent Press, Feb. 18, 1910

→•←

When Madison was a little village of 200 people, Sixth avenue was sprinkled and the dust kept down. Now when the town has become a city with a population close up toward the 2,000 mark no effort is made to sprinkle. The loss to merchants on stocks would pay their sprinkling three times over.

Madison Independent Press, June 17, 1910

→•←

Two or three brainless galoots carrying an overload of the stuff that made Milwaukee famous kept the people of the southwest corner of this city awake about all

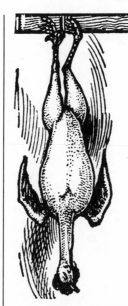
night last Saturday night.

Madison Independent Press, Aug. 12, 1910

→•←

The Preacher — We tried a phonograph choir.

The Sexton — What success?

The Preacher — Fine. Nobody knew the difference till a deacon went to the loft to take up the collection.

Madison Independent Press, Dec. 9, 1910

→•←

Dean Taber, who has been

"A very novel and interesting sight is the milking of cows by machinery."

considered one of the best young athletes in Park Rapids, is now barred from all athletic sports, and his condition is such as to cause serious concern on the part of his parents and friends. Dean had been as well as usual, and went to Cass Lake with the ball team last Saturday expecting to participate in the game of ball between the high school teams. Dean discovered while at Cass Lake that there was something wrong, and on being examined by a doctor it was learned that he had leakage of one of the valves of the heart. Dean did not participate in the game and since returning home has on the advice of his doctor given up all sports. This is something of a hardship on a youngster of Dean's inclination, but he will have to make the best of the situation and take good care of himself.

Park Rapids Enterprise, May 11, 1911

–➤•◄–

SURPRISED HIS FRIENDS
Ben Glantz and Miss Nettie Bloom Married Tuesday in Minneapolis

Ben Glantz the popular proprietor of the Bell Clothing Store has decided that there are things in this world that are better than single blessedness and has taken unto himself a wife. The fortunate young lady is Miss Nettie Bloom, daughter of Mr. and Mrs. F.H. Bloom. The wedding took place Tuesday evening at the home of the bride's cousin, Mr. and Mrs. B. Trenblat, and the wedding service was read by Rabbi S.M. Silber in the presence of members of the immediate family. Miss Celyae Glantz, a sister of the bride groom, attended the bride.

The marriage of Mr. Glantz comes as a surprise to his many friends in this vicinity. While it has been known that Mr. Glantz had business matters in Minneapolis that required his attention

GROCERY SPECIALS

AT

Johnson's Department Store

Canned Corn, per can........................... **8c**
90 cents per dozen.

Good Peaches, 8 pounds for...... **$1.**00

Seeded Raisins, 1 lb. package............. **10c**
3 packages for 25c.

Canned Tomatoes, fancy, per can...... **12½c**

Canned Tomatoes, standard, per can... **10c**

Fancy Toilet Soap 3 bars for...... .... **10c**

Red Globe Onions, per peck................. **20c**

Norway Herring, 12 pounds for.... **$1.**00
Our Herring is very good.

Good Rice, 4 pounds for........................ **25c**

frequently, the nature of the business was not revealed to his friends until notice of the engagement was read.

Mr. and Mrs. Glantz are now

taking a two weeks trip to places of interest, after which they will return to Park Rapids. The Enterprise joins with their many friends in congratulations.

A happy pre-wedding event for the bride was given at the home of one of her friends on Sunday evening. About twenty-five of her lady friends were entertained by Miss Jennie Sineberg in her honor, and a very pleasant evening was spent there. None of the parties knew that the wedding was to take place soon, and all were surprised when the news of the wedding reached them.

Park Rapids Enterprise, July 6, 1911

–➤•◄–

A very novel and interesting sight is the milking of cows by machinery. The power or suction is furnished by a small engine. A rubber tube is fastened to the four teats of each cow that is to be milked and the gentle suction milks them rapidly and cleanly, the milk flowing into a large covered receptacle. Four cows can be milked at the same time, and they do not seem to mind at all.

Montevideo Leader, Jan. 12, 1912

–➤•◄–

Some of the church people are pretty sharp. F'rinstance they announce an "Avoirdupois" [a system of weights and measures] and get all the fat young ladies and matrons to attend. Each is weighed on platform scales, and tickets with name and weight, are put into a hat. Then the young men draw for partners at supper and pay at the rate of half a cent a pound, dressed weight. Some of them get out of it for 75 cents, but others have to pay as high as a dollar and a half.

Montevideo Leader, March 1, 1912

–➤•◄–

Have you observed a slight tilting of the earth towards St. Paul this week? If so don't get ex-

"The physicians removed by actual count 1,700 gall stones."

cited. It is only the result of seismic disturbances there, due to the sudden gathering together of large bodies of legislators, office-holders, and politicians. This old earth of ours may wobble a bit occasionally from such causes, but it has never yet been permanently upset.

Montevideo Leader, June 7, 1912

→·←

Two Kinds of Farmer. Better copy the farmer who produces his yields at the lowest cost than the man who produces the largest yields.

Montevideo Leader, July 19, 1912

→·←

Miss Wanda Gag, who is teaching school southeast of this city, is spending a two weeks' vacation at her home in New Ulm.

Springfield Advance, Jan. 2, 1913

[This is the same Wanda Gag, pronounced "Gog," who won international fame as artist in the 1920s. She began writing and illustrating stories for children when she was a child herself in New Ulm. Her peasant characters show the influence of her hometown, which had many immigrants from southern Europe. Gag's most famous work is the children's book called "Millions of Cats," for which she did both story and pictures.]

→·←

This is the age of women. We find all the avocations, professions and trades of life opening their doors to admit the enterprising woman. Some are going into their own and some are going into other people's business. In our admiration for the new woman there is danger of forgetting the wife and mother and woman's true sphere as a homemaker.

Springfield Advance, Feb. 6, 1913

→·←

Minneapolis Tribune, May 6, 1916

On Tuesday morning Mrs. A.J. Weldon of Wabasso, was operated upon in St. John's hospital for gall stones. The result proved that an operation was most timely, for the physicians removed by actual count 1,700 gall stones, fully twenty of which were about half the size of a walnut. She is now doing nicely and her full restoration to former good health is anticipated.

Springfield Advance, Feb. 6, 1913

→·←

The Wonder of Story Telling.

The good mother who gathers her children from the streets for a twilight, firelight story telling hour is developing in the soul of those young ones a beauty and an ideal and a love of the nobler things that will in after years hold her children honorable men and virtuous women when others less cared for stumble and fall. And story telling was healthful for all ages. Adults should frequently renew their youth in the magic story telling circle. Love of story telling could keep them children long after they numbered the

"It's the only occupation in which a man can get fired by the imagination and not lose his job."

years of life counted by the psalmist. On the day that we burn the books and take to story telling by the blazing pile, the forgotten joys of the olden world will gather to warm themselves by the blaze while they listen, entranced as of yore. And they'll not depart again.

Springfield Advance, May 22, 1913

-›-‹-

Summer Outing. The folks who wait procrastinate. What are you going to do with the halcyon [calm and peaceful] days of summer? School boys have picked out their swimming hole and all the dimple chin lassies know where the flowers and berries are tucked away along the Cottonwood. Urban and rustic belles are cleaning their pretty white canvas shoes and diaphanous [delicately transparent] hose. Old strollers on the marriage market are going to make the season hum with the dainty slashes in skirts and sleeves.

The rest of us will have to pick plums and watch the proceedings. Unless of course we pitch a tent or build a bungalow. How about the days on the lake, the fishing and trolling, the picnic lunches on Sunday afternoons down along the Suwannee River, the summer reading of magazines and breezy novels, the long auto trips, and all those other outdoor dreams that tinted the long winter evenings with gold? What about all those deep salt breaths we were going to take this year? A summer in Minnesota is not very apt to abide with us very long; so let us get into our little "Slumber Boat" and glide down the stream of summer's sun kissed tides into the twilights and gloamings of vernal days and unto the raptures of June's circumambient [encompassing] love. Let's go out and sing "The Honey Moon Express," "Peg o' my Heart," "Under the Old Ap-

ple Tree," and "Annie Laurie."

How is that for poetry; it's the only occupation in which a man can get fired by the imagination and not lose his job.

Springfield Advance, June 12, 1913

-›-‹-

When you hear a man glorifying the past and dwelling on the good old days, you may be sure that man's physical and intellectual powers are wavering and that he is straggling farther and farther behind in the rush of the world's progress. The best thing about the good old days is that they have not a return ticket.

Springfield Advance, June 26, 1913

Grove City Times, Aug. 12, 1910

THE FAMOUS

OVERLAND CARS

The Car With the Trouble Left Out

ABSOLUTELY THE BEST FOR SIMPLICITY AND RELIABILITY.

The Overland Cars have certainly forged to the front for 1911—comprising now 22 models—ranging in prices from $775.00 to $1675.00—built in one of the largest and best equipped factories in the world, insuring value received for your investment.

NOTHING FINER THAN THE TORPEDO BODY OVERLANDS

The Overland fore door cars are elegant---and it is a brand new fore door machine---with flush body giving an extra six inches to each seat. Not one of those out-of-date 1910 open front models with a pair of doors patched on the front.   The Overland fore door is a brand new creation.   Be careful when you purchase your fore door and see that you don't find yourself with an antiquated model. The safe way is to buy an Overland.

But aside from our fore door feature the backbone of the Overland is worth your consideration. It is a car truly built to last and work.   The daily performance of the motor has no equal of a given size.   Always ready---always willing and anxious to work like a beaver--- steady, regular and economically,   Note all the specifications--- the inside facts---and see how much you get for your money.

OVERLAND MODEL 52
WITH FORE DOORS

OVERLAND MODEL 45

OVERLAND MODEL 53

OVERLAND MODEL 50

OVERLAND MODEL 54

Your Inspection of These Cars Earnestly Solicited.

JAMES H. STRONG,   -   Atwater, Minn.

Agent for Kandiyohi County and the Western Part of Meeker County.

Atwater Republican Press, March 17, 1911

"Housecleaning may be hard for a woman but it is the blackness of despair for the man."

Many of our town people seem to have the impression that any amount of Traverse county land can be bought at $50 per acre. This, however, is a mistaken idea, as it is a well known fact that land is now selling all the way from $60 to $85 per acre and there are some tracts that cannot be bought at the latter price. Several farms have changed hands here recently at $75 per acre and it seems certain that another advance in land prices will surely come in the future.

Wheaton Gazette-Reporter, July 25, 1913

-ᐳ-ᐸ-

Buster Brown and his dog, Tige, spent several hours at A. Wells Co.'s store Wednesday afternoon, entertaining the children and many of the grown-ups. The object of his visit was to advertise Buster Brown shoes, which are sold in Wheaton by the firm named above.

Wheaton Gazette-Reporter, Oct. 3, 1913

-ᐳ-ᐸ-

New York, Jan. 28 — "Every woman has one great ambition," James J. Hill [president of the Great Northern Railway Co.] said today, during a lull in an unusually heavy rush of business. "She may live in a cot or in a castle, she may be mediocre or brilliant, she may have done much or nothing at all, but she has one great ambition — to find the right man.

"Her ambition goes further. It includes a home and family. At no time does she lose sight of this goal. She may persuade herself she wants a career more than anything else, may even come to believe it means more to her than the right man, but let the man come along, and see how quickly she turns aside from everything else to him.

"This is as it should be. When

Grove City Times, April 22, 1910

woman places business before the family, it will be a sorry day."

Mr. Hill also talked cheerfully of business and industrial prospects.

St. Paul Pioneer Press, Jan. 29, 1914

-ᐳ-ᐸ-

Now is the time when life is a burden for the average man. When he reaches home on an evening not unlikely he finds the house upside down with the annual housecleaning in full swing. Instead of expecting a welcome and a comfortable time he may think himself lucky if he is not asked to beat carpets and do a

thousand other things. Housecleaning may be hard for a woman but it is the blackness of despair for the man. He needs all the sympathy that can be meted out.

Two Harbors Journal-News, April 2, 1914

-ᐳ-ᐸ-

Mrs. Anna Norberg, South avenue, has requested this paper to extend her sincere thanks to the many generous people of the city who contributed to the fund of $80.50 which was used to pay the special assessment levied against her lot to pay the cost of install-

"The angel of death grows busier among the old pioneers who laid the foundation for Traverse county's present prosperity."

ing a sanitary sewer. The money has been paid over to Thomas Martin, city treasurer.

Two Harbors Journal-News, April 2, 1914

—›-‹—

A number of Two Harbors fishermen went to Tower last Saturday for the purpose of removing fish from Lake Vermillion. Some of the boys made a serious mistake by removing some fish that were not up to standard length. Deputy Game Warden Wood happened to be in that locality. While he was examining and measuring the fish in the possession of one of the bold fishermen, other members of the party hurriedly disposed of their small fish and thus escaped arrest. The pleasure of extracting the little fish cost one of the boys $13.50.

Two Harbors Journal-News, May 21, 1914

—›-‹—

Death of Gust. Johnson

As each year rolls by, the angel of death grows busier among the old pioneers who laid the foundation for Traverse county's present prosperity. The latest to be summoned to his final rest is Gust. Johnson, who for thirty-five years past has done his full share toward advancing conditions from the wild state that existed when he came and that have been supplanted by the beautiful homes and modern conveniences and comforts that we see about us today. Those hardy pioneers are well entitled to the nation's praise and gratitude, second only to those who faced death in defense of the flag. The generation that has since entered the field of activity will never know nor realize the bravery and perseverance required to suc-

cessfully pass through the privations and hardships incident to pioneer life, when these men faced the future with little equipment and no other capital than willing hands that knew but little rest except during the few hours that tired nature demanded for sleep. Gust. Johnson was one of these, and richly earned the reward awaiting in the better land for those who faithfully discharge the duties imposed upon them in this life.

Gustaf Johnson was born in Elfsborgslan, Sweden, on March 9th, 1842, and came to America in 1871. He first located at Lake City, Minn., and resided there until the spring of 1880, when he came to Traverse county, settling on a homestead south of where Dumont now stands. A few years later he moved to a farm five miles south of Wheaton, where he resided until the year 1900, when he disposed of his personal property and moved with his family to Wheaton and has since made his home here. On November 19th, 1878, he was united in marriage to Marie Lindstrom and five children were born to them, only one of whom survives. For some time past, Mr. Johnson had suffered from internal disorders and a few weeks ago he went to the hospital at Graceville and submitted to a surgical operation, which for a time it was hoped would prove successful, but the middle of last week a change for the worse came and on the evening of December 25th he passed away.

His widow, one daughter and three grandchildren are the immediate members of the family here, and an aged brother and sister who live at the old home in Sweden.

Mr. Johnson was a member of the Swedish Lutheran church and the funeral service took place there Tuesday, Rev. J.W. Lundgren officiating. Many were pre-

sent to pay their last sad respects to one whose friendship they prized.

Wheaton Gazette-Reporter, Jan. 1, 1915

—›-‹—

If you notice any of the stalwart men around with a peculiar look due to a hirsute appendage on their upper lip, do not be alarmed. They do not belong to the "Black Hand" society but have joined the Mustache Club. Not all people wearing mustaches belong to this new organization but it is not difficult to tell a member when you see him. They will carefully foster, nurse, trim and groom their new adornments until April 1, when we understand the photographer will use a special lens to take the picture of those who have been brave enough to withstand shaving off these precious possessions in spite of the jests and jeers of their friends. After the pictures are taken the faithful members will partake of a banquet.

Mille Lacs County Times, Milaca, Jan. 14, 1915

—›-‹—

Cars of household goods belonging to settlers coming to this community are beginning to arrive in considerable numbers. It is expected that considerably over a hundred families will come this spring to make their homes in "the land of cream and clover."

Mille Lacs County Times, Milaca, March 11, 1915

—›-‹—

A little girl at Ostlun, near Mille Lacs lake, had been troubled for several days with a pain in her ear. Finally it was discovered that a wood tick had lodged itself within and in the meantime

"Berney Bierman, left halfback, is the new captain of the university football team."

Grove City Times, Feb. 18, 1910

---

had grown to a large size. A physician soon removed it.
Mille Lacs County Times, Milaca, June 3, 1915

→•←

Warning to Bathers. Notice is hereby given that anyone caught bathing in river inside of village limits without bathing suits will be prosecuted.

By order of Village Council.
W.A. Erickson, Clerk.
Mille Lacs County Times, Milaca, Aug. 12, 1915

→•←

Julius Schmahl, secretary of state, announces that there are 86,000 licensed automobile owners in Minnesota. On a basis furnished by the Wall Street Journal, he says the cars are worth $84,280,000, while the accessories and other appliances will increase this amount materially. Waseca has 946 autoes valued at $927,080. The average price of an automobile, according to the Wall Street Journal, is $980.
Waseca Herald, Sept. 2, 1915

→•←

Clerk Gets Boss in Bad. A clerk in the Eatwell Restaurant sold a package of cigarettes to a little boy last Wednesday and the matter coming to the attention of officer Lyttleton, he swore out a warrant for the arrest of J.L. Hasbrouck, the proprietor, who was brought before Judge McDonnell and fined $10 and costs, the fine being remitted. Although technically guilty, through the act of his clerk, Mr. Hasbrouck says the sale was unauthorized and that he is against the sale of cigarettes to minors as much as anyone. This law, however, is one that should be strictly enforced.
Graceville Enterprise, Sept. 10, 1915

→•←

Bierman Elected Captain. The following item taken from Sunday's Minneapolis Journal will be read with interest by the friends of Berney Bierman, who formerly resided in this city:

Berney Bierman, left halfback, is the new captain of the university football team. The election took place in the armory just before the team went on the field for the start of the game with Iowa.

Bierman is a resident of Detroit, Minn., a student of the aca-

"Once upon a time there was a man who was too busy to eat."

demic college, and one of the best halves in the west. He is personally very popular on the campus.

The disqualification of Solon [as captain] had a somewhat discouraging effect upon the team, coming as it did just before a game, but the election of the new captain and the talks of the alumni and coaches just before they went on the field is believed to have brought them back to the fighting pitch. The new captain took charge of the field work and the toss when the teams went out for the preliminary warmup before the game.
Waseca Herald, Oct. 28, 1915

[Bernie Bierman was the hero of this game against the Iowa Hawkeyes; Minnesota won, 51 to 13. He went on to coach the University of Minnesota football teams from 1932 to 1950, except for two years when he was on active duty with the U.S. Marines. In the period from 1934 to 1941, the Gophers won six Big Ten championships and five national championships.]

->-<-

No Sunday school was held Sunday morning so that teachers and scholars might take advantage of the opportunity to hear Miss Westling, a returned missionary from China. None that attended this meeting at the Mission church regret that they spent that time listening to an account of events in the lives of the Chinese people. Miss Westling certainly held the attention of the audience while telling of her work as a missionary of the Chinese Inland Mission. The collection taken up and money from subscriptions to a Missionary paper called the "Chinese Inland Mission" amounted to more than $10. The church was more than filled, even the aisles being filled

---

DON'T FORGET
To Pay
YOUR TAXES

AT THE

Farmers & Merchants State Bank of Oklee

Capital and Surplus $16,000

T. Anderson, President   J. A. C. Torgerson, V. P.

W. B. Torgerson, Cashier

Oklee Herald, Oct. 31, 1918

---

with attentive listeners.
Mille Lacs County Times, Milaca, Dec. 16, 1915

->-<-

Once upon a time there was a man who was too busy to eat. In the morning he swallowed a cup of coffee and smeared half a soft boiled egg on his mustache. At noon he allowed himself 15 minutes for luncheon, and as it takes the average waiter longer than that to walk to the kitchen and

back, the 15 minutes was about all the nourishment he got. He usually got home late for dinner in the evening, because he hated to tear himself away from his place of business so long as there was the slightest possibility of making another nickel before he closed down his desk, and when he did sit down to the table he devoured the stock market reports in the evening paper instead of digging into the fodder. He couldn't see any sense in

"The sunset of life . . . does not glow rose-blue for Nellie E. Hamlin."

wasting his time on food while there was so much money in the world that did not belong to him. At the age of 40 he died of what the doctors called acute indigestion, but I know better. It was just plain starvation. Anyhow, he left his family well provided for. The moral is: Perhaps it was all for the best.

Chisago County Press, Lindstrom, Aug. 24, 1916

—>-<—

The sunset of life, when marriage and giving in marriage is usually seen in retrospect, does not glow rose-blue for Nellie E. Hamlin, age 78, in her efforts to obtain a divorce in district court before Judge Cant yesterday from her husband, Charles B. Hamlin, age 80.

Testimony was taken in the case and while no decision was made by Judge Cant it will be forthcoming within a few days, as soon as certain adjustments are made.

Mrs. Hamlin is the widow of a civil war veteran and when she met Charles B. Hamlin, an old soldier at Lynn Bay, Fla., in 1913, they decided to wed. After a year of married life Mrs. Hamlin states that her husband deserted her. She is said to be in needy circumstances now. Before marriage she received a pension of $12 a month as a soldier's widow. When she married she lost this.

Duluth Herald-Tribune, Sept. 1, 1916

—>-<—

Changes in the parking regulations put into effect Aug. 28 may prohibit horses standing on certain streets, according to Commissioner Silberstein last night. Objections made by property owners to horses standing on Fourth avenue West between Michigan and Superior streets resulted in Commissioner Silberstein considering further regulations to prevent the hitching of

horses where the parking of autos is prohibited.

Duluth Herald-Tribune, Sept. 7, 1916

—>-<—

A Mr. Wahlstrand, of the senior class of Gustavus Adolphus College, St. Peter, has been spending several days looking up students for the college. He has created considerable interest among some of the boys and several of them may decide to go there. Gustavus Adolphus is a first class institution recognized as such by the state. It has a busi-

"Just try inside-bathing every morning for one week."

ness department, a five years' course in music, an academic department equal to an accredited high school, and a fully equipped college with a number of optional courses in languages, sciences, and higher mathematics. The next school year begins September 11.

Chisago County Press, Lindstrom, Sept. 7, 1916

→-›-‹-

Because thousands of "snuff drunkards," principally laboring men, are wrecking mentally and bodily health, and the snuff chewing habit, it was said, is assuming alarming proportions, the Minnesota Medical association, in session in Minneapolis Friday of last week, was asked to recommend legislation that would prohibit the use of snuff in Minnesota. Thousands of men and not a few women are victims of the habit.

Chisago County Press, Lindstrom, Oct. 19, 1916

→-›-‹-

To see the tinge of healthy bloom in your face, to see your skin get clearer and clearer, to wake up without a headache, backache, coated tongue or nasty breath, in fact to feel your best, day in and day out, just try inside-bathing every morning for one week.

Before breakfast each day, drink a glass of real hot water with a teaspoonful of limestone phosphate in it as a harmless means of washing from the stomach, liver, kidneys and bowels the previous day's indigestible waste, sour bile and toxins; thus cleansing, sweetening and purifying the entire alimentary canal before putting more food into the stomach. The action of the hot water and limestone phosphate on an empty stomach is wonderfully invigorating. It cleans out all the sour fermenta-

ALL GIRL SHOW

LET'S GO TO THE

LYRIC

Friday, Sat., and Sun. December 15, 16, 17th

VICTORIA TRIO
A Lyric Luxury

Catherine Chalmers & Company
Comedy Sketch Uninvited

KITTY & FLYNN
The Girl From Brighton

Six Crinoline Girls
In a Musical Fantasy
SIX GIRLS FROM DIXIE

BILLIE BURKE
In GLORIA'S ROMANCE

HARRY WATSON
In MUSTY SUFFER, Comedy

Matinee 2:30; Sundays 1:30, 3:30
Evening Performance 7:15; Sundays 6:30
Special Matinee for Ladies Friday
ADMISSION   15 and 25c

The Virginian, Dec. 8, 1916

tions, gases and acidity and gives one a splendid appetite for breakfast.

Daily Virginian, April 5, 1917

→-›-‹-

Modern Improvements. Pa-

tient — Doctor, I'm having an awful lot of trouble with the gas in my stomach. Doctor — Yes, yes; I know. Those old fashioned fixtures are giving people a lot of unnecessary trouble these days. Just step into the next room, and I'll have my engineer wire you for electric lights.

Daily Virginian, May 3, 1917

→-›-‹-

Fritz Melvey, the seventeen year old son of Mayor Melvey, was sentenced to the St. Cloud reformatory Thursday to serve an indeterminate term at hard labor. Fritz has never appeared to be a bad boy at heart, but appears to have gotten into the predicament that old dog Tray got into, "caught in bad company." He has been on probation here for the past few months under the guidance of the Rev. Martin Anderson and other men of this city, and it appears that they were not satisfied with his conduct and turned him over to the mercy of the court who then had no alternative but to send him to prison where he is quite likely to languish for the next five years.

Clay County Leader, Moorhead, Nov. 2, 1917

→-›-‹-

Child is Cooked to Death. Raymond, 12 year old child, a cripple and helpless, son of Mr. and Mrs. Beugh of Prior Lake, was cooked to death at the state school for the feeble minded at Faribault, where he was a patient, according to a report made to the state board of control. Last Thursday the child was being given his bath by an attendant, John Baker, [who] failed to test the temperature of the bath water and placed the child in it. A few minutes later he was rushed to a hospital badly scalded.

Clay County Leader, Moorhead, Nov. 23, 1917

→-›-‹-

"A person born in St. Paul is not required to take out naturalization papers in order to become a citizen of the United States."

It is to be noted that the horrors of war have mitigated the asperity [harshness] of the atavistic [outmoded] feud existing between the Twin Cities. The Minneapolis Tribune has admitted, in answer to a correspondent, that a person born in St. Paul is not required to take out naturalization papers in order to become a citizen of the United States. Let us hope that some St. Paul paper will be broad gauged enough to make a similar admission regarding the natives of Minneapolis, and a great step forward will have been made.

Irish Standard, Minneapolis, March 9, 1918

-→•←-

One of our well-known [Winnebago] farmers started to town over the frozen roads Monday morning with a cargo of cream. When he arrived he had some of the finest butter you ever saw in your life. The humps in the roads are so high that it is just like leaping from precipice to precipice.

Mapleton Enterprise, Jan. 3, 1919, reprinted from the Winnebago Enterprise

-→•←-

Let's Walk.

Why don't we walk more?

Since the advent of the street car, the motor car and various other modes of locomotion, we seem to have forgotten what feet are for. The man or woman who rides to and from work on the crowded street car, probably gets the idea that the pedal extremities were created for other persons to trample on, while the fortunate owner of a flivver imagines they are expressly designed to push the clutch lever and service brake.

Doubtless half of our population do not know how large and how shady are the woods a mile or two from town; how clear the water in the little stream.

The Best Beverage under the Sun—

Drink Coca-Cola

A welcome addition to any party— any time—any place.

Sparkling with life and wholesomeness.

Delicious Refreshing Thirst-Quenching

Demand the Genuine— Refuse Substitutes.

At Soda Fountains or Carbonated in Bottles.

THE COCA-COLA COMPANY, ATLANTA, GA.

Whenever you see an Arrow think of Coca-Cola.

New London Times, Aug. 21, 1913

"This is a grand time of the year for a stroll in the country."

When we hear the old inhabitants speak of walking 30 and 40 miles in a day, we gasp and wonder how they could do it.

This is a grand time of the year for a stroll in the country. It is neither hot nor too cold. And when we get out and away from the town where old Dame Nature has a comparatively free hand, we see things that cause us to stop and ponder.

Grass that was dead a few weeks ago is springing into new life. The trees that stood bare all winter long now are shooting out the buds or blossoms. It is the resurrection.

But walking does not benefit the intellect alone. It stimulates wonderfully the physical man. If you hear a fellow say, or if you say to yourself: "I do not need the exercise. I work six days a week and I need rest more than anything else," just try a walk some evening or on a Sunday morning before church, of eight or ten miles. Don't stroll — WALK. Throw back your shoulders, draw in the oxygen and move along, putting pep into every stride. And the next morning you will crawl out of bed and you'll realize that you are the possessor of a few dozen muscles you never knew existed. Muscles that had been loafing so long they had become flabby and tender. But if you have the nerve to repeat and let them harden up, you will turn up your nose at the fellow at the steering wheel and thank heaven you can look to the side of the road without danger of wrecking the car.

Cook County News-Herald, Grand Marais, April 9, 1919

-➤-◄-

Postmaster Dietz has received notice of the increase in the salaries of the rural mail carriers at the local post office. The increase amounts to $200 each yearly, giving M.H. Stroebel a sal-

Atwater Republican Press, April 1, 1910

"The Royal Hotel is known to be a good place to stop, as a woman autoist from Finlayson thoroughly demonstrated last Sunday afternoon."

---

ary of $1820, F. Kline $1796, Walter McKinnon and Burton Ackerman $1772 each and G.J. Wolff $1796. The amount of salary received by each carrier is rated according to the length of the route traveled. With this increase the carriers say they are no better off than several years ago when they received considerable less pay, but paid out much less for feed for their horses and the general upkeep of the rigs.

Mapleton Enterprise, Nov. 21, 1919

->-<-

There will be a children's Christmas Program in German and English at the Lutheran church Christmas Eve at 7 o'clock.

Finlayson Register, Dec. 19, 1919

->-<-

PERSONALS.

Herb Day, mail carrier on Route No. 1, is enjoying a two weeks vacation and left Friday morning for Hartford, Michigan, where he will visit with relatives and friends.

Park Rapids Enterprise, Aug. 17, 1911

->-<-

Miss Dora Dobberstien has resigned her position as saleslady in the ready-to-wear department of Herter's store. Her place has been taken by Miss Mayme Praxl.

Waseca Herald, June 24, 1915

->-<-

The new school house in district No. 4 will be dedicated with appropriate exercises tonight (Friday). Senator Edward Rustad, County Agent H.E. Kiger and County Superintendent Miss Bessie L. Caswell will take part in the dedication exercises. Refreshments will be served. Miss Ruth Amundson is the teacher in district No. 4.

Wheaton Gazette-Reporter, Dec. 3, 1915

We handle a complete line of supplies and do all kinds of auto repairing.

Nelson-Tellander Garage

Worthington Republican, Oct. 31, 1912

->-<-

The Royal Hotel is known to be a good place to stop, as a woman autoist from Finlayson thoroughly demonstrated last Sunday afternoon. While turning the corner she was unable to turn short enough or to stop the engine and landed squarely against the hotel building with such force that a piano on the inside was moved a foot or more, and the Ingraham baby who was sitting in a chair beside the piano was sick for some time from the fright. A hole was punched through the wall, but the auto was little damaged as it was protected by a bumper.

Pine County Courier, Sandstone, July 10, 1919

->-<-

Through the agency of Gene Williams, the J.J. Waller, Sr., farm in town of Whiteford has been sold to Dave Dundas of Argyle. It has only been a matter of two or three years since Mr. Dundas sold a Rollis farm, which was originally his homestead. But

seeing the present upward trend of real estate he concluded a piece of eastern Marshall county land is good property to own. When our local citizens begin picking the lands offered by the neighbors it is a sure indication that the country is getting onto a solid basis of prosperity.

Middle River Pioneer, Marshall County, July 24, 1919

->-<-

Argyle people who are in California and other western states will not envy us to know that the thermometer has been down to 8 below zero and that this early we have snow enough for sleighing.

Marshall County Banner, Argyle, Oct. 30, 1919

->-<-

A.J. Norholm, who has been in Colorado for the past two years and two or three weeks in California, returned to Finlayson yesterday morning. He says California is all right but the cost of living there was too much for him.

Finlayson Register, Dec. 12, 1919

->-<-

1910s
—>•<—

World War I

World War I began in 1914, and three years later the United States entered the war. Minnesotans had been for "peace and plenty," but they did their bit when the crisis came. More than 125,000 entered the military. Civilians poured money into Liberty Loans, had meatless days and volunteered for hundreds of tasks. At home, a Public Safety Commission adopted repressive tactics to hold down dissent. On Nov 11, 1918, the war was "over, over there" and the celebrations began.

Without Doubt. "Did you see where France is going to make all her fat men do military duty?"

"That confirms the claim that they are going to continue a stout fight."
Wheaton Gazette-Reporter, Sept. 17, 1915

—>•<—

The soldier boys at Camp Dodge [Iowa] are evidently not suffering for want of food. One of the Clay county boys sends home the bill of fare for September 27th. The menu was as follows: Dinner — Boiled Vienna sausage and sauerkraut, boiled potatoes, mustard, chocolate pudding, bread, coffee, sugar, milk; supper — roast beef, hash, boiled potatoes, tomatoes, bread, tea, sugar, milk; breakfast — September 28th, hot biscuits, butter, syrup, fried potatoes, corn crisps, coffee, sugar, milk.
Clay County Leader, Moorhead, Oct. 26, 1917

—>•<—

Wants Boys to Come Home Pure. There is one thing that every father and mother hopes and prays for who has sons in the army and that is if they come back alive they want them to come back as pure and clean as when they went into the army. They know the great temptations that lie in wait for the boys at the concentration camps and especially in France, where wine and women are in evidence. Every parent who has a boy in the service is mighty glad for an opportunity to give something for the Army Y.M.C.A. which is the great connecting link between the boys and their homes. It is the business of the Army Y.M.C.A. to furnish the boys wholesome recreation, good reading matter, and a comfortable place to write letters home and in every way encourage the boys to keep themselves clean and every inch the men they were before they went into service.
St. James Plaindealer, Nov. 17, 1917

—>•<—

The Bijou theatre was filled to the doors Tuesday and Wednesday eve., by an eager crowd that watched, in breathless silence, the exhibition of the screen play, "The Fall of a Nation," which, as teaching America the lesson of preparedness, is not equalled by any play now shown on the screen. . . . It was noticeable that, when the kaiser's soldiers seemed to be having everything their own way, an ominous silence prevailed but when the American boys, raw and untrained recruits tho they were, performed some particularly brilliant stunts, the audience broke into hearty applause and handclapping. That Manager Lakie's efforts to put only the best plays that can be obtained on the screen are appreciated is attested by the fact that every seat was sold for both performances.
Clay County Leader, Moorhead, Nov. 23, 1917

—>•<—

Since the Draft. Jones — How are you?

Smith — Are you speaking as a friend or as a member of the exemption board?
Clay County Leader, Moorhead, Dec. 7, 1917

—>•<—

"The sailor has somewhat been neglected in the flow of recent patriotism."

[Letter to the editor]

... I am sure all will agree with me when I say that the sailor has somewhat been neglected in the flow of recent patriotism. ... In almost every city or town when a soldier leaves for the training camp he is given a great sendoff. When a detachment leaves for the front, they leave amid cheers and a great display of flags, bands and the fond good-bye. When a naval unit moves, it moves under the cover of darkness or many other deceiving ways. We can't write to the "Old Folks" and say where we are going. Our work is silent but sure. ...

When you sit by your warm fires at night and think of the boys "Over There," please also think of the boys somewhere on the Atlantic, as the same kind of a heart beats under the sailor's jacket as the khaki coat of a soldier. ...

Yours truly,

Geo. B. Koktavy, Quartermaster 1st Class, U.S. Navy

New Prague Times, Jan. 3, 1918

-><-

Six young men of Hawley are alleged to have entered the home of George H. Peters, a farmer living in the outskirts of the village of Hawley, last Friday night at about 10 o'clock and removed a picture of the Kaiser and his family from a room of the house, and burned the picture in the middle of one of the streets in the village, while Mr. Peters and his family were absent from their home. ...

The county attorney hesitated about assuming the responsibility of starting a criminal action under the circumstances at this time without first obtaining the approval of the attorney general at St. Paul.

Mr. Peters is an American citizen and states he has never said anything against the war nor does

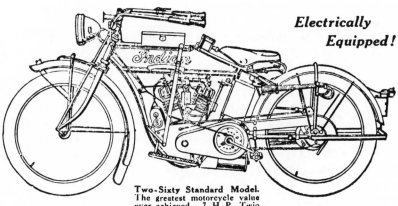

Electrically Equipped!

Two-Sixty Standard Model. The greatest motorcycle value ever achieved. 7 H. P. Twin equipped with Electric Head Light, Electric Tail Light, Electric Signal, Two Sets Storage Batteries and Corbin-Brown Rear-Drive Speedometer. Price $260.00. See Catalog for detailed description.

Indian MOTOCYCLES FOR · 1914

60,000 brand - new red machines will go out over the Indian trails during the coming year—the greatest motorcycle production in the history of the industry.

They will flash forth fully armed with "Thirty-Eight Betterments for 1914!" Armed with powerful and beautiful Electrical Equipment! Armed with a New Standard of Value which must completely overturn all existing ideas of motorcycle worth.

All standard Indian models for 1914 come equipped with electric head light, electric tail light, two sets high amperage storage batteries, electric signal, Corbin - Brown rear-drive speedometer.

You cannot fully realize the 1914 Indian without a thorough study of the 1914 Indian Catalog. It makes plain a host of compelling Indian facts that all motorcycle-interested men can consider to their real profit. Send for the 1914 Indian Catalog—the most interesting volume of motorcycle literature you've ever read.

The 1914 line of Indian Motocycles consists of :

4 H.P. Single Service Model	$200.00
7 H.P. Twin Two-Twenty-Five, Regular Model	225.00
7 H.P. Twin Two-Sixty, Standard Model	260.00
7 H.P. Twin Light Roadster Model	260.00
7 H.P. Twin Two Speed, Regular Model	275.00
7 H.P. Twin Two Speed, Tourist Standard Model	300.00
7 H.P. Twin Hendee Special Model (with Electric Starter)	325.00

Prices F.O.B. Factory

ARTHUR SKOGLUND, Agent,

New London, Minn.

New London Times, Nov. 13, 1913

*"With the exception of a few tears shed by one or two of the boys
they did not show a sign of low spirits."*

not intend to. He stated that he got the picture as a free premium with a Chicago newspaper 27 years ago, and that it has been in his home since that time.

Clay County Leader, Moorhead, Jan. 11, 1918

→•←

About 4,000 people from all sections of Clay county and Moorhead were present at the N.P. [Northern Pacific] depot at 9:05 Sunday morning to say goodbye to the 141 selected men who left for Fort Dodge, Iowa, for army training.

The men were gathered at the Comstock hotel before 9 o'clock, after having spent the night with friends in this city or at the various hotels. At 8:45 they gathered on Eighth street between Front street and the N.P. tracks between two lines of Home Guards and members of the Moorhead fire department, who kept back the large concourse of people from crowding in upon the army men and their friends who wished to say their last farewells at the train. With the exception of a few tears shed by one or two of the boys they did not show a sign of low spirits, but kept up their courage to the last, and they were helped in this to a large extent by the courage of their mothers, wives and sweethearts and sisters who were present in large numbers.

Only one of the men called to leave with the quota Sunday deserted, Athanarios Liberopoulos, who was registered at Glyndon. All the others who were called to go and did not go had been excused. Eight alternates were used.

The train left at 9:05 with the boys occupying two coaches. One coach was equipped with storm windows, which could not be opened from the inside, and it is reported that as the train reached Hawley the boys in that coach provided themselves with fresh air by kicking out a few windows. After leaving the county limits they settled down for the long ride to Fort Dodge and amused themselves by reading, card playing, etc.

Clay County Leader, Moorhead, March 1, 1918

→•←

At the Methodist parsonage on Thursday there was held a Mothers' prayer meeting. This meeting is to be held every two weeks, and the mothers of boys who have gone to the defense of their country, and all other mothers, of whatever church or religious belief, will be welcomed.

Clay County Leader, Moorhead, March 1, 1918

→•←

[When the war ended, the rejoicing was unprecedented. The Minneapolis Tribune ran its story about the local celebration on page one of the Nov. 12, 1918, issue, under the headline "Victory Joy Continues to Sweep City."]

At 2 o'clock yesterday morning it began.

At 2 o'clock yesterday afternoon it was increasing.

At 2 o'clock this morning it was diminishing — slightly.

For more than 24 hours Minneapolis forgot everything but that supreme moment in the history of the world when the official news arrived that the war had ended.

Black Shadow Lifted

Blackening with its shadow far more of the earth's surface than any other war in history; costing in lives, suffering, energy and wealth so dearly that the price of all other wars fades into insignificance; marking the end of right upon the scaffold and wrong upon the throne, remaking the human scheme of things, the lifting of its noisome cloud sent the sunlight of happiness over nearly the entire face of the globe and the sorrowing sons of men lifted their faces to the radiant sky in a world-wide song of praise and of thanksgiving.

"The world is free!"

This was the pean [usually spelled paean; a surging joyous song or hymn] heard in the lifted voices of the victorious Allied countries, and this is the knowledge shared by all humanity, which will make Peace Day an international holiday forever, taking a place above all single national holidays and standing with New Year's Day, with Easter Day and with Christmas Day.

Flashed Across City

The news reached Minneapolis shortly before 2 o'clock yesterday morning. Within a few minutes it sang across the sleeping city from the court house chimes. Hundreds of whistles took up the echoing message and sent it to the edges of town and beyond.

Minneapolis instantly awoke to full realization of its meaning. Lights flashed, windows and doors opened, people began pouring into the streets and in less than half an hour a multitude of men and women were down town renewing their celebration of world peace: singing, shouting, laughing,

"America does not go in very much for carnivals,
just as she does not go in very much for war."

weeping, ringing bells, blowing horns, pounding impromptu cymbals and bestowing affectionate felicitations upon those who were strangers the day before, but were all brothers and sisters of freedom in the bright hour that had come at last.

Carnival Spectacle Presented

It is estimated that the downtown crowds increased at the rate of 200 per cent every hour, and by the hour usually designated as "breakfast time" (though few stopped for breakfast yesterday), Nicollet and Hennepin avenues and all the cross streets below Tenth presented the rare spectacle of an American carnival in full swing.

America does not go in very much for carnivals, just as she does not go in very much for war; but when she celebrates she does it as hard and as tirelessly as she fights, and yesterday was her high tide of celebration, not only in Minneapolis but in every community of every state in the Union.

Parades Appear Quickly

The deafening din of joyousness lasted all day and far into the night. Early in the day parades began to appear, made up of the serried [pressed together] ranks of employes of factories and shops that had closed for the great day; of civic and fraternal organizations led by blaring bands; of orderly ranks of young soldiers and sailors who had hoped to march against the Huns, but were generously celebrating the achievements of their more fortunate comrades whose better luck had taken them overseas. Other parades had no particular excuse for being; they simply sprang into noisy existence because everyone felt just like being in a parade.

Automobiles and auto trucks, covered with flags and bunting, sounding continuous horns, dragging clanging metal tails of tin and iron along the protesting pavements and overflowing with shouting boys and girls, filled the streets until all traffic was blocked, and nobody cared. Paper streamers, scraps of torn paper and rainbows of falling confetti made the dizzy air as noisy to the eye as it was to the ear.

Former Kaiser in Effigy

Small boys dragged stuffed effigies of William Hohenzollern, former kaiser of Germany, along the asphalt and shrieked with glee as an automobile ran over their dummy enemy. Impromptu community sings and dances went on all over the place, wherever a band played a singable or a danceable tune — and all tunes were singable and danceable during that memorable yesterday.

By evening the din was indescribable and the streets well nigh impassable. Some one said it was like a thousand New Year Eves and Halloweens rolled into one; but America doesn't think in thousands any more, but in billions.

It was appropriate that Minneapolis should have joined hands with the world in the greatest celebration in history, for the greatest day the world has ever known called for such a festival.

There were 6,000 of them, soldiers and sailors,

". . . the greatest celebration in the city's history"

representing every army and navy training school in Minneapolis, that marched to military music through solid lines of cheering, happy Minneapolitans yesterday as a uniformed climax to the greatest ever celebration in the city's history. . . .

With an absolute "lid" on saloons, soda fountains and cafes maintained throughout the whole of the celebration yesterday, restaurants, cafeterias and lunch rooms, which alone stood the brunt of thousands of hungry Minneapolitans, were forced to close early when their supplies became exhausted. At midnight but three eating places in the Loop remained open and these were then filled.

Drug stores did a Christmas business at their candy counters and these cases were likewise depleted long before midnight. Sales of talcum and toilet powders were enormous, it was said, and the appearance of merrymakers and the condition of the streets showed this plainly.

The throwing of powder engendered considerable resentment, especially by women, whose furs and expensive scarves were damaged by this kind of enthusiasm. The police were helpless, however, and but little headway was gained in putting a stop to this practice.

It was long after midnight before the crowds began to show any marked signs of dispersing. Reams upon reams of confetti lay upon the sidewalks and pavements while heaps of what were once washtubs, boilers, milk cans, dishpans and other utensils used for noise making, littered the thoroughfares. . . .

Downtown Minneapolis was a "great white way" for the first time in more than a year, Fuel Administrator Garfield having lifted the ban in honor of the Yankee and Allied victory. Thousands and thousands of incandescent lamps, arc lights, ornamental lights and the blazing shop windows, made the streets resplendent. . . .

Led by Donaldson's Kiltie band, some 5,000 members of Minneapolis's greatest joy mob, equipped for the celebration with every style, shape and size of tin household utensils, paraded from Sixth street and Hennepin avenue, through the downtown section, and in and out of a dozen large office buildings. . . . Standing on the balcony of the Donaldson store, a cheer leader led the crowd in singing "America." Then came three cheers for Pershing, the boys "over there" and our Allies.

"The Star Spangled Banner," he announced.

Thousands of persons, jammed like sardines in the street below, doffed their hats. The whistles, tin pans, drums all stopped for a moment. Then, with the first words, the entire crowd joined in.

Minneapolis Tribune, Nov. 12, 1918

→•←

[The festivities were so out of control that one man was knocked down by an automobile driven by a "youthful celebrant," another was seriously injured with a skull fracture and more were slightly hurt.]

→•←

"New Prague seemed to be remarkably immune from influenza until last week."

["Spanish influenza," a previously unheard-of disease, spread quickly around the world during World War I and killed more than 21 million people. Here's a Minnesota repercussion.]

New Prague seemed to be remarkably immune from influenza until last week, when it appeared in all parts of town. Dozens of residences carried the warning signs "Influenza."

The schools were closed last week, and this week saloons were closed. The board of health and church authorities conferred and it was decided best that the churches be closed for a time. Crowds are forbidden to congregate anywhere in town.

The epidemic seems to have subsided, all serious cases being on the road to recovery. There are quite a number of cases in the surrounding country, a few of them being quite serious.

New Prague Times, Nov. 28, 1918

→•←

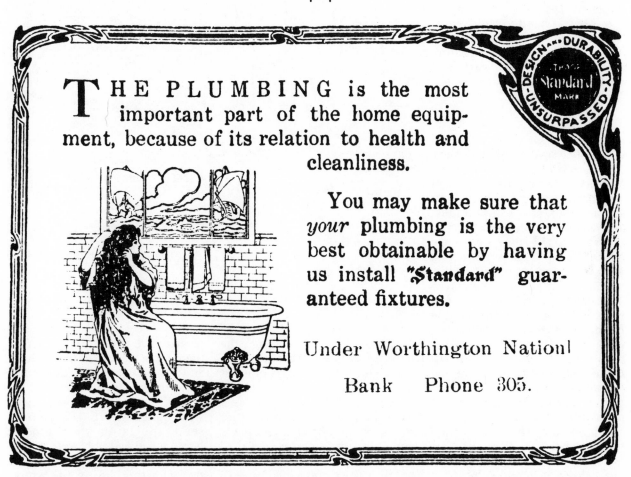

"He says: 'Now I am the only boy left in the family.' "

Red Cross chapters everywhere have been ordered to suspend all knitting. Stocks in all divisions, camp warehouses and national headquarters are sufficient to care for the needs of all men now in camps and those returning from the other side, besides allowing for a generous shipment to Foreign Commissions for civilian relief work. ...

Anyone having unfinished articles please finish as soon as possible and hand to Mrs. Jose so they may be sent in January.

December 19th 6 sweaters and 105 pairs of socks were sent.
Marshall County Banner, Arygle, Jan. 2, 1919

—>•<—

A letter from Walter Pinkham this week conveys the good news that he is once more in America. He came over on a small vessel which was bringing boys from the hospitals, sick and wounded, and which took on a few marines. He stated the marines were packed in like eggs in a case and were fourteen days and nights making the trip. Upon their arrival in the United States the marines were placed in quarantine for nearly a month. He will not receive his discharge for another month or so more and so will come on home rather than spend his time in the east. We will expect to see him in Mapleton soon. ...

Mrs. R. Marske received a letter from her son, Corporal John Marske, written in France Dec. 4th, acknowledging a letter from home with the sad news of the death of his brother George, who passed away while in the government service. He says: "Now I am the only boy left in the family. I am writing this letter with tears in my eyes but mother don't worry about me. I will return safe and sound and will remain at home the rest of my life. It seems hard to think that I came way

over here and went through the horrible battles and am still alive while George thousands of miles from the battlefields had to go, but mother, let's not worry as it was God's will and I am sure He will spare me. Brother George is gone but not forgotten. He died as a soldier, a fact that we should be proud of and the day will come when we shall meet again."
Blue Earth County Enterprise, Mapleton, Jan. 10, 1919

—>•<—

Harold Stroebel writes his parents from Daspich, Lorraine, saying that they made the trip on foot from their last stopping place, the hike being a distance

of sixty-five miles. He says that the people were glad to see them and "had their homes decorated with flags, mostly French and British banners, although there were quite a few U.S. flags to be seen, the latter were mostly home made and they were not always made right, noticed one or two with the blue in the wrong corner and some had gold or silver-gilt stars. But no matter how they were made they gave evidence that they were aware that Uncle Sam was here. The people here talk mostly German, although there is considerable French spoken. We are certainly glad the war is over but when we get home is another thing. We have a good mess sergeant so we

"About the only thing we can get here is vegetables."

have plenty to eat. Food is much higher here than it was in France, in fact about the only thing we can get here is vegetables."
Blue Earth County Enterprise, Mapleton, Jan. 31, 1919

—‣-‹—

Sergeant Edward P. Nowacki returned home Sunday morning, discharged from the army after three and a half years in the service. He was accompanied from Minneapolis by his sister Julia who will remain here for a couple of weeks visiting with home folks. Edward was overseas for eighteen months. He was wounded July 20th, 1918, in the battle of Chateau Thierry, and after several weeks in the hospital he again went to the front with his company. He was in five of the major engagements in which the American forces fought.
Marshall County Banner, Argyle, Oct. 9, 1919

—‣-‹—

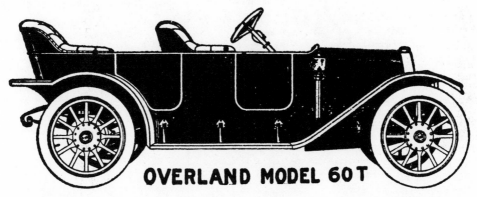
Worthington Republican, Aug. 8, 1912

Women got the right to vote in 1920. Charles Lindbergh, who spent boyhood summers in Little Falls, became the nation's darling for flying the Atlantic nonstop and solo. Radios came into common use. The Panic of 1929 sent the country into its worst depression.

4 O'CLOCK EXTRA Little Falls Daily Transcript **4 O'CLOCK EXTRA**

LINDBERGH ARRIVES IN PARIS

Little Falls Goes Wild As Favorite Son Lands Safely

SUCCESSFUL PLANE BUILT FOR SERVICE

"Lucky" Lindbergh Carries Picnic Lunch On Long Flight

WHISTLES, BELLS PROCLAIM BIG NEWS TO CITY

Crowds Follow Flight By A. P. Dispatches Received Here

He Made It!

LITTLE FALLS BOY ALIGHTS, 3:15 AT LE BOURGET FIELD

FLASH

Lindbergh landed safely at 3:15 P. M.

BULLETIN

FLIER FAVORED "GREAT CIRCLE"

Lindbergh Flew Grandly Into Great Ocean Spaces

VALUABLE MATERIAL WILL BE CONTAINED IN STATE EDITION

Alexandria Golfers Come Here Sunday

SHOT AT SORLIE STRAY BULLET

Youths Shooting at Pigeons Blamed For Stir At Bismarck

ANDREWS QUITS DRY FORCE POST

Haynes Also Will Resign; No Change In U. S. Policy

Big Ku Klux Klan Meeting Scheduled

SHANGHAI STRIFE GROWING WORSE

Fighting With Hankow Reds Is Expected To Break Soon

1920s
–>•<–

Lynching in Duluth

Duluth had about 100 black residents in 1920, many of them former field hands from the South who had been imported by U.S. Steel as strike-breakers. Shortly after a circus left town that June, a young white woman from Duluth and her boyfriend told authorities that she had been raped by six black workers from the circus. Officers stopped the circus train and arrested 13 blacks, some to testify against the others. Seven were released within hours. Here's what happened to three of the others that night in Duluth.

DULUTH had the first lynching in its history last night.

A mob estimated anywhere from 1,000 to 10,000 bent on avenging an assault on a young West Duluth girl, lynched three negroes held as suspects, two of whom, it is claimed, had confessed to the crime and the third who was being held as a material witness, hanging them to an electric light pole in front of the Shrine auditorium. The mob wrecked police headquarters and wounded several policemen in taking the negroes.

The three negroes whose dead bodies are today at Grady & Horgan's undertaking rooms are Isaac McGhie, age 20, Elmer Jackson, age 20, and Elias Clayton, age 19. McGhie is the only one of the trio who, to the last, claimed innocence of the crime.

The gathering of the mob started early in the evening. It is claimed that a truck on which was the label "city truck" came from the western end of the city shortly after 7 o'clock carrying a gang of young men. Attached to the truck and dragging behind was a long rope. The truck traveled through the streets slowly while those on the truck shouted, "Come on fellows, join the necktie party."

Men and boys grabbed the rope and marched behind the truck through the streets, finally stopping opposite police headquarters on the upper side. The crowd gathered rapidly. Truck loads of others joined, many of these truck loads coming from the western end of the city. The truck riders coming later made no demonstration. Apparently no attempt was made to stop them.

Youth Incites Crowd

When the first truck stopped, a young man, whose age was judged at about 20 years, got up on the top of the truck and began to address the crowd. His talk is said to have been exceptionally inciting. He told the crowd that the girl who was attacked by the negroes laid in the hospital at death's door and called on the crowd for vengeance.

The police barricaded the door of police headquarters and called every man off duty to report. A reserve of twenty-five policemen was at the station when the mob began its assault on the jail. Sergeant Oscar Olson was in charge. The police were holding the fort, both front and back, when the crowd flanked them by climbing the fire escape between the city hall and police headquarters and breaking in through the windows. Before the police knew what was taking place, several hundred men had forced their way in and begun the process of battering the jail.

A fire hose turned on the mob by the fire department, which was called out to disperse the mob, apparently only added to the fury. The mob took the hose out of the hands of the firemen and turned the water on the police. Hundreds of feet of fire hose was destroyed.

Bricks, paving blocks, rails and heavy timbers were used in battering the way into the jail. After breaking into the main cell house, the mob tore loose the locks on several of the cells. Finding only

227

"McGhie was the first to be strung up.
He begged for mercy, stoutly declaring his innocence."

Photo courtesy of the Minnesota Historical Society

one of the negroes downstairs, the mob went up-stairs to the boys' department where the other five were being held.

Steel saws were used when it was found that the battering ram was of no avail. Two steel bars holding the big door were sawed through. This process was too slow for the mob, which took another battering ram and broke through the wall, making a hole three feet wide by two feet high. The wall at this point is sixteen inches thick. Through this hole the terrified negroes were dragged.

Negroes Dragged to Doom

The negroes were taken up the hill to First street, following a mock trial held just outside of the cell room.

McGhie was the first to be strung up. He begged for mercy, stoutly declaring his innocence. Father W.J. Powers and Father P.J. Maloney pleaded with

the crowd to allow the law to take its course, but were greeted with hoots and yells and with the remarks "remember the girl" and "lynch him."

The first of the negroes to hang, Isaac McGhie, fell to the ground when the rope broke, the mob members nearest to the victim kicking him and jumping on him until he was about dead. Elmer Jackson, the next to die, met death calmly. He threw some dice to the crowd with the remark that he would not need them where he was going. The crowd cheered during his dying convulsions. When dead, he was lowered to within a few feet of the ground and left hanging, stripped of most of his clothes and covered with blood.

Begs Mercy; Gets Brutality

Elias Clayton, the third negro who had witnessed the hanging of the other two, wept and begged for mercy, but there was no mercy in the

228

"That there is a possibility that the mob has killed an innocent man was brought to light by Chief Murphy."

crowd and he was quickly hoisted high and, with hands lifted in supplication, received the kicks and blows aimed at him as his body dangled against the pole. One young man, who, it was claimed, was the brother of the assaulted girl, stood high up on the pole and kicked repeatedly at the face and head of the dying wretch.

When the hanging was over the crowd stood and, with the aid of a searchlight focused on the two men dangling in the air, viewed the results of its defiance of all law and order with calm satisfaction. The mob slowly dispersed and it was about 1 o'clock when the police were able to get close enough to the bodies to cut them down and turn them over to a local undertaker. Two were still hanging to the pole and one was lying on the ground, battered and bruised, where the mob had stamped and kicked the body fiendishly.

Headquarters a Wreck

The headquarters station is a wreck from basement to the third floor. The mob apparently was insane with desire to destroy and wreak vengeance. Windows, furniture, office records, and even the battery room on the third floor were destroyed. Everything was soaked with water from the hose handled by both sides and the floor of every room was ankle deep in water. Hardly a whole window is left in the building. . . .

One May Be Innocent

That there is a possibility that the mob has killed an innocent man was brought to light by Chief Murphy, who declared that one of the six prisoners was being held simply as a witness against the others and was in no way connected with the crime. Whether one of the men lynched was this man, Chief Murphy had no time to investigate before spiriting them away last night. He declared this morning that one of the men killed was one who had confessed and implicated the others and had given most of the information of the assault to the police.

With the death of this man, the police are without means of fastening the guilt on the remaining three, outside of the statements made to the police by the prisoners during their first examination by the chief yesterday morning.

Duluth Herald, June 16, 1920

→·←

[An even greater injustice was committed than this article would indicate. Not only is it unlikely that any of the lynched men were guilty of assault,

Duluth Herald, June 16, 1920

but also it is doubtful that the young woman was assaulted at all. A medical examination did not substantiate rape.

[Nonetheless, the surviving black men, all insisting they were not guilty, were brought before a grand jury in July. They were not advised of their right to refuse to testify, and no attorneys were present. The jurors didn't do much about the blacks' predicament, but they blasted police for handling of the incident. Several white men later were convicted of rioting and served a few years in prison, but all murder charges were dropped.

[One of the black men was convicted of assault and served four years of a 30-year sentence at Stillwater State Prison. Another was found not guilty. The remainder were dismissed.

[For the story on the Duluth lynchings, see "They Was Just Niggers" by Michael W. Fedo, published in 1979 by Brasch and Brasch.]

"Listen, women voters! Now that equal suffrage is an assured fact, what will you do with your vote?"

On Thursday evening the two and one half year old son John, of Mr. and Mrs. Edward Rozum, was burned to death at their home southeast of this city. The father had gone to the barn to do the evening work and the wife followed later with the milk pails, but before leaving she gave the little fellow some candy and nuts to keep it busy during her absence. She was gone just long enough to milk two cows. When she returned to the house she found the little one lying over a chair, its clothing in flames. She called her husband who came with a pail of milk and put out the burning clothing. On investigation it was found that the child had taken a small piece of wood and standing on a chair had pushed a small lid off the stove and lighted the wood, setting fire to his clothing with the above results. The sympathy of the entire community is extended to the heartbroken parents.

Pine County Pioneer, Pine City, Jan. 16, 1920

—⟩•⟨—

[When the Tennessee House voted in August 1920 to allow women to vote, the required number of states had passed women's suffrage and, as the Moose Lake Star Gazette put it, "all ladies will have the same right to the ballot this fall as the men. This includes all offices." The same paper ran an unsigned column, apparently written by a woman, headlined, "A Straight Talk to Women Voters."]

Listen, women voters! Now that equal suffrage is an assured fact, what will you do with your vote? We are to have a share in deciding what the policies of our government are to be, we want legislation which will protect the rights of all and we should fight any attempt to enact class legislation. We want legislation which will make for better homes, give

HOT CROSS BUNS

THURSDAY, FRIDAY AND SATURDAY

INTERNATIONAL BAKERY
Or at Your Grocer's

International Falls Daily Journal, April 1, 1926

our children more opportunities, throw barriers of protection around them. In order to get this we must come into one of our political parties, help make them what they should be, demand the legislation we should have. Home means much to us and the ballot should be to us another weapon with which to safeguard the home. Contented, prosperous homes are an enduring foundation for our nation to build to greatness on.

These things, the problems of state and national government, are before us. The future of our state and nation is virtually placed in our hands, for if the women whose vote will be for the right become slackers, as so many men have in the past, if they refuse to exercise their right on the ground that politics are dirty, that they will be contaminated by mixing in them, that they will some way be exposing themselves to jeers and sneers, as some seem to think they will, if they say they did not ask for suffrage, nor want it, so will not exercise it, the wrong will be sure to triumph.

Don't let us be slackers! Resolve right now that you will at once study the past accomplishments of the two political parties, their present promises and what they stand for, the men who are in nomination for our legislative and executive offices, are they clean men, men of right vision and right ideals, men who will enact and enforce legislation for the good of the country and the home. Make your choice of one

"Dress her in skirts that the sun won't shine through."

of these parties and enroll as a member. Then work for the success of your party. And don't neglect your vote.

"Pack up your powder in your small hand bag,
And vote, girls, vote.
This year the men have got their eyes on you,
A slacker gets their goat,
There's no use in worrying,
Just vow to be in style — so
Go to the polls and do your duty — then
You'll smile, smile, smile."

Moose Lake Star Gazette, Aug. 26, 1920

→·←

Backward, turn backward, oh Time in your flight. Give us a maiden with skirts not so tight. Give us a girl whose charms, many or few, are not exposed by too much peek-a-boo. Give us a maiden, no matter what age, who won't use the streets for a vaudeville stage. Give us a girl, not so shapely in view; dress her in skirts that the sun won't shine through. Then give us the dances of days long gone by, with plenty of clothes and steps not so high. Oust turkey trot capers and buttermilk glides, the hurdy-gurdy twists and the wiggle tail slides. Then let us feast our tired optics once more on a genuine woman as sweet as of yore. Yes, Time please turn backwards and grant our request, for God's richest blessing — but not one undressed.

Moose Lake Star Gazette, Sept. 9, 1920

→·←

The attention of people patronizing the public library is called to the fact that one of the books of the traveling library is missing, and must be returned at once. The book is "Understanding South America" by Cooper. Please look over the books at home and if you have the above

..Fourth Annual..
Exhibition

OF THE
Redwood County Poultry Association

Redwood Falls Armory,
..December 6, 7, 8, 1921..

EXECUTIVE BOARD.

J. C. Jackson, President............................ Morgan
Mrs. R. A. Cooper, Vice-President.............Redwood Falls
E. H. Albrecht, Treasurer.........................Morgan
Max R. H. Treu, General Supervisor............Redwood Falls
Oscar A. Goetze, Secretary........................Redwood Falls
Arthur Hassenstab, Ass't. Secretary.............Redwood Falls
Frank A. Japs, Superintendent ....Redwood Falls

The officers are hustling to make the coming County Poultry Show one of the best of its kind ever held in Southern Minnesota.

Redwood Falls Sun, Dec. 2, 1921

"Today is national fish day. You are supposed to eat a fish."

HERES SOMETHING FOR YOUR HEADACHE

You'll feel better as soon as you swallow the first one. Two or three pills usually stop all the pain.

DR. MILES' ANTI-PAIN PILLS

are absolutely free from all narcotics and habit-forming drugs. They relieve without danger and without bad after effects. **Your druggist sells them.**

Redwood Falls Sun, Aug. 21, 1921

mentioned one please return it to the library at once.
Cottonwood County Citizen, Windom, Oct. 27, 1920

–›‑‹–

The tooth pick girls [young women at the tooth pick factory] gave a party at Fuller's hall New Years Eve. Lunch was served and the girls enjoyed themselves at dancing and games. Mesdames Mallory, Chisholm and Prange were the chaperones. There were about thirty-five girls present and all reported a fine time.
Cloquet Pine Knot, Jan. 7, 1921

–›‑‹–

A number of cases of prolonged hiccoughs have developed in this city recently, in a few instances the patient suffering from the malady for a period of from six to ten days, while the more numerous cases were of little more than ordinary duration. The disease is one which has baffled medical science as to cause, preventative and cure. In some localities recently it has reached epidemic proportions. Local vic-tims of the affliction seem to be recovering without serious complications, which are usually more pronounced when the trouble develops in connection with other forms of illness.
Rock County Herald, Luverne, Jan. 28, 1921

–›‑‹–

A Thing to Encourage. Today is national fish day. You are supposed to eat a fish.

. . . A fish a day is something we of Northern Minnesota should encourage for the reason that we have the fish. Get people thinking about our fish and they will think about our big ones that are now getting themselves in shape for a season of struggle. Those big fellows down in the bottom of the lake are strong and healthy and awaiting an angler who is impatiently looking forward to the opening of the season. One cannot eat fish without thinking of exciting moments, outstanding events of a lifetime, not in importance, but in pleasure.

To eat roast beef does not stir one's sporting blood. A leg o' lamb doesn't excite one's imagination. But a taste of good fish — it is a better spring tonic than dandelion wine.
Grand Rapids Herald-Review, March 9, 1921

–›‑‹–

The Next War. Somebody said a number of years ago that the only thing that will stop war is the horrible inventions that will make warfare so destructive that it becomes impossible to carry on war. To engage in warfare will mean practically destruction for both sides.

The following clipping from a current magazine makes it appear that we have reached such a stage of destructive warfare:

"A prominent French general, Maitrot, says that a new projectile has been invented by the French army that would destroy the city of Berlin with a dozen shots. New poison gases have also been invented which will eat through any gas mask and also through any human being quickly and thoroughly. Airplanes are being perfected which can carry suffi-

*"It is easy to see that the next war, if it comes,
will wipe out not only armies but whole peoples."*

cient death dealing bombs of one kind or another to make a cemetery out of a city over night.

"It is easy to see that the next war, if it comes, will wipe out not only armies but whole peoples. Women and children will not escape. Young men by the tens of thousands will be eaten up by poison gases. Civilization will be nearly destroyed by another general war. Do you want your boys strangled to death by poison gas? If not, there is one thing to do and only one, and that is to see that there is no next war."

Rushford Star-Republican, March 10, 1921

—>-<—

Art Meyers returned Thursday from an extended tour of the South. Mr. Meyers reports a very interesting trip. While at Hot Springs, Ark., he saw Babe Ruth in his first work-out of the season, clouting the first two balls pitched him, over the fence.

Cloquet Pine Knot, March 11, 1921

—>-<—

It only seems like yesterday that anybody who would could have a job. People were promoted right and left. Salaries were raised. Wages soared. Good, bad and indifferent, we have all been riding the wave together, and thinking all the time that we were the grand little swimmers. Any kind of a lawyer could get cases. Any kind of a doctor could get patients. Any kind of a teacher could get a school. And so on, and on, and on — Get all you can — give as little as you can! That seemed to be the unspoken slogan of millions. But the competent workers, whether they are brick-layers or bankers, are going to set the pace from now on and they are going to get the reward

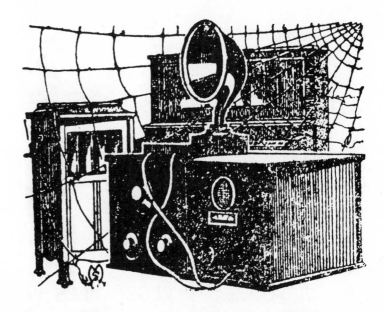

Duluth Herald, Jan. 12, 1923

"Don't jump to the conclusion that she is mailing the child."

that is due them.
Browns Valley Tribune, March 31, 1921

→·←

There are still some folks who sigh for good old times. But who would welcome them were they to come back? Subtract from modern life the movie, porcelain bathtubs, vacuum sweepers, electric lights, instantaneous hot water and telephones. Take out phonographs, motor cars, electric irons and washing machines and sanitary plumbing. Banish these things and you have again what people like to call "good old times." Who really wants the good old times back? Occasionally a cynic declaims against the modern improvement, but he never means it. The modest home of the average middleclass American is infinitely more comfortable than the mansion of those other days called "the good old times." The average housewife, relieved of much of the old drudgery of handwork, has more time for leisure and recreation. Her family has more recreational opportunities. The new times have their faults, but they are the golden age, when contrasted with the "good old times." They cost us more than the "good old days" of yore, but aren't they worth the price?
Rock County Herald, Luverne, April 15, 1921, reprinted from Farm and Home magazine

→·←

Permanent Color Improvement. "Your face is no longer flushed with drink."

"No," replied Uncle Bill Bottletop. "When they proclaimed prohibition, I turned pale and never got over it."
Cloquet Pine Knot, June 10, 1921

→·←

First Airplane Wedding
Elk River has had its first air-

International Falls Daily Journal, April 15, 1926

plane wedding. It happened on Tuesday when a Curtiss airplane arrived in the afternoon from Minneapolis with a would-be bride and groom. The plane was piloted by Walter Bullock, well known Minneapolis aviator, and a landing was made on Houlton's field across the Elk river, the trip from Minneapolis to Elk River having been made in twenty minutes.

Lloyd E. Fraser and Miss Margaret W. Stone, both of Minneapolis, accompanied by Mr. Bullock, appeared before Judge Bailey of the Probate Court and asked to be married. Judge Bailey, however, advised them to go to a minister and as the young lady was a Congregationalist he recommended Rev. Jones. The party then went to Rev. Jones' home and there the marriage ceremony was performed, Mr. Bullock and Mrs. Jones acting as witnesses.

Afterwards the party returned to the airplane and Mr. Bullock piloted them back to the city. Whether or not they were a runaway couple is not known, but they certainly appeared to be in a good deal of a hurry.
Sherburne County Star News, Elk River, Aug. 4, 1921

→·←

"Main Street," which eminent literary judges decided was the best contribution to letters of last year and which brought Sinclair Lewis the Pulitzer prize of a couple thousand dollars, has been ousted from the public library of Alexandria, Minnesota. Possibly somebody up that way read the book and came to the passage where Gopher Prairie was located a day's journey for an ox team from Sauk Centre, which might fit Alexandria. The library board of that city is taking itself too seriously, and there is always humor in asinine solemnity.
St. Cloud Journal-Press, Aug. 29, 1921

→·←

If mother is caught shoving baby through the window of the cabinet at the postal station, don't jump to the conclusion that she is mailing the child. Don't assume that baby is in for a parcel post ride even if the postal clerk is seen weighing the infant.

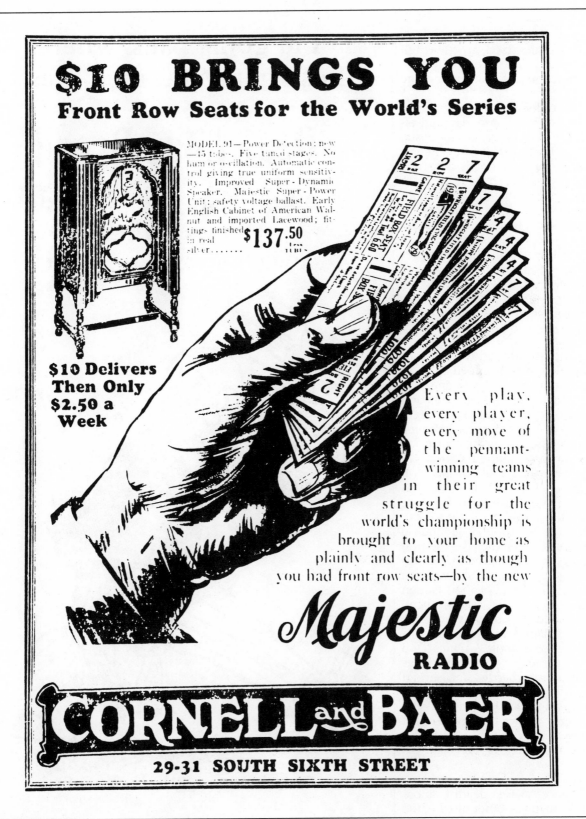

$10 BRINGS YOU
Front Row Seats for the World's Series

MODEL 91— Power Detection; new —15 tubes. Five tuned stages. No hum or oscillation. Automatic control giving true uniform sensitivity. Improved Super-Dynamic Speaker. Majestic Super-Power Unit; safety voltage ballast. Early English Cabinet of American Walnut and imported Lacewood; fittings finished in real silver.......

$137.50
less tubes

$10 Delivers Then Only $2.50 a Week

Every play, every player, every move of the pennant-winning teams in their great struggle for the world's championship is brought to your home as plainly and clearly as though you had front row seats—by the new

Majestic RADIO

CORNELL and BAER

29-31 SOUTH SIXTH STREET

"The fame of their garden has spread, but it has not been over-rated."

For the St. Paul postoffice, now "humanized," will weigh babies as well as attend to its usual functions of distributing the mails.

An order issued by Postmaster Charles J. Moos Monday, and effective at the fifty-seven postal substations in St. Paul this morning, instructs all heads of branch offices to be in readiness to weigh the babies of the neighborhood. Knowing accurately the weight of infants is so important a consideration in safeguarding their health that the postmaster regards it an obligation to society to make the office scales available.

St. Paul Pioneer Press, Feb. 14, 1922

→›•‹—

The Herald editor allowed himself to be kidnapped by Thos. Dyer and Gus Buboltz one evening this week and taken out and inspected the garden and field crops of the Simmons brothers, about eight miles west of Cook the town of Linden Grove. He had heard much about this farm but half had not been told. It is on the Little Fork river, and comfortable farm buildings have been erected on high ground on the west side of the river. Several large pine and spruce trees furnish ample shade for their farm home. The fame of their garden has spread, but it has not been over-rated. It not only contains all vegetables incidental to this section, but apples, plums, and grapes show a fine growth, as well as strawberries and several varieties of raspberries are demonstrating that they can be successfully grown in Northern St. Louis County.

Cook Herald, Aug. 10, 1922

→›•‹—

Cancer causes death in more adults than any other disease, the death rate from this disease in the past two years in the state of

I'm going back where I can get some nice fresh

Real Loaf Bread

bought at the Grand Marais Bakery

Frank Cherry, Proprietor

"One of the most serious consequences of the blizzard last week was the complete isolation of a family of five all ill with influenza and without help of any kind."

Minnesota surpassing that from tuberculosis. In Minnesota 2,193 people died from cancer in 1921. As yet the cause of this malady is unknown. In an effort to combat its increasing death rate the American Society for the Control of Cancer is conducting an intensive educational campaign, that the early signs and symptoms of cancer may be familiar to all.
Mankato Free Press, Nov. 10, 1922

→-<-

There is Nothing Wrong with Minnesota. Except — That entirely too many of us get up in the morning at the alarm of a Connecticut clock, button a pair of Chicago trousers to Ohio suspenders, put on a pair of shoes made at Lynn, wash in a Pittsburgh tin basin, using Cincinnati soap and a cotton towel made in New Hampshire; sit down to a Grand Rapids table, spread with Vermont maple syrup and Kansas City bacon fried on a St. Louis stove; buy fruit put up in California seasoned with Rhode Island spices; put on a hat made in Philadelphia; hitch a Detroit tin mule fed on Texas gasoline to an Ohio plow and work hard all day long on a Minnesota farm covered with a New England mortgage; send our life insurance money to New York, Milwaukee, Indianapolis and Bogota and at night crawl under a New Jersey blanket and be kept awake by a damned dog — the only home product on the place — wondering all the while why ready money and prosperity are not more abundant in this wonderful state of ours.
Madison Western Guard, Jan. 19, 1923

→-<-

Isolated in Blizzard. One of the most serious consequences of the blizzard last week was the complete isolation of a family of five all ill with influenza and without help of any kind. The family of Ralph Henderson, liv-

We have a Limited Supply of these Durable little Wagons *on hand*

Which we were Fortunate Enough to get at less than WHOLSALE PRICE and Which

We Are Giving to Our Customers at Exact Cost to Us

If you buy 12 cans of Fruit, Vegetables or assorted if you like. Buy a load and have a Toy for the boy.

J. C. Murphy's Store

Cook County News-Herald, Dec. 14, 1922

ing on a farm about five miles west of Montevideo, underwent this experience and for four days suffered terribly.

Mr. and Mrs. Henderson and their three children, ages 3, 4 and 6, were all ill. The storm had put their telephone out of order and they were unable to go out in the blizzard Tuesday. One of the little children was delirious Tuesday and Tuesday night. Fi-

nally on Friday afternoon Mr. Henderson crawled out of bed and managed to hitch up and drive to the nearest neighbor about half a mile away. Mrs. Ole Haugen responded at once to his appeal for help and returned with him. Mr. Henderson was forced to return to bed and was not able to get up again until Monday.

Altho circumstances looked

"All these years she had been on the lookout for somebody who could tell her where I went to."

dark all members of the family survived their illness and are now able to be up and around.
Montevideo News, Feb. 23, 1923

→•←

The highest medical authorities and records of the hospitals bear testimony that no man can drink beer safely, that it is an injury to any one who uses it in any quantity, and that its effect on the general health is far worse than that of whiskey.

But the physical effect is not the worst feature of beer consumption; the most pernicious thing is its demoralizing, brutalizing influence on those who habitually use it.
Madison Western Guard, March 2, 1923

→•←

Johnny Weismuller [later Tarzan in the movies], the crack Illinois Athletic Club swimmer, whose record breaking feats of the past few months are the talk of the swimming world, arrived in St. Paul last night to compete in the meet at the Athletic Club tonight.
St. Paul Pioneer Press, March 4, 1923

→•←

Finds Mother. Our readers will be interested in a letter the Bulletin received the past week from Mrs. C.L. Rairdin, whose maiden name was Florence Beltz, the adopted daughter of Mr. and Mrs. F.A. Beltz of this village. The letter is self-explanatory and is as follows:

"St. Paul, Minn., March 28.

"When I read in the Bulletin of Earnest Ruf finding his sister I thot I would look up my record. Spent about four days hunting. Found an old lady, seventy-six years of age, who had taken care of me at one time, and thru her I got trace of my mother. It was a terrible shock to her when she was told who I was. All these

St. Cloud Daily Times, April 7, 1928

years she had been on the lookout for somebody who could tell her where I went to. On my birthday in February she had been crying and wondering if I was still living. So her mind is at rest now. Her health is very poor. I have three brothers and one sister. She has a very nice home but nothing like the home I had. She

"Toast can be served in 21 different ways."

can never take the place of my adopted mother in my heart. No one could have been a better mother to me than she was.

"Hope everybody is well and happy back in the old home town. Best wishes to all.

Florence Rairdin."

Boyd Bulletin, April 6, 1923

—>-<—

The anti-saloon league is to be commended for its effort in proposing the passage of a law to prohibit doctors from prescribing liquor as medicine and ministers from using fermented wine at the communion table. Would that every minister of the gospel from now on would enter this fight, and be on the dry side. If we want any reform work done, it must come from the church.

Madison Western Guard, April 13, 1923

—>-<—

The Real Issue. "Doggone it, Bringsley, I don't know what is going to become of the country. Things are going to the dogs."

"Your business slow?"

"No, not that; but last night my partner led the king when I held the ace, and when I came back with the ace to hold lead and kill the suit she trumped my ace, and then got the idea diamonds was trumps when I had made it hearts. I tell yuh, women are getting too darned independent."

Madison Western Guard, June 8, 1923

—>-<—

A nation-wide campaign to promote the more extensive use of toast by the American public and thereby increase the domestic consumption of wheat foods will get under way on December 3, under the auspices of the Wheat Council of the United States.

"Eat It With Toast," is a slogan for the new campaign which

St. Cloud Daily Times, April 18, 1928

is a patriotic movement to help the impoverished wheat farmer and also restore the national dietary to the proper balance. . . .

Toast, in its many combinations with meats, jellies, jams, butter, cheese, milk, eggs and other foods will be set before the public by all the interests concerned in the campaign. Dairy, cheese, butter, coffee, bakery and milling interests coupled with local individual firms will feature recipes furnished housewives how toast can be served in 21 different ways. Radio will be used to broadcast some of the recipes.

Madison Western Guard, Nov. 23, 1923

—>-<—

1920s

—>•<—

Lindbergh's Nonstop Flight

Charles Lindbergh spent his boyhood summers at his family's farm at Little Falls, Minn. After his solo, nonstop flight of 33 1/2 hours across the Atlantic in 1927, Little Falls claimed a world hero. Newsmen flocked there, and so did curiosity-seekers, who helped themselves to anything they could carry away. Any number of cities — Detroit, Washington, St. Louis among them — took credit for Lindbergh, but here's what the Little Falls Transcript had to say, starting with bulletins of his progress toward Paris.

LITTLE FALLS BOY ALIGHTS, 3:15 AT LE BOURGET FIELD

FLASH

Lindbergh landed safely at 3:15 P.M.

BULLETIN

An aeroplane believed to be that of Captain Lindbergh was sighted approaching the Le Bourget flying field at 10 o'clock tonight.

The crowd on the field was so large that the police could not hold them, and there was some doubt whether the aviator would be able to land, so densely were they packed. The crowd burst into cheers even before the plane could be definitely identified.

While trying to locate the plane, which was circling the lower end of the field, the crowd was in a tremendous uproar, and the police were having utmost difficulty in keeping them from the danger zone.

Plane Passed over Bayeaux

Paris, May 21: The French Cable Co. announced receipt of an official advice saying Captain Lindbergh's transatlantic plane passed over Bayeaux on the French coast at 8 o'clock tonight, French time. . . .

Local Storm Arises At Field

Le Bourget Flying Field, May 21, (AP): A storm, apparently local, passed over the flying field here late this afternoon.

There was a sharp shower with the sky a leaden grey, but it soon blew over and at this time the weather is clear. A stiff breeze [is] blowing from the northwest.

Near Cork at 11:30 This Morning

Belfast, Ireland, May 21: Lindbergh's plane was reported sighted over Dingle Harbor, County Kerry, southwestern Ireland, at 5:30 o'clock this afternoon (11:30 a.m. Little Falls time) flying in the direction of Cork.

Dingle Harbor juts into the western coast of County Kerry, which is on the course platted by Captain Lindbergh for his flight to Paris.

His reported arrival there at 5:30 p.m. also coincides with the time schedule of the plane as computed at New York.

Cable Company Gets Notice

New York, May 21: The Paris Cable Co. this afternoon announced receipt of official advices from the English government stating that Captain Lindbergh was over Ireland headed in the direction of Cork at 5:20 o'clock this afternoon, Irish time.

Steamer Sights Lindbergh's Plane

Valencia, Ireland, May 21: The government army

"He has made it."

station here is advised by the steamer, Collier Nogi, that she sighted a gray aeroplane headed east by southeast while the Nogi was approximately 52.45 north latitude, 12.5 west longitude. The plane was flying rather low.

Reached Ireland at 7 A.M.

Halifax, Nova Scotia, 10:05 A.M. — Captain Charles Lindbergh's aeroplane passed over Valencia Island, southern Ireland, at 7 a.m., Little Falls time, according to a report broadcast by station WYM, Catham, and picked up at the radio station at Yarmouth, Nova Scotia, and relayed to the government station here. (Valencia is some 600 miles from Paris.)

France Cheers at First Report

Flying field Le Bourget, France, May 21: The exultant cries of "He has made it," ran rapidly from

Photo courtesy of the Minnesota Historical Society

crowd to crowd upon hearing the report that Charles A. Lindbergh has been sighted off Ireland.

Crowds waited his coming although it was known that the transatlantic flier could not reach here for several hours.

The crowd was small at 5 o'clock tonight consisting only of two or three hundred persons, most of whom were cameramen and reporters. Big cars containing pompously dressed women were beginning to arrive with their pet dogs and a few patient souls who had brought books seated themselves where they could see the field.

Strong Wind Behind Lindbergh

Paris, May 20, (AP): Captain Lindbergh will come into France tonight with a strong quartering wind from the southwest behind him.

Weather reports this afternoon bore out reports last night indicating that favorable conditions existed over the English channel, which will probably last until The Spirit of St. Louis is well over Paris.

Every available light will be blazing the way to Le Bourget flying field, near Paris, while from Mount Valerian, at Suresnes, the greatest searchlight in the world will throw its powerful beam in a complete circle every five seconds. This light can be seen from the coast when visibility is good.

This afternoon weather reports indicated that it would be cloudy in the Paris region tonight with perhaps a bit of fog or rain, but not enough to affect the landing.

Lindbergh's fearlessness and his will to win have aroused the admiration of the French people. "Magnificent!" "What daring!" "I hope he succeeds!" These are some of the excited exclamations heard everywhere.

However, some expressed disgruntlement that an American may win where Nungesser and Coli [two Frenchmen who attempted to fly from Paris to New York] seem to have failed and perhaps lost their lives. [They were never found and were presumed dead.] But the remainder of the people are watching with interest and show admiration for the courage of the man who started modestly and alone.

The flying field at Le Bourget is in readiness to receive the intrepid flier. All other planes will be kept from the air as far as possible when Lindbergh approaches to avoid confusion or accident.

Preparations have been made against the possibility of an unsuccessful landing. The fire department and ambulance crews have been ordered to be ready on the field and the American hospital in Paris is sending doctors and nurses and an ambulance.

A constantly increasing pile of telegrams and cablegrams is waiting for the flier and plans to entertain him are growing hour by hour.

"Little Falls slept fitfully last night."

WHISTLES, BELLS PROCLAIM BIG NEWS TO CITY

Crowds Follow Flight By A.P. Dispatches Received Here

Little Falls went wild today when her favorite son became the world's hero by flying from New York to Paris.

An Associated Press flash was the tip for the whistle's shriek at the Hennepin paper mill and every sounding device in Little Falls immediately took up the cue. Church bells, in vast contrast to the Sunday morning stateliness, pealed forth with greatly increased tempo. Tin horns and wild cries of "Hurrah for Lindbergh" filled the air.

Plans for the big pow wow were laid last night when a Board of Commerce committee confidently prepared for the greatest celebration in Little Falls since 1918 when another flash from France proclaimed the end of the war.

Little Falls Sends Greetings

The American Legion firing squad was ready for action and the city band was prepared with its most spirited march when the news broke.

"Greetings from Little Falls. You have accomplished that which your home town knew you could do. Little Falls is celebrating your achievement," is the cablegram which young Lindbergh received as he alighted from his plane in Paris. The message was sent by the Board of Commerce in care of Ambassador Myron T. Herrick, who was on the reception committee.

Lindbergh also will receive a cablegram of congratulations from the students of his alma mater. Little Falls high school this afternoon filed a message to Paris.

Little Falls slept fitfully last night. "I dreamed about Lindbergh a dozen times," one businessman said, while scores of residents said substantially the same thing.

Although he does not know it, Charles Lindbergh is an honorary member of the Little Falls Hunting club, the aim of every sportsman in the city. The executive committee at a meeting last evening broke the hitherto hard-and-fast rule by increasing the membership from 18 to 19. All the privileges of the hunting lodge at Leech lake are at the disposal of the intrepid young flier and the members of the club are hoping that he will join them in a hunting expedition next fall.

Go where you will, you'll find fresh evidence of Chesterfield's constant appeal to men who know good tobacco

Chesterfield

Chesterfields are made by the Liggett & Myers Tobacco Company

International Falls Daily Journal, Feb. 23, 1926

Many Rumors Adrift

As usual in a case of this kind, the customary "grapevine wire" news was noised around the city. Lindbergh was reported as having landed in Paris a dozen times. These rumors promptly were dispelled by Associated Press dispatches. The public kept its head and refused to let out a war-whoop at every rumor, relying on the Associated Press to give the authentic news.

At 11:45 a.m., a dispatch stated that Lindbergh was flying toward Cork. He was almost in a direct line with his proposed route and within 800 miles of his goal.

With Lindbergh on everyone's mind, "home town" stories continued to crop out today. Charles Farrow, an automobile salesman, told about giving

"It is hard to say which suffers worse."

the youngster his first auto driving lesson. Mr. Farrow in 1917 sold the Lindberghs the Saxon six that Charles drove at such a furious rate. The deal was made through correspondence with the elder Lindbergh, who was then in congress. Fifteen-year-old Charles naturally became the family chauffeur and Mr. Farrow pointed out the "whys and wherefores" of the gas buggy. "He sure took to it like a duck to water," Mr. Farrow said. "He learned it all the first day."

While Little Falls citizens sat around and talked about Lindbergh's hard ride in the dark last night, they recalled that the elder Lindbergh was a man of great physical endurance frequently poring over his law work most of the night, and banked on young Charles to withstand the ordeal and come through triumphant. More and more, father and son appear to be "moulded from the same clay" and the name

of Lindbergh is indeed illustrious in Little Falls.
Little Falls Daily Transcript, 4 o'clock Extra, May 21, 1927

-><-

[In 1931 the Lindbergh family gave the Little Falls house and 110-acre farm to the state. The house and an interpretive center on the Mississippi River are run by the Minnesota Historical Society and are open to the public.

[Be sure to read Charles Lindbergh's account of his flight, the Pulitzer Prize-winning book, "The Spirit of St. Louis," published in 1953 by Charles Scribner's Sons. It's good reading, even for people not fascinated by aviation. A less-accurate but captivating tale of the flight is the 1957 movie, also called "The Spirit of St. Louis," starring Jimmy Stewart.]

->•<-

It is hard to say which suffers worse: a woman holding her breath while her husband hunts for the hooks on the back of her evening gown, or a man holding his breath while his wife tries to repeat his favorite funny story.
McGrath Tribune, Oct. 21, 1924

-><-

The following people in the primary grades had perfect attendance last month: Fay Bashore, Ruth Ellis, Alfred Genz, Melvin Gilbertson, Alice Heller, Alberta Hengel, Hazel Niskawara, Walter Hahn, Ralph Klingl, Hilda Plowman, William Plowman, Goldie Sloan, Pearle Sloan, Anita Toebe, June Torison, James Tawns, Robert Viviant, Antoinette Worm, Homer Zeismer, Isabelle Zimpel, Celia Genz, Myrtle Thomson and William Isley.
McGrath Tribune, March 24, 1925

-><-

Many Operations. The past week has been a busy one at the hospital. Saturday night Mrs. John Woida of Effington had an operation for appendicitis. Sunday, Mrs. John Lambertz was operated on for appendicitis. Wednesday night, Hertha Betterman, daughter of Gust Betterman,

and Theresa, daughter of Math Grappa, had appendicitis operations. Anna, the daughter of Fred A. Thoennes was operated on last week for appendicitis. Alois Faber is receiving treatments for blood poison in his foot, and Thos. Koep, who had his hand badly cut last week, is also receiving treatment. The Faber young man cut his foot

with an axe. Albin Listrom from Leaf Mountain had his shoulder crushed last week at Urbank, being run over by an automobile and is receiving treatment. Mrs. Ed Pekulik, who recently had an operation for appendicitis, was able to return home today.
Parkers Prairie Independent, Jan. 14, 1926

->•<-

"The high school juniors had the examinations in Economics last week."

The Greatest Woman. A Boston paper offered a prize for the best essay on the question "Who is the greatest woman in history?" The following essay was awarded the first prize and the award was correct, don't you think?

"The greatest woman of history is the wife of a man of moderate means who does her own cooking, washing, ironing, sewing, and who brings up a family of boys and girls to be useful members of society, and finds time for intellectual improvement. This woman is well known. She lives in many communities and in the hearts of many sons and daughters who had their chance in life through her efforts and guidance."
Parkers Prairie Independent, May 6, 1926

–›–‹–

Among Buyers and Sellers of Land . . . A.E. Hanson, 223 Hubbard Street, Crookston, Minnesota, is in the market for a small tract of partly improved land of from 20 to 40 acres in the northern section between Crookston and Duluth which he can develop for raising garden truck, berries, potatoes, and keep poultry. Would prefer something with lake shore, some timber, and not too far from railroad and good town. Owns house in town and has about $500 cash to invest. Mr. Hansen is 56 years of age, married and has three children. Lutheran church should be available.
Verndale Sun, Jan. 20, 1927

–›–‹–

The high school juniors had the examinations in Economics last week. The new course is taught by Prof. Sullivan. The questions were as follows:

I. Define economics. What are the four main divisions? Explain each.

II. Explain the difference be-

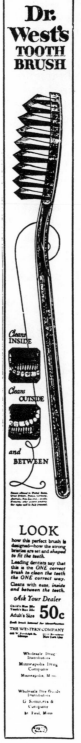

tween wealth and property.

III. What is the difference between capital and income?

IV. Define five of the following:

Marginal utility.
Division of labor.
Law of supply and demand.
Corporations.
Monopoly.
Discount.
Protective tariff.
Railroad tariff.

V. What is money? What determines the value of money? What is an index?

VI. What do you understand the Federal Reserve System to be?

VII. What is a business cycle? Explain how it works.

VIII. Define five of the following:

Speculation.
Risk.
Rent and economic rent.
Shares.
Par value.
Interest.
Profits.
Dividends.

IX. What is a favorable balance of trade? What causes a favorable balance of trade? What is the result to the country of a favorable balance of trade?

X. What is Capitalism? What is Socialism? Which do you prefer?

In this examination all the grades were over 90. The highest, 96, was made by Anna Scott. The other members of the class are Susan Tonheim, Alpha Bakk, Ethel Johnson and Elna Holm. The second highest grade was made by Elna Holm. These students will now proceed to the study of Sociology for the second semester.
Cook Herald, Jan. 27, 1927

–›–‹–

The Verndale band played at the moving picture show Saturday night before a packed house. The show was very good and the

"He is sporting the new car around the roads."

band was proclaimed as being greatly improved.
Verndale Sun, April 14, 1927

—‣•‹—

Lewis Bradford, owner and manager of the Verndale Sun, besides reducing his subscription rate from $2.00 to $1.50 per year on this weekly newspaper, managed to save out money enough the past eight years to pay the difference in money [that] a dealer at Bemidji asked for a 1923 Rickenbacker and a brand new 1927 Hudson Brougham, balloon tires, four wheel brakes and all. He is sporting the new car around the

"Every morning, the big town opens its maw and in pour the suburbanites for their daily grind."

roads at present but if job work and subscription money does not come in regularly he will have to let it stand in the garage as it uses plenty of gasoline. Outside of that it is a very nice motor vehicle.

Verndale Sun, July 14, 1927

—◦-◦—

Give Us the Old Way. Another reminder that change is not always progress is an entirely new way to make turkey stuffing.

Verndale Sun, Aug. 25, 1927, reprinted from Columbus (Ohio) State Journal

—◦-◦—

The Big Town and the Little Town

A city editor of a Chicago daily [newspaper] wants to move to a small town and edit a country weekly.

Sherwood Anderson, novelist, bought the Republican and Democratic newspapers in the small town of Marion, Va., and enjoys recording the "activities" of his fellow townsmen.

A well-known magazine has an article on the advantages of living in a small town.

The last few decades have witnessed an overwhelming migration from the little town to the big town. Some day the migration will switch about and here are some reasons for the prediction.

Every morning, the big town opens its maw and in pour the suburbanites for their daily grind. Every night the big town spews out the suburbanites and they carry with them the stench and the filth that the big town has given them.

The migration to the city has resulted in sprawling, mauling, big towns that are monsters of inefficiency. The average suburbanite spends two hours a day or 600 hours a year going to and coming from work. The engi-

Responding To

The Many Requests

Of Our Patrons

FOSHAY TOWER
RESTAURANT

Is Now Open From

11:30 A. M.

To Midnight

A Cuisine Par Excellence

FOSHAY TOWER
RESTAURANT
FOSHAY MANAGEMENT

Minneapolis Tribune, Oct. 4, 1929

neers who design office buildings have discovered that windows give little light and waste a lot of heat; therefore, there must be fewer windows, or, better yet, no windows at all.

Every morning, the little town wakes up quietly and its workers sit down to leisurely breakfasts, walk to work, come home for dinner, walk to work, and come home for supper. And yet they have done a day's work. A very stupid existence, some call it.

Climb into your cells of brick and steel, Big Towners — we pity

"It was the thrill of a life-time, he said, and it was well worth the price charged."

you. Lock yourself into your apartment Mrs. Big Towner — we feel sorry for you, because we're leaving the baby at the neighbors' while we go to ladies' aid. Some call our existence a stupid one, but we know better; we know!
Montevideo News, March 2, 1928

⇥•⇤

Charley Novak, proprietor of the Crystal theatre, is billing from time to time many of the very best pictures for the entertainment of theatre-goers. He offers them on April 16th, 17th, 18th and 19th, the world's mightiest attraction, "Ben-Hur," and following on the heels of this splendid picture will come "The Big Parade," the greatest of all great pictures, which will be shown on April 30th, May 1st, May 2nd and May 3rd. The announcement of the billing of these two renowned pictures for the Crystal should be happily received.
Glencoe Enterprise, March 22, 1928

⇥•⇤

I. Kaufman, local business man, was among the first ones initiated into the ranks of the St. Paul-Rochester airline fans. After spending a little over a week with his mother, who is ill at the Mayo Clinic in Rochester, Mr. Kaufman hurried to catch a train for St. Paul in order to keep an important business engagement here. When he arrived at the depot, the train had left and Mr. Kaufman wondered vaguely how he would keep his appointment.

Suddenly there entered his mind the new Rochester-St. Paul air route [of Jefferson Airways]. He paid the price, wondering whether he'd keep his appointment alive or just badly crippled, in case the huge tri-motored plane crashed, but there was no other way. Mr. Kaufman left Rochester when the plane left and before he could think much

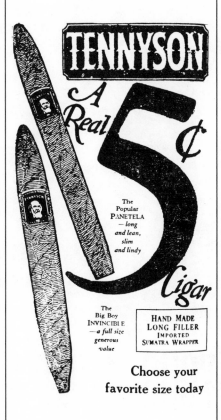

about it he was in St. Paul, after only fifty minutes of flying, and in plenty of time to keep his date.

It was the thrill of a life-time, he said, and it was well worth the price charged, but even though it afforded the biggest thrill he ever had, he is not anxious to try again, for coming down at the landing field was not so good, as it was a severe tax on his nerves.
North St. Paul Courier, July 20, 1928

⇥•⇤

Mr. and Mrs. W.H. Daniels returned home last Wednesday from an extended motor trip through the east to Niagara Falls. They left here about two weeks

ago stopping at Dundee, Ill., where they visited friends. At Marshall, Mich., they were guests of Mrs. Daniels' brother, William Huepenbecker and family, for a few days. From Marshall they drove to Cleveland, O., where they visited with Mrs. Daniels' uncle, Henry Lembke. The next points of interest were Buffalo, N.Y., and Niagara Falls. On their homeward journey they took the Canadian route to Detroit, Mich., where they viewed the Ford plant. From that place they went to Milwaukee, Wisc., and remained for a few days with friends there. The trip, of twenty-four hundred miles, was made without tire or car trouble of any sort.
Glencoe Enterprise, Aug. 23, 1928

⇥•⇤

Hard Times? Maybe

Twenty-two thousand people attended the Ringling Bros. circus at Marshall Saturday. Besides the $40,000 spent by them to gain admission to the "big top," the side-shows, etc., another $40,000 was spent for gasoline, feed, etc.

This vast sum of money would support the public schools and all of Marshall churches for a year. It would support every school in Murray county for a like period. . . .

As always has been the case, we shall continue to give grumblingly to our churches. We shall ever condemn the high taxes. We will never fail to preach hard-times, and we'll always be on the search for new thrills, new ways and means of spending our hard earned money.

Yea, verily, we are a funny and most inconsistent lot.
Slayton Herald, Aug. 23, 1928

⇥•⇤

Is it true? The sins we do by two and two, we pay for one by one.

Don't let child stay bilious, constipated

MOTHER, YOUR CHILD'S BOWELS NEED "CALIFORNIA FIG SYRUP"

Even Cross, Feverish, Sick Children Love its Taste and it Never Fails to Empty Little Bowels

If your child is listless, full of cold, has colic, or if the stomach is sour, breath bad, tongue coated, a teaspoonful of "California Fig Syrup" will quickly start liver and bowel action. In a few hours you can see for yourself how thoroughly it works the constipation poison, sour bile and waste right out and you have a well, playful child again.

Millions of mothers keep "California Fig Syrup" handy. They know a teaspoonful today may save a sick child tomorrow. It never cramps or over-acts. Ask your druggist for genuine "California Fig Syrup" which has directions for babies and children of all ages printed on bottle. Mother! You must say "California" or you may get an imitation fig syrup.

Duluth Herald, Jan. 17, 1923

"Mr. Wetter informed his many friends that there is no place like Minnesota."

"Damaged Goods" [a movie] is a startling expose of social evil — a terrible but necessary warning to the present generation of so-called flappers and cake eaters. And with it all is presented a story of a loving, trusting wife, and her innocent baby who were made the victims of a man's passion and greed. You have seen many so-called "No Children Under Sixteen Pictures" but never one like this.

At the Opera House Monday evening, October 8th. Show for women only at 7:30 p.m. Show for men only at 9:15 p.m. Admission 50c. Children under 16 will positively not be admitted.
Wabasso Standard, Oct. 4, 1928

→>·<—

William Wetter, who spent the past year in California, arrived at his home near Mayer. Mr. Wetter informed his many friends that there is no place like Minnesota.
Waconia Patriot, June 27, 1929

→>·<—

Gust Harthun spend several days here visiting with old friends. Mr. Harthun left here 18 years ago, at one time being the owner of the duplex now occupied by the Rauschendorfer family. Mr. Harthun informed local people that he was surprised at the progress and the improvements made during the past 18 years in this city.
Waconia Patriot, Aug. 8, 1929

→>·<—

Local Boy Killed Here on July 4th

Peter Hauwiller, age 9 years 11 months and 6 days old, youngest son of Mr. and Mrs. Frank Hauwiller, residing on the south edge of this village [St. Bonifacius], met sudden death when he was struck by an automobile, driven by George Specken, of Cologne.

Duluth Herald, Jan. 12, 1923

The accident occurred at about 12:20 P.M. on Thursday July 4th while Mr. Specken was on his way to his home at Cologne. As there was no eye witness to the accident, it is presumed that both the boy and the driver of the car became confused as to which way to turn, resulting in the boy being struck down and thrown to the side of the road. The accident was unavoidable.

The parents were making preparations and were about to leave for an outing at a Lake. The boy was not missed at the time,

*"Almost every woman has something about her which, carefully nurtured,
will make her seem desirable."*

**Can't you taste the ginger cake
Mother's mixing, up to bake,
Of "UNIVERSAL FLOUR" to fill
That empty space in Jack and Jill?**

DULUTH UNIVERSAL MILLING CO
DULUTH
UNIVERSAL
PATENT
DULUTH MINN

Duluth Herald, Jan. 19, 1923

and it was thought that he was out in the back yard playing, but instead he was playing in the front yard which is close to the road and presumably had run onto the road while playing and did not see the approaching car in time to make his escape. Fragments of a toy cap pistol were strewn along the highway. The father heard the crash from inside the house and immediately rushed outside, only to find his own son lying at the roadside with two legs and one arm broken and his skull fractured, he was in an unconscious condition when picked up and carried into the home, a physician was immediately summoned, but the lad died soon after without regaining consciousness. However before he died he received the last sacraments of the Catholic church of which he was a member. Peter Hauwiller was born here on July 28th 1919 and would have been 10 years of age on the 28th of this month. Besides his parents he is survived by four brothers, Raymond, Paul, Francis, and Alex and four sisters, Emelia, Alice, Helen and Yolanda.

Funeral services were conducted on Monday morning July 8th at 9 o'clock from the St. Boniface Catholic church. Rev. Father Schifferer officiated. The pall bearers were his school mates Bernard Dittrich, Clarence Hauwiller, Jerome Gothman, Norbert Ebert, Clarence Ess, and Herbert Logelin. The flower bearers, also his school mates, were: Norbert Simon, Marcel Dittrich, Earl Hegerle, and Francis Klein. . . . A large number of friends and relatives attended the last sad rites.

Waconia Patriot, July 11, 1929

->-<-

Almost every woman has something about her which, carefully nurtured, will make her seem desirable — not, of course, to every man in her world, but to one or two. The charm, which may be anything from piquant conversation to good cooking, will find appreciation somewhere if it be well displayed. . . . There may be men who dislike mere flirtation, and coldly ignore a woman who attracts them, but you will have to look for them in monasteries and other retired places. They are not of this world.

Waconia Patriot, Aug. 1, 1929, reprinted from "The Technique of the Love Affair by a Gentlewoman"

->-<-

1920s
—>•<—

Scandal in the Twin Cities

*The Twin City Reporter was a scandal sheet, but, its editors insisted,
a scandal sheet with a conscience. They stated their position in an
editorial that ran May 13, 1921.*

The Twin City Reporter prints scandal; there is no denying that fact. For instance, if the head of some big department store wants to divorce his wife and marry his stenographer, or his wife discovers that he had been intimate with the stenographer and sues him for divorce, none of the big papers that carry department store advertising will print the story.

So we print it.

And that's "scandal."

If some poor girl, forced by relentless economic laws into a life of shame, discovers that a baby is about to be born and resorts to a crime in order to conceal the evidence of her misstep, the daily papers print that story — and give the girl's name, but NOT the name of the department store where she was forced to slave for a pittance insufficient to maintain life decently.

The Twin City Reporter prints the name of the store, but not the name of the girl.

And THAT'S scandal.

—>•<—

[Here's an example of the Twin City Reporter's fare.]

One month an innocent 17 year old girl, with the bloom of health on her cheeks and the flash of youthful innocence in her eyes — and thirty days later a denizen of a Bridge Square dive, the "woman" of an habitue of vice. That is the pitiable history of the little daughter of a banker in a nearby Minnesota town.

Obviously we will not divulge the girl's name. She has learned her lesson, and has gone back to her home to make amends. The fault was not hers, but that of society in permitting her to attain the age she did in complete ignorance of many of the facts of life.

This unfortunate daughter of wealth and refinement is a typical product of prudishness — the kind of prudishness that we have decried for so many years in this paper, and hope, sometime, to see abolished in America as it has long since been done away with in the Latin countries. She is the product of a society that even today brings up its sons and daughters to believe that babies are brought by storks or in doctor's satchels. Just so long as the vital facts of life are kept from our young, will men like E.I. Wilson, proprietor of a soft drink place [most likely a tavern before Prohibition] at 112 First street south, continue to ply their jackal's trade on the bodies and on the virtue of innocent girls.

Wilson is in jail now. Not because he committed a crime in debauching this young life. He was arrested on a charge of having stolen goods in his possession. There are laws, you see, to protect property — but the laws that should be on our books, and are, in some instances, for the protection of life itself, are too often a dead letter, unenforceable, or laughed at.

When Wilson goes to trial, it will be for having alleged stolen shoes in his possession. But for the crime of having seduced into a life of shame a girl whose youth should have been her protection, he will go scot-free, so far as the laws of the land are concerned. We do not believe that his conscience will bother him greatly, either.

We will call this girl Mary; that is not her real name. Mary was brought up, as most girls in her class of life are brought up, very carefully. Her father and mother exercised careful supervision over what she ate, what she wore, the kind of company and the kind of hours she kept, and what she read and what kind of theatrical entertainment she attended.

"Wilson made violent love to this girl half his age."

Like most parents, they undoubtedly failed utterly to keep Mary in ignorance as to the relation between matrimony and babies. She probably even discovered for herself that there were girls who "went wrong," although if she went to her parents and asked why these girls strayed from the straight and narrow path, she was told that they were "bad" girls.

In due time Mary graduated from high school and then came to the city. She liked the city. The bright lights and the gayety fascinated the simple mind fresh from the less hectic pleasures of a country town. The glamour of the metropolis, its roar of ceaseless activity, its atmosphere of luxury, caught her unsophisticated imagination in the meshes.

In her tours about the city she met E.I. Wilson.

Had she been a city girl, of the poor, self reliant and perhaps self-supporting [type], she would never have been deluded by the sham veneer, the pseudo-polish, of this human vulture. But as it happened, life had treated her but shabbily in failing to warn her that such beasts as this were ever on the watch for girls.

Wilson, we are told, is nearly forty years old. Steeped in vice, old in the myriad evils that grow upon a man who lives among the habitues of the underworld, he would instinctively have repelled a girl whose training was such as to prepare her to meet life on equal terms. The sheltered, carefully protected existence of 17 year old Mary was no preparation in self-defense against the wiles of a Wilson, however.

Wilson's long experience with girls and women of the demimonde [prostitutes] and girls who had not yet fallen, but soon would take the irretrievable step, taught him how to proceed. With all the fervor of an old time cadet who was paid so much a head for every girl he brought into the clutches of some proprietor of an evil resort, he set out to entrap the girl. His metropolitan ways, his "culture" which the girl did not know came from cheap cafes and from vulgar associations, his easy spirit of comradeship, all made their indefinable appeal to a heart too young to know itself, and too unwise in worldly matters to realize the danger.

Wilson made violent love to this girl half his age. His coarseness, his viciousness, his half restrained desires, rang no danger signal in the consciousness of the banker's daughter. Instead of being warned, instead of having wise counsel from her parents to guide her aright, she believed what she heard, and accepted Wilson at his own valuation.

Then — she fell.

Down in the Bridge Square district — The Gateway, as those who are trying to redeem the district

"BEING AS HOW I DONT EXPECT TO LIVE MORE THAN A COUPLE OF HUNDRED YEARS LONGER, AND CONSIDERING ALL THE THINGS I WANT TO DO, I FIGGER I AINT GOT A MINUTE TO WASTE KNOCKING GRUMPING AND WOLFING ABOUT THINGS I DONT LIKE!

CHARLES SUGHROE

Cook County News-Herald, Grand Marais, May 17, 1923

from its evil past and vicious present [say] — there was a new girl behind the bar in Wilson's soft drink parlor. Her skirt was short, as are the skirts of all the unhappy girls who are compelled by one circumstance or another to forget their womanhood in pandering to the evil desires of the floating population of the Northwest. Her blouse was sheer georgette, as are the blouses of all the members of that

"Not even an eye experienced in detecting disguises, and in peering beneath the surface, could have recognized the 17 year old girl beneath her make-up of shame."

NEW NICOLLET HOTEL
MINNEAPOLIS
HOME OF WCCO STUDIOS

When in **MINNEAPOLIS** why not gratify your long felt want of an atmosphere of friendliness, comfort and relaxation by staying at the NEW NICOLLET

600 ROOMS complete in every detail at exceptionally reasonable rates. Restful beds.

Moderately priced Restaurant and Coffee Shop.

Three blocks from both depots.

Tourist Bureau directly opposite.

W. B. CLARK, Manager

St. Cloud Daily Times, April 13, 1928

fallen sisterhood — so that the lustful eyes of the bums, the hobos, and dregs of civilization from Chicago to the Pacific coast, could pierce to the half concealed white flesh beneath.

Beneath the short skirt were silk stockings, lacy with an open work design, and on the feet, tiny pumps that mocked the granite block which paves the streets of that God forsaken district of which the southeast corner is the approach to the Third avenue bridge.

Not even an eye experienced in detecting disguises, and in peering beneath the surface, could have recognized the 17 year old girl beneath her make-up of shame. Gone from the cheeks was the bloom of health, induced by country air and wholesome thoughts. Gone from the eyes was the look of

"Wilson, debaucher of women, had tried his hand at a bolder game, and was caught."

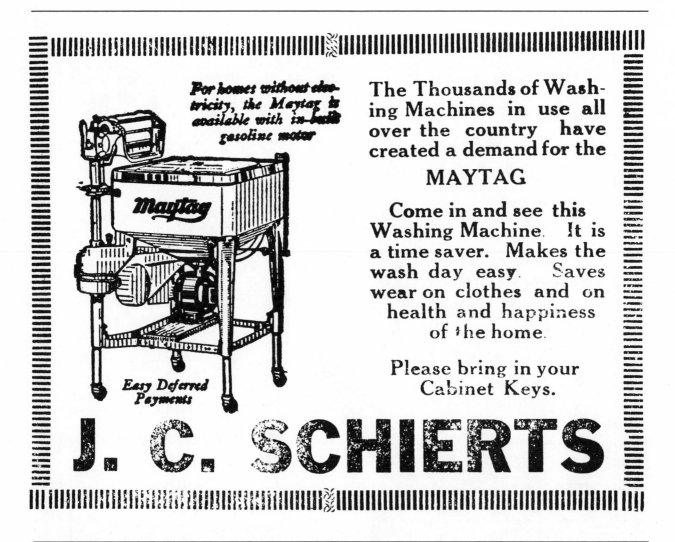

Wabasha County Herald, Kellogg, Feb. 17, 1927

trusting innocence: Rouge sticks and make-up box had destroyed the one, and a month of unrestricted association with the jackals and harpies of the plague spot of the city had taken away, forever, the other.

Leaning familiarly over the counter, in coarse badinage [repartee] with a greasy tramp who had a dollar or two to spend, Mary was not the girl who left her home a short month before to come to "the city." So quickly does vice take hold of its victims. All the horrible assurance, the easy familiarity, the coaxing methods, of the confirmed bar maid, were hers in that brief period.

Whether she ever looked back with regret upon her secluded life at home, whether her illusions about Wilson had been lifted, we have not learned. So strange a thing is the mind of woman — and Mary became a woman on the day that she no longer resisted Wilson's advances — that perhaps the glamour of romance of the wrecker still clung to him, and she regretted nothing.

But Wilson, debaucher of women, had tried his hand at a bolder game, and was caught. The police came to his den and arrested him in connection with the theft of some shoes from a retail establishment in Minneapolis. And when the bedraggled women who lured the Bridge Square floaters into the "soft drink" parlors and then "lure" their scanty savings or earnings from them, were questioned, Mary gave her true name.

That is how she was discovered. Even the hardened policemen whose minds are accustomed to the sight of misery, debauchery, crime, and vice, could hardly believe that in the self-confident young woman behind the soft-drink bar they beheld the banker's daughter whose age was not yet 18 years.

She was taken to the city jail and the police noti-

*"There will be a chapter in her life upon which she will
often wish to draw a veil, and never can."*

fied her parents. Her father hurried to the city and
for the first time in his honorable career, visited the
inside of a city jail. The respectable old banker, for
so many years secure in the thought that his fortune
could ward off all evil from himself and his loved
ones, saw his illusions shattered and his daughter
in the care of a police matron, all in one brief thirty
days.

Both the father and the daughter refused to
prosecute. Wilson will steer clear of the law so far
as this escapade is concerned. The father took his
daughter back home, and in the seclusion of her
childhood home, he will try to build up again from
the beginning Mary's health.

Whatever strides she makes in effacing the past,
there will be a chapter in her life upon which she
will often wish to draw a veil, and never can. Her
mind will always picture that evil month, and if the
time comes, as it probably will, when some man
wants to make her his wife, then she will be up
against a harder problem than she ever had to face
before.

It is time Americans stripped the veils of ignorance from the figure of life, and gave their children a fighting chance to break even in what is a
tough battle at the best.

Twin City Reporter, Minneapolis, Dec. 17, 1920

–>·<–

1930s

☙ THE MINNEAPOLIS JOURNAL

SPA[...]   MONDAY EVENING, MAY 21, 1934   24 PAGES—2 CENTS IN MINNEAPOLIS

Strikers Fight Pitched Battle With Police; 37 in Hospital, Officer Stabbed; 75 Jailed

Federal Labor Board Asked to Intervene

Building Trades Vote Sympathy Walkout To Involve 35,000

Newest Group to Join Strike Will Go Out at 5 P. M. Today—Produce Loads Moved into City

BLOODY RIOTING MARKS EFFORTS TO START TRUCKS NEAR MARKET

Group of 12 Appeals to Washington

Urge Early Action to End Bloodshed in Minneapolis Strike

FEAR CONSEQUENCES IF OLSON CALLS TROOPS

Want Regional Body to Assume Jurisdiction and Direct Hearing

MISSILES FLY IN STRIKE BATTLE ON "COMMISSION ROW"

13 Killed in Plane Fall

Shadowed and Threatened By Gang, May Tells Jury

Dillinger Poked Gun in His Ribs, Physician Claims—Cross-examination Opened

Shoemaker Jailed After Strike Row

Five Killed as Truck Hits Bridge in Texas

Citizens Appeal to Labor Board

Employers' Reply to Governor

Latest Strike Developments

Unemployment, bank failures, bankruptcies and drops in farm prices marked the decade. Extensive federal and state aid projects were started. In 1932 70 percent of miners were jobless, and income of dairy farmers was only 25 percent of what it had been the previous decade. Drought and grasshoppers added to farmers' economic distress. Organized crime moved into the state. Prohibition was repealed in 1933. The Minneapolis truckers' strike of 1934 became notorious and led to the city becoming a union town. Talking movies became popular.

Minneapolis Journal, May 21, 1934

1930s

–>•<–

Minneapolis Truckers' Strike

By 1930 Minneapolis had ended a period of tremendous growth. The lumber and flour-milling industries were declining. The labor situation in Minneapolis already was tense, and the Depression made it worse. Working people were desperate. Small businessmen, near financial ruin, were fighting the unions.
An attempt in 1934 by Truck Drivers Local 574 to gain bargaining rights led to outright war in the streets — club-swinging, rock-throwing and, ultimately, gun-firing clashes between strikers and police. Many men enlisted on the side of the police were businessmen or unemployed men hired as special deputies.

Strikers Fight Pitched Battle With Police; 37 in Hospital, Officer Stabbed; 75 Jailed

VIOLENCE FLARED in the truck strike again today and 37 men were seriously injured in the worst clash between strikers and police since the strike's inception, in a battle at Third avenue N. and Sixth street. Police have jailed 75 in the last 24 hours.

One policeman was stabbed. The officers drew riot guns and threatened the pickets with them to quell the rioters.

The casualty list included 18 police and 19 strikers.

For the first time since the crash, the strikers were nearly all armed today. They were equipped with hundreds of 18-inch lengths of gas pipe and with clubs and sticks.

Nearly 500 strikers and nearly 200 police and special deputies were involved in the fray, which lasted nearly half an hour.

Northwestern hospital was jammed with the injured and its receiving room looked like a World War hospital. Deaconess hospital was also jammed, and General could take no more. As an emergency measure, the hospitals appointed A.G. Stafel, superintendent of Eitel hospital, to take care of the wounded and to assign them to hospitals as they arrived.

At the height of the battle, the Minneapolis Building Trades Council, meeting at the Labor Temple, 614 First avenue N., met and voted to walk out in sympathy with the drivers' union, according to a statement by C. Hagland, secretary of the organization. . . .

Produce trucks had been moving in and out of the market district at dawn with little difficulty. But, by groups, strikers began to concentrate on Third avenue N. and Sixth and Fifth streets. Truckloads of strikers filtered into the district one by one. The men were armed. . . .

Today's bloody riot started in front of the Gamble-Robinson Company, 301 Fifth street N.

Special police had been in the district since 4 a.m.

Two trucks started to move out of the S.G. Palmer & Company warehouse. A group of the strikers stepped in front of it. A policeman pushed one of them and ordered him to "back up."

Someone swung a club. The battle was on.

Police and strikers' clubs beat a tattoo on heads. Men fell in the street to the right and left. There was a roar from the body of strikers and there were pitched shouts of instructions from police officers ordering their men to rush to the trouble spot.

One squad of strikers armed with lengths of brass pipe pushed their way to the front of the strike crowd and went into action. The police centered on this group. There was a bloody hand-to-hand battle.

The screaming of ambulance and police sirens

"Suddenly, there was a cry as one large striker drew a knife from his belt and swung it."

added to the din, and emergency ambulances rushed to the scene to pick up the wounded, and police reserves came speeding into the crowd.

Another detachment of strikers pushed its way through the milling crowd, picking up their own wounded and placing them in trucks to be taken to strike headquarters at 1900 Chicago avenue, from where they were taken to Northwestern hospital.

Sheriff Wall rushed 100 special deputies to the scene. Among the special deputies were many socialites, who had dropped their work in bond houses and the wheat market to join citizens who had volunteered for service to attempt to quell the strike. Typical of these men were Ned Dodge, John Marfield, Jr., Merritt Case and Al Lindley. Lindley, a polo player and athlete, was wearing a padded polo hat to protect his head from blows. Several of the men were wearing football helmets.

Policemen who were injured and taken to General hospital included: Percy Block, Ray Mahoney, Arthur Hesle, Frank Barry, Wilbur Roberts, Gust Smith, Marius Paulson, Ivan Swanson, Earl Richter, A. Danborg, Donald Noard, Ralph Welbaum, Charles Grunewald and five others whose names were not immediately learned.

Of the policemen, Block, Mahoney and Hesle were most seriously injured. Block suffered a broken jaw and a broken arm. Mahoney and Hesle were severely beaten on the heads and shoulders.

Strikers received at Northwestern hospital for treatment included: Glen Snodgrass, 2943 Newton avenue N.; Louis Bobineau, 708 Sixth street NE.; Albert Damerow, 1400 Elliot avenue; Tom Allen, 1515 Stevens avenue; C.W. Anderson, 309 Third street S.; Elmer Johnson, 3617 Fourth avenue S.; John Peterson, Stockholm hotel; John Smith, 4452 Camden avenue; George White, 923 Lyndale avenue N.; Fred Hartshorn, 2801 Chicago avenue; Joe Blais, 519 Third avenue NE.; Raymond Mason, 1509 Portland avenue; Frank Phillips, 29 Eastman avenue; Frank Gray, 3513 Nineteenth avenue S.; Myron Anderson, 306 Twenty-third avenue S.

With 15 in Northwestern hospital, Harry Brown, hospital superintendent, announced the hospital was filled to capacity. Additional strike casualties were taken to Deaconess hospital. Among them were: George R. Riley, 1620 Laurel avenue; H.L. Bolduc, 69 Bedford street SE.; Harvey McCracken, 510 Knox avenue N.; John Skrentny, Princeton, Minn.

Of the strikers, Frank Phillips was most seriously injured. He was still unconscious at noon today, and it was feared he had suffered a fractured skull.

The riot began to quiet down, then, suddenly, there was a cry as one large striker drew a knife from his belt and swung it, flashing in the sun, at a

Detroit Lakes Record, May 6, 1937

policeman. The knife cut a thin gash in the policeman's neck.

The police cried out at the sight and a score of them rushed to nearby squad cars where they seized shotguns. They ran back to the battle and lined up facing the strikers menacingly, their riot guns at ready.

The sight of police armed with guns quieted the crowd, although the strikers fell back growling at it.

"You're going to shoot down your buddies, are you?" someone screamed.

"You're trying to kill us," a policeman cried back.

Chief Michael Johannes ordered every man on the night police shift to report for duty immediately and sent out a further order cancelling all vacations and recalling all men on leave.

"Some violence was recorded through the night in isolated and outlying parts of town."

A few trucks moved in the early morning hours today, but there was no general movement of commercial transport. Both sides seemed to be marking time. A few trucks, all under guard of regular or special police, started out and succeeded in making deliveries without trouble.

Farmers from rural Hennepin filtered into the city under escort of deputy sheriffs and for the first time since the strike started there was sale of garden produce in the market.

Some 500 additional special police were sworn in, bringing the total to approximately 1,600, as employers and the law and order committee perfected plans for running the strike blockade.

A number of employers, it was learned, have received word from truck drivers who have joined the union that they are ready to go back to work. Several employers said their men offered to turn back their union buttons if they could be put to work immediately.

Although a large crowd gathered in the market district and along "commission row," where fierce rioting broke out Saturday, police experienced little difficulty in getting farmers' trucks in to start the day's business. Market business was far from normal, however, but more trucks succeeded in reaching the market and unloading their supplies than at any other time since the strike started.

Both sides claimed victory as the trucks started to move. At strike headquarters it was asserted that there is no general truck movement as yet and that strikers are only waiting for the larger activity to start.

"We are going to have our men at strategic points," a strike spokesman said. "We'll have them at the market and places like that. There'll be plenty doing when they start to move."

At police headquarters, however, Chief Michael Johannes was confident the situation is well in hand. Many police officers regard the disturbances Saturday as the turning point of the strike. They believe the strikers learned they have sufficient resources to handle any future difficulties that may arise.

Some violence was recorded through the night in isolated and outlying parts of town. Windows in several stores and a laundry were smashed with rocks, and several gasoline pumps in filling stations were damaged by marauders.

The threatened strike of truck drivers in St. Paul appeared to be clearing up today as both drivers and employers agreed they are anxious to submit their differences to arbitration to avoid the difficulties experienced by Minneapolis. Both sides were ready to meet with Governor Floyd B. Olson today to start an arbitration session.

Minneapolis Journal, May 21, 1934

Detroit Lakes Record, April 1, 1937

[The violence in the streets continued. The next day 6,000 people clogged the streets and men serving as special officers were fatally injured. Gov. Olson declared martial law. By the time the issues were settled in August, four men had died and many more were badly injured.

[The settlement was an overwhelming victory for the union. To this day, Minneapolis remains a union town.]

→·←

*"The faithful of the Catholic Church, diocese of St. Cloud,
are allowed to eat meat on Friday, July 4th."*

Wilted vegetables can be restored, fresh ones kept in prime condition for many days, and sandwiches held fresh and wholesome for long periods of time in a recently perfected moist air compartment for the electric refrigerator, it was explained today by H.J. Blenker and Nick Ohmann, local Frigidaire representatives, who have just returned from the convention of this company at Chicago. ... Another announcement of this year was that Frigidaire now combines the beauty of porcelain with the strength of steel in all household cabinets.
Albany Enterprise, Feb. 13, 1930

–>•<–

A minister said recently that one cannot throw a stone out of the window without hitting some one with an inferiority complex. Well, aren't they the safest kind of people to hit?
Albany Enterprise, Feb. 20, 1930

–>•<–

By special dispensation by the Rt. Rev. Bishop Busch, the faithful of the Catholic Church, diocese of St. Cloud, are allowed to eat meat on Friday, July 4th. This is in conformity with dispensations granted in other dioceses. Realizing that Independence Day is a day for celebrating and picnicking, the high officials realize the hardship upon the lunch providers and have wisely given them free sway to choose the makeup for their lunch basket — which is heartily appreciated.
Albany Enterprise, July 3, 1930

–>•<–

When times are good in the big city, our city cousins are prone to laugh up their sleeves at us rubes in the country, sticking along on our little old jobs where the wages are no great shakes at the best. Right now, however, our city cousins are beginning to

"Scotch" has come to mean "thrifty" and "saving." Your telephone is Scotch because it's a thrifty investment for you ... it saves you time, money, worry and trouble.

Americans have the world's best bargain in telephone service. No other people get such good telephone service at such low cost.

NORTHWESTERN BELL TELEPHONE COMPANY

East Grand Forks Record, Jan. 20, 1939

flock back among the rubes, tickled to death if they can but draw the modest incomes of rural America. After all, the country and the small town are the best places to live. We never make any big fortunes out here in the sticks but we eat three good meals a day, including fresh eggs and some real cream now and then, whether the times are good or bad. If current reports are true, there are a lot of folks who lived high in the big city who don't know whether they will eat tomorrow or not, right now.
St. Peter Herald, July 18, 1930

–>•<–

The present depression is not without its attendant commensurate object lessons to all of us. For the past 10 years, labor in many instances has grown chesty and critical of its employers, but today the thousands who have

"Reverses are good for all of us or we would never come down to earth."

been forced to seek work elsewhere have begun to realize that
they had pretty good jobs after
all. Out of this crisis will be born
a better understanding between
employer and employe, a more
industrious and better satisfied
citizenry. While conditions now
tend toward political and social
unrest, a few months of pinching
and sober reflection will resolve
itself into a new conservation
that will undo whatever radical
harm in the present may be done.
Reverses are good for all of us or
we would never come down to
earth.

St. Peter Herald, Aug. 6, 1930

→·>·‹·←

*When Noah sailed the waters
    blue
He had his troubles, same as
    you,
For forty days he drove the
    Ark
Before he found a place to
    park.*

Dassel Dispatch, Sept. 25, 1930

→·>·‹·←

It is reported that the work of
laying pipeline like that in process of construction west of town
occupies a crew of 60 men to
maintain a certain rate of speed
per day. Ten years ago, without
the machinery and equipment
now used in the construction
work, the same rate of progress
would have required a crew of
600 men. F.W. Peck, addressing
the recent annual meeting of the
Rice County Farm bureau, cited a
striking example of the elimina-
tion of manpower in manufacturing operations, a Milwaukee concern now making 10,000
automobile frames per day with a
force of 150 men, where formerly
it employed 800 men to produce
2,000 frames. Similar examples of
the substitution of machinery for
manpower might be cited indefi-
nitely, making it easy to understand why there should be an un-

Detroit Lakes Record, Feb. 11, 1937

employment problem. To find
new employment for the vast
number of workers who in the
last decade have been laid off as
a result of improvement in manufacturing and construction proc-
esses has not been an easy task.

Northfield Independent, Dec. 11, 1930

→·>·‹·←

NEW FORD V·8

The Car Without Experiments

THERE'S never any doubt about value when you buy a Ford car. You know it's all right or Henry Ford wouldn't put it out. One thing that never changes is his policy of dependable transportation at low cost.

That's the biggest feature of the New Ford. The reliability and economy of its V-8 engine have been proved on the road by upwards of 1,400,000 motorists. Owner cost records show definitely that the Ford V-8 is the most economical Ford car ever built.

See the nearest **FORD DEALER** *for a V-8 demonstration.*

●

NEW FORD V-8 TRUCKS AND COMMERCIAL CARS ALSO ON DISPLAY.

FORD MOTOR COMPANY

Bird Island Union, Feb. 21, 1935

"It was plainly evident that he was going to pay his own way this time."

Randolph, Minn.
Dear Santy Claus:

I am a little girl 9 years old. I have been in bed since the 29th of Oct. with infantile paralysis and I get awful lonesome laying in bed so long. Please bring me some nice playthings just anything will be alright. I would like a roller skating doll, a Christmas stocking full of toys, and a washing set. Please remember my four brothers and two sisters too, also papa and mamma and Dr. Seeley as they have been very kind to me.

Your friend,
Charlotte Cords.
Northfield News, Dec. 12, 1930

→►◄←

A picture from life: A young man entered a Fairmont eating place one day early this winter. He plainly showed signs of the wear and tear of depression — out of work. He asked the lady waitress if she would please give him a cup of coffee. She did — and something more to eat with it. He came in again, and was treated in the same manner. Then he left and did not come back for several weeks. One day he came in again, but what a difference! He sat down at the counter and said, "Give me a cup of coffee." It was plainly evident that he was going to pay his own way this time. When he had finished his coffee, he asked how much the other feeds were. No track had been kept of them. He put some money on the counter and said, "Put this in the till anyway."
Fairmont Sentinel, Jan. 16, 1932

→►◄←

Having admired the locally built float and seeing it moving eastward Sunday morning for the parade at the Legion convention in Granite Falls was too much for two of our youths to remain on home grounds.

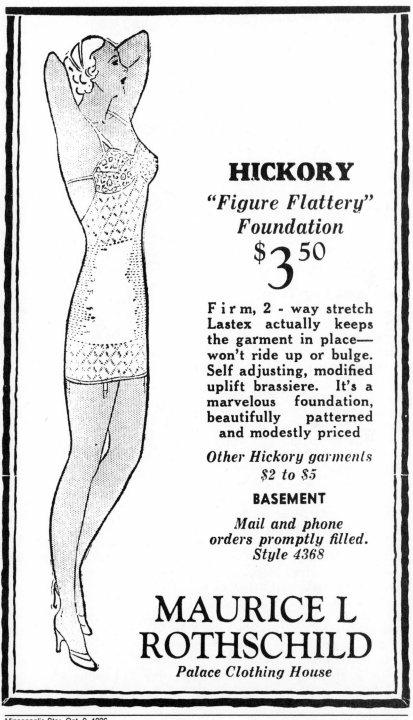

Merle Hahn and Glenn Johnson, five years old and chums, talked things over and decided it just wouldn't do for them to miss seeing the parade. Their decision also included that if there was no other way to get to the convention city they would walk. Keeping their deliberations secret, even unto their parents, they

*"The biggest share of the dancers were of dusky skins,
varying from real black to a good generous tan."*

took off afoot for Granite — 19 miles distant.

A quarter of a mile out, Glenn retraced his steps homeward, with Merle continuing on and on. Raising his right hand in approved manner as a stop signal to motorists, he was unsuccessful until about a mile out, when Mr. and Mrs. Olaf Toftness halted their car to make inquiry of the youthful pedestrian. "I'm going to see the parade," said Merle. "I will give you a ride home," said Mr. Toftness. Arriving home Merle made haste to enter the family car, which was awaiting his presence for the trip "to the parade."

Boyd Bulletin, June 10, 1932

→•←

**Mexican Wedding
Dance Draws Big
Mixed Crowd**

Something a bit unusual was "pulled off" in Bricelyn Wednesday evening. A newly married Mexican couple were host and hostess to the public at a dance given by them in the local dance hall in honor of the momentous event. A three-piece orchestra (clarinet, guitar and violin; Mexicans) from near Blue Earth furnished excellent music, altho a bit weak in volume for such a big and crowded hall.

The biggest share of the dancers were of dusky skins, varying from real black to a good generous tan and of course had snapping black eyes and hair. We noticed that almost all of the ladies were considerably shorter and stouter than their fairer sisters, and most of the men were smaller than their fairer brothers, altho they did not average as stout as the senoritas. . . .

The facial expression of both [bride and groom] and a conversation with them showed them to be intelligent and progressive. The whites with whom they come in contact endorse this ob-

Tri-County Forum, Thief River Falls, Sept. 14, 1939

servation and add that they are fine, dependable and honest young people, and like to have them work for them. The Sentinel wishes to compliment them on the fine clean dance they sponsored. Liquor, drunkenness and rowdyism was entirely absent, and those who attended seemed to be imbued with the spirit of good clean fun. This is something that is seldom done when the whites run a dance.

Mr. Albert Acuta and Miss Juana Rocha A-Acosta were unit-

ed in wedlock by one of the judges at Blue Earth about three o'clock Wednesday afternoon.

They will live on the Julius Hove place the remainder of the beet season at least, and hope to return in the future.

Bricelyn Sentinel, Aug. 4, 1932

→•←

Own Your Own Saloon.

For the married man who thinks he can not get along without a drink, the following suggestion is made as a means of free-

"He found himself in the rather embarrassing position of standing in the middle of a field of corn without even a barrel in which to go home."

dom from the bondage of boot-leggers:

Start a saloon in your own home. Be the only customer. (You will have no license to pay.) Give your wife ten dollars to buy a gallon of whiskey. Remember there are sixty-nine drinks in a gallon. Buy your drinks from no one but your wife. By the time your first gallon is gone she will have $23.50 to put in the bank and $10 to start business again. (She can throw in two drinks on the house.)

Should you live ten years and continue to buy booze from her and then die with snakes in your boots, she will have money enough to bury you decently, educate your children, buy a house and lot, marry a decent man and quit thinking about you entirely.

Boyd Bulletin, Aug. 12, 1932

–>•<–

"When school children are hungry at 10:30, hungrier at 11, and tired and irritable at noon, it doesn't take a wizard to tell that they got up late that morning and hurried off to school before breakfast was half over," says Miss Inez Hobart, extension specialist in nutrition, University Farm, St. Paul. . . .

"Breakfast should include a fruit or tomato juice, hot whole-grain cereal, such as oatmeal or cracked wheat, a breadstuff, butter, cream and milk. If breakfast must be very early, include an egg. The cream, butter and bacon take longer to digest, but 'stay by' longer than the starchy foods, and therefore play an important part in the first meal of the day."

Battle Lake Review, Sept. 28, 1933

–>•<–

Caught in a motor-driven corn picker, Ray Koltes was stripped of all his clothes except one shirt sleeve and his shoes last week. In some manner, his clothing was

Tri-County Forum, June 15, 1939

caught in the machinery and before he was able to shut off the power he found himself in the rather embarrassing position of standing in the middle of a field of corn without even a barrel in which to go home. Although he was badly bruised and suffered somewhat from the shock, he escaped without other injury.

Brooten Review, Nov. 2, 1933

–>•<–

Old Evils Not Wanted. The

"It is the wish of Manager Behrndt that all possible room at the theatre be given the little folks."

American people have voted to end national prohibition, but that does not mean that they want the evils of the old time saloon system restored. They have decided to try some other way of managing liquor. But if a host of men abuse their new privilege and bring destitution to their families, there will be another reaction in favor of strict legislation. ... The thing to do ... is to manage this business as strictly as possible, and encourage weak men to learn self control. A liquor place that encourages people to drink when they show signs of intoxication is a peril to the public, particularly in these times of drunken automobile driving.

Wells Mirror, Nov. 23, 1933

-> - <-

Mrs. Roosevelt and Santa. Mrs. Franklin D. Roosevelt is not one of those very conscientious folks who thinks it demoralizes children to tell them about Santa Claus. "Of course I believe in Santa Claus," she exclaims. Good for her. The children of her family will never feel there is no love in the world at Christmas time.

Some things that are not true are a good deal truer than those that are really true, if such a contradiction can be permitted. Some old fable [may have] never really happened, yet comes nearer expressing the world's great truths than oceans of cold reasoning. Literal folks here in Wells may ridicule the story of fat old Santa descending a narrow modern chimney. But a spirit of good will climbs down into selfish people's hearts at Christmas time, even if it has to worm its way through chinks much narrower than any chimney made of bricks and stone.

Wells Mirror, Dec. 14, 1933

-> - <-

As his annual Christmas treat to the kiddies of the community,

East Grand Forks Record, Feb. 24, 1939

Manager Edwin Behrndt of the Cozy Theatre will give a free matinee, Saturday afternoon, December 23, commencing promptly at 2:30. All children under the age of 15 years will be admitted free. Over fifteen years and adults will be admitted at the usual charge of 25 cents. This party is solely for the little folks hence the charge for adults. It is the wish of Manager Behrndt that all possible room at the theatre be given the little folks. Bring the children and let them enjoy the show while you do your shopping.

Cambridge North Star, Dec. 14, 1933

-> - <-

A dog that is either smart enough to be very valuable, or so smart that it is very apt to become a dangerous nuisance, is owned by Mrs. Victor Peterson, of Isle. With a number of other ladies, Mrs. Peterson called on a neighbor one afternoon last week. The roads were muddy, and all the ladies wore overshoes, leaving them on the steps when they entered the house. The dog went along, but remained outside. When she was ready to return home, Mrs. Peterson could not find her overshoes, and finally had to walk home without them. Arriving there, she found that the dog had selected her overshoes from the pile on the doorstep, carried them home and was guarding them in front of her door. Now, was the dog smart in taking home her overshoes, or was it only smart in making her walk home without them?

Anoka County Union, Anoka, April 11, 1934

-> - <-

Monday morning, Dr. J.H. Frank made his usual trip to the asylum and as he was crossing the tracks near the Eastern Minnesota lumber yards, his machine stopped on the track. In some way the brake was applied, and all of the doctor's efforts to move the auto out of the way of an oncoming freight were unavailing, and the doctor's auto sustained a broken mud guard, twisted auto horn, smashed glass, etc., when it landed in the ditch. Dr. Frank says that when he found he couldn't move the auto, he tried to signal the engineer, who had plenty of time to stop the train, as he was going slowly, but there was not a sign of a man in the cab. The train didn't whistle or ring for the crossing and didn't stop after they struck, nor did he see anyone at all on the train. In stepping to one side he did not allow enough room and was struck by the engine, sustaining a

"Not yet big boy."

broken right arm. He walked to the asylum, attended his patients, and then drove into the country by team, and didn't get the arm set till afternoon.

Anoka County Union, Anoka, April 25, 1934

-›-‹-

Two Seattle, Washington, girls, arrived per auto on Thursday, after what they thought was a very good run across country to Fargo, N. Dak. Driving night and day, taking turn and turn about at the wheel, Eveleth Solberg and Claire Shay made the 1600 miles in about forty-seven hours. That would make just one hour short of two days [and about 34 miles per hour]. Eveleth's father, Mr. H.K. Solberg, a former Clarkfield businessman, made the distance in three days, at his last visit here four or five years ago. Eveleth and Claire are both working girls and have only a two weeks vacation, so they want to make the most of it while visiting relatives and friends here, and in Minneapolis.

Clarkfield Advocate, June 23, 1934

-›-‹-

They tell a good one on E.G. McCuskey, the insurance salesman from Redwood Falls who gets to Morton occasionally and Mac admits it's true. Mac had an operation a while ago and as soon as possible, he was taken home to recuperate. A relapse hit him, and believing he had passed away, his wife called the undertaker. The man in black lifted Mac's eyelids and being fairly confident he was due for some business, sat on the bed. About that time Mac gained a little strength and raised up on his elbows with his eyes wide open, murmured, "Not yet big boy." Said undertaker, who was flustered and embarrassed, beat a hasty exit.

Battle Lake Review, Sept. 20, 1934

East Grand Forks Record, March 17, 1939

-›-‹-

Rev. Carl E. Anderson gave a very good lecture at the October meeting of the Lutheran Brotherhood Thursday night in the N.L. church basement. He spoke on a "United Brotherhood." . . . The wage system, in his opinion, fails to realize harmony so long as selfishness and greed actuate both employers and employed. Lutheranism is moving toward consolidation of all bodies, norwegian, swedish and german, he believed, but it may be some time in the future before it will come about. Until we realize that we are all created equal — until we gather under the banner of the greatest Organizer the world has ever seen, we won't have much success, Rev. Anderson declared.

Clarkfield Advocate, Oct. 11, 1934

-›-‹-

A hundred men were registered under the National Relief Bureau by Harry Roese, head of the district unit, at Spooner yesterday. Mr. Roese brought five stenographers from Bemidji, and they were busy all day. Mr. Roese and his staff will return later to take care of more registrations.

There is no project in sight for this county at present, but there is likely to be work later in the summer. An effort is being made by Representative Gustaf Erickson to have the highway department build a new highway on No. 72 from the Rapid River bridge to Wheeler's Point, and if funds can be found the work is likely to be done.

Baudette Region, June 8, 1934

-›-‹-

New SUMMER DRESSES

2 for $15

They Have Everything!

STYLE

Jacket Dresses, Suits, Two-Piece Effects, Lingerie Trimmings, Sleeves and Sleeveless, Graceful Flaring Skirts, Natural Waistlines.

SMART COLORS

New Prints That Everyone Wants, Glowing Plain Shades, Pastels, Black and Navy.

FINE FABRICS

Flat Crepe, Canton Crepe, Shantung, Plain and Printed Chiffon.

VALUE

Any Two You Select for $15.00!

J. C. PENNEY CO., Inc.

Roseau, Minnesota

Roseau Times-Region, May 7, 1931

"You've had a good time this summer, little man."

The first lutefisk supper of the season will be given at the N.L. [Norwegian Lutheran] church basement next Wednesday night, October 17th, sponsored by the Willing Workers' organization. More than 500 pounds of prime lutefisk have been ordered by Mr. Grinager, thru the Kildahl Fish Company at Minneapolis. . . . Adults 30c; School Children 20c; Under School Age 15c.
Clarkfield Advocate, Oct. 11, 1934

→•←

Clarkfield was well represented at the big football homecoming at the University of Minnesota stadium, Saturday, when the usually invincible "Wolverines" of Michigan University fell before the mighty onslaught of "Pug" Lund and his teammates. Only twice in the last ten or fifteen years has Minnesota been able to whip the Michigan team, and for the entire first half it looked as though the visitors were going to hold Minnesota scoreless. But [Coach Bernie] Bierman's strategy this year has been to withhold his heavy attack until the enemy is growing tired and that was what happened Saturday, according to the dozen or so local fans. In the second half Minnesota opened with a terrific attack that would not be denied. When the game ended the score stood, Minnesota 34; Michigan 0.
Clarkfield Advocate, Nov. 8, 1934

→•←

A Tribute
In calling attention to the requirements of a successful rural teacher, someone has suggested that she (for practically all of them are now girls) must be a primary, intermediate, grammar grade and high school teacher combined; she must be able to build fires, adjust fallen stove pipes, put in window panes, sweep, dust, split kindling, drive a car, keep out of neighborhood

quarrels, know how and where to whip a bad boy, understand the school laws, raise money for libraries, keep all kinds of records, plant trees on Arbor day, be of a good moral character and pass an examination in the branches of modern education. For these accomplishments she receives $40 or $50 a month. Out of this she pays her board, buys her clothes, attends summer school, buys educational papers and books, attends county conventions and furnishes pencils for the pupils. What is left she adds to her bank account or starts a bank if she prefers.
Ortonville Independent, Aug. 15, 1935

→•←

And So, School Begins
You've had a good time this summer, little man. You haven't had to get up very early in the mornings, nor wash behind those ears. . . . All summer long that unruly hair of yours could fly around — a comb, what's that? — no, you never heard of one.

You've been pretty lucky. For three months now, you've done little else than play all day. Swimmin', fishin', playin', hikin' — oh, yes, all that you've done. Those things you know.

But, little man, remember back last year about this time, when mother roused you from your sleep, and called, "Get up,

"It's nice to stay inside."

son, it's almost eight!'' And sleepy eyed, up you got. You dressed, you washed, you combed your hair. You polished shoes, you wore a tie. Yes, you did those things. It was breakfast-time, and so you ate. And then, "Hurry, son, or you'll be late. Stop at the store and get those things — a tablet, pencil or what you need. Say good morning to those you meet — and above all, don't fight!'' Remember when your mother told you that?

And you met your pal from across the street, and said, "Naw, I guess we ain't sissies, even if we are all slicked up. But gosh, hasn't it been swell all summer. **Ortonville Independent, Aug. 29, 1935**

->-<-

On Cold Weather

January and its bitter cold weather — what a blessing, that old kitchen stove. It's one time of the year when many of us would like to discard the new electric or gas range which we time and time again have "showed off" to visitors and explained the convenience of this modern appliance. What we wouldn't give for an old kitchen cook stove with an oven in which to toast our frosted feet.

In another month the temperature will with some consistency stay above zero, but what a trial the past month has been. Rises in temperature mean only another deep drop. Twenty-five below, the wind in the northwest, sweeping down the 30 mile stretch of Big Stone lake, bursting into town to bite the uncovered ears and noses of pedestrians, to pierce that coat and comforter, to tie up traffic and slow down business. Winter is surely a heartless season.

But then, we do come to appreciate the comfort of a warm fire, and find that staying home isn't such a dull life after all. There are unexcelled radio pro-

---

Badgar Herald Rustler, Jan. 2, 1931

---

grams to hear, magazines and books that have been accumulating to read. It's nice to stay inside. That extra work of shoveling coal and chores of 20 below weather, the chilled hands and feet and frosted noses and cheeks, are not so sharply realized when we snuggle up next to the fire — and forget winter. **Ortonville Independent, Jan. 24, 1935**

->-<-

Finds Big Spider
In Banana Shipment

In unpacking a crate of ba-

nanas last Friday morning, John Vik noticed a large tarantula, which jumped from the banana bunch on to the floor. After a hard chase it was finally cornered and captured by Mr. Vik, who placed it in a glass jar of alcohol and now has it on display at the store. This playful little creature, about 5 inches long, covered with hair and equipped with an unbelievable number of legs, is known as one of the most poisonous spiders of the south and evidently has made its home in the fruit shipment since it was

"Television, long considered by many to be no more than a dream as far as the general public is concerned, will be an actuality by spring."

packed for transportation up north.

Bronson Budget, Oct. 3, 1935

→›‹←

Television, long considered by many to be no more than a dream as far as the general public is concerned, will be an actuality by spring, according to Professor James Webb of the department of electrical engineering in the University of Minnesota.

After spending last summer working in eastern electrical laboratories, Dr. Webb returned to Minnesota with assurances that television has been conquered. During the late winter, he said, important manufacturers will place twenty or thirty actual television sets in important public places in the east, such as hotel lobbies, railroad stations and the like. Programs will be sent to these sets from a central transmitting outfit and the general public will be given an opportunity to witness a continuous demonstration of the new science.

The receiving outfits will be relatively small, Professor Webb explained, probably measuring something like eighteen by twenty-four inches. Very short wave lengths will be used in transmitting the images. He said he believed that sound will accompany the pictures. . . .

He believes that within a very few years television sets will be available at a price thousands can afford, and predicts that even the first sets will be probably no more expensive than were the better early radio sets.

Ortonville Independent, Nov. 21, 1935

→›‹←

**Governor's Pig Not
Best, Says Larson**

Minnesota raises much better pigs than "Floyd of Rosedale," the large porker given to Gover-

---

Mother's Day

SUNDAY, MAY 11TH

DINNER, 50c

Cream of Tomato Soup

Wafers

Baked Ham or Swiss Steak

Mashed Potatoes

Gravy

Lettuce Salad

Celery	Radishes

Parker House Rolls

Tea	Coffee
Ice Cream	Wafers

REMARK'S CAFE

Norman County Index, May 8, 1930

*"The much-publicized hog did not equal those which he saw
exhibited by farmers of the Red River Valley."*

Tri-County Forum, June 8, 1939

nor Floyd B. Olson by Iowa's governor on a friendly football game wager last fall.

That's the opinion of Gilbert Larson, president of the Mahnomen Co-operative Creamery association after viewing the exhibits at the Winter Shows at Crookston last week.

He says that the much-publicized hog did not equal those which he saw exhibited by farmers of the Red River Valley, and he was disappointed to find that the Iowa hog did not show all the outstanding qualities of breed that others did.

"Floyd of Rosedale" is a pure-bred Hampshire boar pig won by Governor Olson from Governor Clyde Herring of Iowa over the

"Her hair, which was quite gray, is now turning definitely black."

outcome of the Minnesota-Iowa football game. It is now owned by the University Farm School, Saint Paul.
Mahnomen Pioneer, Feb. 14, 1936

-›-‹-

Mrs. Anna E. Tuttle, who makes her home with Miss Bertha Pusher in Morris, celebrated her 90th birthday anniversary recently, and in honor of the occasion displayed a few new black hairs. Her hair, which was quite gray, is now turning definitely black. As a young woman Mrs. Tuttle had black hair, but for a number of years it was almost white. She is extremely active for her age. Some kind of a record will be established if her hair turns completely black as she nears the 100 year mark.
Mahnomen Pioneer, March 6, 1936

-›-‹-

The first vacation in 30 years of Mr. and Mrs. Charles Johnson of Elbow Lake was cut short last week when they were summoned home to be advised that every building on the place except the house had been burned to the ground. In addition to the fine farm buildings, they lost a number of head of stock, a large quantity of grain, pigs, chickens, harnesses and other farm equipment. No one was at the farm home when the fire started, the Johnsons being in Evansville which was to be the initial part of the long awaited vacation. They had been gone for only a day. Although the buildings were insured, Mr. and Mrs. Johnson suffered a large loss.
Moose Lake Star Gazette, July 30, 1936

-›-‹-

Schliep & Kalass, well known shoe dealers at Zumbrota, announces . . . a free demonstration of Dr. Scholl's scientific shoes on Monday, August 9, and invite everyone who is looking for foot

comfort to attend this demonstration and learn what expert shoe fitting can do for them.

Mr. Kalass says: ". . . We invite people of the Wanamingo district to come to our store and have Pedo-graph prints made of their stockinged feet."
Wanamingo Progress, July 29, 1937

-›-‹-

Telephone calls about the "War of the Worlds" dramatization broadcast [a too-real radio broadcast depicting a fictitious invasion of Martians] continued to pour in at WCCO Monday. But, Earl Gammons, general manager of WCCO, said instead of protests, the great majority of the calls were requests for a rebroadcast of the program, from persons who did not hear the Sunday night broadcast which caused

such extensive excitement.
Minneapolis Tribune, Nov. 1, 1938

-›-‹-

[The Baudette Region published a long string of quips and local glories on page two each week. For instance:]

A city man got his picture in the paper the other day with a 25-pound muskie. There are muskies in Lake of the Woods that would chase that one clear up on shore if he let a peep out of him about being a real fish.
Baudette Region, June 22, 1934

-›-‹-

Mae West's salary is $10,000 a week. That's a big figure, but so is Mae's.
Baudette Region, June 29, 1934

-›-‹-

"Old Man Prosperity has found his way back to Baudette."

There isn't a night up here when you can't tuck a blanket under your chin and enjoy a peaceful snooze. Why stay in the cities to become chummy with sunstrokes?
Baudette Region, July 6, 1934

–>-<–

These days children are being taught to swim at five and six years of age. It's different from the old days when kids got tanned in more places than one as a result of sneaking down to the river for a swim.
Baudette Region, July 13, 1934

–>-<–

The average citizen is meek and mild, but if he ever runs into the guy who told Hoover that prosperity was just around the corner, there will be trouble.
Baudette Region, Aug. 14, 1934

–>-<–

A man south of Baudette is starting a skunk farm. He may make a lot of money, but we fear that he is committing social suicide.
Baudette Region, Oct. 19, 1934

–>-<–

Hauptmann, the Lindbergh kidnaper suspect, is having a tough time proving where he was on the night of March first, 1932. By the way, where were you on the night of March first, 1932?
Baudette Region, Oct. 26, 1934

–>-<–

Traffic in the Rex Hotel lobby is the heaviest it has been in years, which is the best evidence that Old Man Prosperity has found his way back to Baudette.
Baudette Region, Nov. 16, 1934

–>-<–

Time to Stop. The news is floating around that a certain man in this county is in the habit of rough-housing his wife. He

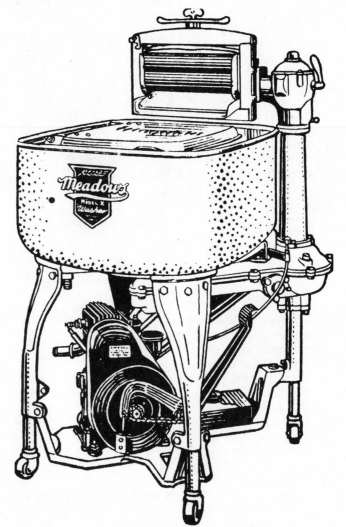

"Now he is three months behind with the pills and three months ahead with the whiskey."

can take this as a hint.
Baudette Region, Feb. 22, 1935

→›•‹–

A local man last summer was instructed by a doctor to take some prescribed pills three times a day and a drop of whiskey every other day. Now he is three months behind with the pills and three months ahead with the whiskey.
Baudette Region, March 26, 1937

→›•‹–

[For a look at Minnesota in the 1930s, see "The WPA Guide to Minnesota," originally published in 1938 and republished in 1985 by the Minnesota Historical Society Press. The book is still useful today.]

For Shaves That Look And Feel Like "A Million," Try This New Gillette Blade

At ½ Price!

Radically Improved Kind Of Cutting Edges Make New Thin Gillette Blade Out-Perform And Outlast Ordinary Blades Two To One!

4 for 10c
8 for 19c

YOU get good-looking, comfortable shaves every time . . . and save money too . . . when you use the new Thin Gillette Blade. This blade is made of easy-flexing steel hard enough to cut glass. It has super-keen edges of an entirely new kind. You whisk through tough beard quickly, easily, and protect your face from smart and burn caused by misfit blades. Gillette alone, with its world-renowned facilities, could produce...and sell at only 10c for four...a blade so superior as this. Buy a package from your dealer today.

Thin Gillette Blades Are Produced By The Maker Of The Famous
Gillette Blue Blade
5 for 25¢

OUTSELLS ANY OTHER RAZOR BLADE

Tri-County Forum, Aug. 3, 1939

1940s

World War II took many of Minnesota's men, some of its women and much of its iron ore and farm crops. Minnesota mines surpassed all previous production levels. Hybrid corn became an important crop. Soybeans were planted for the first time. Of the 300,000 Minnesotans who served in the war, about 6,000 died. For the first time, in 1948 the dollar value of Minnesota's manufactured goods exceeded cash farm goods.

Minneapolis Star Journal, Nov. 12, 1940

1940s
–>•<–

Armistice Day Blizzard

One of the most powerful and destructive winter storms on record struck the Upper Midwest on Nov. 11, 1940. Called the "Armistice Day Blizzard," it hit without warning and caught many people inadequately dressed. Duck hunters along the Mississippi River between Red Wing and La Crosse were in shirtsleeves in the morning's 60-degree weather; they soon found themselves in a driving snowstorm with plummeting temperatures. Women office workers in the Twin Cities regretted wearing high heels rather than snow boots. This article was written in Minneapolis when the strength of the storm was not yet fully assessed.

MINNEAPOLIS and the northwest today dug out of the worst November snow storm in history.

With transportation paralyzed throughout the state as high winds piled up drifts, city dwellers straggled to work on the few streetcars and buses that were operating, while others hiked or arrived in the loop on skis.

Although the record breaking snowfall of 16.2 inches stopped during the early hours of the morning, the high wind continued to whip the fallen snow into huge drifts in the city and throughout the state.

No immediate relief from the cold was in sight. . . .

Ten persons were reported dead in Minnesota, three more were dead in Wisconsin and countless persons were unheard from.

Among the latter were eight hunters marooned on a sandbar in the Wisconsin river near Portage for whom little hope is held; the three fliers whose plane is believed to have crashed in Spirit lake, Iowa, and several parties of hunters marooned in the wilds, as well as a large number of persons marooned in automobiles. . . .

The storm's suddenness caught thousands unprepared, and transportation and communications services suffered heavily.

A rain which had fallen almost without lapse over the week-end yesterday turned briefly to sleet and then to driving snow, while the wind increased to 32 miles an hour, and, in gusts, to 40 and 60 miles an hour.

Drifts were piled up with such suddenness that thousands of cars became stalled to block streets.

At 3:30 p.m. and later the visibility for drivers was virtually nil. Cab companies suspended operations late in the day and at 9 p.m. the streetcar company gave up attempting to maintain schedules.

Train service was seriously hampered and to some points in the south and west was stopped. Bus lines out of the city were stopped completely. Airplanes were grounded. Communications were seriously hampered as sleet and snow broke down wires. Power service was interrupted in sections of the city and in many Minnesota towns. . . .

The storm stopped most state traffic virtually where it was. As a result, many small towns were crowded with marooned travelers. Near New Brighton, 30 cars piled up at one point due to low visibility, and a dozen persons were slightly hurt. . . .

The blizzard had reached such intensity by the time of the usual homegoing rush that thousands of downtown workers crowded loop hotels to the limits in both Minneapolis and St. Paul, sleeping on davenports and in chairs. Many who managed to reach home were unable to get to work today. . . .

Fire Chief Earl A. Traeger called all off-duty firemen to work at 6 a.m. today, and the full roster was ordered to remain on duty until streets were

"The mezzanine floor of the Nicollet hotel looked like a refugee shelter."

Minneapolis Tribune, Nov. 13, 1940

cleared and the situation returned to normal. . . .

Damage to rural districts was incalculable today since many of them were still out of communication with metropolitan points. In some sections of the southern state, where the blizzard struck worst, part of the corn crop was still unharvested.

Thousands of turkeys fattened for the Thanksgiving trade froze to death. There were heavy casualties also among young lambs on the ranges, and among other livestock. . . .

Free blankets, free pillows and an invitation to bunk anywhere they could find room kept hundreds of storm-stranded persons comfortable at Nicollet hotel last night.

Virtually every hotel in the downtown section was jammed in the early hours of the evening as thousands finding they were unable to reach their homes sought shelter for the night.

The mezzanine floor of the Nicollet hotel looked like a refugee shelter as stranded persons took advantage of the hotel management's invitation.

This morning they were given breakfast free by the hotel. Many attempted to pay for their accommodations but payment was refused.

Minneapolis Star Journal, Nov. 12, 1940

[By the 12th of November, subzero winds had roared into southwest Minnesota, and snowdrifts up to 20 feet high were reported around Willmar. The Twin Cities recorded 16.2 inches. Winds gusted to 63 miles an hour in Duluth. In many areas snow drifted so much that it was days before even main roads were cleaned. The National Weather Service says that 49 people died in Minnesota and that damage to livestock, turkeys and property was heavy.

[For more on the 1940 Armistice Day Blizzard, read "All Hell Broke Loose" by William H. Hull, which he published in 1985.]

→·←

1940s
-˃•˂-

World War II and Peace

On "the day of infamy," Dec. 7, 1941, Japan made a surprise attack on Pearl Harbor. The United States quickly found itself deep in World War II, a bitter, prolonged war with incredible demands on the country. More than 6,000 Minnesotans gave their lives. Labor, industry and individuals joined in a concerted effort. Here's a look at life in the 1940s — before, during and after the war.

There's one thing to be said for the climate here. There's a lot of it.
Winona Republican-Herald, Feb. 20, 1941

-˃•˂-

The three children of the Richard Maxwells were excited to receive a card from their mother who wrote it in the air just before landing at Indianapolis. Mr. and Mrs. Maxwell left Chicago two weeks ago last Sunday on one of Eastern Air Lines' great Silver liners. After a leisurely vacation on the western coast of Florida, they are expected home this afternoon. On the trip down, the Maxwells left Chicago at 8:30 in the morning and arrived at Tampa at 6:55 p.m.
Winona Republican-Herald, March 5, 1941

-˃•˂-

[Over the 26 years Cedric Adams wrote for the Minneapolis newspapers, his column was always among the best-read features. He also was loved for his program on WCCO radio, aired from 1931 to 1961. Airplane pilots flying over the Midwest said that lights in small towns and farmhouses went out just after Cedric's Nighttime News. But he started as a newspaper writer and told Edward R. Murrow on the "Person to Person" national television show, "I make the most money in radio, television is the most fattening, and I like newspapering best." His folksy column ran in the Minneapolis Star from 1935 and the Minneapolis Sunday Tribune from 1941 until he died in 1961. Here's what Adams wrote the day after Pearl Harbor:]

A touch of war drama occurred in the Nicollet's [Nicollet Hotel's] Minnesota Terrace last night that few diners caught. During a dance session, Reggie Childs, the orchestra leader, was called off the stand by a long distance telephone call. It came from his brother in Toronto who is a captain in the Canadian air force. "I'm leaving in the morning, going east with 2,000 planes," the brother told Reggie, "and this may be the last time I'll get to talk to you." They visited for a moment. Childs returned to the stand and had his boys play "My Buddy." So strong was the emotional tug that Reggie had to put down his baton and leave the stand.

•

A letter to Santa that appeared in ... a weekly newspaper published by the [army] lads, has some pointed information about shopping for soldiers' gifts. No neckties, no plaid socks, please, say the boys. And no electric razors. They can buy cigarets cheaper. You might enclose a little cash on the line for smokes, though. Stationery with your soldier's camp address printed on both the letters and stamped envelopes, please, are very acceptable. A portable radio, a camera, a deck or two of cards are all good. Magazines and their home town newspaper subscriptions are most welcome, the boys themselves say. (And don't forget to put your magazine subscriptions through your local druggist or news dealer.) Film, the right size; scrap books, pen and pencil sets — all very good. Have the boys helped you?

•

National efficiency in a national crisis such as yesterday is indicated by the fact that exactly

279

"One of our own Montgomery boys had made the supreme sacrifice."

MONTGOMERY, MINNESOTA, FRIDAY, NOVEMBER 20, 1942.

EGISTRATION SET FOR YOUTH OF THE NATION

Announcement from Washington is set three separate registration periods for the young men of our country, who will reach their 18th birthday in the last half of this year. The young men, who reach their 8th birthday in July and August will register the week of December 11th to December 17th. Those reaching that age in September and October will sign up the following week and those becoming eighteen in November and December will register during the week of December 26th to December 31st.

Under the plan there will be continuous registration, who reach their eighteenth birthday after the first of the year.

Pioneer Merchant Died Early Sunday Evening

eter Plonchinsky Passed Away At Family Home In This City; Funeral Held Wednesday.

Peter Plonchinsky, who operated a wagon shop in this city for a period over thirty years, passed away at the family home in this city at 5 o'clock last Sunday evening fol-

Corporal Robert E. Richter Killed In European War Zone

The people of our city were shocked and sorely grieved Wednesday evening, when a message reached here announcing that one of our own Montgomery boys had made the supreme sacrifice. Corporal Robert E. Richter, son of Mr. and Mrs. Paul W. Richter, of Montgomery township, had been killed in an airplane accident in the western European area.

30 Govt. Washington, D. C. 6:25 P. M. Nov. 18th, 1942

Paul W. Richter
RFD No. 1, Dely Special Messenger
Advise Messenger Charge
Montgomery, Minn.

THE SECRETARY OF WAR DESIRES ME TO EXPRESS HIS DEEP REGRET THAT YOUR SON, CORPORAL ROBERT E. RICHTER, DIED NOVEMBER 12 IN WESTERN EUROPEAN AREA IN AIR PLANE ACCIDENT LETTER FOLLOWS

ULIO The Adjutant General
5:39 P. M.

Aside from the notification contained in the telegram, little of the details are known. "Bobby", as he was well and favorably known by everyone in the community, left with a Le Sueur county contingent on February 9th, 1942. After his induction he was assigned to the U. S. Air Corps. After completing the course of training in the camps in this country, he was sent overseas about three months ago. He had been advanced to the rank of Corporal and was a bombardier with the U. S. Forces in England.

A requiem high mass for the repose of his soul will be celebrated at the

AMERICAN LEGION TO STAGE BIG KLONDIKE DAYS PARTY

A special committee has been busy the past week completing arrangements for the American Legion Klondike Days Party, which will be held at the city hall on Saturday evening and Sunday afternoon.

The party will open at 7:00 o'clock tomorrow evening and choice poultry will be awarded as prizes. There will be cards and other attractions on Saturday and Sunday.

As a special feature two choice turkeys will be given away on Saturday evening and Sunday afternoon.

Here is your opportunity to get your turkey for the Thanksgiving dinner. Plan on attending, because everybody else will be there both Saturday and Sunday.

Farmers Signing Up To Purchase War Bonds

Committees At Work In Rural Areas In Campaign To Receive Pledges Between Now and Thanksgiving.

Minnesota farmers this week signed up to buy millions of dollars in war bonds, pledges ranging as high as $8,000 in the special drive being pushed to completion before Thanks-

Montgomery Messenger, Nov. 20, 1942

---

four hours after the Pacific doings had popped, the FBI had instructed every aviation unit in Minneapolis that has private planes for rent, hire or sale that no Japanese could become a customer from then on. It's rather gratifying to Mr. and Mrs. Joe Citizen to see just a single little detail like that carried out with such startling dispatch.

Minneapolis Star Journal, Dec. 8, 1941

⇢•⇠

It's getting to the point where the only man who can break even is the one out of a job.

Warroad Pioneer, Feb. 12, 1942

⇢•⇠

Ed. Phorte Grows Hair on his Chest

Ed. Phorte, redoubtable game warden of Baudette, grew a crop of hair on his chest the other night that would have made the Philistine giant turn green with envy. He was sleeping in a dugout in the forest south of Spooner when he awoke, and felt something on his chest. An exploratory touch revealed that his chest was covered with spines. A porcupine had decided to snuggle into bed with him.

Warroad Pioneer, May 21, 1942

⇢•⇠

The people of our city were shocked and sorely grieved Wednesday evening, when a message reached here announcing that one of our own Montgomery boys had made the supreme sacrifice. Corporal Robert E. Richter, son of Mr. and Mrs. Paul W. Richter, of Montgomery township, had been killed in an

airplane accident in the western European area.

Aside from the notification contained in the telegram, little of the details are known. "Bobby," as he was well and favorably known by everyone in the community, left with a Le Sueur county contingent on February 9th, 1942. After his induction he was assigned to the U.S. Air Corps. After completing the course of training in the camps in this country, he was sent overseas about three months ago. He had been advanced to the rank of Corporal and was a bombardier with the U.S. Forces in England.

A requiem high mass for the repose of his soul will be celebrated at the Church of the Most Holy Redeemer in this city at 9:00 o'clock on Saturday morning. The members of the Ameri-

"The Japs bombed us every night."

can Legion and all veterans of World War I will attend the funeral in a body and a special invitation is extended to soldiers of the present war, who are home on furlough, to be present at the services.

Montgomery Messenger, Nov. 20, 1942

–>–<–

Pipestone Boys Meet on Far Away Shore

A letter received by Mrs. Marion Colby from her son, Cpl. Charles Colby, brings the interesting information that by chance he recently met and visited with Roy J. Tatman, also of Pipestone.

Cpl. Colby is in north Africa, and when on a 24-hour pass a short time ago, met two sailors. As is the custom, each told the other of his home town, and when Charles mentioned "Pipestone," the sailors at once told him Roy Tatman was there. The Pipestone boys met and Charles had dinner with Roy on the latter's ship. Roy is the son of Mr. and Mrs. G.R. Tatman of Pipestone.

It was the first time in seven months, Cpl. Colby writes, that he had seen anyone from home.

Pipestone County Star, Jan. 7, 1944

–>–<–

The following is an excerpt from a letter which Mrs. F.W. Lindquist recently received from her son, Willis, who is a Merchant Marine. Willis recently arrived in San Francisco around the holidays but expected to be shipped out again soon. . . .

**Berkeley, California
December 17, 1943**

Dear Mother,

About my last trip. I sailed as a deck hand on a large troop transport. We went to Hawaii and then on down to the Southwest Pacific to an island in the Ellis group close to Tarawa, bringing supplies and troops for the inva-

Let's blast Japan—and Germany—and Italy—with the chain lightning of destruction that can be built from the scrap in our cellars, attics and garages, on our farms and in our places of business.

Scrap iron and steel, other metals, rubber and waste materials. It will all be used to make tanks, ships, planes and the fighting weapons our boys must have. It is needed at once.

Sell it to a Junk dealer—give it to a charity or collection agency—take it yourself to the nearest collection point—or consult the Local Salvage Committee . . . If you live on a farm, and have found no means of disposing of your Junk, get in touch with the County War Board or your farm implement dealer.

Throw YOUR scrap into the fight!

This message approved by Conservation Division
WAR PRODUCTION BOARD
This advertisement paid for by the American Industries Salvage Committee (representing and with funds provided by groups of leading industrial concerns).

Local Salvage Committee Phone: Lindstrom, No. 2

MARVIN KAUFMAN, Chairman   TELFRED JOHNSTON, Shafer
RALPH JOHNSON, Center City   L. ANDERSON, Chisago City

Chisago County Press, Aug. 27, 1942

sion of that island. Some thirty ships were at anchor in our little lagoon together with many invasion barges. The Japs bombed us every night. They usually destroyed a few planes on the island and killed a few men and sank a few barges, but that was all. Their bombs came close enough to us to rock our ship, but we were sending up so much

stuff at them that they didn't come down to effective bombing range.

I'll never forget that morning when the fleet and barges sailed out of the lagoon to conquer the Japs at Tarawa. As you know, that battle was the hottest one in the history of the U.S. Marines.

Coming back we were loaded with the wounded of that battle.

There's the whistle…Have a Coca-Cola

…*lunchtime is friendly time in the plant*

Everybody likes company when lunchtime rolls around. It's always a sociable spot in the busy day — a chance to talk, to laugh, be friendly and refreshed. And the big red cooler is the place to meet for it. At the words *Have a Coke* things pick up and good-fellowship begins.

BOTTLED UNDER AUTHORITY OF THE COCA COLA COMPANY BY

COCA COLA BOTTLING CO., ST. PAUL

-the global high-sign-

You naturally hear Coca-Cola called by its friendly abbreviation 'Coke'. Both mean the quality product of The Coca-Cola Company.

South St. Paul Daily Reporter, Sept. 19, 1945

"An army fights on its stomach."

Most of those poor fellows were as happy as larks because at last they were "going home," the reward that every soldier on the distant battle front prays for every lonely day.

Love,
Willis

Winthrop News, Jan. 13, 1944

→›‹←

Men! Women! Boys! Girls!

You are urgently needed for work on the farm.

Today, in and near Lanesboro, there's a crop of grain waiting to be shocked.

Today, the boy in your family who's fighting your fight, needs all the food we can get to him, to keep him healthy and strong.

Gathering in the crops, helping the farmer is now your part of the fight. It's the battle for food now going on right in your back yard.

Remember, food is as mighty a weapon of war as tanks and planes. "An army fights on its stomach." And a fighting man needs 1½ times as much food as a civilian.

So let's join hands and keep those supply lines busy. Let's help the farmer who grows the food in every hour of spare time we have. Every day, every weekend, every week is time well spent for you — and for that soldier boy you love.

Time is precious! Call on O.J. Mindrum at Village Hall and make yourself available as a member of the shocking crews.

Lanesboro Leader, July 27, 1944

→›‹←

Wonderful Response

The emergency shocking crews of the several county trade centers have responded wonderfully in coming to the assistance of the busy farmers and helped them shock up their small grain, most of which has been done by crews of from three to six mem-

South St. Paul Daily Reporter, Oct. 23, 1945

bers working evenings.

According to A.I. Swenson, Farm Help Assistant, in one instance, 17 men shocked up a field of 40 acres of oats in a little over one hour. This is a fine example of the friendly spirit that exists in the several communities

"It hasn't been so very long since clothespins were plentiful."

Minneapolis Sunday Tribune and Star Journal, Jan. 4, 1942

in the county, as well as the patriotic spirit. Let the good work prevail.
Lanesboro Leader, Aug. 10, 1944

–>–<–

Hash by Hannah column: It hasn't been so very long since clothespins were plentiful and could be bought for a song. Whenever I broke one in hanging up the clothes I would carelessly toss it away and think nothing of it. But no more. They are too hard to get and whenever I happen to split one, I have my husband take some fine wire and wire it together again and it is just like the ones we used to buy.

A little thing, but how important.
Ellendale Eagle, April 18, 1945

–>–<–

A beautiful wedding service took place by candlelight Thursday evening, April 12, at the home of Mr. and Mrs. H.J. Scharmer.

Miss Florence Bonine, daughter of Mr. and Mrs. Fred Ruschmeyer of Stewart, exchanged marriage vows with Leroy Scharmer of the Navy, son of Mr. and Mrs. H.J. Scharmer of Buffalo Lake.

Rev. H.E. Walker performed the single ring ceremony at seven o'clock in the presence of only

immediate members of the family. . . .

Attired in a light blue spring suit with brown accessories, she carried white and pink carnations and sweet peas. Her maid of honor was her sister, Miss Geraldine Bonine of Stewart, who wore a suit of light rose with brown accessories and carried white, pink and yellow carnations.

Wearing his dress uniform of the Navy, the groom was attended by his brother, Henry Scharmer. . . .

A reception given by the parents of the groom followed the service. Decorations were carried out in navy blue and white with a

"There was little of wild rejoicing at first, just relieved smiles."

three-tier wedding cake gracing the bridal table.

Mr. and Mrs. Scharmer left immediately afterward on a brief honeymoon, which took them to Minneapolis and Winona, returning here Saturday evening.

Mrs. Scharmer has been employed as a secretary in Minneapolis the past couple years and expects to continue her work for the present. The groom returned to Great Lakes this week where he is in charge of trainees in the boot camp. In service for several years, he was overseas for more than two years.

The many friends of the couple extend them every wish for much happiness in their wedded life.

Buffalo Lake News, April 19, 1945

→>-<←

[Peace, at last. Here's the report from St. Paul:]

Ting! Ting! Ting! Ting! Ting!

That frenzied tinkling of the bells on press association teletype machines in St. Paul newspaper and radio offices signaled the "flash" bulletin just after 6 p.m. Tuesday that marked the end of the most horrible war in history and launched St. Paulites on a victory celebration that will continue through today for almost all the city's residents. . . .

For a few minutes after the first radio announcements were barked over the air and the first newspaper extras hit the streets, the crowds were calm. There was little of wild rejoicing at first, just relieved smiles as the people absorbed the news for which they had been waiting so long.

Many of them, let out of work an hour or more earlier, had been waiting downtown expectantly for the announcement that the peace which had been shattered for America back on that fateful Dec. 7 of 1941 had come back all over the world.

After the first shock of the an-

Pillager Herald, April 9, 1943

"Within an hour or so the din was general over the loop."

nouncement that IT WAS TRUE AT LAST wore off, the crowd began to "thaw out" and the carnival spirit took over.

A group of servicemen clambered atop a parked automobile at Seventh and Wabasha and opened a quart bottle of whisky with lusty whoops. The laughing crowd cheered.

Automobile horns began honking, accompanied by the rising shouts of the crowd. . . .

A jalopy occupied by some teen-age youths started circling around the block. Other cars followed. In no time the cars joining this impromptu parade were too many for a single line, and drivers started circling the block two abreast to the constantly increasing din from their horns and shouts from gay celebrants loosening up to the spirit of the occasion more as each minute passed.

As soon as word was flashed out that President Truman had announced Japan's acceptance of the surrender terms, all on-sale liquor establishments in the city closed, to remain so for 24 hours.

But before they locked their doors, they had been packed with expectant celebrants waiting for the signal to let off the pent-up urge of several days of anxious waiting through false peace reports, atomic bombings and alarms that the Japs might be trying a last bit of trickery. . . .

Within an hour or so the din was general over the loop, with merrymakers parading their cars through the streets with an abandon that ignored completely all the lean years of rationed gasoline and tires.

The autocade soon was four abreast in some places and attempts of a few drivers to proceed in orderly fashion according to traffic rules were futile. Typifying the jammed traffic was the experience of a Pioneer Press photographer who had to take half an hour to drive from Ninth

"Mayor Hubert H. Humphrey, in tribute to those who paid for the victory with their lives, stated: 'We shall be ever indebted.'"

I'M GOING TO <u>CAN</u> ALL I POSSIBLY <u>CAN</u> SO MY FAMILY <u>CAN</u> EAT BETTER THIS WINTER!

Pillager Herald, July 27, 1945

st. to the Pioneer Press and Dispatch building on Fourth st.

And as the celebrants circled giddily around block after block, they were showered with confetti, torn-up bits of newspapers, ticker tape and anything else that persons leaning out of office windows found convenient to toss at them.

St. Paul Pioneer Press, Aug. 15, 1945

→>•<←

[Meanwhile in Minneapolis . . .]

Crowds on sidewalks overflowed to the streets, and police finally blocked off the central loop area for pedestrians. Strangers clasped hands, pounded backs and hugged and kissed each other. Many men took advantage of the patriotic atmosphere and kissed all girls they met.

Noise makers sold fast, and hucksters soon disposed of their supplies.

Car horns, streetcar whistles and bells and every other device added to the din of the celebration.

For thousands of others, the surrender news was occasion for solemn rejoicing and thanksgiving.

Many churches were open although services in most were delayed until 8 p.m. today.

Mayor Hubert H. Humphrey, in tribute to those who paid for the victory with their lives, stated:

"We shall be ever indebted to those who made the supreme sacrifice in battle and to those who carried our flag to triumph.

"America has proved her right to greatness — a greatness that comes from devotion to duty, a love of liberty, an irresistible power in the cause of human freedom."

Heaviest traffic in history was recorded at Northwestern Bell Telephone Co., with 23,843 attempts to place long distance calls during the 24-hour period ending at midnight Tuesday.

Minneapolis Star-Journal, Aug. 15, 1945

→>•<←

The free outdoor movie that was to have been shown in Ellendale this week Monday evening had to be cancelled when the picture film went astray. Mr. Fette usually receives his film on Sunday morning, and when it did not show up by Monday morning he immediately got in touch by telephone with the firm that supplies his pictures and made arrangements with them to send a substitute film to Owatonna on an eight o'clock bus, but when the bus arrived and was met by Mr. Fette, there was no picture film on it. The substitute shipment had also gone astray or had by mistake been sent out by train and would arrive too late. So there was nothing else to do but cancel the show. This was the first time this had ever happened to Mr. Fette in his seven years in show business.

Ellendale Eagle, Aug. 22, 1945

→>•<←

A V-Mail letter was received by this corner last week from Cpl. Harvey O. Kamrath, stationed in the Malucas Islands group in the South Pacific. Harvey says he is assigned to the 13th Air Force, better known as the Jungle Air Force. The weather isn't too hot if one doesn't have to work in the sun. It rains plenty there, but the land is mostly coral, so it doesn't

"Red Owl will celebrate the Grand Opening of its new super food market."

get too muddy. He is employed in the radar section.
Buffalo Lake News, Sept. 20, 1945

→·←

Today, and during the balance of this week-end, Red Owl will celebrate the Grand Opening of its new super food market in the remodeled Hoemberg building located at the corner of Fourth street and Second avenue. The reconstruction of this property has been under way for some time and since it involved the remodeling of two buildings in order to accommodate Red Owl's requirements for a new 50 by 80 super market, many architectural changes were necessary.

This new super food market will open at 9:00 a.m. Thursday, February 14, and the Red Owl folks predict that you will not recognize the former buildings.

New Front and Interior

This super market's new front consists of a combination of modernistic corrugated metal and polished plate glass — a fine addition to the buildings on our main street.

The interior of the store has been completely decorated in their modern combination of green, yellow and red. The new store is completely self-service in operation, with all of the newest accommodations, including new, low-type shelving, wide aisles, convenient gondola displays and market-baskets-on-wheels. Daylight-fluorescent lighting will illuminate the sales floor so that all products will be readily recognizable and easy to select.

A New Meat Department

In this new Red Owl store, families in Staples and the surrounding area will have a completely new meat market. Fully 28 feet of meat cases have been installed and will regularly offer fresh, smoked and cured meat products of all kinds. In addition, fresh, frozen and spiced fish, as

South St. Paul Daily Reporter, Sept. 6, 1945

"Announcers who call out the arrival and departure of trains at large railway stations got a close-up of the sorrow caused by the war."

well as cheese and other delicatessen products will be available.

Other Departments

This complete food market includes such features as a self-service, open-style dairy case, complete bakery department and an electric light bulb display.

Red Owl's new fresh fruit and vegetable department is so planned that customers may serve themselves and select their choice of fruits and vegetables. Included in the new store is a large, walk-in fresh fruit and vegetable cooler. This innovation makes it possible to take fresh produce directly from the delivery truck and retain its field-fresh appearance and flavor until it is ready to be placed on display for customers' selection.

Red Owl managers, Willis H. Fuder and Donald Black, invite you to visit their new store this week-end and take advantage of the ample food supplies obtained especially for the opening sale, announced in this issue.

Staples World, Feb. 14, 1946

-→•←-

Announcers who call out the arrival and departure of trains at large railway stations got a close-up of the sorrow caused by the war. At the St. Paul union depot the other day we asked one of the announcers about it and he told us it was almost unbearable day after day to see sobbing wives, children, parents and sweethearts hanging onto servicemen leaving for camp and overseas. "I thought I would have to give up my job — I couldn't take it — but when the men started coming home again it changed the picture and I stuck to my job," he said. We were thinking that if all the train announcers of all nations formed some kind of a peace unit, they would have

Reddy Says: "Let me help you relax at breakfast-time before you start your busy day. Just plug in your electric coffee maker at the table and in a jiffy I'll make the best coffee you've ever tasted. No fuss, no bother for you ∴ and no watching the pot either. I'll do that for you because it's MY job to save you time and work. So put me to work and use the time I save you for your wartime activities."

Yours obediently, *Reddy Kilowatt*
YOUR ELECTRICAL SERVANT

NORTHERN STATES POWER COMPANY
Buy More U. S. War Savings Bonds

Chisago County Press, May 28, 1942

Come and Taste Our Ham Before You Buy!

Armour's STAR **HAM** FOR *Easter*

SPARE RIBS, lb.	22c
SIDE PORK, lb.	25c
RING BOLOGNA, lb.	20c
BRANDED BEEF ROASTS, lb.	25c
LEAN BACON SQUARES, lb.	20c
LEAN PORK CHOPS, end cuts, lb.	29c
PORK LOIN ROAST, lb.	29c
LONGHORN CHEESE, lb.	32c
STEWING VEAL, lb.	18c
FAT ROASTING HENS, lb.	27c
SALT PORK, lb.	25c
HOME MADE HEAD CHEESE, lb.	35c
FRESH PORK NECK BONES, lb.	10c

FRESH—Fish, Oysters, Veal and Lamb

CHISAGO COUNTY CO-OP. CO.

LINDSTROM, MINNESOTA

Chisago County Press, March 26, 1942

"Exercise is a poor way to reduce your weight."

plenty of steam back of their desire and demand for no more war.

Dakota County Tribune, Farmington, April 19, 1946

—›-‹—

Exercise is a poor way to reduce your weight, because it increases your appetite and you have a tendency to eat that much more. A New York magazine says that to lose one pound, a 155-pound lass would have to (a) wrestle for five and a half hours, or (b) saw wood for 10 1/2 hours, or (c) walk 144 miles, or (d) climb the Washington monument 48 times, according to Prof. Arthur Steinhaus of the George Williams college, Chicago. If you want to lose weight, eat less and save yourself a lot of sweat and tears, he says.

Dakota County Tribune, Farmington, May 10, 1946

—›-‹—

Many restaurant eaters have been surprised recently when they have been served one slice of bread with their meal rather than the customary two. This practice is in keeping with President Truman's Famine Emergency Relief program for conserving food to help feed the starving millions in Europe. Anyone wishing the regular serving may request it and receive the full amount.

Winthrop News, May 16, 1946

—›-‹—

Sheer Nylons will soon be coming back. These "Very Sheers" will be under a price ceiling of $1.70 per pair, OPA [Office of Price Administration] announced.

Winthrop News, June 27, 1946

—›-‹—

With widespread cancellation of fairs and other public gatherings and postponement of open-

The Dayton Company.

★ OVALROOM

PHILIP MANGONE

conveys distinction with his hand-stitched scroll motif, $115.

Minneapolis Star-Journal, May 2, 1945

"Leaders in the fight against polio expressed hope this week that the epidemic had reached or was near its peak."

ing dates for the schools in many parts of the state, leaders in the fight against polio expressed hope this week that the epidemic had reached or was near its peak, and asked that the people continue to avoid crowds wherever possible and take other precautions to reduce spreading of the disease.

McIntosh Times, Aug. 22, 1946

→·←

The Blessed Mother of God must have kept special watch over the nine children of Mr. and Mrs. Frank Andres of St. James' parish here [in Randall].

All nine of them were stricken with infantile paralysis within less than three weeks last fall — but now every one has almost completely recovered.

Every day in their farm home three miles southwest of Randall, voices could be heard rising in prayers as they wove the crown of the Holy Rosary in honor of the Mother of God. One by one those voices were silenced — but only for a while — as polio struck first the eldest, Donald, 18, and then went on to claim Jim, 15; Cecilia, 14; Richard, 12; Margaret, 10; Christine, nine; Walter, seven; Robert, four; and little Charley, one. . . .

All but two of the children were hospitalized; Donald, the hardest hit, returned home from the Gillette hospital, St. Paul, just the day before Christmas. . . .

While Mrs. Andres was trying to do her usual housework and watch over those at home, applying hot packs and other remedies, Mr. Andres was breaking records from Randall to the Twin Cities — 1,230 miles in all — with 12 round trips in two weeks that put him "a little behind in the farm chores" with 18 Holsteins on a twice-a-day milking schedule.

Mrs. Andres became proficient in the Kenny method, fol-

South St. Paul Daily Reporter, Sept. 6, 1945

"Mr. Andres insisted on paying the bills as long as he was able."

Pillager Herald, Nov. 12, 1943

lowing instructions she received from University hospital. Many letters reached the Andres home from bewildered parents, asking Mrs. Andres for "secrets" on the treatment of polio.

Mr. Andres insisted on paying the bills as long as he was able. But the $400 to which his hospital insurance entitled him was quickly exhausted.

At that point the "March of Dimes" fund for polio victims stepped in. The fund paid and is paying costs of treatment, expected to run a total of several thousand dollars.

St. Cloud Register, newspaper of the Catholic bishop, Jan. 10, 1947

—>-<—

On Thursday afternoon a large crowd of friends and relatives gathered at the new home [in Tenney] of Mrs. Al Raguse for a house-warming party. The afternoon was spent in solving some new and interesting contests and games and in visiting. Attractive trays were used for the 5 o'clock luncheon, on which were placed pretty doilies, with favors of tiny flags well anchored in the base of a gumdrop. Warm buns and butter, potato salad, cake and coffee made up the tasty menu for the lunch which was eaten on the lawn. Mrs. Raguse was presented with a cash gift, with which to purchase something for her new home in remembrance of those in attendance. Those from a dis-

"A very pleasant afternoon was spent."

tance who attended were Mrs. Lloyd Derrick of Minneapolis, Mrs. Ralph van Tassell of Breckenridge, Mrs. Clara Budke of Wheaton and Mrs. Milton Kinker of Toledo, Ohio. A very pleasant afternoon was spent.

Breckenridge Gazette-Telegram, July 8, 1948

-→-←-

Chisago County Press, March 12, 1942

Minneapolis Times, Dec. 13, 1941

–>•<–

Want More?

Are you intrigued with old newspapers? Oh good.

You may want to do some more reading. Minnesotans are fortunate to have access to most of the newspapers ever published in our state. The Minnesota Historical Society — founded even before Minnesota became a state! — has copies of some 3,000 Minnesota newspapers published since 1849. That's not just 3,000 different days of a few dozen papers. That's newspapers with 3,000 different names, many running more than 100 years.

Most of the papers are preserved on microfilm. Visitors to the Minnesota Historical Society near downtown St. Paul may read the microfilm there, no charge. Persons living outside the Twin Cities metropolitan area may ask their librarians to order microfilm copies of newspapers from the Minnesota Historical Society; there is a nominal fee for the interlibrary loan. Microfilm of newspapers from other states also may be ordered through your library.

Your county historical society or city library may have old copies or microfilm of your local papers.

Here are suggestions on how to use old newspapers:

Look up the date of your birth. Or, as a gift for someone on a birthday or other special day, make copies of a few ads and news stories from the appropriate newspaper. Almost anything you copy will be fun for you and the recipient. Don't limit this idea to old people. Even children get a kick out of reading what the world was like when they entered it.

Think about which newspaper stories of recent years could be included in a book like this 100 years from now. How about an account of the Oct. 27, 1987, parade for the World Champion Minnesota Twins? The Hormel strike in Austin? Prince and the Minneapolis sound? The summer flood of 1987? You decide.

Teachers might consider newspaper research. Send your history and social studies students to the primary source of newspapers. Journalism and English students enjoy the antiquated language of papers long ago. Have students rewrite in today's style one of the old articles — for example, the Northfield bank robbery or the explosion of the flour mills. What are the advantages and disadvantages of the old and the new versions?

Business people might remember that customers enjoy old advertisements and display some for their stores or products.

Artists and designers can learn from the old ads.

Newspaper reporters might take the time to find and quote old newspaper reports when working on articles about past events.

New parents can put aside copies of the newspapers published on the days their babies are born. The papers will be of no monetary value, but they might be treasured someday. Meanwhile, they don't take up much space. Newspapers are best preserved away from heat and humidity, so basements and attics aren't as good as first-floor closets.

Kids can help their folks feel *really* old by finding accounts of their births or wedding days in the newspaper.

I hope you have fun poking around in the past.

–>•<–

Thanks

I'm privileged to have had a wonderfully talented team of newspaper colleagues to work with me on this book. They are: Michael Carroll, book designer; Brian Cravens, typographer; Carol Evans-Smith and Jarrett Smith, cover designers; Stormi Greener, photographer of the newspaper advertisements; Linda James, researcher and indexer, and Ingrid Sundstrom, editor.

Also, I want to thank the historians who found newspaper items for me and guided my search; my supervisors at the Star Tribune who gave me a leave from my job and the encouragement to undertake this project; my family, and my business advisers.

Heartfelt thanks to my friends — the best bunch of friends on earth — who put up with my constant refrain, "Wow, read this one!"

These are the names of some of the people to whom I am grateful:

John Addington, Billy Anderson, Nina Archabal, Norton Armour, Terry Austin, Tino Avaloz, Mary Beaudoin, Terrie Blair, Steve Brandt, Jean Brookins, Mary Cannon, Ken Carley, Jane Curry, John Edson, Zina Emanuele, Nancy Eubank, Bette Fenton, Russell Fridley, George Hage, Gloria Haider, Patricia Harpole, Annie Henry, Helen Henton, Arlinda Hildebrand, Julie Himmelstrup, Nordis Heyerdahl-Fowler, Marilyn Hoegemeyer, Roberta Hovde, Robert Jansen, Kris and Dick Jensen, Sarah Jordan, Lucile Kane, Anne Kaplan, Beverly Kees, Mary Klauda, Joel Kramer, Gretchen Kreuter, Pat Hirl Longstaff, David Lund, Marti Markus, Lynda McDonnell, Tim McGuire, Ruth Meier, Debbie Miller, Stephen Osman, Rosemary Palmer, Roger Parkinson, Kate Parry, Susan Peterson, Bob Phelps, Emma Phillips, Linda Picone, Wiley Pope, Sharon Rask, Ann Regan, the Rockstads (Mary, Dean, Beth and Karen), R.T. Rybak, Bud Schaitberger and Jenny Rosencrans and Associates, Dona Sieden, Brigid Shields, Al Sicherman, Mike and Jo Smith, Mary Sorensen, Jean Spraker, Cynthia Stark, Chuck Stone, Deborah Swanson, the Tackies, Becky Skinner Toevs, Jon Walstrom, Jim Whalen, John Wickre, Alissa Wiener, David Wiggins, Ann Wilhelmy, Julie Williams, Bonnie Wilson, Carolyn Wilson, Alan R. Woolworth, Dave Wood and Margaret Zack.

–>•<–

Index

"Coffee Made Her Insane" may be ordered by mail from:

Neighbors Publishing
P.O. Box 15071
Minneapolis, Minn. 55415

The price of $16.50 includes postage, handling and tax.